TEACHING ACADEMIC ESL WRITING

Practical Techniques in Vocabulary and Grammar

ESL & Applied Linguistics Professor Series
Eli Hinkel, Series Editor

Birch • *English L2 Reading: Getting to the Bottom*

Fotos/Browne • *New Perspectives on CALL for Second Language Classrooms*

Hinkel • *Second Language Writers' Text: Linguistic and Rhetorical Features*

Hinkel • *Teaching Academic ESL Writing: Practical Techniques in Vocabulary and Grammar*

Hinkel/Fotos, Eds. • *New Perspectives on Grammar Teaching in Second Language Classrooms*

Teaching Academic ESL Writing

Practical Techniques in Vocabulary and Grammar

Eli Hinkel
Seattle University

LEA Lawrence Erlbaum Associates
Taylor & Francis Group

New York London

Cover design by Kathryn Houghtaling Lacey

Library of Congress Cataloging-in-Publication Data

Hinkel, Eli.
Teaching Academic ESL writing : practical techniques in vocabulary and grammar / Eli Hinkel.
p. cm.
Includes bibliographical references and index.
ISBN 0-8058-3889-9 (cloth : alk. paper)
ISBN 0-8058-3890-2 (pbk. : alk. paper)
1. English language—Rehtoric—Study and teaching. 2. English language—Study and teaching—Foreign speakers 3. Academic writing—Studying and teaching. I. Title.

PE1404.H57 2003
808'042'071—dc21 2003046234
CIP

Books published by Lawrence Erlbaum Associates are printed on acid-free paper, and their bindings are chosen for strength and durability.

Printed in the United States of America
10 9 8 7 6 5 4 3 2

To RH with love and gratitude

Contents

Part III Text and Discourse Flow: The Sentence and Beyond

Preface

Language is power.
—Angela Carter

Power to the people.
—A slogan from the 1960s

Since the late 1970s and early 1980s, a great deal of time, energy, and resources have been devoted to teaching non-native L2 writers the rhetorical features of written academic discourse in English. In addition, to meet market demands and the expectations of professional training and preparation for English as a Second Language and English for Academic Purposes teachers, teacher-training and graduate programs have set out to address teachers' on-the-job skills that pertain to teaching L2 academic writers how to generate and organize ideas into coherent essays and compositions, as is expected of practically all students at undergraduate and graduate levels.

There is little doubt that L2 writers need to be familiar with many rhetorical and discourse features of written English and that the teaching of college- or university-level writing cannot do without them. In teaching L2 writing to academically bound learners, what has become of smaller importance, however, is the language tools (i.e., the grammar and vocabulary that L2 writers must have to construct academic text, which in turn can be organized into a coherent written academic discourse). To put it plainly, no matter how well discourse is organized or how brilliant the writer's ideas may be, it would be hard to understand them if the language is opaque.

The purpose of this book is to bridge an important gap that exists in teacher training today: the teaching of the second language and its grammatical and lexical features that are essential for any L2 writing teacher and student writer to know. The teaching of rhetorical and discourse properties of academic writing in English can be made far more effective and efficient if L2 learners have language tools with which to build the text. The ultimate goal of this book, however, is to benefit language learners who aspire to success in academic degree programs beyond their ESL and English courses. Few EAP students set out to major in intensive English study and obtain degrees in English composition, and practically all have other educational, professional, and career goals in mind.

This book deals with techniques for teaching L2 writing, grammar, and lexis that can inform L2 instruction and effectively target specific areas of L2 text that require substantial improvements. ESL teachers are usually keenly aware of how short the course and class time are. The scope of material is designed to be taught during one or, at most, two courses at the high intermediate and/or advanced levels of learner proficiency. In such courses, the teacher's goal is usually to provide the critical preparation for students who are *almost* ready to begin their studies in regular college and university courses. Teaching strategies and techniques discussed here are based on a highly practical principle of maximizing learners' language gains by employing a few shortcuts. This book—based on current research and, in particular, a large-scale research of almost 1,500 NNS (non-native speakers) essays (Hinkel, 2002a, *Second Language Writers' Text: Linguistic and Rhetorical Features*, Lawrence Erlbaum) in addition to 25 years of ESL teaching and teacher-training experience—works with several sets of simple rules that collectively can make a noticeable and important difference in the quality of NNS students' writing.

The philosophical goal of this book is to focus the attention of practicing and preservice ESL/EAP teachers on the fact that without clear, reasonably accurate, and coherent text, there can be no academic writing in a second language. The practical and immediate purpose, however, is to provide a compendium of teaching techniques for the grammatical and lexical features of academic language that "every teacher (and student) must know."

Several key differences between this book and many other books on teaching ESL should be highlighted:

- The decision about what a L2 writing course has to address and what L2 writers must know is based on the findings of research into academic text and the text produced by L2 writers. Therefore, the material sets out to address the gaps in current curricula for teaching L2 writing. In addition, the aspects of L2 that are traditionally included in L2 teaching, but hardly ever found in academic text, are highlighted throughout the book.
- Because academic vocabulary, the grammar of formal written English, and specific features of academic prose represent integral aspects of academic writing in a second language, curriculum and teaching techniques presented in this book work with these concurrently.
- The curriculum and its elements discussed herein are not based on an incremental progression of material, such as "first, the course

> covers the present tense, then the present perfect tense, and then the past tense." Although the curriculum is organized in a particular order, instruction on academic L2 writing and language has to include all its elements. For this reason, the material and teaching techniques discussed here can have a variety of logical organizational structures, all of which could be more or less appropriate for a specific course or particular group of students in a particular context. It is a widely known fact that few ESL teachers follow the order of curriculum developed by someone else, and this book does not expect to be an exception.

This book is oriented for teachers of high intermediate and advanced academic ESL students. One of its fundamental assumptions is that learning to write academic text in a second language takes a lot of hard work, and that for L2 academic writers, the foundations of language must be in place before they can begin to produce passable academic papers and assignments.

To this end, the teaching materials, teaching activities, and suggestions for teaching are based on a single objective: The quality of language teaching and student language learning must improve if non-native writers are to succeed in their academic careers.

ORGANIZATION OF THE VOLUME

The volume is divided into three Parts. Part I begins with chapter 1, which explains the importance of text in written academic discourse. It also provides a detailed overview of the essential ESL skills that every student must have to function in the academic milieu. Chapter 2 delves into the specific student writing tasks that all students must face—and deal with—in their studies in the disciplines. Chapter 3 presents the guidelines for a course curriculum that addresses the specifics of academic vocabulary, grammar, dealing with errors, teaching students to edit their text, and other fundamental writing skills essential for students' academic survival.

The chapters in Part II plow into the nitty gritty of the classroom teaching of language. This section begins in chapter 4 with a core and expanded analysis of the English sentence structure to enable writers to construct reasonably complete sentences and edit their own text. The chapters on the essential sentence elements largely follow the order of the sentence. Essential academic nouns and the structure of the noun phrase are dealt with in chapter 5, followed by the place and types of pronouns in academic prose in chapter 6. Chapter 7 works with the teaching of a limited range of English verb tenses and the ever-important uses of the passive voice. Lexical types of foundational academic verbs and their textual functions are the focus of chapter 8. The construction of adjective and adverb phrases, as well as the essential adjective and adverb vocabulary, follow in chapter 9.

The teaching of academic text building beyond the simple sentence is the focus of Part III. Chapter 10 outlines instruction in the functions and types of subordinate clauses: adverbial, adjective, and noun. In chapter 11, the classroom teaching of elements of cohesion and coherence (a famously neglected aspect of L2 writing instruction) is specifically addressed. Chapter 12 concludes with the teaching of hedges and their crucial functions in academic text.

The three chapters in Part I are different from the rest of the chapters in the book. Chapters 1 and 2 are intended to provide the background for the rest of the volume, and chapter 3 presents a sample of course curriculum guidelines to meet the learning needs of L2 teachers of writing and L2 writers.

The chapters in Parts II and III include the key elements of classroom teaching: what should be taught and why, possible ways of teaching the material in the classroom, common errors found in student text and ways of teaching students to avoid them, teaching activities and suggestions for teaching, and questions for discussion in a teacher-training course. Appendixes included with the chapters provide supplementary word and phrase lists, collocations, sentence chunks, and diagrams that teachers can use as needed.

As with all the material in the book, suggestions for teaching and teaching activities exemplified in one chapter can be perfectly usable in another chapter: If a particular activity works well for teaching academic nouns, it is likely to work well for teaching lexical types of academic verbs.

ACKNOWLEDGMENTS

My sincere thanks to Robert B. Kaplan, who over the years has become a mentor and friend and whose idea this book was in the first place. I owe a debt to my long-suffering friends of many years who read earlier drafts of chapters and provided many helpful comments that greatly helped to improve the book: Mary Geary, formerly of Seattle University; Bruce Rogers, Ohio State University; Peter Clements, University of Washington; and Bethany Plett, Texas A&M University.

My devoted comrade and software executive, Rodney Hill, receives my undying gratitude for not only creating a large number of computer programs that enormously eased my life, such as statistical tools, bibliography software, and text macros, but also enduring the reading of countless versions of chapters and formatting the text and layout.

When the book was almost cooked, Jeanette DeCarrico, Portland State University; and Marcella Frank, New York University, served as reviewers and provided helpful comments and suggestions for the style and content. Naomi Silverman, Senior Editor at Lawrence Erlbaum Associates, deserves a special word of thanks for her friendship, invaluable support, patience, and insight.

I

ACADEMIC TEXT AND TEACHING SECOND LANGUAGE WRITING

Chapters 1, 2, and 3 establish some of the groundwork for the book. Chapter 1 presents the main assumptions of the book, which may seem fairly obvious, but are often overlooked in the teaching of L2 writing: (1) Learning to write in an L2 is different from learning to write in an L1, so (2) teaching L2 writing the way L1 writing is taught is not effective. (3) The knowledge-transforming type of writing expected in academic disciplines is different from personal experience narratives or conversational discourse and cannot be developed through conversational or interactional activities—whether written or spoken. On the contrary, (4) extensive, thorough, and focused instruction in L2 academic vocabulary, grammar, and discourse is essential for developing L2 written proficiency.

More groundwork is covered in chapter 2, which discusses writing requirements in a university, characteristics of academic writing and academic text, as well as common writing tasks students need to perform in their mainstream studies in particular disciplines in the university.

Chapter 3 examines the importance of accuracy in academic writing and how to approach the teaching of NNS writing so that accuracy can be achieved.

1

The Importance of Text in Written Academic Discourse: Ongoing Goals in Teaching ESL Skills

OVERVIEW

- NNS academic writing skills in English.
- Key assumptions of the book and support for the assumptions.

In the past several decades, the proliferation of college- and university-level courses, textbooks, and all manner of learning aids for second language (L2) academic writers has become a fact of life that most English as a Second Language (ESL), English for Academic Purposes (EAP), and writing teachers have had no choice but notice. The rapid rise in the number of L2 teacher-training courses, workshops, and MA-level programs in TESL (Teaching English as a Second Language) has also become commonplace in U.S. education.

The emergence of L2 writing courses, teacher-training programs, and textbooks is not particularly surprising given college/university enrollment statistics. During the 2000–2001 school year, approximately 547,867 international students were enrolled in degree programs in U.S. colleges and universities (i.e., 4% of the entire student population; Institute of International Education, 2001). In addition, U.S. intensive and preparatory programs teach ESL and EAP skills, including writing, to another 866,715 L2 learners, some of whom return to their home countries, but many of whom seek admission to institutions of higher learning.

In addition, U.S. colleges enroll almost 1,800,000 immigrant students—that is, 6% of all students (U.S. Census, October 2000). Together international and immigrant students represent about 10% of all college and university enrollees in the United States. In the next 4 years or so, a large proportion of the current 3 million immigrant high school students (up from approximately 2.3 million at the time of the 1990 U.S. Census) are expected to continue their education in U.S. colleges and universities.

ACADEMIC WRITING SKILLS IN ENGLISH

In the past two decades, a number of publications have emerged to point out that, despite having studied English as well as academic writing in English in their native and English-speaking countries, non-native speaking students experience a great deal of difficulty in their studies at the college and university level in English-speaking countries (Hinkel, 2002a; Johns, 1997; Johnson 1989a; Jordan, 1997; Leki & Carson, 1997; Prior, 1998; Santos, 1988). These and other researchers have identified important reasons that the academic writing of even highly advanced and trained NNS students continues to exhibit numerous problems and shortfalls.

For instance, Johns (1997) found that many NNS graduate and undergraduate students, after years of ESL training, often fail to recognize and appropriately use the conventions and features of academic written prose. She explained that these students produce academic papers and essays that faculty perceive to be vague and confusing, rhetorically unstructured, and overly personal. In the view of many faculty Johns interviewed, NNS students' writing lacks sentence-level features considered to be basic—for example, appropriate uses of hedging,[1] modal verbs, pronouns, active and passive voice (commonly found in texts on sciences), balanced generalizations, and even exemplification. As an outcome of the faculty views of the NNSs' overall language and particularly writing skills, many NNS university students experience frustration and alienation because they often believe the faculty to be unreasonably demanding and exclusive and their own best efforts unvalued and unrecognized (Johns, 1997).

Information regarding the high failure rate among NNS students in various U.S. colleges and universities abounds. For instance, dropout rates among foreign-born college students are more than twice that of students born in the United States (U.S. Department of Commerce, Bureau of the Census, 1995). Similarly, analyses of student enrollment data carried out in many large universities in Pennsylvania, California, and New York, as well universities in other states, attribute the dropout rate among NNS students, even at the PhD level, directly to the shortcomings in their academic English skills (Asian American Federation of New York, 2001; Hargreaves, 2001).

The effectiveness of ESL and EAP writing courses in preparing NNS students for actual academic writing in universities was discussed by Leki and

[1]*Hedging* refers to the uses of particles, words, phrases, or clauses to reduce the extent of the writer's responsibility for the extent and truth value of statements, show hesitation or uncertainty, and display politeness and indirectness. Hedging in academic writing is discussed in detail in chapter 12.

Carson (1997). They found that, "what is valued in writing for writing classes is different from what is valued in writing for other academic courses" (p. 64). Leki and Carson further emphasized that the teaching of writing in ESL and EAP programs needs to provide students with linguistic and writing skills that can enable the learners to "encounter, manage, and come to terms with new information" and expand their knowledge base. Other researchers such as Chang and Swales (1999) investigated specific discourse and sentence-level writing skills of highly advanced NNS students. These authors indicate that even in the case of advanced and highly literate NNSs, exposure to substantial amounts of reading and experience with writing in academic contexts does not ensure their becoming aware of discourse and sentence-level linguistic features of academic writing and the attainment of the necessary writing skills. Chang and Swales concluded that explicit instruction in advanced academic writing and text is needed.

> A large number of extensive and detailed studies carried out since 1990 have demonstrated that mere exposure to L2 vocabulary, grammar, discourse, and formal written text is not the most effective means of attaining academic L2 proficiency (e.g., Ellis, 1990; Hinkel, 2002a; Nation, 2001; Norris & Ortega, 2000; Schmitt, 2000).

Since the early 1980s, the predominant method of instruction in the teaching of L2 writing has remained focused on the writing process similar to the pedagogy adopted in L1 writing instruction for native speakers of English (Johns, 1990a; Reid, 1993; Zamel, 1982, 1983). The process-centered instructional methodology for teaching writing focuses on invention, creating ideas, and discovering the purpose of writing (Reid, 1993). Within the process-centered paradigm for teaching L2 writing, student writing is evaluated on the quality of prewriting, writing, and revision. Because the product of writing is seen as secondary to the writing process, and even inhibitory in the early stages of writing, issues of L2 grammar, lexis, and errors are to be addressed only as needed in the context of writing, and L2 writers with proficiency levels higher than beginning are exposed to text and discourse to learn from them and, thus, acquire L2 grammar and lexis naturally.

On the other hand, outside L2 writing and English composition courses, the evaluations of the quality of NNSs' L2 writing skills by faculty in the disciplines and general education courses has continued to focus on the product of writing (Hinkel, 2002a; Johns, 1997; Santos, 1988). In academic courses such as history, sociology, business, or natural sciences at both the undergraduate and graduate levels, evaluations of NNS students' academic skills are determined by their performance on traditional product-oriented language tasks—most frequently reading and writing (Ferris & Hedgcock, 1998; Johns, 1997; Leki & Carson, 1997; see also chap. 2). However, outside ESL and English department writing programs, the faculty in the disciplines are not particularly concerned about the writing process that affects (or does not affect) the quality of the writing product (i.e., students' assignments and papers that the professors read, evaluate, and grade; Dudley-Evans & St. John, 1998; Horowitz, 1986a; Johns, 1981, 1997; Jordan, 1997). The skills required for NNS students to succeed in mainstream general education courses, as well as those in the disciplines, have remained largely unchanged despite the shift in the writing instruction methodology.

Similarly, the assessment of L2 writing skills by ESL professionals on standardized and institutional placement testing has largely remained focused on the writing product without regard to the writing process (ETS, 1996; MELAB, 1996; Vaughan, 1991). The disparity between the teaching methods adopted in L2 writing instruction and evaluation criteria of the quality of L2 writing has produced outcomes that are damaging and costly for most ESL students, who are taught brainstorming techniques and invention, prewriting, drafting, and revising skills, whereas their essential linguistic skills, such as academic vocabulary and formal features of grammar and text, are only sparsely and inconsistently addressed.

KEY ASSUMPTIONS

In this book, teaching techniques and approaches to teaching L2 writing to academically bound NNS students are based on four key assumptions about learning to write in an L2.

---

(1) Learning to write in an L2 is fundamentally different from learning to write in an L1. NS writers already have highly developed (native) language proficiency in English, whereas most NNSs must dedicate years to learning it as a second language—in most cases as adults. To date research has not determined whether a majority of NNS students in colleges and universities can succeed in attaining native-like English proficiency even after years of intensive study that includes exposure to English-language interaction, text, and discourse.

(2) Research has established that applying the writing and composition pedagogy for NSs to teaching L2 writing to NNSs—even over the course of several years—does not lead to sufficient improvements in L2 writing to enable NNS students to produce academic-level text requisite in the academy in English-speaking countries (Hinkel, 2002b; Johns, 1997; Silva, 1993).

(3) The knowledge-telling and knowledge-transforming model of the writing process developed by Bereiter and Scardamalia (1985, 1987, 1989) stipulates that exposure to conversational language experi-

ences and access to written text apply to practically all language users. However, proficiency in L2 conversational linguistic features, familiarity with L2 writing, and "telling" what one already knows in written form do not lead to producing cognitively complex academic writing that relies on obtaining and "transforming" knowledge (i.e., logically organizing information and employing linguistic features and style that attend to audience expectations and the genre).

(4) Extensive, thorough, and focused instruction in L2 academic vocabulary, grammar, and discourse is essential for developing the L2 written proficiency expected in general education courses and studies in the disciplines.

These assumptions are based on a large body of research, some examples of which are cited next.

Assumption 1: Unlike Learning to Write in an L1, Learning to Write in an L2 First Requires an Attainment of Sufficient L2 Linguistic Proficiency

In the past several decades, studies of L2 learning and acquisition have shown that, although the rate of L2 learning and acquisition depends on many complex factors, adult learners' ultimate attainment of L2 proficiency does not become native-like even after many years of exposure to L2 usage in L2 environments (Bialystok, 2001; Celce-Murcia, 1991; d'Anglejan, 1990; Dietrich, Klein, & Noyau, 1995; Larsen-Freeman, 1993; Larsen-Freeman & Long, 1991; Schmidt, 1983). Other researchers have distinguished between advanced academic language proficiency and basic conversational and communication proficiency necessary to engage in daily interactions (Bratt Paulston, 1990; Cummins, 1979; Schachter, 1990). Conversational fluency does not carry with it the skills necessary for the production of academic text.

In addition, much research has been carried out indicating that a substantial and advanced L2 proficiency in lexis and grammar may not be possible to achieve without explicit, focused, and consistent instruction (Celce-Murcia, 1991, 1993; Celce-Murcia & Hilles, 1988; Coady & Huckin, 1997; N. Ellis, 1994; R. Ellis, 1984, 1990, 1994, 1997, 2002; Hammerly, 1991; Hinkel, 1992, 1997a, 2002a; Huckin, Haynes, & Coady, 1993; Larsen-Freeman, 1991; Lewis, 1993, 1997; Nation, 1990, 2001; Norris & Ortega, 2000; Richards, 2002; Schmidt, 1990, 1994, 1995; Schmitt, 2000; Schmitt & McCarthy, 1997, to mention just a few).[2]

[2]Because this chapter establishes much of the theoretical groundwork for the book, a large number of references are necessary. The author promises, however, that the rest of the book will not be as reference heavy as this chapter.

A large number of studies have also established that learning to write in a second language and, in particular, learning to write the formal L2 academic prose crucial in NNSs' academic and professional careers requires the development of an advanced linguistic foundation, without which learners simply do not have the range of lexical and grammar skills required in academic writing (Berkenkotter & Huckin, 1995; Bizzell, 1982; Byrd & Reid, 1998; Chang & Swales, 1999; Grabe & Kaplan, 1996; Hamp-Lyons, 1991a, 1991b; Hinkel, 1999a, 2002a; Horowitz, 1986a, 1986b, 1991; Hvitfeld, 1992; Johns, 1981, 1991, 1997; Jordan, 1997; Kroll, 1979; Nation, 1990, 2001; Nation & Waring, 1997; Ostler, 1980; Paltridge, 2001; Poole, 1991; Raimes, 1983, 1993; Read, 2000; Santos, 1984, 1988; Swales, 1971).

Assumption 2: Writing Pedagogy for NSs with Highly Developed (Native) Language Proficiency, Which NNSs (By Definition) Do Not Have, Is Not Readily Applicable to L2 Writing Instruction

Prior to the 1980s, the teaching of university-level rhetoric and composition was predominantly concerned with analyzing literature and the students' writing style, lexical precision and breadth, grammar, and rhetorical structure (e.g., the presence of thesis and rhetorical support, coherence, and cohesion). The teaching and evaluation of student writing focused almost exclusively on the product of writing without explicit instruction of how high-quality writing could be attained. In reaction to rigid and somewhat restrictive views of stylistic quality and evaluations of writing, L1 methodologies for teaching writing and composition began to move away from a focus on the product of composing, classical rhetorical formality, study of literature, and accepted standards for grammatical accuracy (Hairston, 1982). Instead the humanistic teaching of composition began to emphasize the writing process with a reduced emphasis on rhetorical structure, vocabulary, and grammar.

In the late 1970s and early 1980s, some specialists in the teaching of L1 basic writing observed that a number of similarities exist among the strategies used by basic NS and NNS writers. Therefore, they concluded that if the writing behaviors of both types of writers exhibit similarities, the approaches to teaching writing to NSs can be applied to the teaching of NNSs. Although at that time the research on the applicability of L1 writing pedagogy to learning to write in L2 consisted of only a small number of case studies and student self-reports, the methodology for teaching basic L1 writers took hold in the teaching of NNSs. Following the methodological shift in L1 writing pedagogy, the process-centered paradigm was similarly adopted as the preeminent methodology in teaching L2 writing (i.e., in L2 instruction focused on the process of writing, the quality of writing is evaluated based on prewriting, drafting, and revising; Reid, 1993). The process methodology further presupposes that issues of L2 grammar and lexis are to be addressed only as needed in the context of writing, and that if NNSs with proficiency levels higher than beginning are exposed to text and discourse to learn from, they will acquire L2 grammar and lexis naturally. Teaching ESL writing through the writing process and revising multiple drafts also permitted many ESL practitioners to hope that over time, as L2 writers developed and matured, their L2 errors and concerns about linguistic accuracy in grammar and vocabulary use would decrease (Zamel, 1982, 1983).

Another reason for the enormous popularity of process instruction for NNSs lies in the fact that the teaching of L1 writing relied on the research and experience of the full-fledged and mature discipline of rhetoric and composition. Theoretically, the teaching of the writing process allowed ESL teachers and curriculum designers to accomplish their instructional goals based on solid research findings and pedagogical frameworks (Leki, 1995), which were developed, however, for a different type of learners.

In addition, because many ESL practitioners were trained in methodologies for teaching the writing process, employing these approaches, techniques, and classroom activities entailed working with known and familiar ways of teaching.

However, the new instructional methodology centered squarely and almost exclusively on the writing process that fundamentally overlooked the fact that NNS writers may simply lack the necessary language skills (e.g., vocabulary and grammar) to take advantage of the benefits of writing process instruction. Furthermore, the process methodology for teaching focused disproportionately on only the first of three components that are essential to produce good academic writing: (1) the process of writing with self-revision and editing, (2) formal rhetorical organization, and (3) quality of language (e.g., grammatical and lexical accuracy). In addition, although the methodologies for teaching L2 writing changed, in the academic arena assessment of student writing has remained focused on the end product without regard to the writing process required to arrive at the end product.

Differences Between L1 and L2 Writing

The differences between L1 and L2 writing are so extensive that they can be identified in practically all aspects of written text and discourse. According to numerous studies of L1 and L2 written discourse and text, distinctions between them extend to:

- discourse and rhetorical organization
- ideas and content of writing
- rhetorical modes (e.g., exposition, narration, and argumentation)
- reliance on external knowledge and information

- references to sources of knowledge and information
- assumptions about the reader's knowledge and expectations (e.g., references to assumed common knowledge and familiarity with certain classical works)
- the role of audience in discourse and text production, as well as the appraisal of the expected discourse and text complexity (e.g., reader vs. writer responsible text)
- discourse and text cohesion
- employment of linguistic and rhetorical features of formal written text (e.g., fewer/less complex sentences, descriptive adjectives, passivization, nominalization, lexical variety, and more conjunctions, conversational amplifiers and emphatics, simple nouns and verbs) (Bickner & Peyasantiwong, 1988; Byrd & Nelson, 1995; Carlson, 1988; Connor, 1996; Connor & Carrell, 1993; Connor & Kaplan, 1987; Davidson, 1991; Friedlander, 1990; Grabe & Kaplan, 1989, 1996; Hamp-Lyons, 1990, 1991a, 1991b; Hinds, 1983, 1987, 1990; Hinkel, 1994, 1995a, 1995b, 1997b, 1999a; Hyland, 1999, 2002a; Hyland & Milton, 1997; Hvitfeld, 1992; Indrasuta, 1988; Johnstone, 1989; Kachru, 1999; Kaplan 1983, 1987, 1988, 2000; Kroll, 1990; Leki, 1995; Matalene, 1985; Silva, 1990, 1993, 1997).

In addition to numerous studies of the L1 and L2 writing product, other studies have identified fundamental and substantial differences between approaches to writing and writing processes in L1 and L2 (Jones, 1985; Jourdenais, 2001; Widdowson, 1983). For instance, Raimes (1994) reported that although writing ability in an L1 is closely linked to fluency and conventions of expository discourse, L2 writing requires a developed L2 proficiency, as well as writing skills that pertain to the knowledge of discourse conventions and organizing the information flow. Similarly, Cumming's (1994) empirical study pointed out that L2 proficiency and expertise in writing are in fact two "psychologically" different skills; as individuals gain L2 proficiency, "they become better able to perform in writing in their second language, producing more effective texts" (p. 201), and attend to larger aspects of their writing production. He further underscored that L2 proficiency adds to and enhances L2 writing expertise.

An extensive study by Warden (2000) found that "implementing a multiple-stage process" of draft revising in writing pedagogy represents a mismatch with the reality of "social, cultural, and historical trends" (p. 607) in non-Western countries, where the emphasis is placed on vocabulary and grammar accuracy rather than revising one's writing for meaning and content. In his study, over 100 Taiwanese students revised multiple drafts, showing that redrafting essays results in generally unproductive writing strategies, such as correcting incremental phrase-level errors. Warden also pointed out that "direct application of multiple drafts and non-sentence-level feedback" results in a lower level of student motivation for revision and "increased dependence of reference material," when students simply copy directly from sources.

Silva's (1993) survey of NNS writing research includes 72 empirical studies published between 1980 and 1991. He concluded that, "in general, compared to NS writing, L2 writers' texts were less fluent (fewer words), less accurate (more errors), and less effective (lower holistic scores) ... and ... exhibited less lexical control, variety, and sophistication overall" (p. 668). Silva summarized his research overview by stating that, "the research comparing L1 and L2 writing ... strongly suggests that ... they are different in numerous and important ways. This difference needs to be acknowledged and addressed by those who deal with L2 writers if these writers are to be treated fairly, taught effectively, and thus, given an equal chance to succeed in their writing-related personal and academic endeavors" (p. 668).

Assumption 3: Writing Personal Narratives/Opinions ("Telling" What One Already Knows) Is Not Similar to Producing Academic Writing, Which Requires Obtaining and Transforming Knowledge

In their examination of the writing process, Bereiter and Scardamalia (1985, 1987, 1989) distinguished two types of writing: knowledge telling and knowledge transforming. They explained that "telling" about personal experiences or opinions represents the easiest form of writing production that is accessible to practically all language users, who often perform such tasks in conversations. For example, writing assignments such as *My first day in the United States, My most embarrassing/happiest day,* or *My views on abortion/animal research* do not require writers to do much beyond telling what they already know and simply writing down their memories or opinions in response to the prompt. To produce an essay, writers need to organize information, often in a chronological order, according to a form appropriate within the structure of composition and in accordance with a few prescribed conventions for discourse organization (e.g., overt topic markers and/or lists of reasons—*my first reason, the second reason, the third reason, ... in conclusion ...*) that are also retrieved from memory. In the case of L2 students, such writing tasks can be produced even within the constraints of limited vocabulary and grammar because the degree of textual simplicity or complexity demonstrated in the writing is determined by the writer.

Opinion essays (Bereiter & Scardamalia, 1987) include only two main elements: statement of belief and reason. Some assignments of this type may involve multiple reasons and, at slightly more advanced levels of writing, anticipation of counterarguments, as is often expected of ESL writers in L2 writing instruction dealing with what is often called *written arguments* (Leki,

1999; Lunsford & Ruszkiewicz, 2001). Opinion writing also necessitates knowledge telling because stating one's views requires little information beyond the writer's personal beliefs or thoughts. In these types of essays, writers can produce text on practically any topic within their available knowledge without external information or support. Opinion-based written assignments or essays report personal thoughts in the form of a simple discourse organization that usually meets the expectations of the genre.

It is important to note that the teaching of L2 writing focuses predominantly on topics purposely designed to be accessible for L2 learners. Writing prompts in many L2 writing classes are often highly predictable and may actually require students to produce personal narratives and experiences (e.g., *why I want to study in the United States, holidays in my country, the person who influenced me most, my family, my favorite sport/pet/book/movie/class/teacher/relative*). Opinion essays are also ubiquitous at high intermediate and advanced levels of pre-university ESL/EAP instruction because they appear to be pseudoacademic and are based on short readings: *Please read the article/text and give your reaction/response to (its content on) pollution/gender differences/racial discrimination/the homeless/urban crime/TV advertising/teenage smoking/human cloning/gays/women in the military*. However, a counterproductive outcome of topic accessibility is that NNS academically bound students have few opportunities to engage in cognitively and linguistically advanced types of academic writing expected of them in their university-level courses (Leki & Carson, 1997).

In addition to knowledge telling in writing, the Bereiter and Scardamalia model of writing also addresses a far more psychologically complex type of writing that they called *knowledge transforming*. Knowledge transforming necessitates thinking about an issue, obtaining the information needed for analysis, and modifying one's thinking. This type of writing leads writers to expand their knowledge base and develop new knowledge by processing new information obtained for the purpose of writing on a topic. Knowledge transforming is considerably more cognitively complex than knowledge telling because writers do not merely retrieve information already available to them in memory, but derive it from reading and integrate with that already available to become obtained knowledge.

Bereiter and Scardamalia emphasized that knowledge telling and knowledge transforming require different rhetorical and text-generating skills for producing written discourse. Such important considerations of writing as content integration, expectations of the audience, conventions and form of the genre, use of language and linguistic features (e.g., lexis and grammar), logic of the information flow, and rhetorical organization are all intertwined in knowledge transforming (e.g., defining terms, explaining ideas, and clarifying). In general terms, Bereiter and Scardamalia described the classical academic model of writing expected in the disciplines when students are required to obtain, synthesize, integrate, and analyze information from various sources, such as published materials, textbooks, or laboratory experiments.

Advanced cognitive and information-processing tasks entailed in transforming knowledge and demonstrating knowledge in writing place great demands on l2 writers' language skills.

Assumption 4: Intensive and Consistent Instruction in L2 Vocabulary and Grammar, as Well as Discourse Organization, Is Paramount for Academically Bound NNSs

Instruction in L2 vocabulary and grammar improves learners' receptive and productive skills and provides important means of expanding NNS lexical and syntactic repertoires necessary in L2 reading, constructing academic text, listening, and other fundamental facets of functioning in the academy. The effectiveness and necessity of teaching L2 vocabulary has been demonstrated in a large number of studies such as Channell (1988), Coady (1997), Cowie (1988), Coxhead (1998, 2000) , Dudley-Evans and St. John (1998), N. Ellis (1994, 1997), N. Ellis and Beaton (1993), Harley (1989), Huckin, Haynes, and Coady (1993), Hulstijn (1990, 1992, 1997), Hulstijn and Laufer (2001), Jordan (1997), Kelly (1986), Laufer (1994), Carter and McCarthy (1988), Nation (2001), Paribakht and Wesche (1993, 1997), Santos (1988), Sinclair and Renouf (1988), Schmitt (2000), and Schmitt and McCarthy (1997).

For instance, Laufer and Nation (1995) identified significant positive correlations between learners' gains on vocabulary tests based on Nation's (1990) University Word List (see also chaps. 5, 8, and 9) and the increase of academic vocabulary in the compositions written by the same group of learners. Similarly, Laufer (1994) reported that persistent instruction in L2 vocabulary increases learners' vocabulary range in writing to include the foundational university-level vocabulary and progress beyond it. However, Nation (2001) cautioned that productive knowledge of vocabulary requires more learning and greater motivation for learning than receptive knowledge, in which effective and measurable gains can be made within a matter of days.[3]

The fact that consistent grammar instruction is important to develop learner language awareness and improvement in the quality of L2 production has long been established in the work of, for example, Allen, Swain, Harley, and Cummins (1990), Celce-Murcia and Hilles (1988), R. Ellis (1984, 1989, 1990, 1994, 1997, 2001), Fotos (1994, 1998, 2002), Fotos and Ellis (1991), Kumaravadivelu (1993), Mitchell and Martin (1997), Norris and Ortega (2001), Muranoi (2000), Rutherford (1984), Rutherford and

[3]As research has confirmed, it follows from this observation that vocabulary teaching can result in improvements in L2 reading comprehension earlier than in the increased quality of writing production (Huckin, Haynes, & Coady, 1993; Nation, 2001).

Sharwood Smith (1985), Sharwood Smith (1981, 1991, 1993), Schmidt (1990, 1993, 1994), Swain (1985), and Williams (1999).

A recent study by Norris and Ortega (2000) undertook probably the most comprehensive analysis of published data on the value of grammar instruction. These authors stated that in many cases it is not easy to tell whether communicative, explicit, or meaning-focused instruction led to greater degrees of L2 learning and acquisition because of the disparate sample sizes and statistical analyses employed in various research studies and publications. Thus, to make sense of research findings published in the past two decades, Norris and Ortega standardized the results of 49 studies on L2 learning, acquisition, and grammar instruction. The outcomes of their substantial undertaking show clearly that in L2 teaching, "focused instructional treatments of whatever sort far surpass non- or minimally focused exposure to the L2" (p. 463).

It is important to emphasize that the purpose of this book is *not* to enable teachers to help students attain the skills necessary to become sophisticated writers of fiction or journalistic investigative reports. The narrow and instrumental goal of instruction presented here deals with helping NNS writers become better equipped for their academic survival.

Furthermore, outside of a brief nod in chapter 11, the contents of the book do not include the teaching of the macro (discourse) features of academic writing, such as introductions, thesis statements, body paragraphs, and conclusions. Dozens of other books on the market, for both teachers and students, address the organization of information in academic and student essays according to the norms and conventions of academic writing in English.

Although both discourse- and text-level features play a crucial role in teaching L2 writing, the curriculum and teaching techniques discussed in this book focus primarily on lexical, syntactic, and rhetorical features of academic text. The importance of these features in text and discourse serve as the organizing principle for instruction, narrowly targeting their pedagogical utility. Whenever possible, variations in the uses of the features across such different disciplines as business, economics, psychology, or sociology are discussed throughout the volume.

This book presents a compendium of many practical teaching techniques, strategies, and tactics that a teacher can use in writing and composition classes to help students improve the quality of their academic text. These include the teaching of phrase and sentence patterns that are commonly found in academic writing and can be taught in chunks. The teaching of academic nouns and verbs in the book centers around the basic core vocabulary students must learn to produce writing more lexically advanced than can be attained by means of exposure to spoken interactions and the conversational register. In addition, the material in this book covers the textual and discourse functions of such important features of academic writing as essential verb tenses, passive voice, and necessary main and subordinate clauses, as well as adjectives, adverbs, hedges, and pronouns.

FURTHER READINGS ABOUT WRITTEN ACADEMIC TEXT AND DISCOURSE, AND TEACHING ACADEMIC ESL WRITING

L2 Written Academic Text and Discourse

Atkinson, D. (1991). Discourse analysis and written discourse conventions. *Annual Review of Applied Linguistics, 11*, 57–76.

Bereiter, C., & Scardamalia, M. (1987). *The psychology of written composition.* Hillsdale, NJ: Lawrence Erlbaum Associates.

Bereiter, C., & Scardamalia, M. (1989). Intentional learning as a goal of instruction. In L. Resnick (Ed.), *Knowing, learning, and instruction* (pp. 361–391). Hillsdale, NJ: Lawrence Erlbaum Associates.

Bratt Paulston, C. (1990). Educational language policies in Utopia. In B. Harley, P. Allen, J. Cummins, & M. Swain (Eds.), *The development of second language proficiency* (pp. 187–197). Cambridge: Cambridge University Press.

Byrd, P., & Nelson, G. (1995). NNS performance on writing proficiency exams: Focus on students who failed. *Journal of Second Language Writing, 4*, 273–285.

Carlson, S. (1988). Cultural differences in writing and reasoning skills. In A. Purves (Ed.), *Writing across languages and cultures: Issues in contrastive rhetoric* (pp. 109–137). Newbury Park, CA: Sage.

Grabe, W., & Kaplan, R. B. (1996). *Theory and practice of writing.* London: Longman.

Johns, A. (1991). Faculty assessment of ESL student literacy skills: Implications for writing assessment. In L. Hamp-Lyons (Ed.), *Assessing second language writing* (pp. 167–180). Norwood, NJ: Ablex.

Johns, A. (1997). *Text, role, and context: Developing academic literacies.* Cambridge: Cambridge University Press.

Jordan, R. (1997). *English for academic purposes.* Cambridge: Cambridge University Press.

Poole, D. (1991). Discourse analysis in enthnographic research. *Annual Review of Applied Linguistics 11*, 42–56.

Teaching Academic ESL Writing

Chang, Y., & Swales, J. (1999). Informal elements in English academic writing: Threats or opportunities for advanced non-native speakers. In C. Candlin & K. Hyland (Eds.), *Writing texts, processes and practices* (pp. 145–167). London: Longman.

Grabe, W., & Kaplan, R. B. (1989). Writing in a second language: Contrastive rhetoric. In D. Johnson & D. Roen (Eds.), *Richness in writing* (pp. 263–283). New York: Longman.

Grabe, W., & Kaplan, R. B. (1996). *Theory and practice of writing.* London: Longman.

Hamp-Lyons, L. (1991a). Reconstructing academic writing proficiency. In L. Hamp-Lyons (Ed.), *Assessing second language writing* (pp. 127–153). Norwood, NJ: Ablex.

Hamp-Lyons, L. (1991b). Scoring procedures for ESL contexts. In L. Hamp-Lyons (Ed.), *Assessing second language writing* (pp. 241–277). Norwood, NJ: Ablex.

Paltridge, B. (2001). *Genre and the language learning classroom.* Ann Arbor: The University of Michigan Press.
Santos, T. (1988). Professors' reactions to the academic writing of nonnative-speaking students. *TESOL Quarterly, 22*, 69–90.
Shaw, P., & Liu, E. T. K. (1998). What develops in the development of second language writing. *Applied Linguistics, 19*(2), 225–254.
Silva, T. (1993). Toward an understanding of the distinct nature of L2 writing: The ESL research and its implications. *TESOL Quarterly, 27*(4), 657–676.
Silva, T. (1997). On the ethical treatment of ESL writers. *TESOL Quarterly, 31*(2), 359–363.

2

Student Writing Tasks and Written Academic Genres

OVERVIEW

- Writing requirements in the university
- Most important characteristics of academic writing
- Most common written academic assignments and tasks
- Essential features of academic text and importance of teaching them
- Research findings on explicit instruction in L2 academic text
- Types of writing tasks in commonly required academic courses

Although ESL instruction to non-native speakers (NNSs) takes place in various domains of language skills, such as reading, speaking, listening, and pronunciation, L2 learners who undertake to become proficient L2 writers are usually academically bound. In light of the fact that most students who prepare to enter degree programs dedicate vast amounts of time and resources to learn to produce written academic discourse and text, the teaching of English to academically bound NNS students must include an academic writing component. Although it is a verifiable and established fact that NNS students need to develop academic writing skills, ESL teachers in EAP, intensive, and college-level writing programs do not always have a clear picture of the types of writing and written discourse expected of students once they achieve their short-term goals of entering degree programs. In particular, students rarely need to be proficient narrators of personal experiences and good writers of personal stories. In fact what they need is to become relatively good at displaying academic knowledge within the formats expected in academic discourse and text. More important, NNS students' academic survival often depends on their ability to construct written prose of at least passable quality in the context of academic discourse expectations. This chapter presents an overview of those written discourse genres and formats common in the academy in English-speaking environments.

WRITING REQUIREMENTS IN THE UNIVERSITY

Undergraduate students in U.S. colleges and universities are required to take general education courses in such disciplines as the sciences, history, philosophy, psychology, and sociology prior to their studies in their chosen majors. One implication of this structure in U.S. college education is that the greatest demand on students' language skills occurs during the first 2 years of their academic careers, when they are expected to read large amounts of diverse types academic text, write many short and long assignments, and take numerous tests and exams.

In the academy in English-speaking countries, the purpose of written assignments and of examinations and testing is to require students to display their knowledge and familiarity with the course material. Examinations vary in types and formats, ranging from multiple-choice tests to lengthy term papers, including essay tests and short essay-like responses. Outside multiple-choice tests, a great deal of writing is expected in most undergraduate courses, and it is not unusual for students to have to produce up to a dozen written assignments per term (Horowitz, 1986a). Even some multiple-choice tests—such as the TOEFL, ACT, or SAT—incorporate an essay component designed to measure test takers' writing proficiencies.

It is important to note that practically all writing assignments necessitate more than one writing task, such as exposition in the introduction, followed by cause/effect or comparison/contrast rhetorical structures, and possibly back to exposition in the conclusion. For instance, most types of writing assignments can include summaries of published works or syntheses of multiple sources of information or data. In this case, the writing tasks would include synthesis (or analysis) of information, paraphrasing, and restatement skills.

Beginning in the early 1980s, several studies undertook to investigate the types of writing assignments and tasks required of undergraduate and graduate students in academic mainstream courses in various disciplines, such as the natural sciences (e.g., biology, chemistry, and physics), engineering, business, and the humanities including English.

MOST IMPORTANT CHARACTERISTICS OF ACADEMIC WRITING

A survey of 155 undergraduate and 215 graduate faculty in 21 U.S. universities specifically identified the essential NNS students' L2 writing skills in courses that ranged from history, psychology, business, chemistry, and engineering (Rosenfeld, Leung, & Oltman, 2001). The responses of undergraduate faculty (Table 2.1) clearly indicate that organizing writing to convey

TABLE 2.1
Undergraduate Faculty Assessments of Some Writing Tasks

Task Statement	Mean Importance Rating
Organize writing to convey major and supporting ideas.	4.19
Use relevant reasons and examples to support a position.	4.09
Demonstrate a command of standard written English, including grammar, phrasing, effective sentence structure, spelling, and punctuation.	3.70
Demonstrate facility with a range of vocabulary appropriate to the topic.	3.62
Show awareness of audience needs and write to a particular audience or reader.	3.33

Note. Mean Importance Rating on a scale of 0 to 5.

major and supporting ideas and using relevant examples to support them occupy top priority in the quality of academic discourse[1] (ranks 4.19–4.09, respectively, out of 5).

In addition, demonstrating command of standard written English, "including grammar, phrasing, effective sentence structure, spelling, and punctuation," is another high-priority requirement (rank 3.70), as well as demonstrating "facility with a range of vocabulary appropriate for the topic" (rank 3.62). On the other hand, showing awareness of audience needs and writing to a particular audience/reader was not found to be as important (rank 3.33). In addition to the faculty, undergraduate students ranked written discourse organization skills at 4.18; grammar, phrasing, and sentence structure at 4.15; and appropriate vocabulary at 3.69.

[1]The teaching of academic discourse organization is crucially important in L2 writing instruction, and a large number of textbooks are available that focus on discourse. It would be no exaggeration to say that the teaching of L2 academic writing focuses predominantly on the features of discourse organization. However, markedly few course books on L2 writing for either students or teacher training address the importance of text features in L2 instruction. As mentioned earlier, however organized the information flow can be in student writing, it may be impossible to understand without an essential clarity and accuracy of text.

Graduate faculty (Table 2.2) identified largely similar priorities in student writing with regard to the importance of information/discourse organization and examples (ranks 4.46 and 4.34, respectively), grammar, phrasing, and sentence structure (rank 4.06), and appropriate vocabulary (3.74).

On the other hand, graduate students ranked discourse organization and exemplification at 4.32 and 3.96, respectively; grammar, phrasing, and sentence structure at 3.83; and vocabulary 3.56 (i.e., below the importance rankings assigned by graduate faculty in practically all categories).

In a separate subset of survey items, both undergraduate and graduate faculty also specified the specific writing skills that in their experiences determined the success of NNS students in their courses. For undergraduate faculty, the top three L2 writing skills included (in declining order of importance):

- discourse and information organization (2.40 out of 3)
- standard written English (i.e., grammar, phrasing, and sentence structure; 2.35)
- vocabulary (2.26).

Among graduate faculty, the top three skills essential for success in academic courses consisted of:

- information/discourse organization (2.49 out of 3)

TABLE 2.2

Graduate Faculty Assessments of Some Writing Tasks

Task Statement	Mean Importance Rating
Organize writing to convey major and supporting ideas.	4.46
Use relevant reasons and examples to support a position.	4.34
Demonstrate a command of standard written English, including grammar, phrasing, effective sentence structure, spelling, and punctuation.	4.06
Demonstrate facility with a range of vocabulary appropriate to the topic.	3.74
Show awareness of audience needs and write to a particular audience or reader.	3.62

Note. Mean Importance Rating on a scale of 0 to 5.

- command of standard written English (2.37)
- using background knowledge, reference materials, and other resources to analyze and refine arguments (2.35).

The employment of appropriate vocabulary received a ranking of 2.27.

The Rosenfeld, Leung, and Oltman (2001) study demonstrated unambiguously that L2 grammar and vocabulary skills play a crucial role in student academic success (and obviously survival).

MOST COMMON STUDENT WRITTEN ACADEMIC ASSIGNMENTS AND TASKS

The most comprehensive study of academic writing tasks was carried out by the Educational Testing Service (Hale et al., 1996), which surveyed eight large comprehensive universities in the United States. The information discussed in this investigation is summarized next.

Major Writing Assignments

Major academic essays typically have a specified length of 5 to 10 or more than 10 pages. These papers predominantly take the forms of out-of-class assignments and are required far more frequently in humanities courses such as psychology, economics, history, and English than in the sciences, engineering, or computer science. Most of these projects also necessitate library research and syntheses of literature and relevant information from a variety of sources. According to the Hale et al. (1996) findings, undergraduate courses in the sciences and engineering rarely expect students to write papers as long as 5 to 10 pages, and most of these types of essays are expected in English department courses.

Medium-Length Essays and Short Written Tasks

Medium-length essays between 1 and 5 pages are required as in-class and out-of-class assignments in practically all disciplines, with the exceptions of undergraduate courses in physics, mathematics, and engineering. In social science and humanities studies, they are expected in a majority of undergraduate courses. Similarly, short written assignments of about 0.5 to 1.5 pages represent course components in approximately half of all undergraduate courses, including physics, math, and engineering, and 94% of English courses (Hale et al., 1996). These essays are assigned both in and out of class in undergraduate and graduate studies alike. Among these assignments, library research reports, laboratory or experiment reports with or without interpretation, and book reviews represent the most common types of writing.

Short writing tasks (also called *expanded answers*) found in many written in-class and out-of-class exams, laboratory reports, case studies, annotations of literature, and computer program documentation assignments constitute the most common type of writing across all disciplines and courses. Furthermore, short writing assignments are significantly more common in undergraduate than graduate courses and in in-class than out-of-class assignments.

English Composition Writing Tasks

English composition instruction often provides the model for teaching writing in EAPs. According to the Hale et al. (1996) study, short writing tasks are far less common in English than in social or natural sciences (29% of all in-class assignments vs. 53% and 79%, respectively). On the other hand, out-of-class essays are required in 94% of all English courses, for example, compared with 53% in social and 47% in natural sciences. Among the assignment types, summaries and unstructured writing genre defined as free writing, journal entries, or notes, all which consist of writing down one's thoughts and experiences, are found almost exclusively in English courses, as well as twice as many assigned library research papers as in other disciplines. Major papers of 5 to 10 pages in length are assigned in 41% of English courses and only rarely in social science courses. Similarly, 1- to 5-page essays are required in 82% of English courses versus 39% of those in social sciences and 21% in physical/natural sciences.

FEATURES OF ACADEMIC GENRE AND TEXT

Research into various types of discourse and text (Biber, 1988; Biber, Johansson, Leech, Conrad, & Finegan, 1999; Swales, 1990a) showed explicitly and clearly that academic discourse and text are constructed differently than other types of text, such as fiction, news reportage, or personal correspondence. In fact, Swales (1990a) identified what he called "the academic discourse community" (p. 5), which prescribes somewhat rigid forms of discourse construction and organization combined with similarly inflexible expectations of vocabulary and grammar uses. Biber et al. (1999) examined a large corpus of specific microfeatures of texts in diverse spoken and written genres, and their findings are described in a 1,200-page volume. Their analysis includes the cross-genre uses of nouns, determiners, pronouns, verb tenses, and semantic classes of verbs, adjectives, adverbs, and clauses. Textual uses of practically all features indicate that written academic text is markedly distinct from many other types of texts, such as personal narrative, conversation, and even academic lectures.

Other corpus studies investigated frequencies of use of various lexical and syntactic features employed in academic and other types of text to elucidate the differences between the academic and other types of written genres. For example, these examinations focus on various hedges, modal verbs, epistemic adjectives, adverbs, and nouns (Collins, 1991; Hoye, 1997; Hyland, 1998), as well as classes of collocations, idioms, synonyms, adverb clauses, and text-referential cohesion (Partington, 1996). These studies expanded the current knowledge base regarding specific structures and lexical features of written academic text, as well as other common features of text such as noun and prepositional phrases, stock phrases, and collocations (Kennedy, 1991; Kjellmer, 1991; Renouf & Sinclair, 1991).

For instance, analyses of large corpora have led to the development of pattern grammar to identify combinations of words that occur relatively frequently in academic texts and that may be dependent on a particular word choice to convey clear and definable meaning (Hunston & Francis, 2000). Because of great strides made in corpus analyses in the past few decades, today much more is known about frequent patterns of verb, noun, and adjective uses and variations in their meanings, as well as the syntactic and lexical contexts in which particular lexical and syntactic features occur.

Although findings of text and corpus analyses of the written academic genre may not be directly applicable to classroom instruction and studies of student texts, they provide insight into discourse and text conventions of published academic and other types of texts. Furthermore, they often help explain how written academic prose is constructed and, by implication, can inform writing instruction and pedagogy. An additional benefit of corpus studies is that they shed light on how enormously complex and frequently lexicalized the uses of language and text in the academic genre actually are.

TEACHING ACADEMIC TEXT FEATURES

Several researchers have identified English composition essays and the pedagogical essays (Johns, 1997) ubiquitous in English for Academic Purposes (EAPs) programs to be dramatically different from those students are required to write in the disciplines. Among other researchers, Horowitz (1986a) identified some of the writing tasks in undergraduate humanities courses. According to his findings, these included:

- summary/reaction to a journal article or reading
- annotated bibliography in such disciplines as biology, lab, and experiment reports
- connections between theory and data
- synthesis of multiple literature sources
- various research projects

Horowitz further noted that these assignments do not include invention and personal discovery and "the academic writer's task is not to create personal meaning but to find, organize, and present data according to fairly explicit instructions" (p. 452). According to the author, sentence-level grammar, use of discourse markers, and clarity of academic text remain "vital" (p. 454) in the teaching of academically bound NNS students.

In the 1980s, several studies endeavored to learn about the reactions of faculty to particular features of NNS students' text (Johns, 1981; Ostler, 1980; Santos, 1988; Vann, Lorenz, & Meyer, 1991; Vann, Meyer, & Lorenz, 1984). Most professors in the disciplines are not well versed in the complexities of ESL instruction or L2 learning and acquisition. Nonetheless, their perceptions of text quality are important because they are the ones who grade students' assignments. According to the results of these studies, the employment of syntactic, lexical, and discourse features of text and errors in the uses of these features have an influential effect on the perceived quality of students' text. Although sentence- and phrase-level errors are often seen in relative rather than absolute terms, the problems in students' uses of verb tenses, word order, subordinate clauses, passive voice, and impersonal constructions have been found to obscure the text's meaning. In the view of faculty in various disciplines, such as physical and natural sciences, humanities, business, and the arts, accuracy in the uses of these and other syntactic and lexical features is very important and, in most cases, syntactic and lexical errors result in lower assignment grades.

When thinking about the importance of accuracy in the academic writing of NNS students, many ESL and EAP teachers believe that syntactic and lexical errors in L2 texts are not particularly damaging because NS writers also make numerous mistakes in their texts. However, several studies have found that faculty in the disciplines have a far more critical view of ESL errors than those of NSs (Santos, 1988; Vann et al., 1984, 1991). Although the indications of error gravity vary across disciplines and even vary according to the age of faculty, the conclusions in all investigations largely remain similar: ESL errors in students' texts are costly in terms of grades and overall evaluations of work quality.

To determine whether the needs of academically bound NNS learners were adequately addressed in EAP writing instruction, Leki and Carson (1997) interviewed a large group of students who began their ESL training and then continued their studies in various disciplines, such as engineering, biology, business, communications, and social work. The students reported great differences between the demands of writing in EAP classes and those in the disciplines. Among other important considerations, many students identified shortfalls in their vocabulary repertoire and a lack of familiarity with the *dry* academic textual style. Most important, the students spoke about the fact that EAP writing instruction represents what Leki and Carson called "non-text-responsible writing" (p. 63), whereas in the disciplines students are held accountable for the context of the text they read and the content and accuracy of the text they produce. The authors concluded that what is valued in writing classes that emphasize personal growth and experience is distinct from that necessary in academic writing in the disciplines. They further stated that EAP writing instruction has the responsibility for preparing students for "real" academic courses because without adequate exposure to the demands of academic writing students are essentially left to their own devices once their EAP training is completed.

Johns (1997) explained that the narrow focus of writing instruction in EAPs and its focus on experiential essays is often based on the principle that, "if you can write [or read] an essay, you can write [or read] anything" (p. 122). She pointed out that in mainstream courses the expectations and grading of writing are different from those of ESL/EAP faculty. In fact she commented that when NNS students are exposed to largely one type of writing task, they come to believe that "this is the only way to write." Such limited experience with writing actually does students a disservice and causes problems in their academic and professional careers.

Like Horowitz, Johns emphasized the importance of text in students' academic writing. She emphasized that faculty often complain that students do not use vocabulary and data with care. However, in her view, because personal essays are highly valued in ESL and EAP writing instruction and because many instructional readings are in story form and/or simplified specifically for NNS readers, students are not exposed to the precision often expected in much of the academic prose. Furthermore, considerations of academic objectivity often conveyed by lexical and syntactic means, such as uses of personal pronouns and passive voice, are in conflict with those features of text encouraged in personal essays. Johns emphasized that formal academic register requires writers to be guarded and personally and emotionally removed from the text. She underscored that the hedged and depersonalized register of academic text is rarely addressed in ESL/EAP writing instruction, but should be if students are to attain the proficiency necessary for their success in mainstream academic courses.

In other studies, Dudley-Evans and St. John (1998) also stated that "the process approach [to teaching L2 writing], although extremely valuable in helping students organize and plan their writing has failed to tackle the actual texts that students have to produce as part of their academic or professional work" (p. 117). They also noted that in the United States, most of those who advocate a process approach see the teaching of generalized strategies of planning, writing, and revising as sufficient and believe that a detailed analysis of academic texts lies beyond the job of the writing teacher (Raimes, 1993; Zamel, 1983). However, according to Dudley-Evans and St. John, the considerations of end-product quality in L2 writing is important in academic and professional writing, and combining the strengths of both the product- and process-oriented approaches to the teaching of writing can lead to overall improvements in L2 writing instruction.

THE NEED FOR EXPLICIT INSTRUCTION IN L2 ACADEMIC TEXT

In an important study that surveyed 77 published research reports on the effectiveness of explicit grammar instruction, Norris and Ortega (2000) normed the results of investigations in an attempt to achieve consistency across various investigative and analytical methodologies. Their meta-analysis shows that in grammar learning focused instruction of any sort is far more effective than any type of teaching methodology based on focused exposure to L2 without explicit teaching. They further found that focused L2 instruction resulted in large language gains over the course of the instructional term and that the effects of the instruction seem to be durable over time. Furthermore, Norris and Ortega explained that explicit instruction based on inductive or deductive approaches leads to greater L2 gains than implicit instruction of any sort. Thus, given that academically bound L2 learners need to make substantial L2 gains to begin their studies, it seems clear that L2 grammar and vocabulary should be taught thoroughly and intensively.

When students matriculate from ESL/EAP programs, the quality of their writing and text is evaluated by non-ESL specialists who are faculty in the disciplines. Furthermore, when students' academic studies are completed, the accuracy of their text production is continually appraised by subsequent non-specialists in on-the-job writing whenever college-educated NNSs write e-mail, notes, reports, and old-fashioned memos. Considerate, understanding, and compassionate ESL teachers who seek to benefit their students have to teach the skills and language features that students must have to achieve their desired professional and career goals. In fact, this is what ESL teachers are hired to do. If instruction in the essential language skills is not provided, students are largely left to their own devices when attempting to attain L2 proficiency needed for their academic and professional endeavors.

Much recent research has shown that exposure to daily and classroom interactions, as well as fluency-oriented instruction, does not represent an effective pedagogical approach to developing syntactic and lexical accuracy (Chang & Swales, 1999; Dudley-Evans & St. John, 1998; Ellis, 2001; Jordan, 1997; Richards, 2002). Although teachers in academic preparatory and writing programs often believe that they set out to develop learners' academic reading and writing proficiencies, in actuality few are closely familiar with the types of writing assignments and tasks that NNS students need to perform once they complete their language training. For example, a list in chapter 5 includes the most frequently encountered nouns in course materials across all disciplines in college-level general education courses and contains such words as *ambiguity, anomaly, apparatus, appeal,* and *aristocrat*. In all likelihood, few practicing ESL teachers in EAP programs have undertaken to teach the meanings of these words unless they are fortuitously used in student reading texts. Fluency development activities in writing that require students to keep personal journals or carry out journal-centered correspondence with the teacher are not designed to increase learners' academic vocabulary or grammar repertoire, with its almost requisite uses of passive voice, impersonal construction, and complex hedging. In fact such fluency-based activities encourage the use of immediately accessible lexicon and grammar structures without a means of language gains and perpetuate learners' misunderstanding and confusion with regard to the high degree of accuracy expected in formal academic prose.

A teacher of writing would do a disservice to academically bound NNS students by not preparing them for academic writing assignments, particularly those in the more common forms the students are certain to encounter later in their studies. Within these academic assignments and tasks, students must produce text that is academically sophisticated enough to demonstrate their understanding of and familiarity with the course material. Yet few ESL/EAP programs undertake to at least expose their students to various types of academic assignments and require production of written academic (rather than personal) prose (Chang & Swales, 1999; Johns, 1997; Leki & Carson, 1997).

TYPES OF WRITING TASKS

The discussion of writing tasks in this section relies on the findings of Hale et al. (1996) to survey the writing requirements in eight comprehensive U.S. universities. Overall the types of writing expected of undergraduate and graduate students do not seem to vary greatly with regard to the rhetorical and discourse patterns they elicit. Most assignments combine several rhetorical tasks (e.g., exposition and analysis in business case studies or history essays).

The most common types of rhetorical formats found in in-class and out-of-class assignments represent (in declining order of frequency):

- **Exposition** (short tasks required largely in introductions and explanations of material or content to follow, and thus it is a component of all assignment types)
- **Cause–effect interpretation** (by far the most prevalent writing task, found in over half of all writing assignments)
- **Classification** of events, facts, and developments according to a generalized theoretical or factual scheme
- **Comparison/contrast** of entities, theories, methods, analyses, and approaches (in short assignments)
- **Analysis** of information/facts (in medium-length assignments)
- **Argumentation** based on facts/research/published literature (in medium-length assignments)

Less common writing tasks include:

- **Expanded definition** (least common in medium-length and out-of-class assignments)
- **Process analysis** in such disciplines as political science, economics, sociology, psychology, accounting, marketing, and management (hardly ever found in out-of-class assignments)
- **Fact-based exemplification** of concepts and theoretical premises and constructs (overall least common in both in-class and out-of-class assignments)
- *Not found in any assignments*—**narration/description** in the disciplines or English courses

In general, the frequency of rhetorical patterns does not seem to differ greatly among the writing tasks in undergraduate and graduate courses. Specifically, cause–effect essays can be found in over half of all written tasks in in- and out-of-class assignments, with exemplification, process analysis, and definition being comparatively least common.

Exposition rhetorical tasks require writers to explain or clarify the topic/subject. In general terms, exposition is entailed in expressing ideas, opinions, or explanation pertaining to a particular piece of knowledge or fact. For example,

1. *What nonverbal cues communicated the most conflict in the newlywed study?* (Psychology) (Epstein, 1999, p. 291)
2. *Discuss the various types of accounting information most companies routinely use.* (Business) (Zikmund, Middlemist, & Middlemist, 1995, p. 447)
3. *Which forms of government predominated among the Italian city-states? In the end, which was the most successful? Why?* (History) (Perry et al., 2000, p. 322)

Cause–effect interpretation tasks deal with establishing causal relationships and are based on causal reasoning. Most assignments of this type include a discussion or an explanation of a cause–effect relationship among events or problems, identification of causes or effects, and a presentation of problem solutions in the case of problem–solution tasks.

Examples of cause–effect interpretation assignments can be:

1. *Pabst Blue Ribbon was a major beer company when I was in college. However, recently it has lost market share, and now you hardly even hear about it. What happened at Pabst and why?* (Business) (Adapted from Bean, 1996)
2. *Why does culture arise in the first place? Why is culture a necessary part of all organized life?* (Sociology) (Charon, 1999, p. 105)

3. *Why is the Renaissance considered a departure from the Middle Ages and the beginning of modernity?* (History) (Perry et al., 2000, p. 322)

Classification of events, facts, and developments assignments involve cognitive tasks in which writers are expected to determine what types of group members share particular features or characteristics. Therefore, students are required to classify clusters or groups of objects, events, or situations according to their common attributes, create a system to classify objects or events, and list them based on this classification. For example,

1. *In what ways can a company maintain good relations with its union employees without being unfair to its nonunion employees?* (Business) (Zikmund, Middlemist, & Middlemist, 1995, p. 421)
2. *What do Elaine Walster and Ellen Berscheid say are the ingredients for love?* (Psychology) (Epstein, 1999, p. 326)
3. *What was the traditional relationship between the people and their rulers during the Middle Ages? How and why did this relationship begin to change in the sixteenth century and with what results?* (History) (Perry et al., 2000, p. 376)

Comparison/contrast tasks expect writers to discuss or examine objects or domains of knowledge by identifying their characteristics/properties that make them similar or different. In general, the purpose of such assignments is to identify the specific points that make objects, events, or situations similar and/or different as well as explain one in terms of the other.

Examples of these assignments can be:

1. *Compare and contrast medieval universities with universities today* (History) (Perry et al., 2000, p. 278)
2. *What distinguishes the philosophy of religion from theology?* (Philosophy) (Schoedinger, 2000, p. 225)
3. *Compare the reaction of Olaudah Equino on first encountering Europeans with that of the Spaniards encountering Aztecs.* (History) (Perry, Peden, & Von Laue, 1999, p. 351)

Analysis of information or facts (in medium-length assignments) requires writers to separate a whole into elements or component parts and identify relationships among these parts. Other types of analysis assignments include applying theories or interpretive methods to the object of analysis or a particular school of thought, distinguishing facts from theories, evaluating the validity of stated or unstated assumptions and/or various types of relationships among events, identifying logical fallacies in arguments, or specifying the author's purpose, bias, or point of view. For example:

1. *How does the bourgeoisie gradually undermine its own existence according to Marx?* (Philosophy) (Schoedinger, 2000, p. 215)
2. *How do the elasticities of supply and demand affect the deadweight loss of a tax? Why do they have this effect?* (Economics) (Mankiw, 2001, p. 176)
3. *If class, race, and gender are positions within social structures, we should be able to describe them in terms of power, prestige, privileges, role, identity, and perspective. Can you do this?* (Sociology) (Charon, 1999, p. 86)

Argumentation assignments largely represent a form of exposition that includes an element of persuasion. Therefore, the rhetorical purpose of these writing tasks extends beyond the presentation, explanation, or discussion to convince the reader of a particular point of view. In argumentation tasks, the writers are required to recognize that issues have at least two sides and present the facts or information to develop a reasoned and logical conclusion based on the presented evidence. In practically all assignments, presentations of unsupported assertions are not considered to be argumentation (Hale et al., 1996).

1. *Human beings are social to their very core. How does the material covered in Chapter xxx/this term so far support this proposition? What do you think of this argument?* (Sociology) (Adapted from Charon, 1999)
2. *What is freedom? What is individuality? To what extent do you think human beings are free or individuals? What do you think is the origin of freedom and individuality?* (Sociology) (Charon, 1999, p. 148)
3. *Why would removing trade restrictions, such as a tariff, lead to more rapid economic growth?* (Economics) (Mankiw, 2001, p. 262)

Less Common Rhetorical and Writing Tasks

Three types of writing tasks appear markedly less common than those discussed earlier: definition, process description, and exemplification.

Expanded definition assignments consist of explanations of exact meanings or significance of a phrase or term. Usually these assignments consist of defining the term, listing the concept to which the term belongs, and specifying the attributes that distinguish it from others in its class. For example:

1. *What is social order?* (Sociology) (Charon, 1999, p. 147)
2. *Explain the meaning of <u>nominal interest rate</u> and <u>real interest rate</u>. How are they related?* (Economics) (Mankiw, 2001, p. 237)

Process analysis involves directions on how someone should do something or how something should be done, including chronological details in a series of steps/operations/ actions necessary to achieve a particular result or happening. In most cases, a discussion of reasons for the steps and negative directions are needed. For example,

1. *Suppose that you were to set up an organization—for example, a club, a church, a school, or a small community. What would you do to try to ensure that social order would successfully be established?* (Sociology) (Charon, 1999, p. 147)
2. *What is the business value chain? Use frozen pizza sold in supermarkets to explain your answer.* (Business) (Zikmund, Middlemist, & Middlemist, 1995, p. 17)

Exemplification and illustration largely deals with expanding on theories/concepts/ ideas and providing reasonable amounts of detail to explain a type, class, or group of objects or events by presenting examples. These assignments largely rely on general-to-specific discourse organization flow. For example,

1. *Give at least two examples of what children can learn from playing peek-a-boo.* (Psychology) (Epstein, 1999, p. 258)
2. *What is a simple idea, according to Locke? Give examples.* (Philosophy) (Adapted from Schoedinger, 2000, p. 351)

QUESTIONS FOR DISCUSSION

1. What are the key writing tasks with which NNS writers need to be competent based on research and interviews with undergraduate and graduate faculty? What kinds of instruction can help NNS writers improve these skills?
2. What are the most common forms of academic writing assignments? How can a teacher in an ESL or EAP writing course help students prepare for these kinds of assignments?
3. What can be possible reasons that the common types of essays/writing tasks required of students in ESL/EAP writing courses are distinct from those in courses in the disciplines? If you were in charge of the curriculum in preparatory ESL writing courses, would you change the types of writing tasks required of students? If yes, in what way? If no, why not?

FURTHER READINGS ABOUT WRITING TASKS AND WRITTEN ACADEMIC GENRES

Writing Tasks

Johnson, D. (1989a). Enriching task contexts for second language writing: Power through interpersonal roles. In D. Johnson & D. Roen (Eds.), *Richness in writing* (pp. 39–54). New York: Longman.

Leki, I., & Carson, J. (1997). "Completely Different Worlds": EAP and the writing experiences of ESL students in university courses. *TESOL Quarterly, 31*(1), 39–70.

Ostler, S. (1980). A survey of needs of advanced ESL. *TESOL Quarterly, 14*(4), 489–502.

Rosenfeld, M., Leung, S., & Oltman, P. (2001). *The reading, writing, speaking, and listening tasks important for academic success at undergraduate and graduate levels* (MS 21). Princeton, NJ: ETS.

Swales, J., & Feak, C. (2000). *English in today's research world.* Ann Arbor, MI: The University of Michigan Press.

Written Academic Genres

Berkenkotter, C., & Huckin, T. (1995). *Genre knowledge in disciplinary communities.* Hillsdale, NJ: Lawrence Erlbaum Associates.

Johns, A. (1997). *Text, role, and context: Developing academic literacies.* Cambridge: Cambridge University Press.

Johns, A. (2002). *Genres in the classroom: Multiple perspectives.* Mahwah, NJ: Lawrence Erlbaum Associates.

Paltridge, B. (2001). *Genre and the language learning classroom.* Ann Arbor: The University of Michigan Press.

Swales, J. (1990). *Genre analysis.* Cambridge: Cambridge University Press.

3

Curriculum for Teaching the Language Features of Academic Writing

OVERVIEW

- The importance of accuracy in academic writing
- Recurrent features of academic discourse in English
- The benefits of written academic discourse conventions
- Instructed L2 grammar and noticing
- Vocabulary size and academic text
- Incidental learning of grammar and vocabulary
- Self-editing skills development
- Unimportant features of academic text

The purpose of this chapter is to establish a research-based framework for teaching academic writing courses that focus on just the core, academic survival-level skills students need to be successful in their university work. To this end, the L2 writing course curriculum needs to be designed around the key areas that deal with accuracy in grammar and lexis, intensive vocabulary instruction, and fundamental editing of one's own text. In addition, the chapter also discusses the benefits and shortfalls of incidental vocabulary learning and the grammatical and lexical features of academic text that are customarily taught in ESL classes, but that may be relatively unimportant.

The essential elements of the course that must be addressed can be designed to be flexible within the curriculum structure, and the amount of effort and time devoted to each can be adjusted for a particular group of students. This chapter presents an overview of research to show why core components of the course are critical in teaching L2 academic writing and lays the groundwork for the teaching approach developed in the subsequent chapters on sentence and phrase structure, nouns, pronouns, verb tenses, verb lexical classes, and rhetorical features of text such as cohesion and hedging.

The curriculum design outlined in this chapter centers on current research findings about what it takes to attain viable academic L2 writing skills and presents dozens of techniques for teaching them. The teacher's workload and the student's "learning burden" (Nation, 2001, p. 23)—that is, the amount of effort required to learn L2 grammar and vocabulary—are expected to be realistic, but certainly not very light. Although activities to develop learners' conversational fluency or invention techniques are typically less work and more fun for both teachers and students, they have not demonstrably equipped students for success in university-level academic courses (Hinkel, 2002a; Hyland, 1996, 2002a).

ACCURACY, ACADEMIC TEXT, AND PRACTICAL GOALS

As the teaching of English became increasingly important during and after World War II, Charles Fries developed one of the first U.S. textbooks for training ESL teachers. In 1945, his definition of syntactic and lexical accuracy in L2 use was flexible and pragmatic:

> The "accuracy" which is advocated here does not mean the so-called "correctness" of the common handbooks.... The accuracy here stressed refers to an accuracy based upon a realistic description of the actual language as used by native speakers in carrying on their affairs.... It is fruitless to argue in the abstract concerning the relative merits of the various types of English.... In learning English as a foreign language it is necessary to decide upon a particular type to be mastered, for there is no single kind that is used throughout all the English speaking world. The practical approach is to decide for the kind of English that will be used by the particular group with which one wishes to associate...." (Fries, 1945 pp. 3–4)

The important point made by Fries more than half a century ago is that L2 learners need to identify their goals for learning L2 and the types of the NS population with which they wish to associate. In the case of academically bound NNS learners, these populations consist of the university faculty in mainstream courses who evaluate the assignment quality of the NS and NNS students enrolled in the same classes.

> If NNS college and university students are to succeed in competition for grades and attain their educational objectives, the level of accuracy in their L2 writing needs to at least attempt to approximate that of NS students of similar academic standing.

Without a doubt, this is an ambitious goal. It goes without saying that NS students have been socialized in, schooled in, and exposed to their L1 throughout their entire lives, whereas most NNS students have studied EFL in their native countries and began their ESL/EAP studies as adults. The fact that NNS writers have a reduced English proficiency compared with their NS counterparts further underscores the need for thorough L2 training and instruction. In light of the fact that L2 writers' vocabulary and grammar ranges are usually greatly limited compared with those of NSs, for NNS students, producing academic writing proximate to that of NSs is not a trivial task. Without instruction in and learning how to construct L2 academic text, NNS students often find themselves at a great disadvantage in their academic and professional careers (Horowitz, 1986a; Johns, 1981, 1997; Leki & Carson, 1997; Nation & Waring, 1997; Santos, 1984, 1988).

The curriculum outline for teaching the essential features of academic text in English is based on the research findings discussed in the book *Second Language Writers' Text* (Hinkel, 2002a). That volume presents detailed analyses of NNS students' texts and their quantitative comparisons to the types and frequency rates of textual features in NS students' texts.

> Research has demonstrated that English-language academic writing is governed by several rigid conventions in its discourse structure and language features. Based on the findings of numerous studies and in simple terms, the teaching techniques and strategies discussed in this book aim for maximum gain for minimal work by capitalizing on the rigidity and conventionalization of written academic prose in English.

> The fundamental principle of the L2 academic writing curriculum presented in this volume centers around acceptable and contextually relevant lexical substitutions within a limited range of lexical and syntactic constructions (i.e., text and sentence chunking and focused instruction in replacement parts for chunk components).

DISCOURSE AND TEXTUAL FEATURES OF ACADEMIC WRITING

To some extent, the uses of specific linguistic features may depend on the discipline for which an assignment is written. Predictably, an essay in history, business case studies, or descriptions of experiments in psychology may contain a greater number of past-tense verbs than a paper that discusses generally applicable observations and interpretations of research data. For example, most introductory textbooks in philosophy, sociology, economics, or biology include high numbers of present-tense verbs.

Despite some amount of variation that can be identified in the linguistic features of texts across disciplines and particular academic subgenres, many represent what Johns (1997) called "recurring features" (p. 27) of the academic genre and text—that is, "formal features of text in this genre do not appear to vary considerably from class to class, nor ... have the genre requirements varied much since the mid-1980s" (p. 29). Based on the findings of Swales (1990a), Johns explained that some of these recurring features are at the discourse level of academic text and largely consist of four purposeful introductory moves to prepare readers to read and understand text efficiently. These moves include:

1. establishing or introducing the topic and discussing its importance,
2. reviewing published (or other) sources of information,
3. preparing the ground and reasoning for the present analysis and/or synthesis of information (or demonstrating how the present examination can accomplish what has not been accomplished previously), and
4. introducing the present examination and stating its purpose.

In addition to the discourse-level features of the academic genre, Johns also noted that linguistic features of text are also recurrent and can be found across practically all disciplines and subgenres. She emphasized that these are often neglected in the teaching of L2 writing and suggested various ways to include them in L2 writing instruction.

In particular, Johns summarized the findings of text analysis and research on academic text and pointed out that several lexical and syntactic features are highly valued "in general expository academic prose" (pp. 58–59):

- Lexical precision and careful use of vocabulary
- Careful and purposeful uses of text "maps" and "signposts," such as discourse and metadiscourse markers (e.g., *First this essays discusses xxx and yyy and then presents solutions to the zzz problem*)
- Appearance of the writer's objectivity and impersonal register (e.g., avoidance of first-person pronouns and use of "author-evacuation," the strategic passive voice, and *it*-cleft constructions; e.g., *it is/seems/appears that* ...)
- Nonjudgmental interpretations of information, findings, and events (e.g., avoidance of emotive descriptors—nouns, adverbs, and adjectives such as *great, wonderful, exciting, terrible*)
- A guarded stance in presenting argumentation and results (e.g., employment of frequent hedges such as modal verbs, adverbs of frequency, or linking verbs)

Other studies of L2 written academic text have identified a range of lexical and grammar features that required focused instruction and concerted effort from both teachers and learners (Dudley-Evans & St. John, 1998;

Johns & Dudley-Evans, 1991; Jordan, 1997; Nation, 1990, 2001). Among the most urgent are:

- Expanding the accessible repertoire of common **academic** nouns, verbs, adjectives, and adverbs (e.g., analysis, develop, dramatic, evidently)
- Contextual functions and uses of verb tenses in discourse
- Functions and uses of the passive voice in academic text
- Functions of adverbs in pivoting discourse and information flow
- Regularities in phrase and sentence construction
- Backgrounding information in subordinate clauses
- Textual features of cohesion and coherence in discourse
- Functions and uses of hedges in academic prose (based on Hinkel, 2002a)

Although at first glance producing academic assignments and papers may seem difficult and daunting, the greatest advantage of the fact that written academic discourse is highly conventionalized and its features are recurrent is that, with the groundwork in place and consistent practice, producing academic writing is actually relatively easy.

THE IMPORTANCE OF LANGUAGE PROFICIENCY FOR WRITING

In the production of academic writing, various L2 skills have divergent degrees of importance. For instance, P. Johnson's (1988) study of international undergraduate students' GPAs and TOEFL scores in listening comprehension, grammar, and reading sections established strong positive correlations between students' academic performance and grammar and reading proficiencies. The correlations between listening scores and undergraduate GPAs were not significant, and Johnson concluded that L2 grammar and reading skills play a highly influential role in students' abilities to perform well in humanities, social sciences, and business courses.

Celce-Murcia (1991) emphasized that for educated, academically oriented, and advanced L2 learners, grammar instruction is essential if they are to achieve their educational and professional goals. She commented that, "the importance of a reasonable degree of grammatical accuracy in academic or professional writing cannot be overstated" (p. 465). Celce-Murcia cited a study that indicates that a high frequency of grammar errors in NNS students' academic writing can make essays unacceptable to university faculty, and an average of 7.2 grammatical errors per 100 words in L2 academic prose was judged to be nonpassing by professors in mainstream courses.

Other researchers also identified the critical role of grammatical accuracy in L2 academic writing and stressed that instruction in grammatical features of formal written genres is paramount. Without teaching and extensive practice, many learners are unable to develop a full range of L2 advanced grammatical features essential in formal and written discourse (Celce-Murcia & Hilles, 1988; R. Ellis, 1994; Hammerly, 1991; Schmidt, 1994; Shaw & Liu, 1998). R. Ellis (1990) explained that "formal classroom teaching with its emphasis on linguistic accuracy will engage the learner in planned [spoken or written] discourse and develop the corresponding type of competence" (p. 121).

It is important to keep in mind, however, that the teaching of grammar essential for the production of L2 writing is not intended to develop NNS students' overall native-like proficiency (Pica, 1994). For instance, in her overview of L2 learning research, Larsen-Freeman (1991) concluded explicitly that "for most adult learners, complete mastery of the L2 may be impossible," and that the purpose of L2 teaching and learning is to enable "learners to go as far as they are capable of going in the L2, but [ESL] teachers should be realistic in their expectations" (p. 337).

PREFABRICATED SENTENCES AND LEXICALIZED CHUNKS

Grammar instruction that has the goal of preparing students for academic studies in English-speaking countries needs to be designed to develop learners' practical and useful skills that are directly relevant to producing academic text. Teaching grammar for writing cannot take place in isolation from the lexical and discourse features of text (e.g., the verb tenses in academic prose are determined by the type of context in which they are used: The present tense is useful in citations of sources, but not descriptions of case studies; Swales & Feak, 1994).

Most important, grammar instruction has to take place in tandem with instruction on vocabulary and academic collocations. A great deal of research carried out on the effectiveness of learning grammar in contextual lexicalized chunks and sentence stems (i.e., whole sentences and phrases, and recurrent patterned expressions) has shown that these are fundamental to both L1 and L2 learning and use (N. Ellis, 1997; R. Ellis, 1994; Lewis, 1993, 1997; Nattinger & DeCarrico, 1992). Stock grammatical and lexical chunks can become an efficient means to expand L2 writers' arsenals particularly when learners are also taught how to substitute discrete elements appropriately and in practical ways. For example, the fact that the function of noun clauses is similar to that of simple nouns can be addressed by means of substitutions in patterned expressions common in academic prose:

The experiment/ data/study shows that xxx increases(with yyy) / an increase of xxx/ the growth/rise of xxx.

As Wilkins (1972) commented, learning an L2 in lexical and grammatical units (chunks), instead of discrete words or word elements, can often "cover in half the time what is ... expected from a whole year's of language learning" (p. 102). Peters (1983) pointed out that, despite the linguistic and psycholinguistic evidence that memorizing language chunks represents an effective and unrestrictive means to expand learners' lexical and grammatical ranges, a cultural and pedagogical bias exists against the idea of memorization of long chunks of text. She further underscored that making substitutions within formulaic expressions is objected to "on the grounds that they are so mindless that they are ineffective in promoting second language learning." Peters' research, however, showed that memorizing long chunks of text "is at its simplest the equivalent of memorizing so many long 'words,' but only if no grammatical analysis (e.g. segmentation) is ever performed on these items" (p. 109)—a virtual impossibility in the contexts of creative second language learning.

An important confirmation of Peters' (1983) empirical study of the role chunks in first and second language learning came from the work of Cowie (1988), who analyzed a large body of authentic English data. He found that thousands of multiword units of language (or chunks) remain stable in form across much of their range of occurrence, and thousands of others "tolerate only minor variations" (p. 131), which are themselves regular and predictable in their uses.

In light of the fact that L2 instruction almost always takes place under great time constraints for many teachers and learners, it is important to maximize language gains and make learning as efficient as possible. Using language chunks in instruction and learning is likely to be one of the few available expedient routes to relative L2 accuracy and fluency that leads to production and subsequent automatization (DeKeyser & Juffs, in press; Wood, 2001). For example, according to Wray and Perkins (2000) and Wray (2002), in L2 teaching prefabricated chunks can and should be treated as various types of "word strings" that are to be stored and retrieved whole from memory. Many adults can recite L1 or L2 poems or texts that they learned several decades earlier, and there is little reason to doubt that L2 learners are quite capable of similar feats in their L2 writing.

According to N. Ellis (1997, pp. 129–130), collocational chunks can consist of entire memorized sentences or phrases that include from 4 to 10 words, and these can allow learners to create new constructions to add to their stock of expressions. In this sense, for learners, grammatical constructions such as commonly occurring sentences, clauses, and phrases can be "viewed as big words" and memorized as lexicalized stems. Following Pawley and Syder (1983), Moon (1997) called many of these preconstructed sentences and phrases "institutionalized" because they occur more frequently in certain types of discourse than in others.

Throughout this book, appendixes for most chapters include stock lexicalized sentence stems and phrases that can be very effective and efficient in teaching skeletal frameworks in academic papers and written discourse.

INSTRUCTED L2 GRAMMAR AND NOTICING

Grammar teaching can be made productive for learners if it is cumulative—when the curriculum is designed to build on the structures that learners already know or from the formally and functionally simple to more complex constructions (R. Ellis, 2002; Larsen-Freeman, 1991). To this end, grammar curriculum even at the intermediate levels of student proficiency can begin with an examination and analysis of structures in formal written discourse. Initially, the goal of instruction is to develop learners' awareness and noticing of common grammatical features; building on this foundation, the regularities in grammar structures can be explicitly addressed and practiced in the production of academic writing (R. Ellis, 1990, 1994, 1997, 2002; James, 1998).

For example, at the high intermediate and/or advanced levels, grammar teaching can focus on constructions typically found in introductory academic textbooks (e.g., history texts heavily rely on the use of the past tense, and political science and sociology books can be practical in instruction on the present tense and passive voice). At higher proficiency levels, instruction can also highlight the effects of grammatical features on context, discourse, and text (e.g., tense uses in generalizations or the important difference between *totally* and *a great deal*). In addition, the discourse functions of referential and impersonal pronouns, the hedging functions of modal verbs, and parallel phrase constructions found in abundance in practically all academic prose can be noticed, analyzed, and practiced. The goal of practice (practice, and practice) with grammar constructions is to help learners develop productive fluency in academic writing and, to some degree, automaticity in generating academic prose. Practice activities can include brief restatements of chapter/section contents, objective summaries, paraphrases, explanations, or using sources as thesis support in short pieces of writing at lower proficiency levels or longer essays for advanced learners.

Heightening learners' awareness of the structure of complete sentences in academic prose (as opposed to fragments), as well as important distinctions between conversational and formal written register, should represent ongoing instructional objectives at all levels of proficiency. Because in English-speaking countries most learners are exposed to a great deal more conversational discourse than formal written prose, they usually employ conversational grammar and lexis in their academic essays (Hinkel, 2002a, 2003a, 2003b; Shaw & Liu, 1998). Thus, when they are encountered in reading or speaking, noticing and analyzing the differences between the features of casual spoken and formal written text is vital (Biber, 1995; Hinkel, 2003b; Hyland, 2002a; Hyland & Milton, 1997).

While working with written academic discourse at any level of learner proficiency, it is crucially important to take opportunities to bring learners' attention to global features of academic discourse and discourse moves, vocabulary uses in context, and definitions of important, discipline-specific terms usually provided in almost all introductory academic texts for first- or second-year students.

VOCABULARY AND L2 ACADEMIC TEXT

Nation and Waring's (1997) research outlines the enormous task entailed in learning the vocabulary needed to produced academic text in an L2. As a point of reference, they explained that a complete dictionary of the English language contains around 55,000 word families. A word family includes the base form of a word, its inflected forms, and closely related derived forms (Nation, 2001; e.g., *sing, sings, singing, sang, sung*, or *cold, colder, coldest, coldly, coldness*). Nation and Waring also commented that a 5-year-old NS child has a vocabulary range of 4,000 to 5,000 word families, an average university student 17,000, and a university graduate around 20,000. According to the authors' estimates, native speakers add approximately 1,000 word families per year to their vocabulary size.

> Thus, for adult ESL learners, the gap between their vocabulary size and that of NSs is usually very large because adult learners who have typically dedicated several years to L2 learning have a vocabulary size of much less than 5,000 words. It is possible, however, as in the case of educated non-native speakers, to achieve a significant growth in L2 vocabulary with persistent and consistent effort.

Studies on the importance of vocabulary in L2 writing have been carried out by many researchers. For example, Santos (1988) determined that lexical errors were considered to be the most serious in professors' evaluations of NNS student writing, followed by problems with discourse and information organization and syntactic errors, with the matters of content downgraded to being least important of all. Other studies also demonstrated that the proportion of core academic vocabulary in L2 writers' text correlated positively with higher ratings of essays on standardized tests (Laufer & Nation, 1995). On the whole, based on several earlier studies, Nation (2001) concluded that an increase in the amount of academic vocabulary in L2 writing contributes significantly to the higher evaluations of the quality of L2 academic writing. In light of this finding, it is not particularly surprising that NS student writing usually receives higher evaluations and ratings (i.e., NSs simply have ready access to a much greater vocabulary base).

In general, the work of Nation (1990, 2001) has provided a great deal of insight needed to understand the crucial role of vocabulary in L2 writing production. However, one of the most important issues in learning academic vocabulary is its extraordinarily large size. For example, Coxhead (2000) showed that in basic textbooks in various disciplines, such as humanities, business, and the sciences, the academic vocabulary range of common words includes approximately 10% of 3,500,000 of all words included in an academic word corpus.

As Nation (2001) commented, "[a]n impossibly large number of texts would be needed to cover all of the vocabulary of the UWL [University Word List]" (p. 193). Another factor that greatly complicates the learning of L2 academic vocabulary is that it is not the common words that create the greatest difficulties in reading and writing, but the relatively rare words that actually represent the largest number of words used even in basic academic texts.

Thus, for a vast majority of NNS students, the task of becoming proficient users of L2 academic vocabulary may not be attainable within the time commonly considered reasonable for the completion of their EAP preparatory and academic studies. A more reasonable and attainable goal in increasing the vocabulary range in students' L2 writing is to work with lexical items that learners can use in constructing texts in most writing tasks across all disciplines. For example, the number of reporting verbs that can be employed to mark paraphrases is around a dozen, and they can be learned with relative ease while working on a writing assignment (e.g., *the author says, states, indicates, comments, notes, observes, believes, points out, emphasizes, advocates, reports, concludes, underscores, mentions, finds*), not to mention phrases with similar textual functions such as *according to the author, as the author states/indicates, in the author's view/opinion/ understanding,* or *as noted/stated/mentioned*.

Teaching vocabulary and grammar essential for success in the academy may be tedious and somewhat boring because, unlike the fun activities for developing conversational fluency, even the most basic academic lexicon consists of 850 words that include such nouns as *assent, asset, astronomy, atmosphere,* and *atom*. Teaching and learning academic vocabulary extends far beyond field trips and reading short stories.

Not teaching the foundational vocabulary basics puts students at a great disadvantage in mainstream courses in various disciplines when academic proficiency is requisite.

Students who complete their language preparation in intensive English programs may have a vocabulary range of 2,000 words (Nation & Waring, 1997). However, the accessible lexicon in academic studies does not need to include nouns to describe recipe ingredients, names of interesting animals, or current fashions. It includes words not common in daily conversations that are not learned through conversational activities. Academic words and grammatical structures cannot be learned in casual talk because they do not occur there. Essentially, in most people's daily functioning and interactions, academic lexis and advanced syntactic constructions cannot be learned in naturalistic language settings if they are not taught explicitly (R. Ellis, 1994, 1997, 2001; Hinkel, 2001a, 2003a, 2003b; Nation, 1990, 2001).

INCIDENTAL LEARNING AND NOTICING

In general terms, two types of vocabulary and grammar learning have been identified in research: **explicit learning,** which takes place through focused study, and **incidental learning,** when new vocabulary and grammar structures are *picked up* from exposure to and experience with language. However, research has established that learners typically need at least 10 or 12 repeated exposures to a word over time to learn it well (Coady, 1997). To further complicate matters, several studies of adult L2 learners concluded that the long-term retention of words learned incidentally and through exposure in extensive reading can be particularly low (Hafiz & Tudor, 1990; Hulstijn, 1992).

On the whole, because L2 learning is determined by a number of complex factors, such as L1 literacy and culture, personal motivation and goals, as well as L1 and L2 similarities, the processes of L2 vocabulary and grammar learning have not been clearly established (Schmitt, 2000). In all likelihood, an effective curriculum for L2 teaching relies on both explicit and implicit learning and incorporates a balanced amount of focused study and opportunities for exposure to academic language and text (Nation, 2001).

There is little doubt that for incidental learning of academic text features to occur, students have to have extensive exposure to academic reading with repeated uses of words. Extensive reading can be carried out in and out of class, but an important fact is that students need to be interested in the subject matter to sustain reading the material that often requires them to work hard, concentrate, and memorize new vocabulary. In the days when most forms of entertainment rely on visual media, such as TV, videos, and Internet, the number of learners who read for pleasure has declined (Hinkel, 2001b). As a result, a majority of readers, especially when they are reading in a L2, read for information. Hence, to increase learners' motivation in extensive reading, the teacher may need to find out what types of subject matter can be of particular use or interest to a specific group of students. For instance, learners who plan to enroll as undergraduates in colleges and universities in English-speaking countries are required to take courses in the disciplines that range from humanities to the sciences, and their exposure to useful vocabulary can be flexible. However, matriculated or graduate students may be more motivated if they read texts that deal with their chosen specialties rather than general education courses.[1]

One of the crucial features of effective learning is noticing words and grammar structures, their uses and meanings, and contexts in which they occur (R. Ellis, 1990, 2002; Schmidt, 1990, 1994, 1995). To learn different meanings that words and constructions may have in different contexts, learners need to pay attention to textual features as they read or write (e.g., in written academic text, the modal verb *may* rarely has the meaning of permission as is described in most grammar books, but usually has the function of a hedging device).

> The greatest issue with noticing words and features is that, first, learners need to know what specific text features they should notice and, second, what about these features requires attention. Therefore, it is the teacher's job to guide learners and point out the important and necessary vocabulary and grammar constructions and then discuss their uses and meanings in the academic text. Nation (2001) commented that the discussion of vocabulary items, subsequent to noticing, represents a highly productive way to learn new words in reading.

Noticing forms of words and structures can take place while students listen and read, participate in activities, or even look for synonyms. To notice uses, meanings, and functions of words and grammar constructions, learners need to be aware of language as a complex system. For example, they need to be able to identify nouns, verbs, prepositions, and adverbs to notice that sometimes words or parts of words can have different syntactic properties and, therefore, play different roles in sentences. Noticing and identifying the functions of words and structures is a slow and laborious process that affects a student's reading speed and takes away some of the enjoyment of reading because it removes attention from the context/messages to focus it on the component parts.

In many cases, preteaching texts at the appropriate level of difficulty (i.e., providing definitions of words that occur in the text and explaining the text's purpose) can simplify the learner's tasks particularly when the prereading (or prelistening) activities are followed by a discussion or another focused activity. For example, R. Ellis (1994) found that simple and

[1]It is important to keep in mind that what is of interest to the teacher may not be to the students. Most experienced instructors know that political events and ideological controversies, such as elections or political issues—hotly debated in the country where students study—can actually be of little relevance to a majority of L2 students, who are new to their geographical location or community.

short definitions that include only a few important characteristics of a word or structure lead to significant increases in vocabulary gains. Similarly, vocabulary learning from cards with L1 approximations is also effective when accompanied by a contextualized reading/activity in L2. In general, explicit vocabulary and grammar teaching can contribute directly to learners' development of implicit L2 knowledge (R. Ellis, 1990, 2002).

In grammar learning, becoming aware of how structures are used, combined with explicit teaching, can provide an additional benefit because learners can notice structures that otherwise they may simply miss (R. Ellis, 1997). According to R. Ellis (1990), noticing and awareness play a particularly prominent role in developing accuracy in uses of structures and noticing errors. If learners notice correct uses of structures, they can then compare them to those they produce and self-correct. Self-correction or editing are activities that undertake an analysis of errors that begin with noticing (James, 1998). Explanations of structure forms and their regularities further aid language learning (e.g., in English, subject–verb agreement is based on a system of regularities that is so complex it requires teaching even to NSs). It may be unreasonable to expect that L2 learners be able to figure out the systematic intricacies that govern subject–verb agreement on their own. However, noticing combined with an explanation may help L2 writers improve their skills.

When, guided by the teacher, learners are engaged in conscious noticing and learning, explicit teaching of vocabulary and grammar plays a crucial role. For instance, carefully selected thematic writing tasks that require learners to employ specific vocabulary items and grammar structures in text production can lead to increased opportunities to revisit and practice the items learned or noticed earlier. Learners can be engaged in varied tasks to promote vocabulary gains and retention, and teachers can employ diverse attention-focusing techniques when designing classroom teaching activities.

TEACHING L2 WRITERS TO EDIT THEIR TEXT

Editing one's own text and learning to identify mistakes is notoriously difficult even for advanced NNS academic writers. Causes of errors can be numerous and may be an outcome of first-language transfer, incomplete understanding of word meanings or syntactic rules, or casual mistakes. In addition, in different lexical and grammatical contexts, seemingly similar types of errors can have a variety of causes (e.g., a lack of subject–verb agreement can be an outcome of a writer's inability to identify correctly the subject noun phrase, a misconstrual of a count for a noncount noun or vice versa [see chap. 5], or simply omitting the inflection marker *-s* with either a noun or verb). For instance, James (1998) referred to "dictionaries of errors" (p. 97), and Swan and Smith (2001) published a 350-page volume devoted to descriptions, analyses, and approaches to correcting errors made by speakers of approximately 20 languages.

Although similar types of errors can have numerous causes, it may not be particularly important to figure them out simply because causes of learner problems with particular linguistic features can be highly numerous. However, for academic writers, learning to identify and correct their own errors is essential. In composition and writing instruction, peer editing is often employed with the stated learning goal of providing student writers a more realistic audience than only the instructor, developing learners' editing skills, and establishing a social context for writing (Ferris & Hedgcock, 1998; Johnson, 1989a; Reid, 1993, 2000a, 2000b). However, peer editing (also called *peer response*), as a technique for teaching writing, was originally created for NS students who wrote in their L1 and were more socially and culturally open to the idea of reading and responding to their classmates' writing than a majority of L2 writers socialized in collectivist cultures, which place a great deal of emphasis on group harmony and cohesiveness and the importance of saving face (Carson & Nelson, 1994, 1996; Hinkel, 1999b; Hyland, 2002a; see also Silva, 1997; Ferris & Hedgcock, 1998).

Although some researchers of L2 writing believe that the benefits of peer editing outweigh the disadvantages and that peer response to writing can be made effective when used with care, others have voiced concerns about the effectiveness of this technique in light of the fact among various cultural groups, harmony has to be maintained almost at any cost (Carson & Nelson, 1996). For instance, Carson and Nelson (1994) reported the unease of Chinese L2 learners when working on peer response tasks and their reluctance to provide honest feedback. In fact these authors noted that in this case, learners' responses are likely to reflect a need for positive ingroup relationships than a need to improve their peer's writing.

Several studies of peer editing/response in L2 writing classes reported additional complications (Connor & Asenavage, 1994; Grabe & Kaplan, 1996; W. Zhu, 2001). For example, Nelson and Murphy (1993) found that in many cases, NNS students "tended *not* to act upon their peers' comments" and "in fact, writers may actually weaken their drafts by incorporating peer comments" (p. 140). These authors suggested a variety of strategies for conducting ESL peer response groups that rely on instruction, teacher modeling, awareness, and practical training for students to provide appropriate and useful comments, as well as audio- and videotaping peer interactions for subsequent review, with the goal of improving peer feedback on classmates' writing. Similarly, Tsui and Ng (2000) found that "teacher comments were more favored by most students than peer comments and induced more revisions" because teacher comments were more specific, "were able to explain what the problems were, and were better able to make concrete suggestions for revision" (pp. 165–166). Tsui and Ng's study also proposed a number of techniques to train students to make peer response more effective.

On the whole, the results of studies on the benefits of peer response in L2 composition instruction appears to be highly mixed. Although peer feedback may be more effective in the case of graduate students, this technique developed for L1 writers in the United States seems to be of questionable value when it comes to L2 learners.

Zhang's (1995) survey of ESL students found that all prefer teacher comments over peer feedback because ESL peer respondents are not always on the mark when it comes to suggesting revisions. Furthermore, Zhang noted that L1 and L2 students may have distinctly different conceptualizations and priorities in revision (e.g., L2 writers are far more likely to respond to surface-level and morphological errors than to suggest substantive revision). Arndt (1993, p. 111) reported mismatches between teachers' and students' perceptions of the value of peer responses because students largely see them as unhelpful to both writers and respondents, who lack confidence as well as linguistic skills to be effective. However, "teachers tended to ignore or even be unaware of this factor, glibly assuming" peer responses would come "naturally."

Hyland (2002a) summed up the entire issue with the applicability and usefulness of peer response in L2 writing classes: "The benefits of peer response have been hard to confirm empirically, however, particularly in ESL classrooms, and many studies have reported that students themselves doubt its value, overwhelmingly preferring teacher feedback" (p. 169).

Hyland also pointed out that generally ESL and NNS students perceive revision to mean error correction that can be culturally uncomfortable because it entails "criticizing peers' work."

In L2 writing instruction, however, teacher feedback on errors does seem to be effective. Experimental studies (Ashwell, 2000; Fathman & Whalley, 1990; Ferris, 1995) have demonstrated that correcting errors "universally (for every student and every composition) brought about improvement" in the quality of text "and at the same time led to a 44 per cent improvement in content expression" (James, 1998, p. 246). Furthermore, from a different perspective, learners want and expect teachers to correct their errors in almost all cases. For example, Leki (1991) found that, without exception, students strongly preferred that teachers' correct their errors in writing. Thus, an important consideration in teaching L2 academic writing is not whether to correct textual errors and help students learn to edit their text, but how to deal with numerous and sometimes pervasive errors.

First and above all, the purpose of error correction is not for the teacher to edit the student text and, thus, unintentionally promote student reliance on the teacher. Much more importantly, the educational goal of error correction is to help L2 writers become independent editors of their own text. To achieve this objective, both teachers and students need to be aware that all errors are not created equal. Many studies have addressed the gravity of errors in the perceptions of university faculty (Vann, Lorenz, & Meyer, 1991; Vann, Meyer, & Lorenz, 1984). For example, as mentioned earlier, among other researchers, Santos (1988) found that lexical and semantic errors are often considered to be particularly grievous in L2 academic text. Other reports note that grammar errors also vary in their importance to the L2 text quality.

According to studies cited in this section, the **most egregious** grammar errors include:

- word order
- verb tense
- word morphology (word form)
- *it*-deletion in cleft constructions
- relative (adjective) clauses
- subject–verb agreement.

Errors that have less impact on evaluations of student text include:

- articles
- prepositions
- comma splices
- spelling

Above all, however, studies of error gravity and other investigations have established clearly that faculty in the disciplines are far less tolerant of NNS than NS errors and view L2 language-related errors as sufficiently important to negatively affect their overall evaluations (Byrd & Reid, 1998; Ferris & Hedgcock, 1998).

Thus, teaching students to become independent self-editors represents a crucial component of writing instruction. Some approaches to teaching L2 writing advocate text-level editing only as the final stage of writing—after matters of discourse organization and content are addressed. However, because the ultimate objective of editing instruction is to teach students essential self-editing skills that can be useful for the duration of their academic careers, working on lexical and grammar errors can take place at any point of essay development (Ashwell, 2000).

Self-editing instruction can proceed in stages and be selective. The first step is to raise students' awareness of ubiquitous and egregious errors and improve noticing skills. Editing exercises can begin with text/papers that are not students' own and that contain limited and controlled types of errors.

> At the outset, it is reasonable and manageable to begin self-editing work on four to six types of errors depending on their complexity (e.g., countable and uncountable nouns, singular and plural noun choices, repetitious uses of simple nouns [see chap. 5 on nouns], present and past tenses, unmarked tense shifts, and stative verbs [see chap. 7 on verb tenses and aspects]).

Error exercises of the first group of errors can be assigned as homework and followed up by an explicit in-class analysis and discussion, either in small groups or as a whole class. Both research and experience have shown that explanations of how particular structures can be used in context and typical errors that occur with these structures may need to be persistent and even repetitive to be effective. Explanations of erroneous structures and their correct uses contribute to overall instructional input in L2 learning (R. Ellis, 1994, 1997; James, 1998). Subsequent (impersonal) editing exercises assigned as homework or for in-class practice can be expanded to errors in contexts that are directly and immediately relevant to students' own errors in writing. Most teachers usually note the specific structures or discourse features that require additional attention when they read, mark, and grade students' written assignments.

Editing students' own errors can begin in tandem with editing exercises. Ideally the types of errors in exercises should match those addressed in the teacher's marking and/or correction. If the follow-up analysis and discussion of the selected error types takes place in class, the teacher's workload can be greatly reduced when dealing with explanations of errors (e.g., in individual conferences or during office hours).

Although the writing assignments early in the course can be based on two drafts, closer to the completion of the term, only one draft of writing assignments should be evaluated and graded, similar to assignment grading in mainstream courses. Due to the gradual increase in students' responsibility for the quality of their writing throughout the course, significant instructional and learning benefits can be obtained because students are required to pay close attention to language in their writing and editing (additional editing techniques are discussed in chap. 4).

STEPS IN TEACHING SELF-EDITING SKILLS

1. In the first draft of the first assignment, the teacher should correct all errors of the selected types practiced in the exercises.
2. In the second (final) draft, the teacher highlights all remaining errors of these types and corrects many.
3. In the next assignment, the teacher should correct only some errors of these types in the first draft and underline other errors of these

same types, with explicit instructions that the student needs to correct the underlined structures.

4. In the second (final) draft of the second assignment, the teacher should correct only the most complex occurrences of these types of errors, and the responsibility for the rest needs to be shifted from the teacher to the student.

5. It is vital, however, that the first group of error types not be abandoned when editing practice on the second group of errors begins. Rather, students' awareness of and learning to correct errors of various types has to be cumulative.

6. When practice exercises on the second group of errors begin, the teacher should not correct the errors from the first group (except in rare cases of complex constructions), but underline or highlight them in student writing as they occur. Teacher corrections should be limited to the second group of error types (see Step 1).

7. When working on the third (or subsequent) assignment, the first group of errors should become fully a student's responsibility, and the types of errors in editing exercises can be expanded to the next group of four to six types.

8. Again in the first piece of writing that takes place during the work on the second group of errors, the teacher should correct all occurrences and highlight them in subsequent student writing (see Step 2), and then the cycle is repeated.

Throughout the course, it is very important that the teacher be consistent in correcting, underlining/highlighting, and shifting the responsibility for editing errors to students (R. Ellis, 1984). By the end of the course, it is reasonable to expect students to notice and correct 20 to 40 common types of errors in their own writing.

Some examples of the grouped error types, beginning with the most accessible.

The First Group of Error Types

- Uncountable nouns (e.g., *equipment, information, knowledge*)
- Irregular plural forms of nouns (focus on academic vocabulary—see also chap. 5 on nouns; e.g., *criterion–criteria, phenomenon–phenomena, medium–media, analysis–analyses, basis–bases, hypothesis–hypotheses*)
- Quantifiers (e.g., *few/a few, little/a little*), subject noun phrases with quantifiers and verb agreement (e.g., *some/many books* + plural verb or *some/much information* + singular verb)
- Subject noun + prepositional phrase and verb agreement (e.g., *The researcher with two assistants investigate**S*** ... vs. *The researcher and two assistants investigateØ*) ...

- Compound noun phrases (e.g., *a five-credit-hour university composition course(s), a twenty-five-year-old student(s)* vs. *the student is twenty-five years old*)

Subsequent Error Types Group

- Word order in noun and adjective clauses (e.g., *The authors state that they know which way the wind is blowing; It is not clear whether the price will rise; The lab where the research takes place is located in Pennsylvania*)
  - Also, word order in *how-* noun clauses (e.g., *The scientists described how they identified the virus; The scale was used to measure how much the minerals weighed*)
- Word order with adverbs of manner, time, and indefinite frequency (e.g., *Investors need to make decisions quickly; Usually, car mileage (usually) depends on the size of its engine*)
- The placement of *even* and *also* (e.g., *she was even/also elected, (also) she also/even finished the book, ... was high also/even in the 1990s*)
- The placement and uses of *enough* (e.g., *high enough, enough time/funds, enough of that/them, enough to complete the experiment;* optional: the placement and uses of *almost, almost + enough*, e.g. *almost + enough time/funds; almost never, almost the same, almost finished/the tallest, almost + every* [+ noun])
- Quantifiers with prepositional phrases (e.g., *some/many/most managers* vs. *some/many/most of the managers in the accounting department), most* as an adverb (e.g., *the stock price of dot-coms grew the most in 1999*)

L2 writers may not be able to identify and correct all errors covered in the instruction no matter how much effort and time during one or two composition courses is devoted to the task. Teaching learners to edit their writing independently does not have the goal of making their writing native-like, and it is crucial that both teachers and students set realistic expectations of noticeable improvement in student writing, but not the elimination of errors. The goal of the error awareness practice and self-editing training is to enable students to minimize the number and extent of the most egregious types of errors in their texts.

> A key to effective and productive teaching of self-editing skills is to hold students responsible for their errors just as they would be in real coursework.

In many cases, when students receive low grades on their assignments and papers in mainstream courses, they do not know the reasons that their work received a low evaluation, and few would actually endeavor to find out by asking their professors (Johns, 1997). Even in the rare cases when some do attempt to discuss their writing with their professors, university faculty who are not trained in analyses of L2 writing are unlikely to provide detailed explanations that, for example, a student's essay has too many errors in noun clauses, verb tenses, or word suffixes.

It is a fact of life that after learners move from ESL and EAP programs into their university studies, with the exception of the writing center tutors, they are largely left to their own devices in producing academic writing of passing quality. According to Bratt Paulston (1992), a prominent scholar in language teaching, "now the truth of the matter is most normal people don't find language learning tasks very interesting" (pp. 106–107). She added that learning in many disciplines, such as reading or mathematics, "errors and correction are part of school life," but good teaching prepares students to be competent learners—not necessarily always successful learners, but those who are able to achieve success when they are given access to information and skills for how to achieve success.

WHAT NOT TO TEACH—LOW-PRIORITY CONSTRUCTIONS

The following features of academic writing and text have been identified as rare; in fact, some are never encountered in large written academic and NS student writing corpora (Biber, 1988; Biber et al., 1999; Hinkel, 2002a; Quirk, Greenbaum, Leech, & Svartvik, 1985). Although many of these are traditionally taught in practically all ESL grammar courses, the features listed next may have a verifiably reduced importance in teaching L2 learners to become proficient academic writers. These constructions have a low priority particularly when the teacher and learners have a limited amount of time to make maximum gains in improving the quality of students' writing skills.

Nouns and the Noun Phrase

- first- and second-person pronouns and contexts that require their uses (e.g., personal narratives/examples/experiences)
- indefinite pronouns (*someone, anything, nobody, everything*)
- existential *there*- constructions (*there is a view that* ...)
- prepositions with the exception of collocations (see chaps. 4, Nouns, and 8, Lexical Verbs)

Verbs and the Verb Phrase

- progressive and perfect aspects (*is singing, has sung, has been singing*)
- the future tense and the predictive modal *would*
- modals of obligation (*must, have to*)
- contractions (*don't, can't*)
- place adverbials (*here, in the house*)

- emphatic constructions and markers (*I do agree that this method is better; absolutely, all, always*)
- *by*- phrase passives (*the depth is determined by the technician during the experiment*)

Main and Subordinate Clause Constructions

- *Wh*- and *yes/no* questions (*What is the main idea of this article? Does it matter what the public thinks?*)
- *That*- noun clauses in the subject position (*that fruit farming is not profitable is an established fact*)
- Sentential clauses (*she did not recognize me, which was not surprising*)
- Adverb clauses of cause (*because ..., since ..., for ...*)
- Reduced adverb clauses (*when moving the equipment; having moved the equipment*)
- Reduced adjective clauses (*the team developing a new system*)

NEEDS ANALYSIS FOR CURRICULUM DEVELOPMENT

To date much research has been conducted to identify the prevalent features of student academic writing and text (Byrd & Reid, 1998; Chang & Swales, 1999; Coxhead, 1998; Hinkel, 1995c, 1997b, 1999a, 2002a; Hyland, 1998; Hyland & Milton, 1997; Johns, 1997; Laufer & Nation, 1995; Myers, 1996, 1999; Nation, 1990, 2001; Ostler, 1987; Poole, 1991; Santos, 1984, 1988; Scollon, 1991, 1993a, 1993b; Shaw & Liu, 1998; Swales, 1990a, 1990b, to mention just a few). However, as experienced teachers know, students are different in each class, and so are their language learning needs, even when the majority have the same educational goals of becoming successful academic writers and preparing for studies in their disciplines. For this reason, identifying the linguistic and discourse features that need to be taught to a particular group of students represents an important starting point when developing L2 academic writing courses.

A teacher may choose to analyze diagnostic essays that can be very useful in at least the initial course planning (see the appendix in this chapter for a sample of a course curriculum). Although the writing of different students may include a broad range of issues that can benefit from instruction, it is not difficult to identify commonalities.

Realistic expectations of student progress should take into account that:

1. not every problematic issue in student writing needs to be addressed in teaching, just the important ones (see the section on egregious errors earlier in this chapter)

2. problems in student writing can be broadly similar, but not necessarily identical
3. if the writing of most (or even several) students exhibits a specific problem (e.g., sentence fragments, countable/uncountable nouns, or repetitive vocabulary), it should be addressed in teaching even when one or two students' writing does not seem to have this type of problem
4. a flexible course plan can be amended when the teacher concludes that (further) instruction in a particular aspect of language use is not needed

---

Diagnostic essays are similar to other product-oriented pieces of in-class writing that students are expected to generate in their mainstream classes (see chap. 2). Thus, to an extent, what the teacher sees in the diagnostic piece of writing is what the mainstream teacher gets.

In general terms, most teachers can anticipate the following aspects of L2 academic writing to be in need of at least some degree of polishing and additional work for practically all academic L2 learners:

- academic vocabulary and, specifically, nouns and verbs
- sentence boundaries and phrase construction
- verb tenses in academic discourse
- the functions of the passive voice in academic prose
- noun clauses
- hedges
- textual cohesion devices

A FINAL NOTE

One of the crucial issues with learning a second language is that most of it cannot take place in the classroom because learning a second language well enough to be able to write academic papers in it requires a great deal more work than can be done in class. Hence, if learners are seriously intent on improving their L2 writing skills, the greatest portion of the work that, in fact, represents language learning has to take the form of homework. The learning of many L2 academic skills, such as writing, reading, vocabulary, and/or essay editing, is largely a solitary activity.

On the other hand, if students approach L2 learning as being engaged in interactive and social classroom activities, their conversational listening and speaking skills may improve dramatically, but attaining L2 proficiency sufficient to write papers in sociology or political science may appear to be a remote objective. Unfortunately, to date a method of learning an L2 well as an adult more effective than memorizing and practicing vocabulary, practicing grammar structures in writing, producing large amounts of academic writing, and improving one's self-editing skills has not been invented. Students' motivation to study and learn usually increases markedly if the teacher explains that L2 learning takes a great deal of hard work and persistence, and there are few ways known to humanity of how to make it either easier or quicker.

When a teacher develops a course curriculum, it is also helpful to explain it because if learners understand the direction of the course and incremental means of attaining its objectives, they are able to take the responsibility for their own learning. In addition, it is also important that students be informed of weekly and daily learning objectives as the course moves along its path. These explanations do not need to be detailed or justified by research, but they need to be grounded in students' own learning and academic goals.

CHAPTER SUMMARY

A great deal of research on L2 vocabulary learning carried out in the past several decades points to a direct connection between an improvement in learners' vocabulary base and range and the quality of their academic writing (Johns, 1981, 1997; Jordan, 1997; Nation, 1990, 2001). Although much vocabulary instruction focuses on reading as a means to help learners expand their lexicon, some psycholinguistic studies have shown L2 vocabulary learning is different from the acquisition of L1 vocabulary that takes place in daily interaction and exposure to new lexis in reading. That is, L2 lexicon may be processed as an independent entity and, therefore, requires separate and concerted effort and focused instruction. Specifically, expanding learners' lexical range represents an important pedagogical activity in its own right (Channell, 1988; Coady, 1997; Lewis, 1997; Nation, 1990). Teaching reading and hoping that essential academic vocabulary items are encountered can be inefficient and sometimes ineffective because the vocabulary that students must know simply does not occur frequently enough to be learned from mere exposure to L2 text.

In addition, a large body of research on language and discourse features of academic writing, as well as the writing of NNS university students, has identified the paramount role of lexical and syntactic accuracy in the evaluations of writing quality. In general terms, studies of the recurring features of the academic genre have established that, although some variations occur across disciplines, by and large rigid conventionalized norms predominate in academic discourse and text. However, investigations of NNS students' academic writing have determined that it exhibits a number of systematic shortfalls that can be addressed in detailed, focused, and goal-oriented instruction.

- Explicit teaching and analyses of L2 grammar structures, combined with extensive writing practice, lead to marked improvements in NNS students' productive skills. One of the most practical approaches to teaching formal features of L2 grammar entails the learning of lexicalized sentence stems with an itinerary of appropriate replacements for substitutable parts.
- Raising learners' awareness and noticing of grammar and vocabulary in academic writing is essential in reducing the number of NNS writers' lexical errors that have been found to be among the most egregious in L2 writing.
- A vast majority of NNS academic writers who begin to study L2 vocabulary as adults have such a limited vocabulary range that it consists of only a small fraction of that of NS university-level writers. An intensive and concerted effort in learning the core L2 academic vocabulary is key to successful NNS writing in regular academic courses.
- Incidental vocabulary and grammar learning can supplement, but does not replace intensive and focused vocabulary learning by means of vocabulary and sentence-stem memorization and practice.
- Independent self-editing skills require much training and practice (and practice, and practice) for L2 learners. Several experimental studies have shown that peer editing/response represents a culturally biased and ineffective language learning practice.
- In addition to determining what should be taught in L2 writing, research has also identified a number of lexical and syntactic features that play a reduced role in evaluations. Instruction in these features represents a low return on investment of teachers' and students' effort and time.
- A course curriculum that is rooted in L2 proficiency goals can increase motivation when the goals are explicitly articulated in terms of learners' own language learning needs for success in their academic studies.

QUESTIONS FOR DISCUSSION

1. In your opinion, why do some methodologies for teaching ESL emphasize and others deemphasize the importance of explicit grammar and vocabulary teaching?
2. If you were to design L2 writing courses for intermediate or advanced learners, what features of English-language discourse and text features would you consider to be most important? Why?
3. What are the primary differences between the needs of academic and other types of learners in English-speaking countries?

4. The notion of incidental learning of L2 grammar structures and vocabulary has become highly controversial in L1 and L2 instruction. What do you think are the reasons for this development?
5. Extrapolating from the information in this chapter, what are some of the possible frictions between communicative and instructed approaches to language teaching? Which methodology do you personally advocate, and how can opposing arguments be countered?

FURTHER READINGS ABOUT COURSE DESIGN AND ELEMENTS

Course Curriculum

Lewis, M. (1993). *The lexical approach*. Hove, UK: LTP.

Richards, J. (2001). Accuracy and fluency revisited. In E. Hinkel & S. Fotos (Eds.), *New perspectives on grammar teaching in second language classrooms* (pp. 35–50). Mahwah, NJ: Lawrence Erlbaum Associates.

Sinclair, J., & Renouf, A. (1988). A lexical syllabus for language learning. In R. Carter & M. McCarthy (Eds.), *Vocabulary and language teaching* (pp. 140–160). Harlow, Essex: Longman.

Lexical Chunks in Academic Writing

Nation, P., & Waring, R. (1997). Vocabulary size, text coverage, and word lists. In N. Schmitt & M. McCarthy (Eds.), *Vocabulary: Description, acquisition, and pedagogy* (pp. 6–20). Cambridge: Cambridge University Press.

Nattinger, J., & DeCarrico, J. (1992). *Lexical phrases and language teaching*. Oxford: Oxford University Press.

Wray, A. (2002). *Formulaic language and the lexicon*. Cambridge: Cambridge University Press.

Wray, A. (2003). *The transition to language*. Oxford: Oxford University Press.

Teaching Grammar for Academic Writing

Byrd, P., & Reid, J. (1998). *Grammar in the composition classroom*. Boston: Heinle & Heinle.

Celce-Murcia, M. (1991). Grammar pedagogy in second and foreign language teaching. *TESOL Quarterly, 25*, 459–480.

Jacobs, R. (1995). *English syntax: A grammar for English language professionals*. Oxford: Oxford University Press.

Errors and Self-Editing

James, C. (1998). *Errors in language learning and use*. London: Longman.

Leki, I. (1991). The preference of ESL students for error correction in college-level wring classes. *Foreign Language Annals, 24*, 203–228.

Vaughan, C. (1991). Holistic assessment: What goes on in the raters' minds? In L. Hamp-Lyons (Ed.), *Assessing second language writing* (pp. 111–126). Norwood, NJ: Ablex.

Appendix to Chapter 3

The samples of course outlines and weekly plans and daily lesson plans presented here are only examples based on realistic instructional goals.

SAMPLE CURRICULUM GUIDELINES FOR A PRE-ACADEMIC WRITING COURSE

Course Goals

To prepare for the demands of academic writing tasks on the students' language skills, the course is designed to accomplish several main language-building and writing objectives. The development of increased academic lexical repertoire, grammatical accuracy in sentence- and phrase-structure use, and fluency with written and formal academic discourse organization are imperative for pre-academic learners at the high-intermediate and advanced proficiency levels.

Language Work (Ongoing)

- expanding learners' academic vocabulary range at the rate of at least 10 to 15 chunks (or words) per day or 70 to 100 chunks (or words) per week (mostly independent work at home with follow-up as-needed in-class contextual practice, word analyses, and review; mandatory weekly quizzes)
- building a grammar-structure base at the rate of at least three to five essential constructions per week, with as-needed in-class analysis and practice; a combination of work on sentence-stems, as well as select discrete language elements (e.g., countable-uncountable nouns and present and past tenses) leading to increased grammar accuracy
- lexical and grammatical precision is cumulative with additional independent and in-class work as needed (as structures occur in student writing)
- self-editing skills (cumulative)

Initial and Incremental Writing Assignments

(In tandem with major writing assignments and the relevant learning of lexis)

- daily summaries of readings (or sections of larger readings) and/or paraphrase practice (assigned daily as homework for 2 to 3 weeks, 15 to 20 total)

- information synthesis from several or long readings (assigned daily as homework for 2 to 3 weeks, 15 to 20 total)
- writing assignments marked and returned daily

Writing Skills and Discourse-Level Work (Ongoing)

- information synthesis/analysis—from multiple readings on the same topic/issue for each written assignment
- readings assigned as independent work with a follow-up in-class discussion as needed; ideally readings including book length (2–3 weeks per book) on a single and specific topic continue throughout the course
- organizing information in a thesis-driven coherent academic discourse structure—ongoing

Reading Strategies and Tactics

Remedial and as needed (2–6 hours per course). In many cases, reading assignments in three regular university courses combined (a full-time student load) consist of 150 to 300 pages of academic reading per week.

Major Writing Assignments

Seven to 12 (depending on the course length) major writing assignments are based on two drafts (one per week) at the outset and single/final drafts only in the second half of the course. Thus, the first two to three writing assignments require two drafts (one per week), and five to seven subsequent assignments require students to submit a single draft. Within this structure, the teacher has the flexibility to encourage additional and preliminary drafts that are not graded if students choose to submit them. However, preliminary drafts require the teacher to give preliminary drafts a quick turn around to allow students to take advantage of the teacher's comments.

The length of major assignments should range from 750 to 1,500 words each (three to six typed double-spaced pages). Lexical and grammatical accuracy, issues of academic register and audience, and self-editing skills are dealt with in each writing task.

In addition to developing students' language base, the curriculum emphasizes the ability to extract and arrange information from sources to address a particular writing topic, assignment purpose, and audience.

Course Materials

After the course begins, topics for readings can be determined by the interests of the student majority. Traditional favorites include (introductory university course material): sociology of dating, microeconomics, consumer behavior, and psychology of learning, memory, intelligence, or motivation. Topics to avoid: personal matters and beliefs, experience narratives, religion, and politics. All topics of major written assignments have to be cleared with the instructor if they are chosen by each individual student.

Discussion of content topics is a necessary prewriting activity for most writing tasks, as students are usually guided in selecting appropriate and manageable topics, narrowing the thesis, and choosing convincing supporting information. Content from readings can serve as a base for writing assignments and tasks, as well as reading-based in-class writing to prompts and/or expanded essay questions (15–30 minutes per week in the second half of the course).

Course Duration

The class meets for 50 or 70 hours per term (quarters or semesters), and, in all likelihood, it may be the last (or second to last) formal ESL writing class the majority of the students will ever take.

ATTENDANT WRITING CONCEPTS AND SKILLS (REMEDIAL, AS NEEDED)

High-Intermediate Proficiency Level or Review at Advanced Level

A number of features of academic discourse and text in English represent culturally bound concepts that are not shared in non-Anglo-American discourse traditions (including continental European). Thus, these features may seem particularly foreign and difficult to understand or relate to for a majority of L2 writers socialized in different cultures. For this reason, the concepts and written discourse constructs that underlie the production of academic discourse in English often require additional and repeated teaching.

Language Work (As Needed)

- Academic register and audience
- Lexical and syntactic accuracy, increased sentence complexity and clause use, and noun and verb inflections
- Unity (rhetorical purpose: explication and/or persuasion), cohesion of paragraphs and ideas, and logical connectors
- Avoiding lexical and discourse-level redundancy (concept of redundancy).

Discourse-Level Work

- Upfront thesis statement (that incorporates parts of or references to topic sentences as rhetorical supports)
- Information synthesis, extracting information from sources
- Academic argumentation and argument development
- The notion of plagiarism, restatement, and paraphrase
- Contextual relevance of information; one paragraph—one idea discussed and supported
- Introductory paragraph, closing sentence/paragraph (conclusions are optional)
- Body paragraphs: hierarchy/organization and structure or support, relevance and detail

II

SENTENCES AND THEIR PARTS: LEXIS AND GRAMMAR

The chapters in Part II cover the core information that NNSs need to be taught about English sentence and text construction. Chapter 4 introduces the regularities of English sentences and their elements—sentence slots—that can be taught to and used by students to efficiently improve their writing. Chapters 5 through 9 delve into the major components that fill the slots in sentences, how they are used, and how they can be effectively taught to NNS students. Chapters 5 and 6 cover nouns, noun phrases, and pronouns. Chapters 7 and 8 discuss verb tenses and voice, and lexical classes and functions of verbs. Chapter 9 describes the types and functions of adjectives and adverbs, as well as adjective and adverb phrases, in academic writing.

4

Sentences, Phrases, and Text Construction

OVERVIEW

- Rigid and mobile sentence elements
- The order of elements in the noun phrase
- The order of elements in the verb phrase
- Transitive and intransitive verbs
- Compound sentences
- Common errors in sentence construction

In English the structure of a basic sentence is relatively easy to teach because English has rigid word order (e.g., the subject is followed by a verb, which is followed by an object). Although many variations of this skeletal structure are possible, the additions also adhere to somewhat inflexible patterns. For example, a prepositional phrase cannot perform the function of a subject: Only noun phrases can function as a subject, and a verb must be present in every sentence for it to be grammatical. For example, the structure **For most students go to the U.S. to study* is incorrect because a prepositional phrase occupies the subject position.

The simplest approach to teaching the basic sentence structure can take advantage of the relative rigidity in English sentence structure.[1] An example of a basic sentence structure can consist of an optional adverb/prepositional phrase, subject noun (phrase), a verb, and an object if the main verb is transitive (requires a direct object). The essential sentence elements and

[1]In his teaching of composition courses, Kenneth L. Pike originally developed the idea in the 1950s and 1960s. His tagmemics theory was based on the principle that grammatical units are simultaneously marked for two features: the slot that they occupy relative to other units within a structure (e.g., the subject slot or the predicate slot in a sentence) and the syntactic class/type (e.g., noun [phrase], verb [phrase], or adjective [phrase]; Pike, 1964).

their positions relative to one another are sometimes called *slots,* and in many sentences some slots can be empty (e.g., the object slot is not filled if the verb is intransitive—does not require an object). However, in English sentences, for example, the verb slot is never empty because verbs are required for all sentences to be grammatical, and the subject slot can be empty only in the case of imperatives (commands), (e.g., *Ø close the door*).

It is important to note that an approach to teaching sentence- and phrase-structure systems of English does not place a great deal of emphasis on conveying a particular meaning. Rather, the regularities and rigid order of sentence and phrase elements deals with syntactic accuracy as discussed in detail in chapter 3. Also as mentioned, for academically bound L2 learners, a reasonable degree of grammatical accuracy represents a factor of crucial importance in their academic, professional, and social opportunities (Celce-Murcia, 1991; Celce-Murcia & Hilles, 1988; R. Ellis, 1990, 1994; Fries, 1945; Hammerly, 1991; Schmidt, 1994).

RIGID AND MOBILE SENTENCE ELEMENTS

In general, the breakdown of a sentence into ordered and sequential slots is based on three fundamental principles. The **first principle** states that sentence units occur not in isolation, but in relationship to other sentence elements (e.g., in most sentences [other than questions], the subject precedes the verb.

A Minimal Sentence

Sentence Slots	
Subject	**Verb Predicate**
Particles *Commercials*	*expand.* *proliferate.*
Computer technology *The temperature*	*evolves.* *rises.*

According to the **second principle**, the contexts in which sentence elements occur determine the variation among them (e.g., singular subject nouns require singular verbs or transitive verbs [e.g., *construct, develop, make*] require the presence of objects that follow them). On the other hand, prepositional phrases are slippery elements, and they can occur in various slots—at the beginnings or ends of sentences and/or following a subject or an object noun phrase.

Sentence structures are always dynamic, but variations among them follow predictable patterns that should be explained to students.

- Subject or object slots can be filled by all sorts of words or phrases that belong in the class of nouns/pronouns—for example,
  - proper and common nouns (e.g., *John, Smith, desk*)
  - countable and uncountable nouns (e.g., *pens, equipment*)
  - abstract and concrete nouns (e.g., *happiness, a cloud*) or gerunds (e.g., *reading, writing*)
  - compound noun phrases (e.g., *vegetable soup, a grammar book*)
  - pronouns (e.g., *I, we, they, one*)
  - sets of parallel nouns (e.g., *pens, pencils, and papers*; *flowers and trees*)

Noun phrases include all their attendant elements (e.g., articles, possessives, quantifiers, and numerals—*a book,* (Ø article) *information, their book, most of the book(s), three books*).

In fact, subject and object slots are usually filled by a noun phrase rather than a single-word noun because in real language use single-word nouns are relatively rare (i.e., proper, uncountable, and abstract nouns represent a majority of all cases). To explain the noun phrase elements to students, the simplest way to proceed is to practice identifying the main noun and all its pieces (e.g., *vegetable soup/the blue book*—does the word *vegetable* describe the *soup*? the word *blue* describe the *book*? do these two words go together; *most of the book*—do the words *most, of,* and *the* refer to the *book*? do all these words go together?). Similar techniques for identifying elements and their order in the verb phrase and the prepositional phrase are discussed later in this chapter.

An important and simple technique for identifying entire noun phrases, as well as their elements, and the singular versus plural properties of subjects is to replace phrases with pronouns. For example,

Marie Curie studied the chemistry and medical uses of radium.

She studied the chemistry and medical uses of radium.

Mary Peters and John Smith are planning to attend the conference.
[1 + 1] *They* are planning to attend the conference.

The E-commerce seminar and the technology presentation start at 9 am on Saturdays.
They start at 9 am on Saturdays.

The idea to develop a new type of packaging appealed to store managers.
It appealed to store managers.

Once the noun phrase is replaced with a pronoun, subject–verb agreement is relatively easy to check. An important step in locating the subject noun phrase is to find the verb and then go to the left to look for the subject noun.

The Basic Sentence[2]

<table>
<tr><td colspan="4">Sentence Slots</td></tr>
<tr><td>(Adverb/prepositional phrase—Optional)</td><td>Subject noun phrase</td><td>Predicate verb phrase</td><td>Object noun phrase</td></tr>
<tr><td rowspan="2">(In the evening/Every day)</td><td rowspan="2">They/ Stuents/ Group members</td><td>study (intransitive, optional object)</td><td></td></tr>
<tr><td>review (transitive, object required)</td><td>class materials</td></tr>
</table>

Building on this core structure, it is possible to construct more complicated sentences that adhere largely to the same order of elements. It is important to note that this approach to sentence structure analysis is highly flexible in its ability to account for practically any number of syntactic and contextual variations, even though the core sentence elements remain rigid in their order relative to one another.

The third principle of the unit organization in a sentence specifies that sentence elements are organized according to a hierarchy based on their importance for a sentence to be grammatical (i.e., each sentence must have the most important elements, such as the subject and the verb, and, in most cases, an object or a subject complement). Other elements, such as adverbs or prepositional phrases, are mobile and can occur in various predictable locations. For example, the next sentence includes several units (prepositional phrases) that are added to the core structure, two following the subject noun phrase and one at the end of the sentence.

A Sentence With Prepositional Phrases

Subject Noun Phrase	Two prepositional phrases that describe the subject	**Predicate Verb Phrase**	**Object Noun Phrase**	Adverb/ prepositional phrase
Interaction	*among people from different organizations*	*develops*	*social patterns*	*among those organizations*

(Example from Charon, 1999, p. 131)

[2] Shaded slots in the tables are for optional elements in a sentence.

From a practical point of view, for example, explanations of the English sentence structure based on the core elements with other elements added can greatly simplify instruction in learning to identify the subject, predicate verb phrase, and importance of subject–verb agreement (see further discussion later in this chapter). For instance, in the case of a compound noun phrase and/or a compound verb phrase, a similar approach can be useful.

A Sentence With a Compound Subject Noun Phrase and a Transitive Verb

Subject Noun Phrase (parallel nouns)	**Predicate Verb Phrase**	**Object Noun Phrase**	A prepositional phrase that describes the object	Adverb/ Prepositional Phrase
Talent, training, and effort	*affect*	*placement*	*of the individual*	*in professional organizations*

For teachers, analyzing sentences as sequences of units that are relative to one another in their order and importance can provide a practical and useful tool for dealing with diverse large and small features of sentences, from subordinate clauses to the role of nouns as subjects or objects, parallel structures, or effects of verb transitivity on the presence of objects.

> Most important, the slot organization of sentence elements accounts for fluidity in sentence construction and stylistic variation while being sufficiently clear cut for L2 writers to understand how to use it to their advantage in both constructing new sentences or editing their text.

Speaking broadly, noun phrases have a limited number of functions and can play the roles of a sentence subject, object, or compliment; the type of the main verb largely determines the structure of a sentence.

THE ORDER OF ELEMENTS IN THE NOUN PHRASE

Rigidity in the order of sentence slots can be similarly profitable for teaching elements of the noun phrase structure and the verb phrase structure. Articles mark noun phrases, and the article is always the first element in the noun phrase (e.g., *the book, a lunch*). Articles occur in the same slot as proper possessive nouns (e.g., *John's book/lunch*), possessive pronouns (e.g., *his/her/their book*), or indefinite pronouns (e.g., *some, any*), and therefore cannot be used together in the same position—once the pronoun or article is in the slot, the slot is full. Articles and possessives can be followed by quantifiers (*the five books, John's five books*) and quantifiers by adjectives (e.g., *the ten blue books, Mary's/her ten blue books*).

In the case of (general/nonspecific) plural nouns (e.g., *Researchers investigate processes in language learning*) or noncount nouns (e.g., *Health/honesty is more important than wealth*), indefinite articles cannot be used. On the other hand, definite articles are possible in specifically marked contexts, such as *The researchers from the Famous University* ... or *The health of the patient/The honesty of the accountant* .... Articles, plural, count, and noncount nouns of all sorts are discussed in detail in chapter 5.

In general, noun phrases are not very complex. In noun phrases with plural main (head) nouns, all elements are optional except of course the main noun, and in noun phrases with singular head nouns, the article or possessive also represent a required element.

The Basic Noun Phrase

Article Or Possessive Noun/Pronoun	Quantifiers	Adverbs to describe adjectives	Adjectives	**Main (Head) Noun**
The/Ø	*ten*	*really/most*	*important*	*books*
Their/Mary's	*two*	*very*	*good*	*grades*
A		*highly*	*qualified*	*teacher*

THE ORDER OF ELEMENTS IN THE VERB PHRASE

As mentioned, the type of the main verb determines the sentence pattern and its optional and required slots. Main verbs belong to several classes that vary in their prevalence in academic texts.

Biber's, et al. (1999) large corpus analysis of various types of written texts indicates that lexical verbs (e.g., *walk, sing, talk*) are far less common in academic prose than copula *be* in all its forms. Other verb types common in academic texts are linking verbs (e.g., *appear, become, seem*), intransitive verbs, and transitive verbs that require direct objects (e.g., *read a book, write a paper*). The following discussion of the main verb types is organized based on their prevalence in academic prose as identified in various analyses of academic English language corpora (Biber, 1988; Biber et al., 1999; Hyland, 1996; Quirk et al., 1985).

Be-verbs

Copula *be* main verbs can be followed by nouns and noun phrases, adjectives and adjective phrases, or adverbs of time and place (*when* and *where* words and phrases). Main *be*-verbs are often considered to be a subset of linking verbs (see the next section).

Be-verbs	Nouns, Adjectives, OR Adverbs of time/place
is *are* *was* *were* *is/are* *was/were/been*	*a book* (noun) *an important book* (noun phrase) *important* (adjective) *highly important* (adjective phrase) *yesterday/in January* (words and phrases of time) *here/in the text/on the top* (words and phrases of place)
can/will/may be	*the case* (noun phrase) *true/necessary* (adjective) *on time/at the right place* (adverb phrases)

Because sentences with *be*-verbs are easy to construct, many NNS writers overuse them in their academic writing (Hinkel, 2002a). **One of the most common structures that follows *be* is the prepositional phrase (a preposition and a noun/noun phrase—e.g., *in the lab, at the start*).**

The second most prevalent pattern is *be*-verbs with adjectives (also called *predicative adjectives* because they are a part of the sentence predicate). In some texts, predicative adjectives that follow *be*-verbs and linking verbs are also called *subject complements* because they describe (complete) the subject noun. (The function of adjectives is to describe nouns no matter whether adjectives precede nouns or occur behind *be*- and linking verbs.)

A good (attributive adjective) *book* (noun) *is a joy.*

A book *is* *good* (predicative adjective).

The student *is* *very intelligent* (predicative adjective phrase).

Linking Verbs

The most common linking verb, *become*, can be followed by nouns and adjectives, but not adverbs. However, most other types of linking verbs, such as *seem/appear, get,*[3] *prove, remain, sound, smell,* and *turn*, rarely occur with nouns. By far the most prevalent types of structures with these verbs include adjectives (e.g., *get old/cold, seems small/large, proved boring/exciting*). Another prevalent conversational pattern includes an insertion of the preposition *like*:

[3]*Get* is common only in conversational discourse.

He seemed like a nice man.

That seemed like a boring movie.

Linking Verb Patterns

Linking Verbs (become, seem)	**Nouns and Adjectives only**
becomes	*a task/a consideration*
became	*a difficult task/an important consideration*
seems	*a good plan (a noun phrase—relatively rare)*
seemed/remained	*ridiculous/wonderful/cute*

The adjectives and nouns that occur after linking verbs, similar to those with *be*-verbs, are part of the sentence predicate that complement the subject noun. In general terms, because *be*-verbs and linking verbs are the only two types that can be followed by adjectives, identifying linking verbs can be based on the presence or absence of the predicative adjective (i.e., *if a = b, then b = a*). In this case, if an adjective follows the verb, it is probably a *be*- or linking verb.

> The presence a predicative adjective can be used to catch missing *be*-verbs in structures, such as **it possible* or **average temperature high*.

Intransitive Verbs

Intransitive verbs (those that do not require an object or adjective for a sentence to be grammatical) are actually somewhat infrequent and altogether number fewer than 25 (Biber et al., 1999). In fact most verbs in English can be both transitive and intransitive (e.g., *John reads/writes; Mary reads/writes a book*). Because intransitive verbs make for short sentences, they are usually followed by optional adverb phrases (some exceptions, such as *reside* and *glance,* require an adverb—e.g., *Bob resides on/glanced at Market Street*).

What makes intransitive verbs relatively tricky is that they are most often found among two-word verbs (see chap. 8) and are therefore idiomatic (e.g., *turn in, turn up, turn around*). A majority of intransitive two-word verbs occur with adverbs. E.g.,

in—out *John jumped <u>in</u>/slept <u>in</u>, and a fight broke <u>out</u>.*

up—down *Mary cannot come down because something came up.*

over *However, Peter can take over/move over/run over.*

It is important to keep in mind that two- and three-word verbs are highly infrequent in academic prose[4] and may not be worth the effort expended on teaching them unless one goal of the course is to improve students' conversational skills.

Intransitive Verb	Adverbial
remain	*on the job/at rest*
occurred	*regularly/in the library*
look	*carefully/everywhere/up*
gave	*in/out/up*

In general terms, intransitive verbs are simple to use, but they are important inasmuch as they have to be distinguished from transitive verbs, which are far more numerous and complex.

Transitive Verbs

Transitive verbs require direct objects (monotransitive verbs—e.g., *cause an accident*), direct and indirect objects (ditransitive verbs—e.g., *give John a sandwich*), or direct objects and additional noun or adjective complements (e.g., *elect Mary president, consider Jane studious*). The important thing about transitive verbs is that all of them require a direct object (always used without a preposition), similar to the noun complement following *be-* or linking verbs. For example,

John	*reads*	*a novel.*
This book	*is*	*a novel.*
His memoirs	*became*	*a novel.*

The tricky aspect of object constructions is to distinguish between direct and indirect objects (this distinction becomes important in chap. 7 in the

[4]Analyses of written English corpora have shown that two- and three-word verbs are hardly ever used in academic prose (Biber et al., 1999). The most common are *to be set out in* or *to be set up in* used at the rate of 0.002% (20 occurrences per 1 million words).

discussion of passive verbs). All verbs that require two types of objects entail an element of meaning associated with giving and can be called ***giving*** verbs; e.g.,

announce	give	owe	recommend	show	tell
bring	hand	pass	remember	speak	write
deny	lend	pay	report	suggest	
describe	mention	prove	sell	take	
explain	offer	read	send	teach	

Two techniques can be used effectively to tell direct and indirect objects apart. First, to determine which object is direct and which is indirect, a "giving" preposition *to* or *for* may be inserted:

> *The professor sent me an email message.*
>
> *The professor sent an email message* ***to*** *me.*

If you can put the preposition in front of the noun or pronoun, it is the indirect object because direct objects never occur with prepositions. For instance, all verbs listed previously take the preposition *to* and a few others take *for*; e.g.,

answer	catch	design	find	order
build	change	do	hire	prepare
buy	close	draw	leave	save
call	correct	fill	make	

The second technique for distinguishing direct and indirect pronouns is to ask a *what* (or *whom*) question:

Option 1: *The professor sent me* (what?) *[an e-mail message]*

Option 2: *What did the professor send? [an e-mail message]*

Overnight delivery companies fill the market demand.

Option 1: *Overnight delivery companies fill* (what?) *[the market demand]*

Option 2: *What do overnight delivery companies fill? [the market demand]*

The noun that answers the *what* question is the direct object.

Direct objects are important to identify when the voice is changed from the active to the passive: direct objects become subjects of passive verbs, and indirect objects are not affected (see chap. 7). For example,

Advertising	*brings*	*new information*	*to consumers. [active]* →
New information	*is brought*		*to consumers. [passive]*

On the other hand, transitive verbs that require object complements (adjectives or nouns) are relatively easy to figure out. In the case of noun complements (e.g., *consider the book a problem*), the first noun is the direct object, and the second noun is the object complement (e.g., *the book [is] a problem*). With adjective complements (e.g., *consider the book difficult*), the only noun that follows the verb is the direct object (e.g., *consider <u>the book</u> ...*).

A useful technique can be used to decide whether an adjective or adverb should be used after a verb:

Mary considers her job hard/easy. vs. **John finds his course hardly.*

In this case, the insertion of *to be* can clarify the ambiguity:

Mary considers her job [to be] hard/easy. vs. **John considers his job [to be] hardly.*

One of the common learner errors entails inserting ***as*** in the wrong place and with the wrong verbs, such as *consider:*

**We consider our changes in the program design <u>as</u> important*, or

**Locke considered this human talent <u>as</u> a gift.*

With object complements, ***<u>as</u>*** is required with such verbs as *refer (to), know,* and *think (to)* (e.g., *We refer to Locke as the greatest philosopher of our time*), but not with *consider*, which takes *to be*.

The Order of Elements in the Main Verb Slot

Several verbs, such as *be, have*, or *do*, have a variety of syntactic and lexical functions: They can be main or auxiliary verbs.

John is a student, and he does his homework daily. [*be* and *do* are main lexical verbs]
Bob has been working on his term paper. [*work* is the main lexical verb, and *has* and *been* are auxiliary]

The order in which main verb elements occur is also rigid and can be illustrated by means of slots, similar to the elements of the noun phrase. Every English sentence needs to have a verb to be grammatical. However, only the main verb is absolutely essential, and all other slots inside the verb phrase system are optional. For example,

Peter		*cooks/cooked*. [The essential main verb]
Peter	*should*	*cook*. [Optional *should* and the main verb]
Peter	*should have*	*cooked*. [Optional *should* and *have*, and the main verb]
Peter	*has been*	*cooking*. [Optional *has*, *been*, and *-ing*, and the main verb]

Inside the verb system, the optional slot is reserved for modal verbs (e.g., *can, may, should*) or the future tense marker, *will*. If this slot is occupied, the rest of the slots can contain only the *base form* of the main verb (e.g., *I/he should go, we/she can sing*). If the slot is not occupied, the form of the main verb depends on the tense and number of the subject noun (e.g., *I walk, he walks, they walked; I go, he goes, they went*).

Subject Noun Phrase	Modal/Future Verbs (Optional)	The Main Verb
Mary/I/They/Students	*should/may/will*	*come and go*
I/We/They/You/Students		*walk and talk*
MaryHe/She/It		*walkS and talkS/walkED and talkED*
John/I/We/He/Students		*came and went*

However, as noted in the examples earlier, the verb phrase can include more slots than just those for modals/future markers and the main verb. For this reason, the slot system has to allow for more options to account for various tense auxiliaries, such as *was, have/has,* or *been* because all sentence verbs have some sort of tense. For instance, even in the case of modal verbs, two options are possible (e.g., *should cook* or *should have cooked*, not to mention such complex constructions as *will be cooking* or *will have finished/sung*).

In effect, the tense of thc verb is the first thing that needs to be identified because it determines what happens to the rest of the elements in the verb system. For example, *What tense is used in the preceding text—the present or the past? Are time markers and adverbs found to allow the tense switch?* Identifying the tense/time in which to use verbs in a particular context is the first step, followed by marking the verb for a particular tense (see chap. 7).

The tense can be marked (e.g., *talks, talked, goes, went*) or unmarked (e.g., *I/we/you/they talk/go*). Once the tense of the verb is determined, it creates a domino effect in the rest of the verb phrase elements.

Another important element of the verb system is aspect, such as progressive and/or perfect, both of which require auxiliaries:

is singing [progressive]; *has sung* [perfect]; *has been singing* [perfect progressive]

were eating [progressive]; *had eaten* [perfect]; *had been eating* [perfect progressive]

In the case of the progressive verb, the order of the verb phrase elements is as follows:

	be	+ the base form of the main verb	+ *-ing*
present →	*am/is*	+ *sing*	+ *-ing*
	I am/ He is	*singing.*	

Similarly, in the case of the perfect aspect, the auxiliary *have* is followed by the past participle form of the main verb:

	have	+ past participle
present →	*have/has*	+ *spoken/eaten*

In addition, perfect and progressive aspects can occur together in the present perfect progressive (e.g., *have/has been speaking*) or the past perfect progressive (*had been singing*). A quick overview of auxiliary verbs with a few tense and aspect combinations can be:

am/is/was	*sing+ing/cook+ing*	[BE + base verb + *-ing*]
have/had	*talked/spoken*	[HAVE + past participle]
has/had been	*talking/speaking*	[HAVE + BE-en (past participle) + base verb + *-ing*]

To combine the various elements of the verb phrase, such as the tense, modals, and other auxiliaries, a slot system can be created specifically tailored toward the regularities in the verb system:

1. The tense determines the form of verb in the next slot (e.g., present tense → *walk/walks*; past tense → *walked*), including aspect auxiliaries (e.g., present progressive → *is walking*, past progressive → *was walking*, or present/past perfect → *has/had eaten*).
2. The aspect (including zero marked aspect as in simple tenses) determines the form of verb in the slot that follows, usually, the main verb (e.g., progressive—the base verb + *-ing*, and perfect—the past participle)
3. The combination of the tense and both progressive and perfect aspects results in a series of verb elements: the tense, the optional perfect auxiliary *have* or *had*, *be* + *en* (past participle), and the main verb + *-ing*.

The Verb Phrase Slots

Tense/Aspect	Modal (Optional)	HAVE (Optional)	BE (Optional)	**Main Verb**
Present Simple				*cook(s)/speak(s)*
Past Simple				*cooked/spoke*
Present/Past Progressive			be (present/past) *am/is/was/were*	Verb + -ing *cook+ing/speak+ing*
Present Perfect		*have/has*		Verb - past participle *cooked/spoken*
Past Perfect		*had*		*cooked/spoken*
Present Perfect Progressive		*have/has*	be- past participle *been*	Verb + -ing *cooking/speaking*
Modal/Future	*will*			*cook/speak*
Modal/Future Progressive	*may*		*be*	*cooking/speaking*
Modal/Future Perfect	*will/may*	*have*		*cooked/spoken*

As mentioned, the verb phrase has only two essential elements, the tense/aspect and the main verb. In light of the enormous complexity of the English verb system, it is hardly surprising that many advanced L2 learners often have trouble using verb tenses and aspects appropriately in their academic writing. Techniques for teaching L2 academic writers to get around the complexities of the verb phrase are further discussed in chapter 7.

SUBJECT AND VERB AGREEMENT

Based on the system of required and optional sentence slots, in the teaching of subject and verb agreement, two easy techniques can be used. However, both require a successful identification of the main (head) subject noun or noun phrase. For L2 writers, one of the thorniest issues with subject–verb agreement lies in the fact that it is often difficult to locate the head subject noun and separate it from other elements, such as prepositional phrases that obtrusively sit between the subject and verb.

For example, in Sentence (1), the subject noun phrase is obscured by the prepositional phrases that follow it, making the use of the appropriate verb form somewhat difficult.

1. *Current* ***developments*** *in technology and broadcasting* ***are*** *at a crossroads comparable to the early development of television.*

In (1), the main noun phrase includes the plural noun *developments,* which requires the verb *are* also to be plural. However, the prepositional phrase *in technology and broadcasting* contains two singular nouns that obscure a connecting relationship between *developments* and *are*.

The first technique for identifying the main subject noun involves identifying the prepositional phrases and nouns included in them to simply ignore them by, for example, blocking them off with a thumb, piece of paper, or cap of a pen. As noted in the Basic Sentence illustration, prepositional phrases always sit at a lower level than the subject and object phrase.

Locating and "doing away with" the prepositional phrases between the main subject noun or noun phrase is relatively easy. According to Biber et al. (1999), in academic written text, only six prepositions account for 90% of all prepositional phrases:

of in for on to with

An additional six prepositions each account for approximately 1.00% of all prepositional phrases:

about at between by from like

Thus, to identify a sentence subject correctly, all phrases located between the subject and verb and marked with any of these 12 prepositions simply need to be ignored.

For example,

Some improvement in employees' working conditions come about ....

Some improvement *come about ....*

This technique for identifying head subject nouns can also be effectively applied to blocking off adjectives, adverbs, or whole subordinate clauses (see chap. 10).

The second technique for finding sentence subjects can be useful for learners at intermediate and higher levels of proficiency. This technique is based on converting sentences into *yes/no* questions and moving the verb to the front of the question. In this case, the subject is the very first element or phrase that occurs after the verb.

2. *One of the most powerful ways of increasing one's levels of education is reading.*
   Is (main verb) <u>*one*</u> *[of the most powerful ways of increasing one's levels of education reading]?*
3. *Various personal accounts of the events during World War II help the reader to construct a full picture of the impact of war on families.*

   Do <u>*various personal accounts*</u> *[of the events during World War II] help* (main verb) *the reader ...?*

Thus, if the subject noun is singular, the verb needs to be singular (as in Sentence [2]), and if the subject is plural, the verb is also plural (as in Sentence [3]).

Other types of elements that locate themselves between the subject and verb can include adjective phrases and clauses or appositives. All these can be done away with by means the analysis of slots and *yes/no* questions.

4. *Someone who is self-confident is less likely to find a given situation stressful.*
   Is (main verb) <u>*someone*</u> *[who is self-confident] less likely to find ...?*
5. *Psychologists working from a biological perspective point out that similar experiences can lead to different reactions.*

   Do <u>*psychologists*</u> *[working from a biological perspective] point out* (main verb) *that ...?*

COMPOUND SENTENCES

Compound sentences are those that consist of two or more simple sentences. (Similarly, compound nouns and compound verbs consist of two or more parallel nouns or verbs; see chap. 11 for further discussion.) Compound sentences can be joined by the following:

1. Comma Plus Coordinating Conjunction

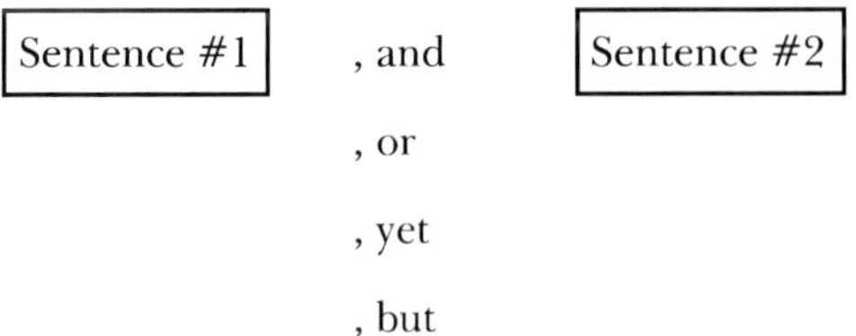

Washington is the nation's top cherry producer, **and** *farmers in the state grew a record 85,000 tons of cherries last summer.*

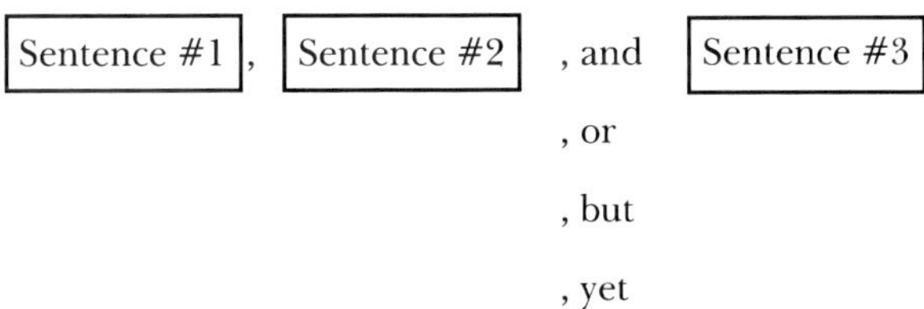

People like to eat sweet cherries, *bakers put them in their pies*, **and** *jam-makers cannot get enough of them.*

In formal academic text in general, according to Quirk et al. (1985), compound sentences may be of limited value, and most are found in informal prose. These authors also noted that formal written discourse highly prefers the use of comma in compound sentences joined by conjunctions.[5]

The use of commas without conjunctions results in one of the most frequent sentence-boundary errors found in L2 writing, usually referred to as run-on sentences (or comma splices).

> **The new advances in technology in the 20th century are amazing, we now have the World Wide Web to connect people for communication, scientists have invented new AIDS drugs.*

Run-ons of this type are relatively easy to fix by simply inserting a coordinating conjunction at the sentence boundary after the comma: The conjunction is necessary to add power to the separate the sentences.

---

[5]The punctuation rules for compound sentences do not apply to compound noun and verb phrases (see chap. 11).

2. Semicolons

Semicolons are used without coordinating conjunctions, but they can conjoin only fairly short sentences.

Sentence #1	;	Sentence #2

Books are sold here; software and magazines are next door.

Semicolons can also be used with sentence transitions (conjunctive adverbs), such as *however, thus,* or *therefore*.

Sentence #1	; however,	Sentence #2
	; thus,	
	; therefore	

When teaching the comma + coordinator and semicolon uses in compound sentences, it is useful to mention that these two patterns largely have the same power to conjoin short simple sentences and mark their boundaries. However, their power is less than that of a period (.). (For complex sentences with subordinate clauses, see chap. 10.)

PUNCTUATION

The easiest punctuation rule of all can be obtained from the system of sentence slots:

> *No single (lonely) commas can be used between required sentence slots.*

Commas are separators of sentence elements, and the essential sentence slots, such as subjects and verbs, verbs and direct objects, and direct objects and indirect objects cannot be separated. No matter how long the subject or object noun phrases can be, the required sentence slots are never separated by single commas.[6] However, **paired** commas (e.g., *Smith [2003], who researched xxx),* mark modifiers of the head/subject noun phrase. Such modifiers are part of the noun phrase.

[6]Appositives, *My father, the scientist,* are discussed in chapter 5. These structures actually occur inside the subject slot and are set off by two commas.

COMMON ERRORS: MISSING OR TOO MANY REQUIRED SENTENCE SLOTS

One of the most common errors in L2 sentences is the missing main verb or its elements. Other types of sentence-level errors frequently found in student writing can be more than one subject noun (phrase; e.g., *Freud, he* ...), prepositional phrases used in place of the subject, missing objects of transitive verbs, and missing subject or object complements. Although some of these errors cannot be completely avoided, students can be taught to edit many of them by identifying the filled or unfilled required sentence slots.

In practically all cases, for a sentence to be grammatical, it must include a subject noun phrase, verb, and, most often, direct object. The following examples from student academic essays demonstrate that teaching students to identify the required sentence slots can lead to correction of many sentence- and phrase-level errors. The following examples of various L2 errors can be corrected relatively easily when sentences are parsed into slots.

Counting Sentence Parts

Checking sentences for grammaticality entails locating all required sentence elements and making sure that they occupy their correct slots.

Step 1. Find all verb phrases and go to the left to locate their subject noun phrases.
Step 2. Block off all the prepositional phrases that sit between the subject noun phrase and the verb.
Step 3. Go to the right of the verb phrase and locate the direct object, the subject complement, or the object complement.
Step 4. Find the required slots and check to see whether they are empty or overfilled.
Step 5. Fill the required slots, if they are empty, or delete overfillers.

The following example illustrates this:

1. *There are differences and similarities between the two theories are easy to notice.*

The Original Sentence							
Subject	**Verb**	**Object/ Comple-ment**	**Prep. Phrase**	**Comma + Conjunct or ;**	**Subject**	**Verb**	**Object/ Complement**
There	*are*	*differences and similarities*	*between the two major theories*			*are [verb without a subject]*	*easy to notice*

The Corrected Sentence							
Subject	**Verb**	**Object/ Complement**	**Prep. Phrase**	**Comma + Conjunct or ;**	**Subject**	**Verb**	**Object/ Complement**
There	*are*	*differences and similarities*	*between the two major theories*	*, and* [comma + conjunction added]	*they* [subject added]	*are*	*easy to notice*

2. *These chemical elements, they combine at a high temperature.*

The Original Sentence		
Subject	**Verb**	**Object/Complement**
1. These chemical elements, *2. they*	*combine*	*at a high temperature*
The Corrected Sentence		
These chemical elements	*combine*	*at a high temperature*

3. *We are work very hard to reach our dream.*

The Original Sentence				
Subject	**Verb**			Object/Complement
	Tense		Main Verb	
		Aux be	+ing	
We	(present)	*are*	*work*	*very hard to reach our dream*
The Corrected Sentences (two possibilities with slightly different meanings)				
We	(present)		*work*	*very hard to reach our dream*
We	(present progressive)	*are*	*working*	*very hard to reach our dream*

For additional examples of sentence correction, see Suggestions for Teaching.

CHAPTER SUMMARY

Rigid and predictable patterns in English syntax provide framework for teaching sentence structure by means of slots that must or may be filled. Once they are understood, students can use the slot patterns to more effectively edit their own writing for grammaticality:

- Sentences must have a verb and a subject (except for imperative sentences with an understood subject *you*).
- In academic prose, adverbs and prepositional phrases are mobile, but subjects and verbs are not.
- Noun phrases must include a main (or head) noun, which can be preceded with, in this order, an article or possessive, quantifiers, adverbs to describe adjectives, and adjectives.
- Main *be*-verbs can be followed by nouns, adjectives, or adverbs/adverbial phrases of time or place.
- Main linking verbs are similar to main *be*-verbs and can followed by nouns or adjectives, but not adverbials of any kind.
- Transitive verbs require a direct object, and some transitive verbs (**giving** verbs) can also take an indirect object. Students can insert the prepositions *to* or *for* or ask a *what* question to identify the direct object.
- The verb phrase has two essential elements: tense (which can be marked or not) and the main verb. Optional verb slots include modals and auxiliary verbs.
- Isolating the subject and the verb helps students check for subject–verb agreement.

STRATEGIES AND TACTICS FOR TEACHING AND TEACHING ACTIVITIES

Teaching suggestions presented here advance in the degree of their sophistication. Their primary instructional objectives are to reduce the frequency of preventable errors and/or fine tune students' self-editing skills. The exercises and teaching activities are designed to focus on the following sentence structure skills:

- Identifying missing or incorrectly added sentence elements based on the regular structural patterns in English (focus noted; e.g., please find and correct all errors in subject–verb agreement).

- Identifying and correcting incorrectly used sentence and phrase elements (focus unspecified).
- Noticing and correcting fragments and run-ons.
- Editing entire text passages written by someone other than the editor.
- Editing one's own essay-length texts.

As mentioned in chapter 3, it is very important that practice with identifying regular sentence patterns be cumulative. When the work with particular focus structures is completed, they cannot be simply abandoned on the assumption that students can productively use these structures for writing and editing. All grammar, lexical, and editing practice must be designed to build on the structures that learners are familiar with or from the structurally and functionally simple to more complex constructions.

Depending on students' proficiency level, the sentences in this exercise can be extracted from authentic texts of varied degrees of complexity. It is important to select somewhat lengthy sentences, such as those in authentic texts or academic textbooks. The sentences should include prepositional, adjectival, and adverbial phrases that sit between the subject and verb.

A realistic degree of sentence complexity represents an important feature of this type of practice. Useful sentences can be reasonably easily adapted from those found in the science and health sections of newspapers; popular print media such as magazines, Internet news, business reports, and movie reviews; and introductory college-level textbooks. All exercises exemplified next can be assigned as individual or group tasks or homework with a follow-up in-class discussion. Students can discuss them with one another or the teacher.

(1) Sentence-Level Practice: Parsing Sentence Slots

In the following sentences, please draw a vertical line to separate subjects and predicates in as many cases as you can identify. Also please mark various parts of the predicate: auxiliary verbs, the main verb, and the object noun or the subject complement.

(a)The experiment proved the point.

(b) Later studies and additional experiments provide additional positive information.

(c) Researchers at Ohio State University report early evidence that berries are actually good for one's health.

(d) Various fruit trees and berry shrubs have been selling quite well in Ohio and neighboring states.

(e) Making phone calls is usually difficult for those individuals who do not speak the language very well.

(f) At this time of year, all over the country, celebrities, politicians, and writers have been asked to give graduation speeches in high schools and colleges.

(2) Parsing Sentence and Phrase Slots

In the following texts, please find all subject phrases and all predicate phrases and all objects/complements in all sentences. Circle the entire subjects and predicates and include all their elements. Please do not forget that sentences can be compound and complex, in addition to simple. After all subject, predicate, and object phrases are found, underline the main subject noun, the main predicate verb, and the main object noun.

(a) Vitamin C and minerals, such as iron, can be found in many types of foods.

(b) Frequently, a shortage of vitamin D occurs during the winter months.

(c) Nationwide, the average commute increased 3.1 minutes from 22.4 minutes to 25.5 between 1990 and 2000. Among the 25 large cities, Seattle's average commute time ranked 15th in 2000, up slightly from 17th in 1990. Los Angeles, Houston, Boston, Philadelphia, and Dallas were ahead of Seattle on the latest list. (Adapted from the *Seattle Times,* June 8, 2002, Local News, Section B, p. 1)

(d) The basic categories of marketing mix elements are product, place, price, and promotion.... The product variable includes the brand name, the package, the warranty, and customer service. Sometimes emotional aspects of the product are very important. We will discuss these topics in the second half of the book.... Decisions about transportation and storage are examples of distribution activities. Price is the amount of money, goods, or services that the customer exchanges for the product. Pricing goods and services involves establishing appropriate price levels.... Using discounts, rebates, and other techniques is a way of adjusting prices to make them low.... Cost, competition, and desired profit determine prices. (Adapted from Zikmund, Middlemist, & Middlemist, 1995, pp. 292–293)

(3) Text-Level Editing Practice With an Explicitly Stated Focus[7]

Identifying Specified Missing or Incorrectly Added Sentence Elements. Depending on students' proficiency levels, the exercise can consist of typed (but not photocopied) short text excerpts from one to four sentences. Typed text can allow the flexibility of deleting or adding elements without visible deletions and omissions.

In the following text, please correct all errors in the subject–verb agreement and object/adjective constructions that follow the verb phrase [explicitly stated foci]. Missing and added elements are included in the square brackets and they should ***not*** *appear in the student copy of the text.*

(a) For many parents, recreation with kids differ[S—deleted] greatly from the days when they could take [object missing—their hiking boots/noun] and

[7]The benefits of various types of editing/error correction practice (sometimes called *negative models* or *negative instances*) have been noted by many researchers, including Corder (1973), Hammerly, (1991), and James (1998).

head out for eight miles on the spur of the moment.... Parents who [ARE—deleted] unfamiliar with the sport or new to the area can join [missing object—activity groups/noun] for ideas on places to go and tips on how to be safe. Many families in the Northwest believes [added -s] that it [IS—deleted] especially important for parents to encourage lifelong exercise habits. Many experts says [added -s] that the best way to do this [IS—deleted] by setting a positive example and being active as a family. (Adapted from the *Seattle Times,* June 8, 2002, Northwest Life, Section E, p. 1)

(4) Text-Level Editing Practice Without an Explicitly Stated Focus

This exercise can be used as an individual or small-group practice, or it can be assigned as homework to be spot-checked and discussed in class as needed.

In the following texts, please correct all errors that you can find. Please be ready to explain each structure that you believe to be incorrect and show how you arrived at your conclusion.

Text 1 Direct mail marketing generate about $244 billion per year in sales. There is at least two issue related to direct mail advertising that needs a thorough examination. Direct mail advertisers, or direct marketing companies, as they are sometimes called, develops and maintains customer information data. Data information include name, address, and estimated income. They also contain a list of products that purchases. Your name is probably on the list, marketers sell to other mailers. You might say, I've never ordered anything by mail. If your have ever fills out a warranty card for an item or if your have ever uses a credit card to purchase something in a store, chance are that the data were transmitted somewhere to add to the list of your preferences in. (Adapted from Leslie, 2000)

Text 2 The human family relationship in the 20th century complex. Society is composed of individuals pursue different goals in life and have different interests and personality. The family is the basic form of society we are from the moment we are born.

Text 3 A big problem in this story. Mathilde in the story "The Necklace," she needs to work very hard for 10 year to earn some money to replace the lost necklace. After she done her jobs, which is work for ten years to replace it, she can breathe freely. Do not see is that, a small problem or big problem.

(5) Sentence Building I

(For additional sentences building practice, see appendix in chap. 4.)

Students can be given stripped-down sentences without optional slots and asked to build them up. For example:

Please add optional elements to these sentences that consist only of filled required slots. You may be asked to explain the differences between the meanings of the original sentences and your own.

1. People dream about two hours every night.
2. Most dreams are quickly forgotten.
3. Dreams are vivid visual and auditory experiences that occur during Rapid Eye Movement periods.
4. Most young children cannot distinguish between dreams and waking experiences.
5. Psychologists have been fascinated by dream activity.
6. Dreams can be made of false or useless information to remove it from memory.

(6) Sentence Building II

Chapters 5 and 8 include lists of academic nouns and verbs extracted from the University Word List developed by Nation (1990). Students can be given a few of these items singly or in combinations and asked to build sentences that include them, paying special attention to required and optional sentence slots. This activity can be carried out in pairs or assigned as homework to be discussed in class or small groups. The same exercise can be repeated for nouns, adjectives, and adverbs (see chap. 9).

Please construct sentences with the following verbs and be particularly careful with required and/optional sentence elements (e.g., some of these verbs require objects and some do not). You can include as many of these verbs as you like in a single sentence:

accumulate	concentrate	contradict	enumerate	function
approximate	conclude	elaborate	establish	generate
challenge	constitute	eliminate	estimate	identify
communicate	cooperate	emphasize	found	integrate

(7) Sentence Building III

This task can be associated with an assignment on a particular topic or consist of individual sentences.

Please complete the following sentences paying special attention to required and optional slots.

1. The first step in a research project ______________________________

2. The statement of a problem can consist of ____________________
3. ____________________ gather data, such as facts and information.
4. ____________________ can be divided ____________________
5. Each research design ____________________
6. The researcher collects ____________________

QUESTIONS FOR DISCUSSION

1. In English, various sentence types belong to several relatively rigid patterns. To make their teaching efficient and clear, how can the patterns noted in this chapter be made even more explicit?
2. Why do you think L2 learners can have difficulty identifying sentence subjects and predicates? Why is it important to teach students to identify sentence elements?
3. The sentences *This sandwich is for you* or *The drinks are for the party* do not neatly fit into the patterns discussed in this chapter. Can you determine why? How can this structure and others like it be taught effectively?
4. In your opinion, which features of the English verb system are most difficult for L2 learners to learn and use correctly? Why?
5. Do you think it is possible to teach the sentence slot system to beginning learners? What could be advantages or disadvantages of teaching the slot system to beginners or advanced learners?
6. Would the sentence slot system be easier to work with for native or non-native speakers of English? Why?

FURTHER READINGS ABOUT SENTENCE AND PHRASE STRUCTURE

Burton-Roberts, N. (1997). *Analyzing sentences* (2nd ed.). Harlow, Essex: Longman.

Celce-Murcia, M., & Hilles, S. (1988). *Techniques and resources in teaching grammar.* New York: Oxford University Press.

Celce-Murcia, M., & Larsen-Freeman, D. (1999). *The grammar book* (2nd ed.). Boston: Heinle & Heinle.

Fabb, N. (1994). *Sentence structure.* London: Routledge.

Jacobs, R. (1995). *English syntax: A grammar for English language professionals.* Oxford: Oxford University Press.

Pike, K. (1964). A linguistic contribution to composition: A hypothesis. *College Composition and Communication, 15*(1), 82–88.

Young, R., Becker, A. L., & Pike, K. (1970). *Rhetoric: Discovery and change.* New York: Harcourt Brace Jovanovich.

Appendix A to Chapter 4

SENTENCE STEMS FOR WRITTEN ACADEMIC DISCOURSE

As discussed in chapter 3, the teaching of sentence and phrase structure needs to co-occur with instruction on vocabulary and common academic collocations. Using stock sentence stems in actual writing can become probably one of the most efficient ways to expand L2 writers' vocabulary and grammatical repertoire particularly when supplemented with substituting their discrete elements. Grammatical constructions, such as commonly occurring sentences, clauses, and phrases, can be "viewed as big words" and memorized as lexicalized stems.

All sentence stems presented in Appendixes A and B can be used for Sentence-Building activities (see Suggestions for Teaching Strategies and Tactics in this chapter), as well as activities in slot structure analysis and replacement of slot elements (see chaps. 5, 8, and 9).

Openings/Introductions

The central issue in xxx is yyy ...
The development of xxx is a typical/common problem in ...
Xxx and yyy are of particular interest and complexity ...
For a long time xxx, it has been the case that yyy.
Most accounts/reports/publications claim/state/maintain that xxx.
According to Smith/recent (media) articles/reports/studies, xxx is/seems to be yyy.
One of the most controversial/important/interesting issues/problems/xxxS (recently/in recent literature/media reports) is yyy.

Thesis/Topic Statements

The purpose of this essay/paper/analysis/overview is to xxx (e.g., *take a look at/examine/discuss yyy*).
The main emphasis/focus/goal/purpose of the/this essay/paper/project is to xxx (e.g., *is to analyze/provide an overview/discussion of xxx)*
This paper describes and analyzes ... xxx.
This paper discusses/examines/investigates xxx.
This paper claims/shows that xxx is / is not yyy.
This essay/paper addresses/examines/ ... is designed to analyze/provide an overview of/take a look at xxx.
My aim in this paper is to ...

In this paper, I/we report on/discuss …
I intend/will demonstrate/show/explain/ illustrate that xxx.
My (basic/main/most important) argument/claim is largely/essentially that xxx.

Secondary Purpose

The primary aim/purpose of this paper is xxx. In addition, it examines/discusses … yyy.
Additionally, yyy is discussed/examined.
A secondary aim of this paper is to yyy.
Another reason/point/issue addressed/discussed in this paper is yyy.

Rhetorical Mode/Discourse Organization Statement

This paper (will) compare(s)/describe/illustrate xxx first by analyzing/comparing/demonstrating yyy (that yyy is zzz), then by yyying zzz, and finally by yyying aaa.
This paper first analyzes/discusses xxx, followed by an examination/illustration/overview of yyy and zzz.

Other Types of Sentence Stems for Essay Development

1. Assertion

It can be claimed/said/assumed that xxx.
It seems certain/likely/doubtful that xxx.
I/we maintain/claim that xxx.

2. Agreement with the author/source

As XXX perceptively/insightfully states /
correctly notes /
rightly observes /
appropriately points out,xxx is/seems to be yyy (adjective/noun).
I/we rather/somewhat/strongly agree with/support (the idea that) xxx.
XXX provides/lends support to YYY's argument/claim/conclusion that zzz.

3. Disagreement with the author/source

I/we rather/somewhat/strongly disagree with XXX/ that yyy.
As XXX states (somewhat) unclearly/erroneously,
XXX does not support YYY's argument/claim/conclusion about zzz/that zzz.
Although XXX contends that yyy, I/we believe that zzz.
However, it remains unclear whether …
It would (thus) be of interest to learn more about yyy/how …

4. Comparison

Both xxx and yyy are (quite) similar in that zzz.
Xxx is like/resembles yyy.
Both xxx and yyy are/seem to be zzz (adjective/noun).
Xxx and yyy have/share some aspects of zzz.
Xxx is similar to / not unlike yyy (with respect to zzz).

5. Contrast

Xxx is (quite) different from yyy (in regard to zzz).
Xxx is not the case with yyy/the same as yyy.
Xxx does not resemble yyy (in regard to zzz).
Xxx contrasts with yyy (with regard to zzz).
Xxx is unlike yyy in that/with respect to zzz.

6. Recommendations

Let me recommend/suggest that xxx be/have/do yyy.
What I want/would like to recommend/suggest is that xxx.
One suggestion is/may be that xxx (do yyy).

7. Citing sources/supporting arguments, claims, conclusions, and generalizations

As proof/evidence/an example (for this), (let me cite/quote xxx).
According to xxx, …
As XXX says/claims, …
XXX provides evidence/support for yyy / that yyy.
XXX demonstrates that yyy shows evidence for yyy / that yyy.
Xxx is an illustration/example of yyy.

8. Citing sources/referring to external sources of knowledge

It is/has been (often) asserted/believed/noted that xxx. (YYY, 2003)
It is believed that xxx.(YYY, 1999)
It is often asserted that xxx.
It has been noted that xxx.

9. Classification

Xxx can/may be divided/classified into yyy (and zzz).
Xxx and yyy are categories/divisions of zzz.
There are xxx categories/types/classes of yyy.

10. Generalization (see also chap. 11)

Overall,
In general,
On the whole,
Generally speaking,
In most cases,
One can generalize that xxx,
For the most part,
With the exception of xxx,
With one exception,

11. Closing statement

In sum/conclusion,
To sum up/conclude,
To tie this (all) together,

(Adapted from Nattinger & DeCarrico [1992] and Swales & Feak [1994].)

Appendix B to Chapter 4

The most common verb/preposition combinations in academic prose (Biber et al., 1999; see also appendix to chap. 7) are:

The Top Most Common:

be applied to	*be derived from*	*deal with*	*refer to*
be associated with	*be known as*	*depend on*	*result in*
be based on	*be used in*	*lead to*	

The Second Most Common:

account for	*be involved in*	*consist of*	*obtain [noun] from*
add to	*be related to*	*contribute to*	*occur in*
be composed of	*be required for*	*differ from*	*think of*
be divided into	*belong to*	*look at*	
be included in	*come from*	*look for*	

5

Nouns and the Noun Phrase

OVERVIEW

- Noun groupings and substitutions to expand vocabulary
- Vocabulary in academic writing
- 380 essential nouns in academic texts
- Required elements of the noun phrase
    - Articles
    - Count and noncount nouns
- Different meanings of singular and plural noun forms
- The importance of gerunds and nominalizations in academic text
- Compound noun phrases
- Strategies for teaching nouns and teaching activities

Most people who have learned a foreign language and attempted to use it for their daily tasks are painfully aware of how an insufficient repertoire with regard to nouns and verbs can become a severe handicap in practically any interaction—even trying to place an order in a restaurant. In academic texts, when students need to demonstrate their understanding of assignments and readings, and in addition explain their ideas on the subject matter, the shortfalls in their lexical repertoire often turn into great obstacles.

Both in reading and writing, many learners are faced with either having to look up numerous words in a dictionary or make do with the lexicon accessible to them. If they elect to look up words, translating dictionaries often provide "matching" items that can render a student's text incomprehensible, while working with English–English dictionaries may take an inordinate amount of time—again due to the simple fact that one needs to have a solid lexical foundation in place to be able to understand distinctions between partial synonyms provided in dictionary entries.

Research on L2 written academic text shows that most NNS students, whose time is limited and who deal with large amounts of weekly reading and writing assignments, fall back on the lexicon immediately accessible to them or found in the reading at hand (Johns, 1990a, 1990b; Vann et al., 1991). Although many books for teaching vocabulary can be found on the market, NNS students often find the task of learning thousands of new words daunting. The laborious processes of vocabulary teaching and learning are further constrained by the fact that many teachers and teacher trainers believe that mere exposure to L2 and reading texts at the level appropriate for students' proficiency eventually results in vocabulary acquisition sufficient for academic studies in colleges and universities.

However, several recent investigations in NNS students' reading, writing, and text demonstrate that even advanced NNS students enrolled in academic programs in U.S. universities do not have the vocabulary range requisite in their degree studies (Hinkel, 2001c; Johns, 1997).

One of the tasks teachers of writing face is trying to build up students' vocabulary to provide them with tools for survival in academic courses and writing tasks. Although today it is widely known that memorizing lists of academic vocabulary is not particularly useful in the long run, other options for learning and teaching vocabulary and lexicalized features of nouns are available. Teaching techniques discussed in this chapter focus on expanding contextualized vocabulary for lexical substitutions, essential and foundational vocabulary for university reading and writing (the University Word List), singular and plural constraints on nouns and changes in their meanings, increasing the range of gerunds and abstract nominalizations, and compound noun phrases.

In each following section, the subheading marks *what* to teach, and the first paragraph following the heading explains *why* to teach it. The reasons that something should be taught are useful not only for teachers, but students as well. Experience has shown that explaining to students why something is taught and how the material and teaching techniques can improve their writing and, consequently, grades in academic courses usually creates a more willing and receptive audience who have their self-interest in mind. In addition, such explanations can improve the teacher's credibility and give the impressions of efficiency, preparedness, and professional competence (assuming that the teacher wants to make such impressions).

CONTEXTUALIZED GROUPINGS OF NOUNS TO EXPAND VOCABULARY

When they write assignments for university classes, students often have a familiar noun or two that they use repeatedly in similar contexts. Such overuse of nouns results in redundant text constructions that create an impression of lexical paucity and awkwardness. For example,

> *(1) The people with higher level of education definitely have a better future than the people who have less. Mostly, people also choose higher education because of its status. People would rather have an average status than a low status. The reason is that the society views these people as underachievers in the community.... In the 21st century, one of the reasons that people will try to get higher education is to have a better status. The other reason is to earn more money. With status and money, people can afford to have a higher standard of living.* (From a student assignment on the economic impact of education on the life of a local community.)

In this excerpt, the noun *people* is repeated seven times, *higher education* three times, and *reason* twice. The lexical redundancy clearly demonstrates the shortfalls in the writer's vocabulary associated with a particular lexical domain. Most NNS students who have taken the TOEFL are familiar with the notion (but not necessarily the term) of lexical redundancy because on the test the section on Structure includes items with redundant meanings. In studies of particularly problematic errors in NNS students' writing, university faculty repeatedly indicated that inappropriate and redundant uses of vocabulary are among the most egregious shortfalls in L2 academic texts—on par with errors in verb tenses and subject–verb agreement (Johns, 1997; Santos, 1988; Vann, Lorenz, & Meyer, 1991).

To help learners expand their vocabulary range in the domain *people,* alternatives can be provided and practiced in context:

People—adults, employees of local businesses, individuals, persons, population, the public, residents, community/group members, workers.

Higher education—college/university education, advanced training, college/ university degree studies, education beyond the high school, professional preparation, professional training, college/university-level training.

Reason—aim, basis, cause, consideration, expectation, explanation, goal, purpose, thinking, understanding.

> An important advantage of teaching vocabulary in semantic and contextually applicable clusters is that students see its immediate uses and practicality. Although to expand students' vocabulary ranges in various semantic domains simultaneously is a gradual and painstaking process, it is much easier and more profitable to work with papers, contexts, and assignments at hand because such an approach meets students' immediate needs for developing a set of interchangeable lexical "plugs" that can be reused from one written assignment to the next.

Another important consideration when providing students with lexical alternatives is that they are essential in maintaining text cohesion by means of lexical substitutions (see further discussion on cohesion in chaps. 7, 8, and 11). A study based on a large corpus of L2 academic essays has shown that even advanced L2 writers employ lexical substitutions significantly less frequently than first-year NS students simply because NNSs rely on a severely restricted lexical repertoire. NNS students who have taken the TOEFL are familiar with lexical replacements (e.g., *The word substitution in line/paragraph 3 is closest in meaning to (1) replacement, (2) restitution, (3) reconstruction, (4) replication*).

To write papers in the disciplines, students need to know key terms used in each domain of studies such as economics, physics, or history. Usually discipline-specific terms are heavily emphasized in courses, lectures, and textbooks, and most students learn them as a part of their coursework. However, even in discipline-specific papers, increasing the vocabulary associated with nouns can be essential. The following excerpt comes from an assignment in basic physics:

> *(2) Density is an important unit and usually used in measuring and calculating amount of material. Density is the mass of a specific compound divided by its volume, such as the density of water is 1 g/cm^3. However, when different subunits represent density, the amount of density becomes different.*

Although the term *density* is used to refer to a particular property of a material, its repetition can be avoided by means of pronouns and sentence combining (e.g., the first sentence in this excerpt can easily be combined with the second; see chap. 6, Pronouns; and chap. 10, Subordinate Clauses). In addition, however, the word *amount* is also repeated, and the redundancy can be avoided:

Amount—computation result, ratio, value.

However, as with uses of dictionaries, the teacher needs to preselect applicable and contextually appropriate lexical items that can meet students' needs without pitfalls. The following example is extracted from an assignment in an economics course:

> *(3) There are at least 2900 companies listed on the New York Stock Exchange, 1000 companies on the American Stock Exchange, 2700 companies traded on the over-the-counter, to name a few. This is only publicly traded companies in the U.S., not to mention the foreign companies. With so many options at hand, how should we decided which company to be our best shot? ... A lot of ratios could be used to measure the company's profitability. The combined use of these ratios can not only tell us if the company is making money but also give us some information such as the expenses and the number of outstanding shares inside the company. ... You are rich because others are poorer than you. If every company in the world makes more than two million dollars this year and your company only makes one million dollars. Your company is still profitable but it is not worth investing.*

It is apparent from this example that, in addition to other problems such as fragments, personal pronoun uses, punctuation, and somewhat informal register, the noun *company* is repeated excessively. However, other nouns are readily accessible and practical for students to use in similar courses and contexts:

> *Company—business, concern* (if large), *firm, enterprise, venture* (if new)

To construct such lists of nouns with similar or contextually appropriate meanings, not much research is required. In many cases, when teachers have trouble coming up with a list of useful alternatives in a particular context, they can resort to looking up words in a thesaurus. Most experienced teachers have discovered that they cannot just recommend that their students use a thesaurus. As with dictionaries, using a thesaurus without the adequate lexical base needed to tell appropriate from inappropriate entries can be difficult. For example, according to the *Roget's Thesaurus* (1994), the noun *company* can have the following partial synonyms:

> *NOUNS 1. fellowship, companionship, society, fraternity, fraternization 2. firm, business firm, concern, house, ... business, industry, enterprise, business establishment, commercial enterprise; cast, acting company, troupe, repertory company, stock company*

Unless NNS writers already know the meaning of such words as *cast, troupe*, and *repertory*, they may simply be unable to tell the difference between a *business company* and *acting company* (does the acting company mean an *active* company?). Furthermore, the distinctions among the meanings of *company, house*, and *industry* are substantial enough to make the student's excerpt in (3) very confusing. As mentioned earlier, a strong vocabulary base is needed to consult dictionaries and thesauri and choose a noun appropriate in a particular context.

Constructing a list of appropriate lexical substitutions that can be used in writing does not have to be complicated. A typical college-educated NS of English has a vocabulary range of 17,000 word families that together comprise about 150,000 words (Nation, 1990; see chap. 3). Thus, when compiling lists of nouns that can be used in similar contexts, most L2 teachers do not need to look much farther than their own lexicon, even if in doing so they stand a chance of missing an appropriate noun or two.

VOCABULARY IN UNIVERSITY WRITING

Research on the vocabulary range needed to write basic academic text has shown that a foundation of 2,000 to 3,000 words can go a long way toward a successful production of assignments and essays in many disciplines. In fact, according to some studies, 95% of all academic texts at the undergraduate level can be understood and written within this lexical range (Nation, 1990). It is important to note, however, that words commonly found in academic texts are different from those used in casual conversation (Biber et al., 1999). Therefore, academic vocabulary and grammar need to be explicitly taught (Norris & Ortega, 2000). In general, the importance of noun usage in academic prose cannot be overestimated. For example, Biber et al. (1999) pointed out that, although pronouns are more common than nouns in conversations, "at the other extreme, nouns are many times more common than pronouns in ... academic prose" (p. 235).

Another important distinction should be made between what has been typically called *productive* and *passive vocabulary*. Productive vocabulary refers to the vocabulary items that learners can use in speech or writing, and passive vocabulary represents the words that learners are familiar with and understand in listening and reading. In written text production, one of the most important instructional goals is to increase NNS writers' productive vocabulary range. A study of NNS advanced academic texts shows that they contain two to three times as many simple nouns (e.g., *people, world, human, man, woman, stuff, thing, way*) than similar prose of NS high school graduates (Hinkel, 2002a, 2003b).

Over the past century, research on various large corpora of English words has identified lists of most common vocabulary items employed in undergraduate and introductory texts across several disciplines (Coxhead, 2000; Nation, 1990). The University Word List (Nation, 1990) and the Academic Word List (Coxhead, 1998; cited in Nation, 2001) include 800 words and 567 head words of word families in academic texts, respectively. The following list includes only 375 words extracted from the University Word List (Nation, 1990). Many of these are frequently used as nouns, but can also appear in noun, verb, or adjective form (for a list of verbs, see chap. 8).

Lists of words, such as the noun list in this chapter, the verb list in chapter 8, or the entire University Word List (Nation, 1990), can be handed out to students with an explanation of what it is and why they need to have it. When the words from the lists come up in readings, exercises, and activities, it important to point them out to provide learners a sense of purpose in light of the amount of tedious and difficult work they need to do to improve their vocabulary. Nation (2001) called vocabulary work "the learning burden."

Most Common Nouns in Introductory Course Texts at the University Level

The words in the **bold font** are found most frequently and in highly varied texts across all disciplines. (Nation, (1990) Extracted[1])

[1]In many cases, noun and verb forms can be identical (e.g., *access, aid, influence, advocate*). These are included on both the list of common nouns and the parallel list of frequent verbs.

abstract
access
acid
adjective
adult
aesthetic
affect
affluence
aggression
aid
alcohol
ally
alternative
ambiguity
analogy
anomaly
anthropology
apparatus
appeal
appendix
approach
area
aristocrat
arithmetic
aspect
aspiration
assent
asset
astronomy
atmosphere
atom
attitude
attribute
auspices
awe
axis
battery
benefit
biology
bomb
bore
breed
bubble
bulk
bureaucracy
calendar
capture
carbon
career
catalog
category
cell
challenge
channel
chapter
chemical
circuit
circumstance
classic
client
clinic
code
coefficient
collapse
column
comment
commodity
commune
competence
complement
complex
component
compound
compulsion
concentrate
concept
conduct
configuration
conflict
confront
congress
conjunction
consent
console
constant
construct
contact
context
contingent
continent
contract
contrast
controversy
convert
creditor
crisis
criterion
critic
crystal
culture
currency
cycle
cylinder
data
debate
decade
decimal
decline
deflect
democracy
denominator
design
detriment
diagram
diameter
digest
dimension
discourse
doctrine
domestic
drain
drama
drug
duration
dynamic
economy
electron
element
embrace
emotion
energy
entity
environment
episode
equilibrium
equipment
equivalent
ethics
exhaust
expert
exponent
export
extract
faction
factor
fallacy
fare
fate
feature
finance
fluid
focus
fossil
fraction
fragment
fraud
friction
frontier
fuel
function
fundamental
fund
fuse
geography
geometry
germ
goal
grant

graph
gravity
guarantee
harbor
hero
hemisphere
heredity
hierarchy
horror
hypothesis
image
impact
implement
import
impulse
incentive
incident
incline
income
index
individual
inflation
innovation
instance
instinct
integer
intellect
interlude
interval
interview
intimacy
issue
item
job
journal
label
laboratory
labor
launch
layer
lecture
leisure
lens
locomotion
logic
luxury
magic
magnitude
major
margin
material
mathematics
matrix
maximum
medium
metabolism
metaphor
method
microscope
military
minimum
molecule
momentum
monarch
morphology
motive
muscle
myth
navy
negative
nerve
network
niche
norm
notion
novel
null
nutrient
objective
odor
option
orbit
outcome
overlap
oxygen
parenthesis
parliament
peasant
pendulum
period
perspective
pest
phase
phenomena
philosophy
planet
plot
pole
policy
pollution
port
portion
positive
postulate
potential
premise
preposition
prestige
principle
priority
process
project
propensity
proportion
proprietor
protest
province
prudence
psychology
quote
radical
radius
range
ratio
rebel
rectangle
reform
region
reign
release
relevance
research
reservoir
resident
residue
resource
reverse
rhythm
rigor
role
route
saint
sanction
satellite
schedule
scheme
score
section
segment
sequence
series
sex
shift
sibling
site
skeleton
sketch
sociology
source
species
spectrum
sphere
statistic
status
stereotype
strata
stress
structure

style	task	theorem	trend
sum	team	**theory**	triangle
summary	**technique**	tissue	**usage**
supplement	**technology**	tone	vein
surplus	telescope	topic	velocity
survey	**tense**	**trace**	version
switch	terminology	tractor	vertical
symbol	territory	**tradition**	vocabulary
symptom	terror	traffic	volt
synthetic	text	trait	volume
tangent	texture	transition	x-ray
tape	theft	treaty	

Given that lists of the most common nouns employed in academic texts are accessible to most interested teachers, finding lexical alternatives is relatively easy in various contexts—for example:

affect—feeling, emotion, sentiment
competence—ability, skill, capability
fragment—particle, piece, bit, shard
sphere—(1) circle, realm, domain, province, field, arena
(2) ball, globe, balloon, bubble

However, unlike the words easily learned in the course of daily interactions, expanding the range of academic vocabulary requires a great deal of work and persistence. The crucial factors in the success of academic vocabulary learning are contextualization (and thematic organization), exposure to appropriate-level academic texts with conscious noticing of how various words are used, and sequencing of easier words to be followed by more difficult ones. For example, such nouns as *triangle, traffic, tradition*, and *topic* can be accessible even to beginners. Similarly, if intermediate learners already know the noun *feeling*, they can be in a good position to learn *affect* and *emotion*.

Learning academic vocabulary, like many other aspects of learning, can become productive through repeated exposure and contextualized repetition. If vocabulary dealing with *planet, policy, pollution, release, research*, and *residue* is worked on during the second week of classes, these nouns need to be reviewed and practiced in context later in the course. On occasion, when teaching a large number of words in a limited amount of time, combining new items with the review of those covered in previous units can lead to a snowball effect. In vocabulary work, it is important to set realistic goals. For example, contextualized exposure to 700 to 1,000 words during one 10- to 12-week term may be reasonable assuming that students are assigned homework or projects outside the class (see following Teaching Suggestions).

Research has demonstrated that gaining initial familiarity with the meanings of 30 words per hour is possible when various vocabulary learning techniques are combined (e.g., word lists, vocabulary logs, and key words; Schmitt, 2000). However, this rate of learning requires learners to be focused and motivated; but as vocabulary grows, so does the ability to increase the vocabulary range. The greater the students' vocabulary repertoire, the wider the possible exposure to new vocabulary through reading. Thus, learners with a vocabulary range of 5,000 service and academic words combined are likely to have an easier time learning new words than those with 1,500.

ARTICLES AND SINGULAR/PLURAL CHOICES

The English article system is highly lexicalized and context-bound. That is, in many cases, it is difficult to tell whether a definite or an indefinite article is appropriate in different contexts or even if an article is required at all. Comprehension is far easier than production. One of the solutions to the article dilemmas in production can be to encourage students to use plural instead of singular count nouns. This teaching technique does not do away with all the article problems, but it reduces their frequencies. For example,

> *Taking risks can produce bad result. For example, the investor buys stocks from new company, and he expects to gain their capital. These people, however, may lose some of their money on stock if their estimation about the stock is false. Stock price declines from $10 to $6 after they bought the stocks at $10 each. Despite the bad result of taking risk, people can succeed and accomplish their goal because the stock market can give them chance to become successful.* (From a student's assignment on investment risk.)

This excerpt contains nine errors in article and singular/plural noun uses. Most of these can be avoided (or corrected) if the excerpt relies on the usage of plural instead of singular nouns.

> *Taking risks can produce bad results. For example, investors buy stocks from new companies, and they expect to gain (break even on) their capital (investment). These people, however, may lose some of their money on stocks if their estimations (evaluations/appraisals/expectations of) (about) the stocks are false (incorrect/inaccurate). [If] stock prices decline from $10 to $6 after they bought[buy] the stocks at $10 each, [investors lose money] . Despite bad results of [from] taking risks, people can succeed and accomplish their goals because the stock market can give them the/a chance to become successful.*

An important difference between learning how to cope with difficulties in production and learning general rules that apply to most (or many) article uses in English is this: In the broad-based approach, the tendency is to gloss over the problem areas that students encounter in real language production. The reason is that, in general, rules are not intended to account for specific occurrences of articles, but rather are designed to serve as overarching guidelines. In the case of employing plural nouns instead of singular and, thus, avoiding at least some of the problems associated with article use, students usually appreciate a tip that they can easily put into practice. The ambitious goal of attaining a broad-based L2 proficiency and near-native performance is usually not the students', but the teachers'.

NONCOUNT AND IRREGULAR NOUNS

Although noncount nouns in English are relatively few, they can play an important role in making text appear idiosyncratic because they are very common in academic texts (see the list of frequent nouns). Many L2 grammar books provide lists of these nouns divided according to their semantic classes (e.g., groups made of similar items, mass nouns, abstractions, or names of recreational activities—*baseball, basketball, soccer, tennis, camping*). Although these semantic divisions seem to be logical and organized to NSs, to L2 learners they do not always make sense. For instance, why should *baggage*, *clothing*, and *furniture* items, which one can easily count, be noncount, and what could possibly be the difference between *baggage* and *bags*? The trouble with noncount nouns is that in English their singularity or plurality is often simply lexicalized and cannot be explained logically.

Most lists of noncount nouns are organized based on their semantic categories (e.g., whole groups made up of similar items—Fluids, Solids, Abstractions, Languages, Recreations, Activities, and Natural phenomena). However, to know that *homework, slang, vocabulary, news, advice, music, laughter,* and *wealth* represent abstract phenomena, one needs to have a relatively good vocabulary range. For this reason, the organization of noncount nouns exemplified next is organized structurally and based on explicit and overt noun markers such as suffixes.

> Although current and popular methodologies for L2 teaching disdain rote memorization and frown on attempts to assign lists to be memorized, unfortunately there may be few means to learn academic vocabulary outside of memorization, followed by extensive contextualized practice. Those who have successfully attained L2 proficiency sufficient for success in academic reading and writing in any L2 (particularly one without L1 cognates) are familiar with the tedious work entailed in learning lists of exceptions to almost all rules provided by instructors.

An important consideration in learning noncount and other irregular nouns is that the actual list of those necessary for producing academic texts is small. For instance, students who do not plan to enroll in veterinarian studies may not need to know that the plural of *calf* is *calves*, and learners who do not play cards should not bother remembering that *poker* does not have a plural form.

Lexical groupings of noncount nouns can be further simplified by organizing the list by their endings. Plural cannot be used with:

- *-work* nouns—*homework, coursework, work, fieldwork* (i.e., all types of work performed by people, but not *framework* and *network*)
- *-age* nouns—*courage, voltage, postage, luggage, baggage, barrage, change (money), garbage* (but not *garage*)
- *-edge* nouns—*knowledge, pledge*
- *-ice* nouns—*advice, juice, practice, malice*, including *ice*
- *-ware* nouns—*freeware, hardware, shareware, software, silverware, flatware, stoneware*
- *-fare* nouns—*welfare, warfare, fare,*
- *-th* nouns—*breadth, health, warmth, wealth, strength, truth, youth (*but not *myth, depth, width*, or *length;* see singular and plural meanings of nouns later)
- many *-a/ence, -ment, -ness, -(s/t)ure, -(i)ty, -ing* nouns, usually called *abstractions* in students textbooks. These derived nouns often have different meanings in singular and plural forms (see Nominalizations and Gerunds).
- nouns that have the same form as verbs—*air, fish, fog (up), help, ice, iron, mail, play, oil, rain, slang, snow, smoke, traffic, water, weather, work* (some nouns are duplicated in these categories based on the *whatever works* principle)
- nouns that exist only in noun form—*art, business, energy, fun, grammar, music, oxygen, trouble, virtue, vocabulary, wisdom*

Languages and People Rule. If a noun ends with *-n* or *-i* (*American, Korean, German, Moroccan, Indonesian, Norwegian; Iraqi, Irani, Emirati, Somali*), the plural marker is required. No plural can be used with any other types of nouns and adjectives that refer to languages and people. For example, *Arabic [language]—Arab [person]* have different adjective–noun forms. On the other hand, *Amharic, Chinese, Japanese, Vietnamese, Burmese, Dutch, French, English, Spanish* refer to both languages and people and do not take plural markers.

It is important to distinguish between the names of languages and people that function as nouns or adjectives. If the name is followed by another noun, as in *Indonesian students/people/professors/culture*, plural markers cannot be used with the first noun (see Compound Nouns) because in this case *Indonesian/American/Somali* has the function of an adjective. However, if a noun follows immediately, the plural form is required (e.g., *Indonesians, Americans, Somalis*).

Nouns that refer to languages and people can also be used in the adjective form (e.g., *American professors, Chinese/Japanese speakers*). If these language/people nouns are immediately followed by another noun, they are used as adjectives. In this case, they never take the plural form no matter what ending they have (see Compound Nouns).

A good rule of thumb is to identify the nouns and adjectives of the people/languages type that frequently show up in students' texts or are simply very common and focus on these particular items instead of trying to work with the entire list of irregular plurals. In this case, the nouns *hair, help, junk, space, music, rain, snow, poverty, news, progress, people, pride, sleep, vocabulary, grammar, slang,* and *life* are highly productive, whereas *flour, chalk, corn, grass, silver, gold, dirt,* and *dust* may be less so.

Possessives. Possessive nouns are relatively rare in academic prose and structures such as: ?*Indonesia's economy,* ?*company's management,* ?*course's assignments* usually sound awkward. In most cases where L2 writers employ these constructions, possessives should be replaced with adjective + noun or compound noun constructions:

Indonesian economy, company management, course assignments. Possessive constructions are usually limited to nouns that refer to humans:

John's lunch, teacher's pet.

However, even in the case of nouns that refer to groups of humans, the use of possessives can be obscure:

**faculty's lounge,* **employee's quarters,* **government's benefits.*

In those cases where possessives can be used, the rule to follow is that if the noun is singular (*a boy/a nurse*), the apostrophe is placed at the end of the singular noun (*a boy's/a nurse's*). However, if the noun is plural (*students/professors*), the apostrophe is still placed at the end of the noun, and only one *-s* is needed (*students'/professors'*). If the teacher has limited time to work on various structures, possessives can be skipped because they are comparatively rare in student texts.

ESSENTIAL NOUNS IN ACADEMIC TEXTS

An important point to remember is that the University Words List and Academic Word List (Nation, 1990, 2001) include only a handful of noncount nouns that are essential for students to use correctly: *alcohol, atmosphere, awe, biology, consent, equipment, ethics, friction, geography, geometry, gravity, hemisphere, inflation, integrity, intimacy, labor, logic, mathematics, minimum, maximum, navy, philosophy, pollution, prestige, psychology, reluctance, research, sociology, trade, traffic, vocabulary, welfare.*

Common Nouns That Are Always Plural. (and, therefore, require plural verb forms, when used in the subject position) include: *clothes, glasses, grounds, jeans, odds, pants, people, savings, shorts, stairs, surroundings, tropics.*

Irregular Plural Forms of Nouns. Other highly common nouns from the University Word List and Academic Word List that have irregular plural forms are: *axis, crisis, criteria, emphasis, focus, hypothesis, index, matrix, media/medium, overseas, parenthesis, pendulum, phenomenon, radius, series, species, strata, thesis.*

All nouns that end in *-is* take the plural marker *-es* (*crises, emphases, hypotheses, parentheses*), *-ex/ix* endings become plural *-ces* (*indices, matrices*), *-um* nouns take *-a* (*medium—media, stratum—strata*), and *-on* endings have the plural form of *-a* (*criterion—criteria, phenomenon—phenomena*). Such nouns as *overseas, series*, and *species* have identical plural and singular forms (*one series—several series, one species—many species*).

These nouns are not likely to be frequent in conversations and daily spoken interactions. For this reason, they probably cannot be learned in the course of routine communications and activities for developing conversational fluency (see chap. 1). This may be one of the reasons that the vocabulary of even advanced and proficient L2 students does not include them. Although teachers may attempt to design activities and exercises to provide students practice with these nouns, it is doubtful that many enjoyable tasks can be constructed with nouns such as *axis, crisis*, and *hypothesis*. Nonetheless, it is essential for students to know the meaning, pronunciation, and spelling of these nouns at least to recognize them when they appear in academic reading and lectures. There are few better solutions to the dilemma of their learning beyond simple memorization and contextualized practice and use. The key to success in students' vocabulary learning is the teacher's insistence that essential vocabulary nouns be used when they are needed.

SINGULAR AND PLURAL NOUNS WITH DIFFERENT MEANINGS

Many essential countable nouns such as *business, development, difficulty, failure, industry, injustice, technology*, and *truth* have different meanings in singular and plural forms. When used in singular they refer to concepts or whole notions, and when used in plural they refer to specific instances, types, kinds, and occurrences of these notions. The singular form *technology* refers to all types of *technology* as a concept, but the plural *technologies* to various types/subsets of *technology* such as computer, automotive, or telecommunication. For example,

> *The development of economy is the most important job of the government in my country.* (From a student text.)

In this sentence, the noun *development* refers to the entire collective notion that consists of many components, such as *the development of agriculture, transportation, and commerce*. On the other hand, the plural form *developments* refers to events and occurrences:

> *Many developments in the political arena point to a possibility of early elections.*

The plural form *developments* refers to small and separate events or occasions. In other words, when used in singular these nouns refer to overall constructs, and in plural to smaller instances/subdivisions of these constructs.

The same principle of identifying meanings of singular and plural forms can apply to other nouns that may be considered noncount, but are employed in both plural and singular:

beer—beers, cake—cakes, change—changes, cheese—cheeses, chocolate—chocolates, coffee-coffees, coke—cokes, hair—hairs, glass—glasses, milk—milks, paper—papers, tea—teas, time—times, wine—wines, work—works, youth—youths

All these refer to whole notions/concepts/mass quantities or one instance of in singular and specific instances in plural:

> *Beautiful hair* [as a total mass/collective] *requires much care* vs. *If you found two gray hairs* [two instances/small occurrences of] *on your head, do not panic. We have a solution to grays.*

Most nouns that can have different meanings in singular or plural are usually (and unfortunately) found in the lists of noncount nouns that are ubiquitous in ESL grammar texts. To avoid confusion on the part of students, some researchers (DeCarrico, 2000, p. 21) have called them "crossover" nouns; if this label is helpful to learners, there is little reason not to use it.

GERUNDS AND ABSTRACT NOMINALIZATIONS

Analyses of written and academic English corpora have demonstrated that gerunds and abstract derived nouns are very common in academic and professional texts (Bhatia, 1993). According to Biber's et al. (1999) findings, abstract nominalizations are encountered far more frequently in academic writing than in news reportage or fiction. On the other hand, conversational discourse has the lowest rates of nominalization occurrences among all other language genre. Biber et al. explained that "academic discourse is much more concerned with abstract concepts than the other registers, especially conversation" (p. 323).

Analysis of L2 text, however, shows that in academic texts advanced NNS writers employ significantly fewer gerunds and nominalizations than first-year NS students without formal training in writing (Hinkel,

2002a, 2003b). The outcome of the NNS shortfalls in the uses of these lexical features is that L2 academic text—both spoken and written—appears to be far less academic than may be expected in college and university settings. In addition, given their lack of academic vocabulary needed to convey abstract concepts, L2 writers may simply be unable to explain their ideas and adequately demonstrate their familiarity with readings and material. Therefore, using gerunds and abstract nominalizations can make students' texts appear less childish and simple and, ultimately, lead to better grades in mainstream courses. Although teaching the uses of gerunds and abstract nominalizations is not particularly exciting, these structures are essential for the development of students' academic language skills.

Both gerunds and nominalizations represent nouns and nounlike forms derived from other parts of speech. Gerunds are always derived from verbs, but nominalizations can be derived from verbs, adjectives, and other nouns (e.g., *read—reading, learn—learning, develop—development, ship—shipment, dark—darkness, warm—warmth*). A gerund can be derived from practically any verb by adding *-ing* to its base form (e.g., *sing—singing, write—writing, listen—listening, speak—speaking*).

An important characteristic shared by nouns (including nominalizations) and gerunds is that they frequently occur as objects/complements of prepositions (e.g., *a chance of obtaining funding/failure, a discussion about learning/equipment, an opportunity for improving teenagers' diet/improvement*). In academic writing, the most common nouns that take of + gerund constructions are in declining order (Biber et al., 1999):

way	idea	problem	experience	form	system
method	possibility	process	purpose	important	
means	effect	cost	advantage	practice	

Derived abstract nominalizations are more complex than gerunds because several various suffixes exist, all of which have the function of converting words, including simple nouns, to abstract nouns: *-age* (*acreage, mileage*), *-ance/ence* (*assistance, dependence*), *-cy* (*accuracy, fluency*), *-ity* (*ability, simplicity*), *-ment* (*predicament, government*), *-ness* (*readiness, cleanliness*), and *-ion* (*solution, intrusion*). Other nominalizers, such as *-er/or* (*teacher, doctor*), *-ee* (*employee, interviewee*), *-ent/ant* (*attendant, student*), are also common, but they are relatively semantically simpler than abstract nouns because in most cases they refer to people or concrete objects that perform a particular action or are from/in a particular place (*senator, New Englander*).

Although lists of these suffixes are found in most L2 reading and vocabulary books, in general terms it is not possible to predict what types of verbs, adjectives, or nouns can be derived by the suffixes *-ment*, *-ness*, *-ity*, or *-ure*.

In academic writing, nouns with the suffix *-ness* refer to characterizations and states, whereas *-ion* nouns are particularly prevalent in the academic genre, where the suffix occurs in frequent and rare words.

The Most Common Nouns with *-tion* Derivations

action	direction	infection	production
addition	distribution	information	reaction
application	education	instruction	relation
association	equation	ooperation	situation
communication	examination	organization	variation
concentration	formation	population	

(Biber et al., 1999)

In terms of their semantic content, most gerunds and nominalizations, which are frequent in generalizations, refer to concepts, actions, and processes that would be difficult to convey by other lexical means. For example,

> *Social structure impacts institutions and culture because those at the top of the structure have the most to gain by developing, teaching, and protecting the prevailing institutions and culture. Culture normally justifies the institutions and structure, and institutions generally work to support the structure and culture. Together, social structure, culture, and institutions are important to what individuals do.* (Charon, 1999, p. 125)

Gerunds, even more than nominalized nouns, refer to processes (some linguists actually call them *process* nouns)—for example:

developing (ideas)—development
creating (software)—creation
observing (animals)—observation
suggesting (new directions)—suggestion

In fact, one of the key differences between gerunds and nominalized nouns is that of a process referred to by means of gerund versus an abstraction, concept, or action expressed in nominalizations. Thus, *instituting* something is different from *an institution* and *organizing* from *an organization*. There are various derivations of both types that exist in only one form (e.g., *reading, writing, teaching, learning, hoping* or *culture, moisture, revolution, possibility, probability*).

Traditionally, practically all L2 grammar books provide lists of verbs that are followed by gerunds, infinitives, or both (e.g., *enjoy* + *swimming* (but not *to swim*), *decide + to go* (but not *going*), or *like to dance/dancing*). Although these lists are essential, in reality the uses of gerunds are a bit more complicated than this. For example, the sentence

**Developing is expensive*

is incorrect because *develop* is a transitive verb, which requires a direct object. Thus, the sentence

Developing software is expensive

is correct. Because all gerunds are derived from verbs, the point of fact is that if gerunds are derived from transitive verbs, which require a direct object, the process nominals retain their transitivity feature.

> A good explanation to give students can be a metaphor: When a verb goes to a new job and becomes a noun, it takes its possessions with it; when a verb is converted to a nominal by means of adding *-ing* to its basic form (*suggest+ing*), it drags the object with it (e.g., *Suggesting a new plan requires preparation*).

For a list of common transitive verbs, see chapter 3.

In addition, another level of complexity is added with gerund singular and plural distinctions when some gerunds can be used in plural and some cannot (e.g.,

*reading—readings, swimming—*swimmings*).

As a general rule, gerunds that refer to concrete objects and events can take plural, and other gerund forms that refer to processes cannot. Therefore, gerunds that can be used in a plural form are far less common than those that are noncount (e.g., *beginnings, endings [of books/movies/stories], markings, paintings* [but not **clothings*]).

COMPOUND NOUN PHRASES

Noun phrases consist of several nouns, among which the first noun or two function as adjectives to describe the main (head) noun:

composition class
university composition class
university-level composition class

In these phrases, the noun *class* is the head noun, and all other nouns describe the *class*.

Compound noun phrases are extraordinarily popular in academic texts, and some linguists call them "notorious" (Bhatia, 1993, p. 148). These structures can come in various forms: Some consist of two simple nouns (*book cover, vocabulary list*), gerund/nominalization and another noun (*listening activities, automobile production*), and fused verb+particle constructions (*setup, handout, wash-back effect*). Corpus studies of academic texts have found that these are far more common in written than conversational genres, that noun compounding represents a highly productive structure, and that formal written texts include more of these constructions than informal varieties (Biber et al., 1999).

In L2 texts, one of the typical errors is pluralization of the descriptive nouns in the compounds (e.g., **a five-credits-hours course*, **a 20-years-old student*). Relatively speaking, avoiding these errors is easy to teach. In English, adjectives do not take plural, and the structures **blues books* and **bigs blue books* are incorrect because only the main (head) noun can be used in plural. Similarly, with compound nouns, the first job is to identify the main noun (usually the last one in the string of nouns) that can take the plural:

a five-credit-hour course(s), a 25-year-old woman (women)

(for an in-depth discussion of adjectives see chap. 9).

> In most compound noun phrases (e.g., *the vegetable garden*), only the last (head) noun takes the plural marker *-s*, and other nouns that describe it do not.

Exceptions to this rule are few, and they almost always include "exclusive plurals" (Quirk et al., 1985) when it is known that the descriptive noun includes more than one entity (e.g., *arts degree, customs officer;* it is also possible to say *art degree* when one type of art is involved).

Another typical problem with compound nouns is that compounding can take place only if an adjective form of a particular noun does not exist:

vegetable soup, noodle dish, rice bowl, table top (there are no adjectives that can be derived from *vegetable, noodle, rice,* or *table*). In contrast, compound structures such as

**nation flag*, **economy data*, **culture norms*

are incorrect because adjectival forms of nouns have to be used if they exist—*national*, *economic*, and *cultural*.

A word of caution is necessary when it comes to adjectives derived from nouns because the meaning of the adjectives can be quite different from that of the noun:

composition teacher vs. *compositional teacher*
book vs. *bookish*
territory vs. *territorial*

CHAPTER SUMMARY

To deal with shortfalls in students' repertoire of nouns prevalent in academic texts, a concerted effort has to be made to increase the learner's vocabulary range. To this end, several simple and effective teaching techniques can be highly productive:

- Contextualized lexical substitutions of nouns that are common and frequently repeated in L2 prose do not require much work beyond the teachers' use of a thesaurus (or even the vocabulary in their own lexicon).
- Provide practice and exercises based on the list of highly common nouns employed in academic textbooks across various disciplines. A reasonable number of words learned during a 10- to 12-week course can range from 700 to 1,000, and the rate of instructed learning can be as high as 10 words per hour (or more).
- Expanding students' academic vocabulary should start at the beginning level of proficiency and continue throughout their language training. Astute text simplification may take the form of omitting rare words, but not lexically and structurally complex common academic words, because learners can only benefit from maximized exposure to frequent and, thus, essential academic words.

Many specific problems that L2 writers encounter in producing academic prose can be explicitly taught through simple explanations and exercises. Research has shown that explicit instruction of any sort leads to significantly greater language gains than no instruction or implicit instructional approaches (Norris & Ortega, 2000). The following teaching techniques have proved to be effective and easy to use:

- Count and noncount nouns that are usually classified based on their semantic features are difficult to learn because L2 writers require substantial vocabulary range to understand the semantic classifications. Categorizing nouns based on their structural features, such as endings, can be more productive. In general, only 32 noncount nouns are frequent in academic texts.
- Abstract plural and singular nouns may have different meanings in singular and plural forms. Most learners are not aware of this distinction, which should be addressed in teaching.
- Gerunds and nominalized nouns are particularly important for academically bound L2 learners because most cannot be acquired through exposure to conversational discourse and fluency-building activities. Research has shown, however, that gerunds and nominalized nouns are two to three times less common in L2 than in L1 academic prose.
- Compound noun phrases are extraordinarily popular in academic texts, but can be structurally complex. A few simple techniques dealing with these structures can help learners overcome some of the problems associated with the uses of these constructions in L2 text.

STRATEGIES AND TACTICS FOR TEACHING AND TEACHING ACTIVITIES

Incidental learning of vocabulary (see chap. 3 for a discussion) represents the least labor-intensive way to expand vocabulary. The learning goals of the teaching suggestions and activities presented next are developed to promote:

- Noticing the uses and meanings of nouns (see chap. 3)
- Incidental learning of words (see chap. 3)
- Discussing contextualized occurrences of nouns and their lexical substitutions

It is crucial that the teacher follow up on the assigned exercises and vocabulary learning tasks. As mentioned in chapter 3, learning 10 new words per hour is not an unreasonable rate, and it is through the discussion and activities that the words are actually learned. In-class discussions and/or follow-up work with nouns and other words provide the most important benefit because they give students additional opportunities to:

- Focus their attention on specific vocabulary items
- Use them in speaking and listening
- Negotiate meaning of nouns and other words
- Refine contextualized meanings and syntactic properties of items
- Develop classroom interactional skills

All teaching activities exemplified in this chapter and others have been used for decades with many types of academically bound students with various levels of proficiency, from beginning to advanced. Although books on teaching academic vocabulary often call for constructing exercises and tests for each lesson, these are laborious and time-consuming. The teaching suggestions presented here are based on using texts easily obtainable from print and written media sources such as advertisements, book cover descriptions, and news reports. In the days of the Internet and Web site proliferation, example texts can be easily obtained in many geographical locations and can be chosen to suite all types of learners—from beginners to highly advanced writers.

As a general rule, if text simplification is needed, it is best to eliminate rare rather than common words, even if they are lexically and structurally complex.

Prefixes and Suffixes—Dictionary Work and Practice

English–English dictionaries are alphabetically organized, and a photocopy of one to three dictionary pages with words that begin with a specific prefix can allow learners to figure out its meaning. For example:

- *incommunicado—if you are kept incommunicado, you cannot see or talk to anyone*
- *incomparable—so good or beautiful that nothing else can even be compared to it*
- *incompatible—two people are incompatible if they have completely different personalities and cannot get along*
- *incompetence—no ability or skill to do a job properly*
- *incompetent—not having an ability or skill to do a job properly*
- *incomplete—not having all its parts*
- *incomprehension—not being able to understand something*
- *inconclusive—not leading to a clear decision or result* (Adapted from *Longman Dictionary of Contemporary English,* 1995).

It is important for dictionary-based exercises to include dictionaries of appropriate levels of difficulty. For example, learners' dictionaries can be used for beginners and intermediate-level students, and advanced learners can work with unsimplified dictionaries. The work on a particular prefix/suffix needs to coincide with other practice with prefixes/suffixes with similar meanings (e.g., *ab-, un-, non-*) and exercises found in all vocabulary textbooks.

While working on prefixes and their meanings, it may be useful to devote at least some amount of attention to parts of speech and their varied suffixations (e.g., noun suffixes *-ion, -ure, -ment* are different from adjective suffixes *-i/able, -a/ent, -i've*). Also the structure of dictionary entries and the practical information contained in them can be examined and discussed (e.g., count/noncount designations, verb-transitive/verb-intransitive, or prepositions typically used with particular nouns).

Graded Exposure to Authentic Texts (Increasing Lexical Complexity)

(a) For beginning students, magazine/newspaper advertisements or book cover descriptions with frequent noun uses can be used to provide exposure to contextualized vocabulary learning. On a photocopy of the advertisement/description, the useful and practical nouns (verbs, adjectives, or prepositions) can be blocked out with adhesive labels or whiteout to create blanks for a fill-in-the-blank practice with authentic language. However, the nouns from the original are listed below the text to be used as prompts for blank filling. For example:

If you sometimes have problems ___________ and adapting to American culture, or have difficulty communicating with ___________ of American English, this book will help you.

Each chapter in this book has two _________ (1) readings and exercises about cross-cultural _______________ and selected areas of American ________; and (2) intercultural communication _________ designed to promote discussion of cross-cultural communication. To help you better understand the material, the book includes

- *reading ___________,*
- *comprehension questions,*
- *discussion questions,*
- *____________ exercises, and*
- *conversational _____________.*

Omitted nouns and gerunds:

sections	*activities*	*exercies*	*culture*	*understanding*
speakers	*communication*	*vocabulary*	*activities*	

(Adapted from Levine & Adelman, 1993.)

Vocabulary expansion practice:

sections—parts, portions
understanding—comprehending
activities—exercises, work, practice, doing something
conversation—speaking, talking, discussing

(b) An activity such as described in (a) can be used without the list of original nouns (or other types of words) when students are expected to come up with lexical alternatives or various possibilities for appropriate context completion. For instance, all appropriate lexical replacement options can be acceptable if students supply them.

In intermediate-level classes, newspaper articles on various topics of interest, as well as science and market reports, can become a good means to increase the level of text complexity and lexical variety (see later example).

If the original nouns/words are not provided, students can work in groups to complete the text and supply as many contextually appropriate fillers as they can. Groups can compete for finding as many lexically appropriate and syntactically correct fillers, and the winner of each blank can be awarded a token (e.g., a piece of colored paper). The group that accumulates the most tokens wins the competition. Students usually enjoy this type of competition, and the amount of discussion associated with appropriate lexical and syntactic choices of words can be highly productive.

(c) For advanced students, this technique can be used with excerpts from introductory texts in the disciplines or literature on any topic that the teacher considers to be useful and appropriate. As intermediate learners, students can work in groups or complete the assignment as homework, followed by a substantial class discussion of their lexical choices. For example,

- Why is a particular word appropriate/inappropriate in this sentence?
- What better word can be found?
- Why is another choice of a word better?
- How many parts does a particular word consist of?
- What are they?
- Is this word a noun, adjective, verb, or adverb, and how do we know?
- What lexical substitutions for this word can we think of?
- Are some better than others and why?

Lexical Substitution Exercises

Restatement and paraphrase are often considered to be essential academic tasks. However, many NNS students lack the necessary lexical and reading skills to restate an idea. Teaching restatement by means of lexical substitutions is simpler than paraphrasing, and lexical restatement can be practiced even with high beginners. For example,

Task 1. Please replace the underlined nouns with other nouns (or phrases) with similar meanings.

1. *Education abroad is rapidly expanding due to an increasing number of adventurous students who take advantage of going abroad to explore their ethnic roots.*
   [*education—studying, going to school, learning; abroad—in a foreign country; expanding—growing, becoming popular; roots—origins, family history*]
2. *Several factors play an important role in this trend.*
   [*facts, points, ideas*]
3. *Colleges and universities in England remain the top destination for U.S. students.*
   [*choice, place, location, goal*]

Paraphrase practice is a little more complex and requires examples for students to complete it successfully. However, if the lexical substitution work takes place prior to restatement, students will have little trouble.

Task 2. Please explain in your own words and in one sentence what these three sentences say together.

Also in writing practice, after students produce a paragraph or an essay, the teacher can underline nouns/words in the students' texts to be replaced with other words with similar meanings.

Editing and Finding Mistakes in Noun Forms and Uses

(a) Noticing and drawing attention

The first step in teaching students to edit their own text is to present one written by someone else with several mistakes of the same or similar types:

> *"You got a mail." Technology can provide various ways for communicate. Most American have already visited WWW, but in my country, people still don't use technologies often. With the technology development, we, people, can get more and more benefit. We use technologies doesn't mean we abandon the traditional way to communicate with other people. I really enjoy to meet with friends and have fun with family. But everybody is so busy today, technology provides a more convenient way for communication. Everybody have different way to communicate, and I believe technology make us having more communicate with other, it also makes our life more beautiful.* (From a student essay on the influence of technology on communication.)

This text can be put on a transparency and the mistakes in it discussed in class. Alternatively, students can work on several similar texts in small groups and then present their findings to the class with explanations for each error they identified. In this case, the entire class may have additional opportunities for noticing and working with problematic nouns.

(b) When proofreading text for structural, morphological, or inflectional errors, most students begin reading their text from the beginning. In doing so, the reader almost immediately gets caught in the flow of the text and stops paying attention to errors in word/noun form. Furthermore, when students read their own text silently, they employ only one type of memory—visual. For students in ESL/EAP programs in English-speaking countries, aural memory (remembering how the word sounds) can provide an additional boost in mistake-hunting power:

- It is far more effective to start reading one's own text from the beginning of the *last* sentence to the end of this sentence. In this way the reader proofs the text by reading it backward, sentence by sentence, to avoid getting caught in the text flow.
- Then move up to the one before the last sentence and read to the end of this sentence.
- Then move up one sentence higher still (the third sentence from the end) and proofread it.
- The proofreading of text should be done aloud (but not necessarily loudly) while paying close attention to word forms.

- This proofreading technique can help students locate and correct about one third to half of the word-form errors in their writing.
- In most cases, students need to be shown this technique only one time because it is simple to understand and use. They just need to be reminded to proofread their text, read it out loud, and follow what is written (rather than what they think is written). Reminding writers to proofread is not a new task for any writing teacher.

For example:

[This is the last sentence to be proof-read (6)] *When I was a child, all the technologies in my hometown were still simple.* [The fifth sentence to the end (5)] *Started from television to computers, all were changed.* [Then the fourth sentence to the end of the sentence (4)] *Basically, all technologies that people discovered in communications were not to make money.* [Then read the third sentence to the end (3)] *They were made for improvements.* [Then continue with the second sentence to the end of the sentence (2)] *It is true that until now there are no technologies that can promote person contact.* [Start reading here to the end of the sentence—(1)] *For example, people can only hear voices from telephone and people can only see the faces and voices through internet.* (From another student's text on technology and communication.)

Gerund Practice

As mentioned, gerunds derived from transitive verbs often retain their objects even when they play the role of sentence subjects. Identifying the sentence subject appropriately when working with gerund constructions is important in subject–verb agreement editing. To raise students' awareness of gerund complexities, many gerund + direct object constructions can be found. Students usually learn a great deal from such practice and enjoy it. For example,

Please explain which verb form is correct and is an appropriate choice in this sentence. How many are possible and why?

Trusting friends becomes/become necessary at the time of trouble.
Eating fresh vegetables is/are recommended for children and adults of all ages.
Reading books is/are essential in learning a second language.
Hiding cookies from children is/are something that many parents do, when they want to control their children's diet.
Writing exercises help/helps students to improve their vocabulary skills.
Choosing universities is/are complicated for teenagers without their parents' assistance.

In general, gerund + direct object constructions are extremely common (e.g., *understanding parents/children/students, building blocks (of houses), buying cars, answering phones, typing letters*), and many similar sentences can be made for practice.

QUESTIONS FOR DISCUSSION

1. In teaching ESL to L2 university-bound students, instruction in vocabulary and grammar usually take place in courses separate from the teaching of L2 writing. Why were ESL curricula and language work designed like this? If you were in charge of the curriculum design, what course structure would you develop?
2. In your opinion, why did Nation (1990) call vocabulary learning *a learning burden*? How can learners acquire academic vocabulary in classroom activities? How can these activities be designed to be productive for learners?
3. Why does the learning of academic vocabulary need to become one of the central foci of classroom instruction? What current L2 teaching methodologies match the needs of academically oriented learners?
4. What methodological and research premise underlies the expansion of learners' range of nouns by means of contextual lexical substitution?
5. Among the L2 learners' problems with nouns addressed in this chapter (e.g., countable–uncountable nouns, articles, names of languages and people), in your opinion which ones are more important than others for L2 learners to be aware of? Why?

FURTHER READINGS ABOUT ACADEMIC VOCABULARY AND VOCABULARY TEACHING

Vocabulary Teaching

Carter, R., & McCarthy, M. (Eds.). (1988). *Vocabulary and language teaching*. Harlow, Essex: Longman.

Coady, J., & Huckin, T. (Eds.). (1997). *Second language vocabulary acquisition*. Cambridge: Cambridge University Press.

Dudley-Evans, T., & St. John, M. J. (1998). *Developments in English for specific purposes*. Cambridge: Cambridge University Press.

Jordan, R. (1997). *English for academic purposes*. Cambridge: Cambridge University Press.

Milton, J. (1999). Lexical thickets and electronic gateways: Making text accessible by novice writers. In C. Candlin & K. Hyland (Eds.), *Writing texts, processes and practices* (pp. 221–243). London: Longman.

Schmitt, N. (2000). *Vocabulary in language teaching*. Cambridge: Cambridge University Press.

Schmitt, N., & McCarthy, M. (1997). *Vocabulary description, acquisition, and pedagogy*. Cambridge: Cambridge University Press.

Academic Vocabulary

Adams, V. (2001). *Complex words in English*. Harlow, Essex: Longman.

Arnaud, P., & Savignon, S. (1997). Rare words, complex lexical units and the advanced learner. In J. Coady & T. Huckin (Eds.), *Second language vocabulary acquisition* (pp. 157–173). Cambridge: Cambridge University Press.
Coxhead, A. (2000). The new academic word list. *TESOL Quarterly, 34*(2), 213–238.
Francis, G. (1994). Labelling discourse: An aspect of nominal-group cohesion. In M. Coulthard (Ed.), *Advances in written text analysis* (pp. 83–101). New York: Routledge.
Nation, I. S. P. (1990). *Teaching and learning vocabulary*. New York: Newbury House.
Nation, I. S. P. (2001). *Learning vocabulary in another language*. Cambridge: Cambridge University Press.

Vocabulary in Discourse

Celce-Murcia, M., & Olshtain, E. (2000). *Discourse and context in language teaching*. Cambridge: Cambridge University Press.
Hatch, E. (1992). *Discourse and language education*. Cambridge: Cambridge University Press.
McCarthy, M. (1991). *Discourse analysis for language teachers*. Cambridge: Cambridge University Press.

Appendix to Chapter 5

LEXICAL CHUNKS WITH VARIOUS TYPES OF NOUNS AND NOUN PHRASES

Negative Openings: Uncountable Nouns

(However),

little information	*is available about xxx*
little attention	*has been devoted to yyy*

Negative Openings: Countable nouns

few reports	*have discussed/examined zzz*
few discussions	*have addressed/noted/examined*
few articles	*have focused on/noted*
few studies	*have investigated/dealt with*

(Adapted from Swales & Feak, 1994)

Most Common Noun Phrases Found in Academic Prose

Nouns with Prepositional Phrases

the relationship between the
the difference between the
an important part in
an important role in
an increase in the
the same way as

Prepositional Phrases Followed by the ***Of***-phrase

as a result of the
as in the case of the
at the end of the
at the beginning of the
at the time of the …
at the time of writing
from the point of view (of)
in the context of the
in the division of labor
in the course of the
in the early stages of

Most Common Noun Phrases Found in Academic Prose

Four-Word Units: Noun Phrases Followed by an ***Of***-phrase

(and) the development of the
different parts of the
one of the main/most
other parts of the
part(s) of the body
parts of the world
per cent of the
point of view of
the ability of the
the absence of a
the base/basis of the
the beginning of the
the case of a/the
the center of the
the composition of the
the context of the
the course of the
the division of labor
the early stages of
and the number of
the edge of the
the effect(s) of the
the end of the
the existence of a
the first of these
the form of a/the
the formation of the
the history of the
the importance of the
the length of the
the level of the
the magnitude of the
the nature of the
the needs of the
the origin of the
the point of view
the position of the
the presence of a/the
both sides of the
the presence or absence of the
the purpose of the
the rest of the
the results of the
the role of the
the shape of the
the size of the
the start of the
the structure of the
the sum of the
the temperature of the
the time of the
the top of the
the total number of
the use of a/the
the value of the
the work of the

(Adapted from Biber et al., 1999)

Five-Word Units: Noun Phrases Followed by an ***Of***-phrase

one of the most important
the aim of this study
the first part of the
the other end of the
the point of view of
the presence or absence of
the rate of change of

(Adapted from Biber et al., 1999)

6

More on the Noun Phrase: Pronouns

OVERVIEW

- The place of personal pronouns in academic text and their associated genres.
- Uses of impersonal pronouns.
- Demonstratives, text cohesion, and lexical substitution.
- The prevalence of indefinite pronouns and learning to avoid them.

Although the term *pronouns* suggests that they can be used in place of nouns, in reality pronouns have characteristics and functions that make them different in important ways. First, unlike nouns, pronouns represent a closed class of words (Quirk et al., 1985)—that is, they are limited in number and functions, and new words of this type are not coined. Unlike nouns, pronouns can be used in place of whole phrases or concepts with nominal functions (e.g., the phrase *the big blue grammar books* can be replaced by a pronoun *they*, which refers to the entire noun phrase). Furthermore, in English pronouns have syntactic properties that nouns do not have: Pronoun forms can vary depending on whether they occur in the sentence subject or object position (*I/me, she/her*) or refer to first, second, or third person, or male or female.

In addition to personal pronouns, various other types of pronouns are very common in English: demonstrative (*this/that, these/those*), indefinite (*somebody, anybody, everything*), and slot fillers (*it/there*). Although many L2 learners believe pronouns to be syntactically and lexically simple, and although words or particles with demonstrative and indefinite functions exist in most languages, various types of problems in pronoun use have been identified in NNS students' academic prose (Indrasuta, 1988; Johns, 1991, 1997; Vaughan, 1991).

Additional levels of complexity arise when L2 writers transfer culturally determined considerations of appropriateness in pronoun use, as is the case, for example, with personal pronouns. In the teaching of L2 writing in ESL/EAP and writing/composition courses, frequent employment of personal pronouns is often perceived to be appropriate and acceptable, particularly in essays associated with expressing personal views and ideas. However, several studies of large corpora of formal academic text have found that in many disciplines uses of personal pronouns are very infrequent. With regard to L1 and L2 essay texts, prominent and significant distinctions have been identified between NS students' uses of various types of pronouns and those encountered in NNS academic prose in English (Hinkel, 2001c, 2002a).

This chapter begins with an examination of personal pronouns in academic texts, followed by slot fillers (*it/there*), and then demonstrative and indefinite pronouns and their functions in academic discourse and text.

PERSONAL PRONOUNS IN ACADEMIC TEXTS

The textual purpose of personal pronouns in written discourse is to refer directly to the writer, the audience of writing, and specific things or persons other than the writer or audience. Corpus analyses of various genres have shown that personal pronouns are orders of magnitude more common than other types of pronouns, and these features are far more common in conversational than in any other type of genres. In addition to conversational discourse, personal pronouns are also encountered in fiction, but only rarely in academic text. As Biber et al. (1999) pointed out, because personal pronouns mostly refer to persons, "human beings are a more marginal topic" (p. 333) in academic prose.

First- and Second-Person Pronouns

In written text, the uses of first-person pronouns usually mark personal narratives and/or examples that are often considered inappropriate in academic writing. Many researchers of academic discourse and prose have noted the highly depersonalized and objective character of academic prose that requires "author evacuation" (Johns, 1997, p. 57). Explicit teaching of features of formal and academic discourse and text requires avoiding personal pronouns, personal tone, and personal references (Jordan, 1997; Raimes, 1992; Swales & Feak, 1994).

In fact, Swales' (1990a) analysis of written academic genre found that academic texts are often expected to project objectivity in presenting information and depersonalize text by various lexical and syntactic means. Swales further argued that the teaching of writing and "student writing in colleges and universities should not be viewed as an individually-oriented, inner-directed cognitive process" (p. 4), but as tasks in discourse and text construction within the conventions of communicating knowledge within the norms of the academic community. According to Swales, L2 writing teachers need to prepare students to write in the disciplines because academic writing is a socially situated act that extends far beyond the writer's analysis of his or her inner explorations and thoughts.

Second-person singular and plural pronouns are also considered inappropriate in academic prose because they are employed to address the reader directly (Smoke, 1999; Swales & Feak, 1994). The use of these pronouns requires a specific individual to whom the text is addressed, indicates a high degree of the writer's involvement with the addressee, and marks the conversational register (Biber, 1988, 1995).

Corpus analyses have shown that first- and second-person pronouns are rare in academic prose. In all the rate of occurrences of *I*, *me*, *we*, and *us* constitutes 0.006% (6 per 100,000 words) in a large corpus of academic text (Biber et al., 1999). The rate of occurrences of *you* is rarer still with 0.001%. Some amount of variation of personal pronoun use has been noted across various disciplines. Prose in philosophy included the highest rates of first-person pronouns of 6.5 per 1,000 words (0.65%), followed by texts in marketing and applied linguistics with 6.2 (0.62%) and 4.8 (0.48%) occurrences per 1,000 words, respectively (Hyland, 1999).

However, in NNS students' academic texts, personal narratives and examples can be common, and rates of first-person pronoun usage varies between 1.89 and 3.97% (Hinkel, 2002a). In addition, the frequency rate of second-person pronouns are also relatively high—between 0.5% and 1.00%. For example, in a senior-level psychology assignment, included next, a student employed several types of personal pronouns to an extent that may make her text appear to be a personal narrative.

Extroversion

(This excerpt starts at the beginning of the third paragraph of the paper.) *Is it possible for everyone to change one's behavior and thoughts by different environmental factors? I believe the answer is no doubt. One's childhood experience and background constitute his disposition for the first period. During this period, his family or school teachers might influence his development of character. Furthermore, he, as an adult in the second period, could transfer whether from introversion to extroversion or from extroversion to introversion, depending on his religion, culture, and personal experience in society. Perhaps, his personality will be changed again in the future. The best successful example is my personal experience to support this approach. I was so isolated and shy that I was not popular in my parents' eyes when I was a child. It won't be changed until I entering high school. Mr. Lee, one of my high school teachers, encouraged me and helped me to understand my own ability in languages that completely decided my future. After I attending many speech contests in school, I have become a self-confidence and talkative girl as a leader. Most friends consider me to be an extro-*

verted person. Nevertheless, I discover that my personality has changing again and again after getting my teaching experience. (The student wrote two more paragraphs to complete the assignment.)

In this excerpt, the use of a personal example as supporting information does not seem appropriate because, for one thing, it does not demonstrate familiarity with course material and/or relevant literature. Furthermore, personal examples cannot be considered generalizable and are most often perceived as anecdotal. For the purposes of an academic course assignment, the writer needs to be directed to cite research, literature, or other types of formal academic evidence that can support her position that extroversion is a variable trait.

Third-Person Pronouns

In addition to first-person narratives, NNS students also employ third-person recounts and stories to support their positions. In many cases, due to the narrative-like character of NNS academic prose and insufficiency of their vocabulary, L2 writers include high rates of third-person pronouns in their text (Hinkel, 2002a). For example, in an essay on the economic benefits and pitfalls of credit cards, the student writer tells the story of his friend.

> (This excerpt starts at the beginning of the third paragraph.) *It is true that credit cards are really popular these days, but it has problems, like debt. For instance, one of my friends, who is Dan, had two gold credit cards. But he didn't concern the budget of his account, while he was using the plastic money. So, he had heavy debt on his account. It took about two and half years to pay off his debt. After he had big trouble with charge cards, he cut his two gold credit cards with scissors. Now he does not have any kinds of credit cards.*
>
> *Moreover, according to the Social Security statistic, in 1996, only 30% of the credit card holders pay full pay amount and another 70% pay only minimum amount or less than a full amount. The statistic shows us how people are abusing the credit card, and the phenomenon gets worse and worse.* (The essays includes three additional paragraphs.)

In this excerpt, the function of personal or third-party recounts is largely the same (i.e., to provide validation for the main points expressed in the essay). Another point to make is that, despite the fact that in many cases, L2 writers are familiar with employing published sources (e.g., *the Social Security statistic*) as a means of rhetorical support, this technique might not be used consistently and appropriately. In the credit card example, the statistic cited by the student does not support the observation that users abuse credit cards or the claim that the phenomenon gets worse and worse. Thus, instruction on the limited power of personal narratives to support essay points should coincide with the teaching of citing elaborated discussions of data and sources, combined with the fact that the citations must validate all points made in the text and not just some of them.

In general terms, NNS students need to be explicitly instructed to avoid the uses of:

- personal examples, narratives, and recounts of personal experiences
- addressing the reader directly and, thus, second-person pronouns
- personal tone and its attendant linguistic features, such as adjectives (*wonderful, great, terrible, horrible, disgusting*), adverbs (*very, much, really, definitely, pretty (good)*), and context-specific nouns (*winner, loser, miracle, magic*)

If these textual features appear in student texts, they can be replaced by common nouns or impersonal/indefinite pronouns.

Highly advanced NNS students employ first- and second-person pronouns in texts written in various disciplines such as business, finance, and management. For example, in the following excerpt from an assignment on Profitability, the NNS student employs first- and second-person pronouns in contexts where common nouns may be more appropriate. As mentioned (see chap. 3), L2 writers who are pressed for time and are dealing with high demands placed on their language skills often resort to employing vocabulary immediately accessible to them. Also as discussed in chapter 5, the vocabulary items used extensively in courses and texts in particular disciplines are acquired incidentally by virtue of their prevalence in academic reading texts, textbooks, and lectures.

An excerpt from a student's academic assignment on profitability illustrates the use of first-person pronouns that do not seem to be necessary:

> *Profitability is especially useful for potential investors. Comparing Martin Marietta to its competitors over the profitability ratios, <u>we</u> can see that it performed well above the industry. The only concern is its business nature. Any political change will influence its business. If <u>our</u> perception toward the world future situation is same as current one, then Martin Marietta is a good buy. If not, then if the money <u>you</u> have is for the rest of <u>your</u> life then try some other industry. Otherwise, in the good time <u>you</u> get stable return and in war time, <u>you</u> get a lot more back. <u>My</u> recommendation is that if Martin Marietta gets new contracts in the new administration, <u>you</u> should buy their stock.* (From a student paper on profitability.)

In this excerpt, the uses of first-person pronouns can be replaced by impersonal constructions:

- *<u>we</u> can see—it is easy to see, one can see, an analysis can show*
- *If <u>our</u> perception toward the world future situation—in the future, if the situation remains the same/all things being equal, if the world does not change much/a great deal, if the present situation continues to hold/remain the same*

Similarly, second-person pronouns can be replaced by the indefinite pronoun *one* (Jordan, 1997) or common nouns such as *buyers/investors*:

- *if the money you have is for the rest of your life—if the money one/buyers/investors invest(s) is/represents their entire savings, if one invests all his or her money*
- *you (should buy their stock)—one/investors/buyers/interested consumers*

According to Biber et al. (1999), in conversation the first-person pronoun *I* is repeated 10 times more frequently than all other personal pronouns combined. Thus, the uses of the first-person pronoun tend to impart conversational and colloquial tone to written academic prose—a point worth making in teaching formal academic writing.

Pronouns as Noun Replacements

In academic essays, the use of third-person singular and plural pronouns can be advisable because they impart detachment, formality, and objectivity (Hacker, 1994; Leki, 1999). Although functions of pronouns are far more complex than mere noun replacement, in L2 academic prose their uses may be necessary when a particular noun is repeated to excess (see chap. 5). For example, in the following excerpt from a student's assignment, the noun phrase *employed women* is repeated several times in a relatively short text:

> *As the number of employed women has increased, marketers and consumer researchers interested in employed women who are young and have great consumption power. Women's employment outside of the home has led to changes the lifestyle which affect consumption patterns. As their lifestyle is changed, the employed women have been dominated by many factors in selecting clothing. What factors influenced the employed women in the selection of apparel? So it is important for marketers to understand the factors that have impact on employed women's clothing decision making.*

However, merely replacing repeated nouns and noun phrases with corresponding pronouns (e.g., *employed women—they*) can lead to ambiguous and unclear constructions. For example,

?*Many stores accept credit cards, but they can be expensive.*

The reason that simply substituting pronouns for repeated nouns may not work well in this example is that the sentence *many stores accept credit cards* contains two plural nouns: *stores* and *credit cards*, both of which can be referred to by the pronoun *they*, resulting in a confusing structure. Another problem with replacing nouns with pronouns can be noted if a relatively lengthy amount of text separates the noun and the pronoun replacement:

> *Some scholars argue that political and economic situations, and ideology affect education. That is, the content and the method of education change not due to the problems*

in education in itself, but due to the political and economic situations, and ideology at the time. The reasons for the change are outside of education. They interpret history of education of the early republic period, the late eighteenth and early nineteenth century. (Excerpted from a student essay on ideology in education.)

In this example, the pronoun *they* in the third sentence refers to *scholars* in the first. However, in the context of the excerpt, it may be somewhat difficult to track back the reference and determine that *they* does not refer to the noun *reasons* or *problems*.

Another important point about pronouns that function as noun replacements is that repeated pronouns may appear to be just as redundant as repeated nouns. For example,

With above context, some scholars believe that poor people or poor classes in our society maintain their own unique culture. Usually, they are dirty and are reluctant to clean their environment. They are also lazy and don't like to work hard. They depend on the income from their daily job or temporary employment or they receive welfare benefits. They are skeptical about life and aggressive to the current social structure. They use alcohol and drugs, and they are criminals. These attitudes of the first generation can be transferred to the next generation and be maintained for a long time. (Excerpted from a student's assignment on socioeconomic stratification and discrimination.)

This and earlier examples illustrate that merely replacing nouns with pronouns can be somewhat tricky and requires detailed familiarity with contextual constraints on pronoun referential uses and functions. As noted in chapter 5, replacing redundant nouns with other contextually appropriate nouns, as well as pronouns, can be a productive way to construct a less repetitious text.

IT-CLEFT AND IMPERSONAL *IT* STRUCTURES AND THEIR TEXTUAL FUNCTIONS

The impersonal pronoun *it* with copula *be* (where *it* is also called a dummy subject because it is empty of meaning) is more common in academic texts than practically any other written or spoken genre (Biber et al., 1999). This structure has several discourse functions, one of which is to focus the sentence on the information provided later in the sentence (see also chap. 8). The most prominent contextual feature of *it+be* is to depersonalize text and create an impression of the writer's distance and objectivity. In many cases, *it*-cleft constructions can be accompanied by adjectives, as in *it is clear/ useful/ important/ advantageous*. Other uses of the impersonal pronoun *it* can be found with such verbs as *seems, appears*, or *looks,* which, like adjectives, provide an element of hedging:

It looks therefore as if proved oil reserves should be enough for forty years ... at the current rate of consumption. (Schumacher, 1999, p. 103)

It-cleft constructions are syntactically complex, and for this reason, they frequently present an area of difficulty for academic L2 writers. In the practical reality of writing academic text to be submitted for a grade, many *it*-cleft structures can be avoided and replaced by other simpler constructions with similar focal and hedging functions.

Typical problems associated with the uses of it clefts and other impersonal constructions often lie in the fact that many L2 writers do not use them when they are necessary, as in the following two student sentences:

> **Companies may be difficult to hire qualified employees when the job market is high.*

> **Students are useful to practice individual notes and scales after they learn the piano keys.*

It-cleft constructions can be confusing because the concept of a dummy subject is not particularly easy to understand for speakers of many languages other than Germanic. (A similar issue may arise with existential *there* subjects, which are often confused with locative adverbials *there*). Although for the teacher the easiest way to correct the first sentence is simply to rewrite it as in *it is difficult for companies to hire qualified employees* ..., another solution can be to provide syntactically simpler options:

(a) *Hiring/to hire qualified employees may be difficult for companies* ...

(b) *For companies, qualified employees may be difficult to find/hire* ...

In these alternative constructions, the focal information of the sentence that follows the *it+be* structures is moved from the beginning of the sentence to the position of the sentence subject, where it continues to play an important informational role.

In general terms, impersonal *it* constructions can be presented as sentence slots, some that are always filled regardless of context, and some that are open for optional informational content (see chap. 4 for an extended discussion).

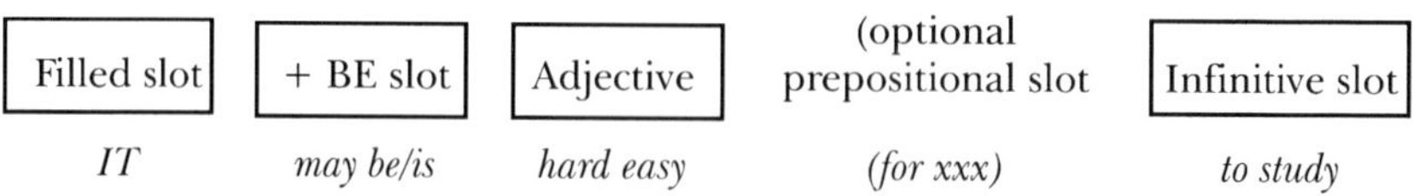

A similar system of slots can be used for other structures with the dummy subject *it*:

An advantage of this visual piece-by-piece constructing of sentences with *it* is that students can see that the subject has no referent (and is thus "empty" of meaning) and that it is a constant and invariable feature of *it*-cleft constructions.

Various analyses of written academic corpora have shown that nonreferential *it* occurs frequently in the following combinations that may be useful for academic writers to become familiar with:

- With adjectives—

it is (not) (im)possible to/that	*it is interesting to*
it is likely/unlikely that	*it is difficult/easy to*
it is important to/that	*it is (not) clear that*
it is necessary to	*it is true that*

- With modal verbs—*it may be that*
- With modal verbs and adjectives—*it may (not) be (im)possible to/that, it should be possible to/that, it may be necessary to/that, it is clear that, it is important to/that*
- With passive verbs—*it can be seen that, it should be noted that, it has been suggested that, it has also been … (determined, found, argued, stated, implied, shown, noted, written)*. Most passive constructions are accompanied by *that*-clauses that contain the focal information.

THERE EXISTENTIAL SUBJECT

Like the nonreferential *it*, the existential *there* has little semantic content. In general, however, the syntactic structure of *there*-constructions is much simpler than *it*-constructions, and the existential *there* is frequent in L2 written texts. The discourse function of existential constructions is to introduce new information and/or topics, and most co-occur with place and time adverbs (e.g., *there are few of them in the world today, there are many such teachers in my country*). It is important to note, however, that the existential *there* structures are particularly rare in most written genre, including academic, where they are encountered fewer than 10 times per million words (Biber et al., 1999). Overall, existential *there* is more frequent in conversational than written discourse. Because *there*-constructions are relatively syntactically simple, L2 academic writers tend to overuse them in their prose (Hinkel, 2003b). For this reason, students may be encouraged to employ them judiciously.

In written text, *there*-subject occurs in such constructions as:

- *seem/appear to be*
- *be supposed to be*
- *used to be* (past time and past tense contexts)
- *exist*—the most common alternative to *be* found almost exclusively in academic prose
- *occur*

These verbs can provide acceptable variations for the uses of *there*-constructions that academic writers may encounter in readings. However, it is important to bring students' attention to the limited uses of *there*-subjects.

REFERRING TO EARLIER TEXT: FUNCTIONS OF DEMONSTRATIVES

Demonstrative pronouns (*this, that, these, those*) play an important role in text cohesion because they have indexal (pointing) and referential functions (Halliday & Hasan, 1976). However, demonstratives can be ambiguous and vague when it is not immediately clear what specific noun or phrase they refer to. Research into academic text has found that demonstratives are comparatively common precisely due to their lack of specificity and their ability to project objectivity (Biber, 1988; Myers, 1989). However, *this* occurs far more frequently than *these, that*, or *those*, whereas the combined frequency rate of all demonstrative pronouns stands at 0.45% per million words of academic prose (Biber et al., 1999).

In general terms, demonstratives are one of the simplest cohesive devices in English. In their attempts to make their text cohesive, L2 writers often misconstrue the limited cohesive capacity of demonstratives or rely on them to excess (Hinkel, 2001a, 2002a). The following example is extracted from a student's academic assignment on the rising costs of farming:

> *Since cows are housed in areas that cannot be kept clean, there is an increased disease incident and other health problems, which result in high input costs. This is the reason why other farming systems are being considered for lowering this cost of milk production.*

In the example, the first occurrence of *this* actually refers to several "reasons" that "other farming methods are being considered" (i.e., a lack of cleanliness in cow housing, increased incidence of disease, and high input costs). However, in English a singular demonstrative pronoun has a limited referential capacity and cannot refer to a number of referential points at one time.[1] The second *this* refers to a plural noun *costs* that is not located in the immediate proximity to the pronoun. In both cases, the use of demonstratives makes the text appear confusing and somewhat obscure.

In general terms, the use of demonstratives requires adherence to largely rigid noun–pronoun agreement in number (i.e., singular pronouns *this* and *that* cannot refer to plural nouns). In most cases, *this* and *these* can "point" to nouns in their close proximity (or a close proximity to the speaker, as in *This is a great computer*, when one is looking or pointing to a computer). However, *that* and *those* are markers of a more distant reference. However, neither type of demonstratives can refer to a sizable portion of text, as can often be encountered in students' texts (Hinkel, 2001a) .

REFERRING TO EARLIER AND FOLLOWING TEXT: NOUNS TO ENUMERATE

In addition to demonstratives, various lexical means of establishing text cohesion have been identified and can be used with greater positive effect and sophistication for the text (Halliday & Hasan, 1976; Tadros, 1994). In English, a number of lexically simple nouns can refer to several textual points or entire classes of nouns at one time. For example,

(1) *Until now, we have not considered social change. Our emphasis has been on order and stability in organization. But social organization also changes. Change is easily as important a topic in organization as order and stability. With all the* <u>*factors*</u> *defending order in organization, how is change possible?* (Charon, 1999, pp. 181–182)

(2) *How does economics relate to the* <u>*problems*</u> *discussed in the previous chapters?* (Schumacher, 1999, p. 26)

Such nouns as *factor* and *problem* have a cohesive property of *catch-alls* because they have enumerative meanings and usually refer to a few points previously mentioned or those that follow. Although not particularly lexically sophisticated, they appear to be more advanced than, for example, demonstrative pronouns (Partington, 1996).

Many highly useful and flexible enumerative nouns are presented next (Tadros, 1994). It is important to note that few of these can be found in conversational register because their functions in text are lexically and semantically complex. However, the explicit teaching of enumerative catch-all

[1]In some contexts, *this* can refer to several points provided that a restatement/paraphrase noun is used to apply to all points covered by *this*. For example, *Senator Smith called members of his party useless civil servants, and* <u>*this gaff*</u> *is likely to cause his resignation* (<u>this tip</u> was suggested by Marcella Frank, New York University).

nouns has an additional benefit of highlighting the differences between informal conversational and formal written registers.

Common Enumerative "Catch-All" Nouns

advance	*drawback*	*practice*
advantage	*element*	*problem*
angle	*episode*	*process*
approach	*event*	*program*
aspect	*evidence*	*project*
attempt	*exercise*	*purpose*
background	*experience*	*reason*
behavior	*facet*	*result*
category	*fact*	*scenario*
challenge	*factor*	*shortfall*
change	*feature*	*stage*
characteristic	*form*	*step*
circumstance	*issue*	*system*
class	*item*	*subject*
consequence	*manner*	*task*
course [of action]	*method*	*technique*
criterion [a]	*objective*	*tendency*
deal	*occurrence*	*term*
difficulty	*phase*	*topic*
dilemma	*period*	*trend*
disadvantage	*plan*	*type*

Some of these nouns have very similar meanings and can be used interchangeably to form semantic and associative networks (and cohesive ties) in many contexts:

aspect—facet	*phase—stage*
category—class	*process—system*
characteristic—feature	*approach—method*
disadvantage—drawback	*difficulty—problem—issue*
element—item	*task—project*

EVERYONE HAS SOMETHING: INDEFINITE PRONOUNS

Indefinite pronouns that consist of *every-*, *no-*, *some-*, and *any-*words (*everybody, everything, nothing, anyone*) are markedly more frequent in L2 academic texts than in comparable NS prose (Hinkel, 2002a). Among these pronouns, *every-* and *no-*words are usually associated with overstatement and exaggerations and considered to be inappropriate in formal written texts (Quirk et al., 1985). However, *some-* and *any-*words are often so vague that they may have little semantic content. For example,

> *People hear the word "information" everywhere any day and usually define "information" as news, facts, knowledge, data, and so on. Everyone wants to have as much information as they can when they make business decisions. However, in every field of business, information is different for many people, and it depends on what people specialize in. Every student using the internet as the information system tries to search for something that they want to gain through it. And the information systems transmit something to learners. People have heard the concepts of facts, data, and knowledge. Although these concepts have different meaning, facts are something that have happened or have been done. This is the type of information that is valuable for everyone in any business.* (Excerpted from a student's academic paper on information technology.)

Studies of written English-language corpora have shown that *every-* and *no-*words are marked exaggeratives, and they are particularly rare in academic prose, although quantifiers such as *some* and *no* are encountered occasionally (2.5 occurrences per 100,000 words—i.e., 0.0025%; Biber et al., 1999). Their uses often create an impression of overstatement, inflation of facts, or hyperbole (see also chap. 12 on Hedges). In the spoken register, however, *every-* and *no-*words occur with greater frequencies.

Studies of L2 text have demonstrated that students often rely on overstatements and exaggerations as a means of rhetorical persuasion common in rhetorical traditions other than Anglo-American (Hinkel, 1997b; Matalene, 1985). In addition, as mentioned in chapter 3, when the NNS writers' lexical range is limited, they rely on the accessible lexical arsenal to produce academic prose. For this reason, instruction on constructing written academic text must focus on the development of learners' vocabulary.

However, *some-* and *any-*words (*someone, something, anybody*) often function as hedges with the goal of expressing vague general truths, commonly held opinions, together with uncertainty and imprecision. In some discourse traditions, such as Chinese and Japanese, indefiniteness and hesitation are considered to be desirable characteristics because they allow writers to state their opinions indirectly without the risk of offending or losing rapport with the reader (Maynard, 1997).

However, in Anglo-American academic prose, neither exaggerations nor vagueness are valued highly, thus the usage of indefinite pronouns is not likely to make a favorable impression on the reader. For instance, in the prior excerpt, the *-body* and*-one* pronouns can be relatively easily replaced with nouns such as *business managers/researchers/students/ community* and *-thing* pronouns with contextually relevant nouns.

> In general terms, it is important that NNS writers learn to avoid *every*- and *no*-pronouns and use *some*- and *any*-words sparingly.

CHAPTER SUMMARY

On the whole, the uses of specific personal pronouns differ by genre and text types. Thus, the work on pronouns represents only one aspect of a bigger picture of teaching students to identify their audience and adjust their text accordingly.

- First-person pronouns are common in personal narratives and occasionally fiction, but they are relatively rare in academic prose.
- By the same token, second-person pronouns are associated with direct appeals to and/or establishing common ground with the audience. This type of text is particularly rare in Anglo-American academic prose.
- Third-person pronouns can be useful in avoiding repetition of proper nouns. However, uses of third-person pronouns require care to ensure that pronouns refer to specific and easily identifiable nouns in the preceding text.
- *It*-cleft constructions are common in academic text because they project authorial distance and depersonalization. However, they represent a persistent problem for students and may require additional and specifically focused work and persistence.
- Because demonstratives represent the simplest cohesive device, L2 students frequently overuse them in their text or employ them in inappropriate contexts. The popularity of demonstratives can be reduced to some extent if learners' lexical repertoire is expanded to include enumerative catch-all nouns.
- Indefinite pronouns with their exaggerative or vague meanings should be avoided.

STRATEGIES AND TACTICS FOR TEACHING AND TEACHING ACTIVITIES

Various written genres can be relatively easily identified by their text features. The goal of the activities described next is to help learners identify and notice pronouns (and other textual characteristics such as adjectives and adverbs) that distinguish various types of genres.

Genres and Pronouns: Personal Narratives or Academic Text

A copy of a couple of pages from memoirs or juvenile romantic fiction can be handed out to students to analyze the uses of personal pronouns and determine the frequency count of first-, second-, or third-person pronouns in a paragraph or page. Then a similar analysis and/or computation can be performed in a text excerpt of a proximate length photocopied (or shown on an overhead projector) from an introductory level textbook or a science or business report from a newspaper.

Why do pronoun counts differ? What is the author's purpose in either text? Is it to tell a personal story or present impersonal information? How many occurrences of the impersonal pronoun *it*, for example, can be identified in each text?

When writing essays or assignments, what is the students' rhetorical purpose? If they set out to tell a personal story, then certainly the use of first-person pronouns is necessary. If it is not, how should they approach the text?

In group activities, students can be handed different types of text (e.g., a student essay/personal narrative may be contrasted with a published argumentation/position essay, a newspaper editorial with company promotional materials, or excerpts on textbooks on philosophy and business/economics). Topics of the materials can differ widely to match students' interests and can range from those on fashion, cars, and computer games to pollution, nutrition, and military history. After students analyze various genres of text, depending on the students' proficiency level, they can present their results to another group or the entire class or they can write a short report to describe their findings and observations. Part of the benefit of this exercise is helping students develop the habit of noticing features of the text they are reading.

Demonstratives and Enumerative Nouns in Text Cohesion

(a) Work with demonstrative pronouns needs to address their limited cohesive power in English and the requisite noun–pronoun agreement in number (e.g., *employees—these workers, the author's argument/claim—this position*). The fact that demonstratives require the presence of identifiable noun or phrase references in the immediate proximity to the pronoun should be emphasized.

Another important consideration in the appropriate use of demonstratives is that they can refer only to nouns, noun phrases, or clauses and cannot be used to refer to entire contexts or implied referents. For this purpose, learners can be asked to identify the specific nouns or phrases to which demonstratives in texts refer. For example, drawing connecting lines or arrows in texts or their own essays can help students understand the highly limited cohesive power of demonstratives in English (as opposed to that in many other languages, such as Arabic, Chinese, or Korean). This exercise can emphasize that if a demonstrative pronoun does not point to any particular noun, phrase, or clause, then this type of pronoun probably cannot be used as an effective cohesive device.

(b) In addition, the textual uses and functions of enumerative nouns can also be discussed, and students can be similarly asked to draw the connecting "strings" to establish lexical ties between particular words or phrases. For instance, nouns such as *advantage, factor, problem, reason, stage, term,* and *type* are expected to have specific identifiable referents in text, to which these nouns are connected. Thus, students can be asked to "tie" each of the enumeratives to the structures, text elements, or text excerpts to which these nouns refer. If such structures or short contexts cannot be easily identified, enumerative nouns may not be the best choice of a cohesive device. For activities to work with indefinite pronouns, see chapter 12 on Hedges.

QUESTIONS FOR DISCUSSION

1. Why should teachers direct students to reduce the number of first- and second-person pronouns in academic writing assignments?
2. If pronouns can make awkward noun replacements, what can be the reasons that in the teaching of writing, pronouns are often "oversold" as noun substitutions? What could be better ways to teach the functions and uses of pronouns?
3. What could be the reasons that indefinite pronouns are far more common in L2 than in L1 academic essays written by NSs of English?
4. What can students do to correct overuse of demonstrative pronouns?

FURTHER READINGS ABOUT PRONOUNS AND TEACHING

Pronouns in Various Genres of Academic Text

Chang, Y.-Y., & Swales, J. (1999). Informal elements in English academic writing: Threats or opportunities for advanced non-native speakers. In C. Candlin & K. Hyland (Eds.), *Writing texts, processes and practices* (pp. 145–167). London: Longman.

Horowitz, D. (1986a). What professors actually require: Academic tasks for the ESL classroom. *TESOL Quarterly, 20*(4), 445–462.

Horowitz, D. (1986b). Process, not product: Less than meets the eye. *TESOL Quarterly, 20*/1, 141-144.

Horowitz, D. (1991). ESL writing assessment: Contradictions and resolutions. In L. Hamp-Lyons (Ed.), *Assessing second language writing* (pp. 71–86). Norwood, NJ: Ablex.

Johns, A. (1981). Necessary English: A faculty survey. *TESOL Quarterly, 15*(1), 51–57.
Johns, A. (1991). Faculty assessment of ESL student literacy skills: Implications for writing assessment. In L. Hamp-Lyons (Ed.), *Assessing second language writing* (pp. 167–180). Norwood, NJ: Ablex.
Johns, A. (1997). *Text, role, and context: Developing academic literacies*. Cambridge: Cambridge University Press.
Swales, J. (1990). *Genre analysis*. Cambridge: Cambridge University Press.

Enumerative Nouns and Text Cohesion

Francis, G. (1994). Labelling discourse: An aspect of nominal-group cohesion. In M. Coulthard (Ed.), *Advances in written text analysis* (pp. 83–101). New York: Routledge.
Halliday, M. A. K., & Hasan, R. (1976). *Cohesion in English.* London: Longman.
Tadros, A. (1994). Predictive categories in expository text. In M. Coulthard (Ed.), *Advances in written text analysis* (pp. 69–82). New York: Routledge.

Impersonal and Demonstrative Pronouns

Diessel, H. (1999). *Demonstratives: Form, function, and grammaticalization*. Amsterdam: John Benjamins.
Haspelmath, M. (1997). *Indefinite pronouns*. Oxford: Oxford University Press.
McCarthy, M. (1994). It, this, and that. In M. Coulthard (Ed.), *Advances in written text analysis* (pp. 266–275). New York: Routledge.

7

Teaching Verb Tenses and Voice in Text Cohesion

OVERVIEW

- Tenses and aspects
- Tense and time
- The simple present tense
- The past tense
- The future tense
- Aspect
- Problems with the uses of tenses and aspects
- Active and Passive Voice in Academic Writing

Much earlier research has demonstrated that, in general, English tenses are often difficult for L2 learners to use appropriately (Guiora, 1983; Hinkel, 1992, 1997a; Riddle, 1986; Sharwood Smith & Rutherford, 1988). However, errors in the uses of tenses are considered to be among the most egregious problems in the quality of academic L2 text (Horowitz, 1986a; Johns, 1981; Ostler, 1980; Reid, 1993; Santos, 1988; Vann et al., 1984, 1991; Vaughan, 1991).

TENSES AND ASPECTS

Although ESL grammar textbooks describe around 12 tenses or more (e.g., the present progressive, the present perfect, or the present perfect progressive), the simplest way to teach tenses is to start by separating tenses and aspects (see also chap. 4). Thus, there are three tenses in English: the past, the present, and the future. In addition, there are two aspects: the progressive and the perfect. The tenses and aspects can combine to create a nice stew that can include such ingredients as the past perfect or present perfect progressive.

Fortunately, in effect, only a few combinations of tenses and aspects are used in academic writing (as opposed to, for example, conversational discourse or ESL grammar classes), and for academic writers the task of using tenses and aspects correctly is greatly simplified. For example, Biber's (1988) study of various spoken, written, and published genre shows that past-tense constructions are relatively infrequent in academic prose compared with, for instance, press reportage, personal letters, or face-to-face conversations.

TENSE AND TIME

In all human languages, time (but not necessarily tense) is divided into three large categories: now (the present), before now (the past), and after now (the future).

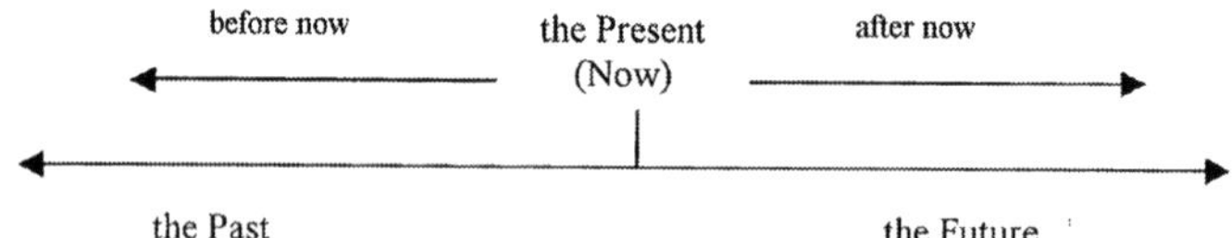

In English, as in other languages, the tense marks the time and connects an action or event to a particular time. For example,

- *Scientists sought knowledge*—the past tense (*sought*) marks a finished action that took place before now.
- *Scientists seek knowledge*—the present tense (*seek*) refers to a general action that took place in the past, takes place in the present, and is likely to continue into the future.
- *Scientists will seek knowledge*—the future tense (*will*) marks an action that did not take place in the past, does not take place in the present, but is certain to take place in the future (the time forward from now).

According to Biber et al. (1999), a vast majority of all verb phrases—over 85%—are employed with tenses. In academic writing, the usage of the present tense is over threefold that of the past tense. Phrases with modal verbs, and hence no overt tense markers, represent 10% to 15% of all verb phrases (see chap. 12 for a detailed discussion). Thus, in light of the fact that the present tense is greatly prevalent in academic writing, the following discussion focuses primarily on its uses and functions and, to a smaller extent, on those associated with the past tense and verb aspects.

THE SIMPLE PRESENT-TENSE USES AND FUNCTIONS

Forms and Meanings

The simple present tense refers to actions and events that are general (i.e., they have no specific [or definite] time to which they refer). In academic writing, present-tense verbs refer to states or habitual (and repeated) activities (e.g., *be*-verbs, linking verbs [*become, seem, appear*], *consist, believe, know;* Quirk et al., 1985).

> The simple present tense refers to actions/events that take place generally in the present, but not necessary at the present moment or time.

For example, in (1), the action *study* refers to general time (i.e., it took place in the past, takes place in the present, and is likely to continue to take place in the future).

1. *Sociologists study social experiences in each stage of life.*

However, the present-tense action *study* may not necessarily take place at this moment if none of the sociologists is at work, at this moment, studying social experiences. In fact, the simple present tense cannot be used to refer to actions and events that take place at this very moment (or at any specific moment).

Simple present-tense verbs are not marked for plural and first-person singular subjects (e.g., *I, we, you, they study*), but are marked by *-s* or *-es* for third-person singular subjects (e.g., *he, she, it studies*).

Functions and Uses

In general terms, in academic writing the present tense is strongly associated with verbs that refer to mental and logical states, whereas the past tense denotes specific actions and events in the past time (Biber et al., 1999). For the purposes of written academic discourse outside of references to specific past-time events, such as those in business case studies or specific events, the present tense provides a relatively safe venue because in academic text the uses of the simple present tense are highly conventionalized (Swales, 1990a) and, hence, may be appropriate in various contexts.

One of the contexts where the past tense can be appropriate—but entirely optional—is citations of earlier research, as in *Smith (2000) found/investigated/reported....* Even in these constructions, the present tense can be used appropriately: *Johnson (1999) finds/investigates/reports....* According to Swales and Feak (1994), the uses of "citational" present are very common in the academic genre. They pointed out that in general, citing, reviewing, or referring to sources allows writers options in their choice of tenses.

For example, the use of the present tense is appropriate in citations and paraphrases of information, as well as a presentation of general facts, opinions, or research findings. For example,

Bobson (2001) points to the recent increases in employment rates among high school students.

Jane Leserman (1981) also examines the socialization processes in medical school.

It is difficult to estimate the number of youngsters involved in home schooling.

Because few occupations are performed in social isolation, work links individuals to others with whom they interact both on and off the job. (Citations from Thompson & Hickey, 2002, p. 444)

As mentioned, with the exception of references to specific actions and events that occurred in the past, for L2 writers the task of constructing academic text can be greatly simplified when large portions of their assignments and papers (if not entire assignments and papers) can be written in the simple present tense.

> L2 writers should be encouraged to use the present simple tense whenever possible in their writing provided that they are also taught how to establish subject–verb agreement and can do so correctly in most occurrences of the simple present.

For example, the excerpt in (1) is extracted from a student's paper on gender and reasoning skills:

(1) Women are a minority in school science classes and in the scientific society in the U.S., which are well-known phenomena. Research on gender and science shows us that gender differences in science education come from achievement, attitude, and motivation, or science course selection. The purpose of the study by Michael Shemesh, a professor in the Department of Education, is to investigate gender-related differences between gender-related reasoning skills and learning interests during the early adolescence stage. His study hopes that the result can help figure out explanations to the differences that exist in school courses participation.

In this research, a videotaped group test is used to measure students development. This test contains 12 videotaped simple experiments and demonstrations. At the end of each demonstration, students answer questions and justify their solutions. Students with correct answers receive two points. Then students are categorized by their points into concrete, transitional, or formal reasoners.

Students also have to write down two subject fields which they are most interested in....

In excerpt (1), which begins with general introductions and then proceeds to discuss a specific experiment, the writer employs the simple present tense throughout. McCarthy and Carter (1994) referred to what they called "the historical present" (p. 100), often considered to be useful and appropriate in introductions and citations from sources to indicate the "now-relevance" (p. 102) of research and information. The flexible and commonplace employment of the present tense in excerpt (1) and other types of academic texts allows L2 writers to avoid pitfalls and complications associated with the uses of other more complex English tenses.

> With the exception of references to time-specific events such as case studies, historical analyses, or biographical sketches, the flexibility and conventionality of the simple present tense in academic writing can help L2 writers simplify tense uses in their writing. Therefore, they should be encouraged to maintain the simple present tense as much as possible in their writing.

Corpus analyses have also identified important clusters of verbs that tend to occur predominantly in the simple present tense. Their numbers are small, and these verbs can simply be learned.

Verbs Predominantly Used in the Present Tense

care	doubt	imply	matter	mind	tend
differ	fancy	know	mean	suppose	want

> An Important Caveat: In academic writing, a lack of grammatically correct subject–verb agreement is considered to be a serious error. For L2 writers, dealing with the subject–verb agreement issue is made more complex because many NNS learners have trouble identifying the head subject noun in a subject noun phrase (see chap. 3 for techniques to teach L2 writers how to locate the head subject noun).

THE PAST-TENSE USES AND FUNCTIONS

In the teaching of ESL grammar, much attention is usually devoted to the formation and meanings of the past tense. However, in academic writing, past-tense verbs represent less than 18% of all verbs that have tense (Biber et al., 1999), and most verbs used in the past tense denote specific, limited-time activities. In fact the English past tense is sometimes called the *definite past* employed largely in "historical or biographical statements which have specific people, places, or objects as their topics" (Quirk et al., 1985, p. 184).

The past forms of regular verbs take the marker *-ed* or the past forms of irregular verbs (e.g., *sang, wrote*), with complete lists found in practically every ESL grammar book or dictionary (for this reason the form of past-tense verb is not examined in any detail here).

Functions and Uses

Verbs used in the past tense refer to actions, events, or states that took place or existed in the past and no longer continue in the present. The meaning of the past tense in reference to specific past-time activities can be somewhat distinct from those in constructions with "state past" (Quirk et al., 1985, p. 186), as Sentences (2) and (3) show. For example,

> 2. *In early American history, the family assumed responsibility for educating its children.*

> The past tense necessarily marks an action or a state for the past time and no longer continuing at the present time. Specifically, the past tense refers to activities and states that are not connected to the present (i.e., the historical past).

In this context, it is important to note the role of time adverbs that can greatly assist in identifying the time of the action or event. Sentence (2) is marked by the past time adverb phrase *in early American history*. However, even if the adverb phrase is omitted, the action remains in the past time—for example,

> 3. *The family assumed responsibility for educating its children.*

The meaning of the past-tense use with the verb *assumed* implies that the action was performed or a state existed in the past and was finished in the past.

> The past tense usually refers to specific and finished past time actions, events, and states.

An important point about past-tense uses is that in academic writing they necessarily require a past time adverb or adverbial phrase/clause (i.e., some type of a past time marker that warrants the employment of the past tense). The past time marker does not apply only to the sentence in which it is used, but can extend to an entire text excerpt until a new time marker is used to flag that the time and the tense can be switched (Hinkel, 2002c). For example,

> 4. *In the summer of 1994, the Gatorade Company introduced Gatobar into test markets. The fruit flavored energy bar was the company's first effort to extent its name beyond its sports drink. Gatobar with only 110 calories was targeted toward active people who sought a low-fat bar for snacking. Gatorade also introduced another product—Sunbolt—which was a caffeinated drink. At present, the company works to find new venues for its products.* (Adapted from Zikmund et al., 1995)

In excerpt (4), the past time adverb phrase *In the summer of 1994* marks the beginning of the past-tense use that continues throughout the text until the present time adverb is encountered: *At present*. The present time adverb marks the beginning of the present-tense use and shifts the entire text to the general present.

> In academic writing, most contextual uses of the past tense are flagged by past time adverbs and apply to the entire context until the time adverb switches the verb tense to the present.

The consistent usage of a tense in a context framed by adverbial phrases or other types of time switch markers is important to establish textual cohesion in the flow of discourse and information. Inconsistent uses of tenses in students' writing is discussed in the section Typical Problems with Tenses later in this chapter.

Case Studies and Specific Past Events

In academic writing, the past tense can be useful in specific and limited contexts, such as business or environmental case studies, specific experiments in, for instance, psychology or sociology, or examples of specific past-time events employed to provide rhetorical support in argumentation ("the event past"; Quirk et al., 1985, p. 186). For example, the text in (5) refers to a specific event that took place in 1994.

> 5. *In 1994, Hilton Hotels Corp. announced plans for a reorganization of its internal operations, including the relocation of some functions of Las Vegas. The new corporate organization includes five key lines of responsibility....* (Zikmund et al., 1995, p. 184)

In contextual examples and descriptions of past time events or states, the uses of the past tense are framed by means of adverbs or adverbial prepositional phrases that specifically refer switch the time to the past—*in 1994*. Within the past time context, the discourse is continued in the past tense until it is switched to the present tense by means of another marker—*The new corporate organization*.

In another example in (6), the switch marker is not an adverbial phrase of time, but a past time event flagged by the past-tense verb *developed*:

> 6. *3M has a strong focus on technology. It developed Post-It note pads and many other unique products. Being a leader in innovation is one of 3M's primary objectives.* (Zikmund et al., 1995, p. 164)

In this excerpt, the discourse switches from a general present statement to a specific past time event (the development of Post-It note pads), which supports the claim that 3M has a technology focus, reverts to a present-tense general statement *Being a leader ... is....*

The switch time markers can take many forms, such as adverbs and phrases (e.g., *now/then, today/at that time, currently/in the past, in today's society/in the early days*) as well as adjectives (e.g., *new/old, recent/past, current/previous/early*) or even other verbs with a different tense.

However, academic texts required of students in some disciplines, such as history and philosophy, seem to be somewhat more prone to the uses of the past tense than those in the natural sciences, political science, psychology, sociology, or economics.

Like the list of verbs employed predominantly in the present tense, the list of specific verbs that occur mostly in the past tense is also very limited.

Verbs Predominantly Used in the Past Tense

bend	lean	remark	set off	turn away
bow	light	reply	shake	wrap

(Adapted from Biber et al., 1999)

THE FUTURE-TENSE FUNCTIONS AND USES

The future tense marks the future time that follows *now*. The future tense is marked by auxiliary verbs *will* or *going to* + the base (infinitive) form of the main verb (see a brief discussion in the Infinitive section of this chapter; e.g., *will sell, will determine*). Another common means of marking the future is the employment of the present tense in conjunction with future time adverbials (e.g., tomorrow, next month, in 2015). The usage of the present simple tense to refer to future activities is particularly prevalent with subordinate clauses of time and condition marked by such conjunctions as *if, whether, when, before* (e.g., *The interest rates will rise* ***when*** *the Federal Reserve Board approves the new fiscal policy*).

When teaching the uses of the future tense, it is important to emphasize at the outset that future-tense markers are never used in clauses of time and condition and constructions such as **when the Federal Reserve will increase the prime rate* result in ungrammatical and obviously non-native sentences (see chap. 10 for further and more emphatic discussion).

The general function of the future tense is to refer to future actions, events, or states. However, the meaning of the future tense expressed either by means of the auxiliary verb *will* or the simple present tense represents "a marked future of unusual definiteness, attributing to the future the degree of certainty" usually associated with the present and the past (Quirk et al.,

1985, p. 215). In academic writing, such definitive references to future activities or states are extremely rare because the writer is usually expected to project "modesty and proper caution," as well as anticipate negative reactions to the "claims being advanced" (Swales, 1990a, p. 175). On the other hand, the future-tense marking by means of *going to* has not been widely accepted in formal written prose.

Thus, an important outcome of various analyses of written academic corpora is that the future tense marked by any type of future verb forms, such as *will, going to*, or the simple present tense, is often considered to be inappropriately definite and/or conversational and colloquial. Instead modal verbs such as *may, can*, or *could* represent the hedging devices of choice to project an appropriate amount of hesitation and cautious claim making (see chap. 12 on Hedges).

Studies of L2 writing and text have noted that NNS academic prose often creates an impression of a high degree of certainty (Hyland & Milton, 1997). Among other textual features that convey an exaggerated degree of definiteness is the fact that L2 writing employs significantly more markers of the future tense than NS college-level writing does. For example, the differences in the degree of certainty and definiteness expressed by means of the future marker *will* and the modal verbs *may* and *can* is readily apparent in the following contrasting sentences:

a.) *When goals are hard to define, managers <u>may</u> tell employees to do their best.*

b.) *When goals are hard to define, managers <u>can</u> tell employees to do their best.*

c.) *When goals are hard to define, managers <u>will</u> tell employees to do their best.*

Sentence (c) clearly expresses definitively what the manager will say as opposed to noting a possibility in (a) or an ability in (b).

> Due to definiteness and certainty constraints associated with the usage of the future tense, it is hardly ever used in academic writing, and L2 academic writers should be encouraged to employ modal verbs such as *may, can*, and *could* instead.

In teaching it is helpful to present excerpts from student texts and ask students to analyze them to determine which displays a higher degree of definiteness and certainty in the future outcomes of events. Excerpt (a) is extracted from a student's paper on the role of the government in a market economy.

a) In countries like Costa Rica, political decisions are based on the economic model. Under this model, the market competition <u>will</u> increase, and the market economy <u>will</u> solve most problems in an efficient way without any interruption of the government.

When markets don't work well, the government will try to fix them, but they will fail because the market cannot be fixed by the government. The market will solve its own problems, and it will benefit the people and create a stable economy. In turn, the stable economy will lead the country to political stability, and the political order will give the people peace for a long time.

In excerpt (a), the uses of the future tense project a high degree of definiteness in the success of the implementation of a market economy without government interference. In this text, the writer appears to be certain about the outcomes of the market policies, which in reality may not be nearly as certain. The same excerpt can be slightly reworded, as in (b), where the definite future tense is avoided and replaced by modal verbs with less definite meanings, as is the convention in academic writing (Swales, 1990).

b) In countries like Costa Rica, political decisions are based on the economic model. Under this model, the market competition may increase, and the market economy can solve most problems in an efficient way without any interruption of the government. When markets don't work well, the government may try to fix them, but they may/are likely to fail because the market cannot be fixed by the government. The market may/can solve its own problems, and it may/is likely to benefit the people and create a stable economy. In turn, the stable economy can lead the country to political stability, and the political order may give the people peace for a long time.

The text in (b) rephrases the same text without the uses of the future tense; in combination, the employment of modal verbs *can* and *may*, as well as the hedge *to be likely to*, help make the text pivot on possibility rather than certainty.

(For "future in the past" constructions—e.g., *Sam Walton predicted that Wal-Mart would turn into the largest discount chain in the U.S.*—see chap. 10, Subordinate Clauses.)

ASPECT

The time of an activity or a state is denoted by means of a tense. On the other hand, the verb aspect marks actions and events for progression or continuity during a particular marked period of time (the progressive aspect) or occurrence during the time period leading up to or prior to another specific time marker, activity, or event (the perfect aspect). Thus, the activity or state expressed by the verb can be marked for tense (and time) and aspect (progressive and/or perfect) to denote the progression of an activity during a period of time, which is always overtly or implicitly marked or up to a particular specific time/event. For example,

- *Television socializes its viewers to become mass consumers*—the (general) present tense, zero aspect (i.e., neither progression nor completion of the activity is marked).

- *Television is socializing its viewers*—the simple present tense (marked by the present tense of the auxiliary verb *is*) combined with the progressive aspect to refer to the progression of the activity at the present moment
- *Television has socialized its viewers*—the present tense (marked by the present of the auxiliary verb *has*) combined with the perfect aspect to refer to the activity up to (or relevant to) the present moment
- *Television socialized its viewers*—the past tense, zero aspect
- *Television was socializing its viewers ... in 1990 and 1991*—the past tense (marked by the past tense of the auxiliary *was*) combined with the progressive aspect to refer to the progression of the activity during a marked period, *1990 and 1991*
- *Television had socialized its viewers ... prior to 1990*—the past tense (marked by the past of the auxiliary *had*) combined with the perfect aspect to mark the completion of the activity up to the time marker, *1990*

(For a detailed discussion of tense and aspect auxiliaries in English, see chap. 4.)

Although a great deal of time and effort is expended on teaching students how to use English tenses and aspects correctly, the point of fact is that this instruction may not be particularly necessarily for the purposes of academic writing. According to Biber's, et al. (1999) analysis, across various types of language use (e.g., news reportage or academic writing), about 90% of the most common verb phrases have zero aspect.

In academic prose specifically, only a small fraction (around 8%) of all verb phrases is used with the perfect aspect, and the progressive aspect is employed with even fewer verbs. In addition, the combination of the perfect and the progressive aspects in all tenses (e.g., *have/had been writing*) is encountered so rarely that Biber's et al. (1999) analysis specifies its proportion at approximately 0.5% of all verbal tense and aspect markers.

The teaching of perfect progressive verb forms and their uses may not be worth the time in L2 academic writing instruction. Furthermore, devoting class time, work, and effort to the teaching of the forms and meanings associated with the uses of the progressive aspect in general can also take a low priority.

In academic writing, a large majority of verb phrases with the progressive and perfect aspects are used in the present tense, but not in the past or future. To this end, instruction in the present perfect may be more worthwhile than teaching the past or future perfect.

The Progressive Aspect

Progressive verb phrases consist of at least two elements: the auxiliary verb *be* and the main verb + *-ing*. The tense of the verb phrase is reflected in the form of the auxiliary verb (e.g., *is/are* [present] and *was/were* [past]). The usage of the progressive aspect is predominately in conversational and informal registers and can be encountered in personal and/or expressive narratives (Chafe, 1994).

The progressive aspect is used to refer to action and events that are in progress during a particular specified period of time or at the time of another specific action and event. When the progressive aspect is combined with the present tense, the activity takes place at the present moment, and this meaning is implicit. For example,

- *The students are conducting an experiment* [at the present moment]
- *The water was boiling steadily from 1:05 to 1:10* [past progressive; time duration/period specified]
- *The technician was mixing the solvents when the chemical reaction took place* [past progressive; the time of another event overtly specified]

As mentioned, progressive tenses rarely occur in academic prose, and the number of verbs that are useful in the teaching of L2 academic writing is actually quite small.

Verbs That Tend to Occur in Progressive Tenses

bring	carry	hold	lock	move	stand	wait
buy	do	listen	make	say	take	watch

A large class of stative and other types of nonprogressive verbs, however, is practically never used with the progressive aspect in any tense. Broadly defined, progressive verbs can refer to actions and events that, by virtue of their meaning, can take place in progression. Conversely, the meanings of nonprogressive verbs fall into three groups (Quirk et al., 1985):

1. states rather than actions (e.g., *believe, know, understand, possess*)
2. actions that are momentary (and, therefore, cannot have progression [e.g., *doubt, note, notice, realize*])[1]

[1]Some verbs that denote momentary actions (e.g., *blink, bounce, explode*) are used in the progressive aspect to refer to a succession of momentary actions.

3. perceptions that are involuntary (i.e., the doer of the action [the grammatical subject] has little control of the action; e.g., *consist [of], contain, hear, resemble, perceive*)

In teaching, whenever possible, it is helpful to contrast the nonprogressive uses of some verbs in formal prose with progressive uses of proximate activity verbs. For example,

know—learn	**is/was knowing—is/was learning*
see—look—watch—observe	**is/was seeing*[2]*—is/was looking—watching—observing*
hear—listen	**is/was hearing—is/was listening*
contain—place/put (into)	**is/was containing—is/was placing*

The complex meanings of nonprogressive verbs, such as stative, may make them difficult for L2 writers to use appropriately. However, the common few items can be simply learned.

Common Non-progressive Verbs

agree	belong	dislike	have	matter	promise	understand
appear	concern	dissolve	hear	mean	realize	weigh
appreciate	conclude	doubt	include	need	recognize	
associate	consist (of)	equal	initiate	owe	resemble	
attain	contain	exist	interest	own	see	
attribute	correlate	fear	invent	perceive	seem	
base	cost	find	know	possess	sound	
believe	desire	guarantee	like	prefer	surprise	

Nonprogressive verbs are important for L2 writers to know because these items can be used only in simple tenses (the simple present or simple past).

> On the whole, progressive tenses are rare in academic prose. However, they are common in conversations and spoken discourse. For this reason, the usage of progressive verbs may impart a somewhat conversational flavor to academic writing. In formal academic writing, simple present (and occasionally simple past) tenses can be much more effective and easier for students to use.

[2]In such constructions as *Mary is seeing John* or *John is seeing a new doctor, see* has the meanings of *date* or *visit*, both of which can take the progressive tense. Also in conversational register, it is possible to say, *I am hearing you*. Such structures, however, may be inappropriate in most contexts.

Research has demonstrated that the meanings of aspects create an additional level of complexity for NNSs (Hinkel, 1992; Sharwood Smith & Rutherford, 1988). In teaching L2 writers to use tenses appropriately, it seems that the simpler is indeed the better.

The Perfect Aspect

As mentioned, the perfect aspect combines with tenses to create for a complex verb phrase forms and meanings, e.g. the present perfect, *has developed*, or the past perfect, *had come*. The most common verbs that are encountered in the **present perfect** in academic writing are (in declining order):

has/have	+	*been*	the rate of 0.1%
		shown	the rate of 0.01%
		had, made, seen, become	the rate of 0.004% each

(All rates here and below computed based on the data cited in Biber et al., 1999)

In addition to the relatively infrequent uses of the present perfect, the **past perfect** verb phrases are hardly ever found in academic writing, and practically all uses entail *be*-copula verb that occur with frequency rates of 0.01% per million words (Biber et al., 1999; e.g., *Prior to the 1980s, public service announcements had been aimed at adults, informing them of possible environmental or military dangers*). In formal academic writing, however, the past perfect verb phrases tend to occur in the adjective clauses of complex sentences (see chap. 10 for more information).

Verbs Rarely Used in Perfect Tenses

accomodate	comprise	depend	illustrate	quit	smell
afford	connect	differ	induce	reflect	suppose
aim	consist	distinguish	inhibit	regulate	want
await	constitute	doubt	lean	relate	
base	contain	ensure	matter	remember	
believe	correspond	entitle	mind	represent	
boil	cost	excuse	need	require	
compete	denote	glance	protect	resemble	

(Adapted from Biber et al., 1999)

> On the whole, the teaching of verb tenses and aspects in L2 academic writing needs to focus first on the meanings and uses of the simple present. In instruction the meanings and uses of the simple past represent the next order of priority, followed possibly by the present perfect tense. Based on the frequencies of occurrences in formal academic writing, the teaching of other verb tenses and aspects may be of reduced value compared with the top three tenses.

TYPICAL PROBLEMS WITH THE USES OF TENSES AND ASPECTS

Inconsistent Contextual Uses of Tenses

In written text in English, the tense system provides an important means of textual cohesion (Halliday & Hasan, 1976; Matthiessen, 1996; see also chap. 11). Inconsistent uses of tenses (aka "jumping" tenses) represent highly common types of errors in L2 academic writing. Fortunately, it is relatively easy to teach students to avoid and correct them.

> The uses of tenses in academic writing are highly conventionalized, and their uses do not necessarily reflect objective reality. For this reason the conventional uses of the "academic" present tense often appear untruthful and incorrect to L2 writers.

In L2 academic writing, tenses are often employed inconsistently because of NNS students' logical analyses of the organization of events along the time continuum.

> Errors with inconsistent uses of tenses are so prevalent in L2 students' academic writing that in the long run it may be helpful and effective to address them in classroom teaching to provide L2 writers a means of correcting or preventing such errors in their own writing.

Some of the most common and logical reasons for writers' errors can include the following:

- Past-tense verbs may be used refer to activities that took place prior to those denoted by present-tense verbs (e.g., **last quarter, the student <u>studied</u> hard, and he <u>gets</u> good grades*). Thus, in those cases when L2 writers feel the need to highlight the sequence of activities and mark an action that precedes another, the past tense seems to be a logical choice to indicate to the reader that one action took place before another.

- To correct these types of errors, a past time adverbial marker needs to be inserted to reframe the context for the present time and tense (e.g., *Last quarter, student studied hard, and* ***now*** *he gets good grades*).

- In other occurrences of mixed present and past tenses, one verb may refer to an activity that takes place in the general present, but another verb denotes a past-tense activity (e.g., **When the market moves up and down every day, the fund manager issued a new policy*). In this sentence, both tenses—present and past—are used logically: *The market moves every day* refers to an action that is generally true, whereas the fund manager took a onetime, past-tense action to issue a new policy. In this case, the inconsistent use of tenses can be corrected in two ways:
  (1) by inserting an adverbial or other marker (such as an adjective) to reframe the context for a different tense (and time) as discussed earlier, or
  (2) by changing the past tense to the general present tense to match the other verb(s) (e.g., *When the market moves up and down every day, the fund manager issues a new policy*).

The problem with merely changing the tense of the verb, as in (2), is this correction may appear factually untruthful to the writer—if it is known that the past time action of the manager's issuing a new policy is a factual past time event.

> It is important to emphasize that the uses of the general present tense are highly conventionalized in academic writing in English and that the verb tenses must meet the requirements of the conventions even when they may appear to be somewhat factually incorrect.

The following extended example demonstrates various inconsistent uses of tenses in an excerpt from a student's paper on efficiency in public administration:

> *Every country in the world has* [simple present] *many problems such as pollution, unemployment, crime, war, and so on. And in most modern countries, the government takes* [simple present] *a role to solve these problems. It is* [simple present] *due to the fact that any individual or organization can't afford* [simple present] *to manage costs to do this. As society becomes* [simple present] *more complicated, the government expanded* [simple past] *its role dramatically.*

> *The fundamental services, which we use* [simple present] *every day such as water, gas, electricity, public transportation were produced* [simple past] *by individual vendors. But there was* [simple past] *a critical problem with these individual suppliers, and in industrial societies the government provides* [simple past] *these services. It is*

[simple present] *a question whether the government really provides* [simple present] *these services as efficiently as possible. Actually, it was* [simple past] *the fundamental question in public administration, since public administration began* [simple past] *as an independent discipline.*

As one solution to this problem, Luther Gulick presents [simple present] *some principles of public administration to improve efficiency. According to his suggestion, a higher level of efficiency can be achieved* [simple present] *by specialization of tasks. Gulick's principles also mentioned* [simple past] *how to improve efficiency in public administration, such as unity of command, process, and clients. These principles are called* [simple present] *the principles of efficiency, and they became* [simple past] *the focus of research. Many scholars present* [simple present] *new principles every day, when public demanded* [simple past] *more public services and goods from the government.*

(Extracted from a student paper on efficiency in public administration.)

Throughout the text, the present-tense verbs are mixed with those in the past tense. Most of the inconsistent uses of tenses can be corrected (or prevented) by employing the types of corrections discussed earlier. For example,

- *As society becomes* [simple present] *more complicated, the government expanded* [simple past] Ø [***expands***—simple present] *its role dramatically.*
- ***In the past/In the 1920s/In the early days****, the fundamental services, which we use* [simple present] *every day such as water, gas, electricity, public transportation were produced* [simple past] *by individual vendors.*
- *But* ***in those days/at that time/during that period****, there was* [simple past] *a critical problem with these individual suppliers, and in* ***today's/current/modern*** *industrial societies the government provides* [simple present] *these services.*
- ***Today/These days/Currently*** *it is* [simple present] *a question whether the government really provides* [simple present] *these services as efficiently as possible.*
- *Actually, it was* [simple past] *the* ***initial/early/original/old*** *fundamental question in public administration, since* ***the time/the beginning (when)*** *public administration began* [simple past] *as an independent discipline.*

Exercises for correcting inconsistent tense errors in actual student writing can be highly productive and useful for practice with conventionalized uses of tense in academic written discourse in English.

Progressive Aspects with Nonprogressive Verbs

A common type of errors with the usage of progressive tenses occurs when L2 writers employ nonprogressive verbs. For example,

This essay is concerning the studies that have shown a sharp decline in the number of recycling plants in the New York area and other U.S. cities. Those people who listen

to the news are hearing about the high cost of recycling that makes it too expensive for the industry to continue collecting metal and paper. The news quote recycling plant owners and operators who are depending on recycling for their jobs and who are complaining that there is simply not enough material to recycle for them to earn a living and that operating too many plants is costing too much. So, the plant owners propose to close down some of their collection centers and reduce recycling. However, the plant owners and news media are dealing with this problem totally incorrectly. They need to educate the public to recycle more instead of closing down plants that will lead to the public recycling less. (Extracted from a student paper on how to educate the public on recycling.)

The progressive tenses are exceptionally rare with verbs such as *concern*, *hear*, *depend*, and *cost*. Thus, their use of nonprogressive verbs in progressive tenses needs to be avoided, and simple tenses can be used instead. However, in real contexts the issue may seem to be more complex than just simply changing the aspect of the nonprogressive verbs because other verbs, such as *complain* and *deal* found in the same context, are perfectly acceptable in the progressive form: *are complaining* and *are dealing*.

Two points are important to remember:

- Progressive verbs seldom occur in academic writing.
- A number of important academic verbs are not used in the progressive aspect, and these verbs need to be learned.

Thus, in academic writing, it may be best to avoid progressive tenses.

THE ACTIVE VOICE AND THE PASSIVE VOICE IN ACADEMIC WRITING

The form and grammatical derivation of passive constructions can be found in all ESL grammar books. For example:

The student bought the book.	→	*The book was bought by the student.*
John helped the boy.	→	*The boy was helped by John*

Because passive derivations are highly regular in their form, L2 learners generally quickly figure out how to convert active constructions into passive ones. Then when it comes to fill in the blank exercises on sentence converting, learners fill in all the blanks, and their learning of how to use the passive voice is thus completed.

Unfortunately, as is often the case with other English structures, the uses of passives in real academic writing are far more complex than doing exercises in an ESL grammar textbook or filling in the blanks.

The Uses and Functions of Passives in Academic Writing

The uses of the passive voice are extraordinarily common in academic writing, and to a large extent the prevalence of passive voice is determined by academic discourse conventions (Biber, 1988; Myers, 1989; Poole, 1991; Swales, 1990a). The use of passive voice in formal writing has a number of important textual functions. One of these is to project an **academic indirectness, detachment, and objectivity** in what Johns (1997) called "the author-evacuated prose" considered to be requisite in Western scientific tradition, and particularly so in natural sciences and engineering. However, in reaction to the conventionalized use of passive in rigidly structured academic discourse in the United States, much writing instruction and many composition texts discourage the use of the passive voice except on rare occasions (Hacker, 1994, 2000; Kennedy et al., 2002; Lunsford & Connors, 1997; Lunsford & Ruszkiewicz, 2001).

In addition to creating an impression of detachment and objectivity, a more sophisticated function of the passive voice is to develop cohesive text by organizing information in sentences along the known/old-to-new/important pattern in sentences. For example:

> *The population problem is most pronounced in Third World nations. The population of the African continent exceeds 650 million.* (Adapted from Thompson & Hickey, 2002)

> *In the 1930s and 1940, live music was generally considered superior to recorded music. Early disk jockeys made a significant contribution to change the public opinion.*

> *The second strategy, known originally as the "spectacular," is today recognized by a more modest term, the "television special." At NBC, Weaver bought special programs, like Laurence Olivier's filmed version of Richard III.* (Adapted from Campbell et al., 2001)

In these examples, the passive voice constructions shift the new/important idea to the end of the sentence and thus help create lexical and semantic cohesive chain by connecting the end of the first sentence to the beginning to the next (see chap. 11 for more information on cohesion).

There are probably few constructions in writing and writing instruction that have been subject to as much debate and controversy as the use of passive voice. The opponents claim that active voice is more emphatic, vigorous, and clear than passive; that in active the doer of the action is placed in the sentence subject position; and that "active verbs are usually more effective because they are simpler and more direct" (Hacker, 2000, p. 241). All these evaluations are undoubtedly true. However, based on the corpus analyses of academic prose, it appears that in real academic writing discourse, outside of the teaching of composition, passive voice is ubiquitous and remains a prevalent feature of academic text in various disciplines (Biber, 1988; Hyland, 1998; Johns, 1997; Swales, 1990a).

A commonsense recommendation is provided in the writing guide specifically geared toward efficiency and clarity in writing (Williams, 2002, pp. 41 and 43; see also chap. 11 on cohesion).

> "The uses of the passive voice should not be avoided merely based on a general principle because they can be highly useful in many contexts. The important use of the passive is that it allows the sentence to focus on what is done rather than who does it and that it can be of great value in developing cohesive text, by means of shifting the most important and new information to the end of the sentence."
>
> To put it simply, if the passive works better than the active in a particular context and for a particular discourse purpose, then use it; if not, then don't.

The Contexts and Uses of the Active Versus the Passive Voice in English

Several studies of the uses of passive constructions in English have shown that the passive voice is very difficult for L2 learners to use appropriately because, generally speaking, many passive structures are lexicalized (Atkinson, 1991; Owen, 1993). That is, many passive constructions and specific contextual uses are idiomatic and cannot be structurally derived in some cases.

However, it may be practically impossible to avoid using the passive voice in academic writing: 25% of all sentence predicate verbs are employed in the passive (Biber et al., 1999). However, analyses of L2 academic texts has shown that compared with NS first-year university students, NNS writers even at advanced levels of proficiency do not use passive structures nearly as frequently (Hinkel, 2002a). (As a side note, it should be mentioned that *get*-passives, such as *get confused/finished/married*, are extremely rare and occur only in conversation, and even then they seem to be highly infrequent.)

For L2 writers, another important complication arises with regard to learning to use passive constructions in English. Passive-like structures exist in many languages, such as Spanish, Chinese, Japanese, Arabic, or Russian. However, also in many languages the doer of the action expressed by the verb must be a person or an animal (i.e., some type of living being that is actually enabled to perform the action; Hinkel, 2002d; Master, 1991). In such languages it would be correct to say, *The man writes well,* but incorrect to use a subject that is not capable of acting on its own (e.g., *The pencil writes well*). The problem with such structures is further compounded by the fact that instruments and abstract concepts as subjects (rather than alive beings) of active verbs are highly common in academic writing (e.g., *the chapter discusses/*

reviews/presents, the program/machine runs, the factory produces, the office develops, the process begins, the forecast compares).

> For L2 writers, a key issue with these constructions is to realize that in English it does not really matter whether the subject of the active verb is alive or not, or whether it has the capacity to perform the action expressed by the verb. Thus, all such structures and sentences are grammatical no matter whether the subject of the active verb actually and effectively performs the action.

In addition, a small number of verbs are never used in the passive voice and are always encountered in the active. These verbs need to be learned because verbs with similar meanings exist in other languages, in which they can be and often are used in the passive voice (e.g., Spanish). Hence, L2 writers need to be particularly careful when employing these verbs in their text.

Verbs That Are Always (or Almost Always) Used in the Active Voice[3]

appear*	**consist**	**happen**	**last**	**resemble**	stay
arrive	**come**	**fall**	**occur**	rest	wait
belong	**die**	**lack**	**remain**	**seem**	

*The verbs in bold are *always* used in the active voice.
(Adapted from Biber et al., 1999; Swales & Feak, 1994)

Transitive Verbs, Direct Objects, and Agents

In teaching it is important to emphasize that only transitive verbs (those that require direct objects) can be used in the passive voice (see chap. 3 for more information). The reason that only the structures with transitive verbs can be converted from active to passive is that only the direct object can be moved to make it the subject of the passive verb:

Managers considered [past tense] *the price* →

The price was [past tense] *considered (by managers)*

In this construction, the direct object "jumps" to the subject position, the verb tense stays the same, the main verb is used in the past participle form (e.g., *written, gone, shown, considered*), and the subject of the active verbs

[3]Linking verbs, such as *appear, become, remain,* and *seem,* cannot be used in passive voice because they are not (and cannot be) transitive.

moves to the back of the sentence and into the *by*-phrase. In passive constructions, the nouns and noun phrases in the *by*-phrase are called *agents* (and the entire phrase is called the *agentive phrase*).

> In English passive construction, all agentive phrases are optional. In fact some of them can be downright incorrect.

A quick check to see whether a verb can be used in passive is to place it in a structure with a direct object:

> *report* → *The book/article/xxx reports the finding*. If the verb can be used with a direct object, the verb can be converted into passive. The verb *report* can be used in passive: *The finding is reported (*by the book/article).*
>
> *hold* → *xxx holds the book* → passive constructions are possible → *The book is held (by xxx).*
>
> *appear* → **The book appeared the page* → passive constructions are not possible.
>
> *last* → *The rain lasted (two hours)* → passive constructions are not possible because *two hours* is adverbial of time and not a direct object (see chap. 3 for techniques to identify direct objects).

Analyses of written academic texts have demonstrated that *by*-phrases occur infrequently, and the presence of a *by*-phrase depends on whether it is needed for cohesion and the continuity of new information from one sentence to the next by means of cohesive chains (e.g., *Most consumer goods are sold by retailers. Many in the retail trade industry have a size standard of 3.5 million in average annual receipts*). In other contexts, however, the *by*-phrase is usually omitted.

In such contexts where the agent is unknown, unimportant to the discussion, or is easily understood from the context, the *by*-phrase needs to be omitted:

> (1) ?*The fuel injector was designed by us to show it at the Engineering Senior Fair.*
>
> (2) ?*We were told by someone that a company in Everett has a similar fuel injector.*
>
> (3) ?*When their original designed was developed by them, they had to re-do it because at first the injector did not work, but the one developed by us worked from the start.* (All examples are from a student assignment in engineering.)

In (1), the *by*-phrase can be understood from the context of a written group assignment; in (2), the writers did not know or did not care to mention the agent, and the sentence can easily do without the by-phrase. In (3), both *by*-phrases—the *by them* and *by us*—are unnecessary because the agent in each phrase can be understood from the context.

A vast majority of passive sentences in formal academic writing do not include the *by*-phrase.

In summary, L2 writers encounter a number of difficulties with appropriate uses of passive constructions in English. Some have to do with various complexities in the meanings and uses of passives and others with the influence of the first language grammar on the learners' uses of passive in English when it is learned as a second language. However, due to the prevalence of the passive voice in academic writing in English, L2 writers need to learn to employ passive constructions correctly.

Several important considerations must be taken into account in instruction on the passive voice in academic writing.

- The greatest difference between active and passive constructions is stylistic, and in English passives have no additional meanings compared with those of active structures.
- Many passive constructions in English are idiomatic, and these need to be learned.
- In English sentences, instruments and abstract concepts can be subject of active verbs even when the sentence subject does not actually perform the activity expressed by the verb. For this reason, for example, such structures as *the book fell, the door is sliding,* or *the newspaper arrives late every time* are perfectly grammatical.
- Only transitive verbs that require direct objects can be used in the passive voice.
- The *by*-phrase is always optional in English sentences, and it is rarely used in academic writing.

Working With Passive Constructions

In light of the many complexities associated with the contextual uses of the passive voice in English, one of the easier techniques that L2 writers can rely on with great effect is to select verbs that almost always occur in passive and learn and practice using them.

The Most Common Passive Verbs in Academic Writing (in declining order)

For all verbs: *be (is/are/was/were)* + the Past Participle Form of the Main Verb (as listed)

made	seen	found	considered
given	used	done	shown

(Lists of common academic passive verbs here and elsewhere are adopted from the research of Biber et al., 1999; Nation, 1990, 2001; Swales & Feak, 1994.)

These especially common passive verbs are usually familiar to L2 writers at intermediate and higher levels of proficiency simply because they are encountered in most academic reading and other types of textbooks. For this reason, the practice with common passives can be combined with other verb constructions, such as modal verbs or infinitive complements (see also chaps. 3 and 12; e.g., *can/may be found, is considered to be,* or *was shown to be;* see additional suggestions for teaching at the end of this chapter).

In addition to these highly common verbs, other important academic verbs include a large number of those noted in chapter 8. Some of these verbs are often accompanied by relatively fixed prepositions, which can be also learned and practiced in contexts.

Other Academic Verbs Predominantly Used in the Passive Voice

For all verbs: *be (is/are/was/were)* + the Past Participle Form of the Main Verb (as listed)

achieved	deemed	formed	measured
aligned (with)	defined	given	needed
applied	derived	grouped (with/by)	noted
approved	described	held	observed
asked	designed	identified	obtained
associated (with)	determined	illustrated	performed
attributed (to)	discussed	inclined	plotted
based (on)	distributed	intended	positioned
born	documented	introducted	prepared
brought	drawn	involved	presented
calculated	entitled (to)	kept	recognized
called	estimated	known	regarded
carried	examined	labeled	related (to)
chosen	expected	left	replaced
classified (as)	explained	limited (to)	reported
compared	expressed	linked (to/with)	represented
composed (of)	extracted	located (at/in)	required
coupled (with)	flattened	lost	said
situated	subjected (to)	transferred	viewed

stored	thought	treated
studied	told	understood

Typical Problems With Passives

Verb Forms. Many, many errors with passive constructions have to do with verb forms:

1. *_The articles on the sociology of crime was write/wrote by John Smith._
2. *_Psychology studies were conduct at Harvard University._

It is important to emphasize that the past participle form of the verb is required in passive constructions following *be*-verbs. Many L2 writers—even those who are highly advanced—do not attribute sufficient importance to the distinctions between the past-tense and past-participle forms of irregular verbs, and both types of forms need to be learned.

Other similar types of problems occur simply because even at the college level L2 writers have not learned the three basic forms of irregular verbs.

3. *_Cheaters are usually catched by their professors._

When such ugly constructions are encountered in academic assignments and term papers, they usually prove to be highly embarrassing regardless of whether L2 writers are actually embarrassed by them.

> Learning the forms of irregular verbs is one of the basic essentials in university-level studies, similar to learning the multiplication table to be able to do such basic math operations as counting the change due.

Intransitive Verbs in Passive Constructions. A very common type of error includes perfectly correct passive structures with verbs that can never be used in the passive:

4. *_This problem was happened in my country._
5. *_The change in climate was occurred in coastal areas._

As mentioned earlier, only transitive verbs (those that require direct objects) can be used in passive. Hence, L2 writers must learn the verbs that never occur in the passive (see the list earlier in this chapter).

Agentive (Who Does It) and Instrumental (by Means of) By-Phrases. These types of errors are encountered occasionally and may be worth mentioning only when necessary:

6. **The students are taught by the Silent Method.*

If this sentence is converted back from the passive to the active voice, the following structure results:

7. **The Silent Method teaches the students.*

As noted, in passive sentences agentive *by*-phrases are located at the end and include nouns and noun phrases that would be subjects of parallel active constructions (e.g., *The solution was mixed by the student* [passive]—*The student mixed the solution* [active]).

In this case, the test question can be used to identify the doer of the verb action: *Does the subject noun of the sentence perform/do the action expressed by the verb?* If the answer is no, then the passive cannot be used (e.g., *Teachers teach the students*). Thus, the sentence may need to be completely rewritten:

8. *Teachers taught the students by means of the Silent Method* [instrumental meaning]
9. *Students were taught by means of the Silent Method* [instrumental meaning]

> When working with passive sentences, it is important that L2 writers learn to identify the differences in meaning and function between the agentive meaning of the *by*-phrase [*the action was done by **whom**?/**who** did the action?*] and the instrumental meaning in the *by means of* phrase (see also chap. 11) [***how** was the action done?/**by what means** was the action done?*].

The agentive *by*-phrase refers directly to the doer of the action, and the sentence subject that did the action can be always reconstructed when the passive sentence is converted back to active, as in (6). On the other hand, instrumental *by means of* (prepositional) phrases can never be sentences subjects of any sentence (see chap. 3).

In general terms, the uses of tenses and aspects in English are complex, and tense-related errors are considered to be one of the most grievous in L2 writing. However, written academic discourse and text are relatively rigid and conventionalized; from this perspective, L2 writers do not need to become excellent users of the entire range of tenses in English, but only some of them. A great proportion of contextualized verb phrases in academic prose employs the simple present tense, and it is probably one of the simpler tenses in English in terms of its attendant verb forms and contextual application. The simple past tense is also not particularly complicated to use. By consistently maintaining these two tenses in appropriate and overtly marked contexts, L2 writers may be able to construct a large variety of reasonably accurate context at least in terms of tenses. However, the contextualized uses of the active and passive voices present a number of problems for L2 writers, who need to become proficient with passive verb forms and meanings. Although the form of passive verbs can become easier to employ with some practice, the meanings and functions of the passive voice in sentences and broader contexts require a great deal of work from students and attention, effort, and knowledge from teachers.

CHAPTER SUMMARY

English tenses are often difficult for students to understand and use appropriately. The simplest way to teach tenses is to start by separating tenses and aspects. There are three tenses in English: the past, the present, and the future. There are two aspects: the progressive and the perfect.

In general terms, the **simple present** tense is very flexible, and its uses are highly conventionalized. For this reason the simple present can be employed even in contexts where, logically speaking, the past tense should be used (e.g., citations from and references to earlier publications). The **simple past** tense can be used in the specific contexts of historical and biographical descriptions of specific people, events, and/or places such as case studies. The **future** tense is rarely used in academic writing—more commonly, modal verbs (e.g., *can, may*) are used to express future expectation. Progressive tenses are rarely found in academic writing, and perfect tenses are employed only occasionally and mostly with a limited class of verbs.

The passive voice is common in academic writing, although some composition books advise against its use. Students need to be taught judicious use of the passive voice—that only transitive verbs can be used in the passive voice, that the *by*-phrase is optional and rarely used in academic writing, and that some passive constructions are idiomatic and must be learned independently of general rules.

STRATEGIES AND TACTICS FOR TEACHING AND TEACHING ACTIVITIES

The following six exercises and practice assignments can help students with verb tenses and voice.

(1) Learning to Notice Typical Errors in the Verb Phrase and Articulate the Reasons for the Errors

This exercise is similar to those found in many ESL grammar books. The primary benefit of this practice is that students need to explicitly indicate what the problems with the sentences are and devise a general rule to avoid making similar errors in their own writing. Students can work in pairs and then compare their generalizations to decide on the most accurate and easiest to remember.

Please correct the errors in the following sentences and create specific rules that can be followed to avoid making such errors in writing. What types of errors have you noticed in these sentences? How many?

1. College graduates will earning more money than people without college degrees.
2. The Internet has everything, the news, shopping, and gossip, and the Internet has reach every aspect of our lives. When I searched for the information for my classes, I have find all the facts I need.
3. The purpose of my essay will be to focus on the work of Pendelton's early paintings that has been giving the credit for founding the still-art school.
4. It is not Pendeltons style that was widely imitating among the local group of painters in the 16th century, but the style of his pupil Johnson (1479–1559).
5. Johnson didn't just only learned painting from Pendelton; he was also often imitated the styles of earlier artists, such as Ellison, Dickerson, and Morris.
6. Abraham Maslow did identified the order of human needs from the lowest to the highest.
7. The interviewer have not spoke to the study subjects in detail, but he should.
8. The topic of the causes of Second World War has been discussing in many articles.

(2) English Is a Strange Language: Strange Subjects of Active Verbs and Strange Active Verbs

This exercise leads to interesting discussions for pairs or small groups of students. It is important that the teacher follow up with a whole-class discussion and explanation.

In your opinion, which of the following sentences are grammatical, which are a little strange, and which are not grammatical? Please explain why you think that some of the sentences seem strange or incorrect and how they can be corrected.

1. It was a dark and stormy night, and students studied in the library because they will have a test tomorrow.
2. Engineers will make a decision about the design for the bridge. They will choose one of the three designs: a floating bridge, a suspension bridge, or an arch bridge. The public vote will approve their choice.

3. The dog ate my homework. The food processor ate my homework. The vacuum cleaner ate my homework.
4. The tree is growing. John's paper is growing. The city is growing. The child is growing.
5. The man is running. The water is running. The car is running. The test is running. The tape is running. Time is running.
6. A barometer predicts the weather. A TV station predicts the weather. A meteorologist predicts the weather.
7. The weather is predicted (by a barometer). The weather is predicted (by a TV station). The weather is predicted (by a meteorologist).

(3) "English Is Not my Native Language and I Can't Write Like Native Students" Practice

The purpose of this practice is to provide L2 writers examples of tenses and passive uses in authentic NS writing. L2 writers often believe that the quality of language usage (and discourse organization) usually found in NS texts is superb and that the standards of quality expected of L2 writing can be unfair and unreasonable. First of all, these beliefs are based on a simple lack of facts: Native students' writing often leaves a great deal to be desired in terms of both the quality of language and discourse organization. An important teaching objective is to demonstrate to L2 students that being a native speaker does not guarantee superb writing, and that the writing of native students, like L2 writing, also varies widely in quality.

Samples of native students' writing can be requested from the Writing Center, a mainstream composition/writing instructor, or even individual students on campus. If the teacher has access to the writing of several NS students, the best way to proceed is to collect three or four pieces of L1 writing: the not-so-good, passable (and passing), and a good one. If the NS papers/essays are written on the same topic (or in similar disciplines), text and discourse analysis can be made very profitable for L2 writers. Most important, however, the analysis of NS essays can address a number of points simultaneously or in the course of a couple of class meetings:

- discourse organization and structure (including thesis and topic supports and the amount of elaboration—see appendix to chap. 11)
- uses of tenses and passives, as well as adverbial time (and tense) markers and frames, and tense shifts
- uses of adjectives and descriptive adverbials such as prepositional phrases (see chap. 6)
- vocabulary range (e.g., nouns, verbs; see chaps. 4 and 8)
- any useful/relevant type of discourse and text features

In addition to highlighting how NS writers of similar academic proficiency employ text features, one of the main benefits of this exercise is that it helps take away the illusions of NS writing perfection that many L2 academic writers have regarding NS academic papers.

(4) Functions of the Passive Voice in Academic Writing

The goal of this activity is to help students identify the functions of passive in academic writing and develop their skills as astute users of the active and passive voices. An attendant objective is to practice revising and editing skills with tenses and passive/active constructions.

Please read the following excerpt from a student assignment. Some constructions used in it contain errors that need to be corrected. In addition, some other constructions are grammatically correct, but they can be written better. Please (1) identify both types of structures, and (2) correct the errors; also please (3) explain which sentences should be improved and why, and then (4) show how they can be rewritten.

As a part of our marketing assignment, we had to go to a small cheese farm where the husband and wife own it. The husband and the wife sent a letter to our marketing professor, and they requested that someone come there to analyze their marketing techniques to help them improve their sales. We went through their entire production chain, and we tried to figure out two things: how they can cut their costs and how they can improve their sales.

In this paper, we analyze how they can cut their costs. We found out that each cheese is poured into a container for ripening and storage. The containers cost 9 cents each and the lid costs 2 cents. So, if they store the containers one on top of the other than they do not need lids, and they can save 2 cents on each lid. Of course, the container on the top needs to have a lid.

Then we analyzed how they can cut their storage costs. They keep all the cheese in a huge refrigerator for ripening, and when it is ready, they take to the market. They keep the new cheese for at least two months and the aged cheese for up to 18 months. They keep the temperature between 40° and 45°. So, we performed a little calculation and figured out that if they keep the temperature at 45° instead of 40°, then they can save about a dollar a day on their electric costs.

Then we analyzed their shipping costs. We asked them to tell us how much they pay for shipping. They told us that the shipping of each cheese is costed them $2.80 because they have to ship the cheese in a special container so it does not warm up and spoil in the truck or when it is waited for the customer to come home and take it inside. Each container costs $1.20, and they have to pay $1.60 for transportation. So, we did some research, and we found out that they can find a cheaper supplier for their containers, and the new supplier will sell them the container for $1.05. We are told them that they can save 15 cents on each container if they will buy it from the new supplier we found. But they said that they have a relationship going with their old supplier and that the new supplier will not like it if they switch.

When we heard that we said to them do you care if your old supplier will not like it or do you care to save money? And then we said that if they will have trouble in their business in the future than their old supplier will have to sell them fewer containers because they will ship fewer cheeses. We recommended that they talk to their old supplier and explain the problem with the price. We said maybe your old supplier will match the price of the new supplier then you'll be in good shape. But they said that they always buy from the old supplier for almost 30 years and that they cannot talk to them about a new price after all this time.

(Extracted from a group student assignment in marketing.)

When you are finished with the revisions, please explain the various functions of the passive voice that you noticed while working to improve this essay.

(5) Subjects of Active Verbs

The goal of this activity is help learners become adept at using active verbs with subjects that are not live beings and that are seemingly unable to perform the verb action.

Please complete the following sentences. The main verbs are provided.

1. Hot weather [lead] ________________________________
2. Ice cream and diary consumption [increase] ______________
3. In some regions, climate [change] ______________________
4. The chapter in the book [lack] _________________________
5. Human eyes [adapt (to)] _____________________________
6. Mixing colors [produce] _____________________________

(6) Mixing Active and Passive Constructions in Academic Writing

The goal of this exercise is to help L2 writers employ both active and passive constructions to the best advantage of their text (e.g., employ varied structures in a reasonably cohesive text). This practice can be particularly useful for paired work when students can discuss their suggested revisions and changes. The teacher needs to be sure to follow up with a whole-class review when students are finished working. Exercises of this type can also be assigned as homework with a follow-up in-class discussion.

Please decide which structures should be used in the active or the passive voice to improve the text. Some structures should be converted (1) from active to passive, others (2) from passive to active, and (3) some should be left unchanged. Also please pay special attention to (4) various types of errors and (5) the uses of by-phrases. It is your decision how to improve this text, but your goal is revise it to help its author get the highest grade possible. Please be ready to explain why you think a particular structure should be rewritten and how your revision improves the original.

When the world population increases dramatically, more food is demanded by all people. Only 40 years ago, the world population was counted at 4 billion, in 1990 it was 5.3 billion, and it expects to grow to 8 billion by the year 2020. However, the speed of food production cannot be kept up the rate of growth of population under the limited farmland, and it is already fallen far behind the demand. This problem could solve by the development of engineered foods. The new biotechnology can be contributed by increasing the productivity of crops and improve diversification in food sources.

It is clear that to eliminate hunger is involved expansion of crop production. The potential yield of existed crops is necessary to decrease or eliminate hunger, and in the process, the environment cannot be destroyed. This be required further scientific advances in food production, and plant biology can play an important role in it. Growing new crops requires the use of various pesticides and irrigation, in addition to fertilizing. Creating new foods is requires changing the local crops by the agricultural scientists because it is possible to obtained certain plants that can be made more productive and better adaptive. A "miracle rice" was developed under this process at the founded International Rice Research Institute in the Philippines in the 1970s by biologists. The researchers created a new shorter rice plant with better crops. The new rice was matured more quickly so farmers did not lost their crops to floods. Engineered plans also have the ability to reduce the use of chemicals. The cost to farmers will be reduced, and the pollution will be decreased as well.

Opponents argue that engineered foods offend nature. They think that the creation of a new type of life form should be left alone and evolution will be taken care of that by itself. They have these ideas only because people are always distrusted new products, particularly food. We should know that traditional creating of new crops is almost as old as agriculture. The first farmer who was bred the best bull with the best cow in the heard to improve the stock, was implemented agricultural engineering in a very simple way. The first baker who used yeast to make bread pie was also used a lining thing to produce an improving product. Science always finds new ways for them to introduce quickly and directly a specific crop, and animal improvements will lead to more people with food by technology. These days, it can take a decade to produce something that was taken by generations of farmers to come up with.

(Extracted from a student assignment on world hunger and biotechnology.)

QUESTIONS FOR DISCUSSION

1. In your opinion, what does the term *conventionalized uses* mean when it comes to English tenses and the passive voice in formal academic writing? Can you think of other conventionalized constructions in academic text? Do textual conventions exist in written genres other than the academic?

2. In the following excerpt from a student assignment, please identify the tense-related (and other types of) errors, and state how these errors can be clearly explained to students so that they can the correct them independently without having to rely on the teacher's corrections.

Around the world, there are numbers of people with diseases that were inherited from their ancestors. Every day, approximately 14% of newborn infants were afflicted by some sort of inherited physical or mental problems when they were born. The diseases dealing with genes are very hard to know who will inherit it. Gene therapy is a medical procedure that treats a disease by replacing a faulty gene. Though many people thought that gene therapy has some side effects, I believe that gene therapy will be important to us for our future. Nowadays, scientists are trying to solve the problem of AIDS. Gene therapy researchers are trying to find a cure for the disease that many infants inherited from their mothers when they were born. There are many developments that were occurred in gene therapy recently that will bring the world around.

(Extracted from a student assignment on the influence of technology on health care.)

3. As discussed earlier in the chapter, the progressive and perfect tenses are rare in academic writing, and, for example, the perfect progressive is hardly ever encountered. In your opinion, why is the teaching of these tenses so common in L2 grammar instruction? Can similar observations also be true about other English constructions?

4. When it comes to tenses and the active and the passive voices, do you think that the findings of corpus analyses of academic writing in English can be applied to L2 student writing? Why or why not? If the findings of corpus analyses cannot be useful in L2 classroom, what should the basis of ESL and EAP curricula be?

5. The information in this chapter explains that many passive constructions in English are idiomatic and have to be learned. Can you come up with a few examples of passive constructions that you believe to be idiomatic or derived and explain your determination? A few examples are provided.

(a) The importance of small business to the U.S. economy cannot be overstated.
(b) The speaker was long winded, and the listeners were quickly lost in his citations of numbers.
(c) Once the production plans are made for the next business cycle, they are continually altered in response to the new information.

FURTHER READINGS ABOUT VERB TENSES AND VOICE AND TEACHING

Carlson, G., & Tanenhaus, M. (1984). Lexical meanings, structural meanings, and concepts. In D. Testen, V. Mishra, & J. Drogo (Eds.), *Papers from the Parasession on Lexical Semantics* (pp. 39–52). Chicago: Chicago Linguistic Society.

Chafe, W. (1994). *Discourse, consciousness, and time.* Chicago: University of Chicago Press.

Croft, W. (1998). The structure of events and the structure of language. In M. Tomasello (Ed.), *The new psychology of language* (pp. 67–92). Mahwah, NJ: Lawrence Erlbaum Associates.

DeCarrico, J. (1986). Tense, aspect, and time in the English modality. *TESOL Quarterly, 20*(4), 665–682.

Deitrich, R., Klein, W., & Noyau, C. (1995). *The acquisition of temporality in a second language.* Amsterdam: John Benjamins.

DeLancey, S. (1985). Agentivity and syntax. *Chicago Linguistic Society, 21*, 1–12.

Hinkel, E. (1997). The past tense and temporal verb meanings in a contextual frame. *TESOL Quarterly, 31*(2), 289–313.

Hinkel, E. (2002). Why English passive is difficult to teach (and learn). In E. Hinkel & S. Fotos (Eds.), *New perspectives on grammar teaching* (pp. 233–260). Mahwah, NJ: Lawrence Erlbaum Associates.

Levin, B. (1993). *English verb classes and alternations.* Chicago: University of Chicago Press.

Master, P. (1991). Active verbs with inanimate subjects in scientific prose. *English for Specific Purposes, 10*(1), 15–33.

Matthiessen, C. (1996). Tense in English seen through systemic-functional theory. In M. Berry, C. Butler, R. Fawcett, & G. Hwang (Eds.), *Meaning and form: Systemic functional interpretations* (pp. 431–498). Norwood, NJ: Ablex.

Owen, C. (1993). Corpus-based grammar and the Heineken effect: Lexico-grammatical description for language learners. *Applied Linguistics, 14*(2), 167–187.

Thompson, P. (2000). Citation practices in PhD theses. In L. Burnard & T. McEnery (Eds.), *Rethinking language pedagogy from a corpus perspective* (pp. 91–101). Frankfurt: Peter Lang.

Vassivela, I. (2001). Commitment and detachment in English and Bulgarian academic writing. *English for Specific Purpose, 20*, 83–102.

Appendix to Chapter 7

DISCOURSE-DRIVEN SENTENCE STEMS WITH THE PRESENT PERFECT TENSE

The increasing interest in xxx has heightened the need for … / to …
Recently, there has been growing interest in
The possibility of … has generated wide interest in …
The development of xxx has lead to the hope that …
The xxx has been / become a favorite topic for analysis /discussion / examination.…
Knowledge of xxx has become an important aspect of …
The xxx has been extensively studied in recent years.
Many educators/scientists/analysts have recently turned to …
The relationship between xxx and yyy has been investigated/studied by many researchers.
Many recent articles/reports have focused on …

(From Swales & Feak, 1994)

8

Lexical Classes of Verbs: Meanings and Text Functions

OVERVIEW

- The most essential academic verbs
- 350 foundational verbs
  - Text functions and syntactic properties of lexical verb classes
  - Activity verbs
  - Reporting verbs
  - Mental/emotive verbs
  - Linking verbs
  - Logical-semantic relationship verbs

Verbs represent one of the most important elements in sentences and text construction (Quirk et al., 1985). In the teaching of ESL grammar, a great deal of attention is typically devoted to such features of the verb phrase as tenses, aspects, and auxiliary fronting (for verb tenses and their uses, see chap. 7). In addition to these syntactic properties of verbs, verb meanings and textual functions play a prominent role in the construction of academic text.

This chapter covers the functions and uses of lexical classes of verb and their specific textual meanings and implications. As with nouns, the prominent role of verbs in academic writing and text cannot be underestimated. Because L2 writers' academic prose often appears to rely on severely restricted vocabulary range, learners need to be taught the functions and uses of a wide range of verbs, without which their writing appears constrained and repetitious. As mentioned earlier in this book, it may not be possible to express many ideas within the confines of a 500-word repertoire. To help L2 writers expand their range of accessible academic verbs, they need to be explicitly and persistently taught.

In this chapter, the most essential academic verbs are highlighted. Then a foundational set of approximately 350 verbs is discussed in some detail because they constitute one of the keys to NNS students' production of university-level text (Jordan, 1997; Nation, 1990). This chapter also deals with context and discourse functions of several lexical classes of verbs that can noticeably improve the quality of students' academic prose.

WHAT ARE LEXICAL VERBS?

In general terms, lexical verbs have been divided into several large classes that have been assigned different labels and components depending on the purpose of a particular classification. Because this book is primarily concerned with functions of verbs in L2 academic prose, the specific labels of constituent verbs are not greatly important. However, because some sort of verb labeling is necessary, whenever possible, the discussion follows the terminology adopted in many ESL student textbooks. In addition, because textbook classifications do not always examine verb types in sufficient detail, some of the labels rely on those developed by Quirk et al. (1985) and Biber et al. (1999). In teaching lexical verbs to L2 learners, the transparency of the labels is of greatest importance.

> Some analyses of lexical verbs identify as many as 30 semantic classes and others around a dozen. However, only five are particularly important in L2 instruction: activity verbs, reporting verbs, mental/emotive verbs, linking verbs, and logical-semantic relationship verbs (the functions and uses of modal verbs are discussed in chap. 12 on hedging). In actual classroom teaching, these labels can be further simplified for students:
>
> - "doing" verbs (activity)
> - "speaking" verbs (reporting)
> - "thinking/feeling" verbs (mental/emotive)
> - "being/becoming" verbs (linking)
> - "relationship" verbs (logical-semantic relationship)

Verbs in different lexical and semantic classes do not play the same role in teaching L2 academic writing, and some are more important than others. For example, few activity and mental/emotive verbs are actually encountered in academic text, but linking and logical-semantic relationship verbs are a great deal more common. In addition, although many simple activity and mental/emotive verbs (e.g., *do, feel, think*) are so common that they can be learned in daily living, logical-semantic relationship verbs are far more advanced and need to be taught.

Another small but tremendously important note needs to be made when it comes to teaching academic verbs. As most teachers know from experience, even advanced university students enrolled in graduate courses continue to make numerous mistakes in the spelling of irregular verbs. In academic texts, however, the number of irregular verbs that are actually used is not particularly large, but such spelling mistakes are usually profoundly embarrassing. Even in the age of ubiquitous spellcheckers, students need to learn to spell irregular verbs because without knowing the correct verb form it is difficult to know which form suggested by the spellchecker should be accepted and which can make the text almost incomprehensible. Furthermore, a large proportion of university-level courses requires students to produce in-class assignments and exams, most of which are written by hand—without spellcheckers.

> It is strongly recommended that teachers insist that students learn the correct spelling of common academic verbs. In many cases, even for students at the low-intermediate level, about a month of persistent effort can do the job.

THE MOST ESSENTIAL VERBS

Various studies of academic prose have determined that certain verbs consistently recur in diverse genres of academic texts ranging from introductory course books to publications of innovative research (Biber et al., 1999; Leech et al., 2001; Nation, 1990, 2001). Therefore, it stands to reason that these verbs are essential for students to know and use in their writing. These verbs number fewer than 100, and they may not be especially difficult to learn, particularly because they are encountered repeatedly.

Such relatively simple and common verbs as *make, give, take, use,* and *show* predominate in the verb vocabulary across all written genres as single words or in combinations with particles as two- or three-word verbs. These extremely common verbs are not included on the following list of the academic must-have verbs because they can be easily learned in the course of daily exposure to English. Other highly common academic verbs (e.g., *describe, imply, refer*) are also not included because they are familiar to practically all NNS university-bound students who are required to take the TOEFL, and they are included dozens of times in test questions and instructions.

Thus, The Most Essential Verbs constitute a somewhat reduced list of core verbs. Without at least some of these, it may not be possible to write an academic essay or paper in any discipline or on any topic.

The 40 Most Essential Verbs[1]

affect	*consider*	*form*	*matter*	*reflect*
allow	*constitute*	*include*	*obtain*	*relate*
appear	*contain*	*increase*	*occur*	*remain*
apply	*determine*	*indicate*	*produce*	*represent*
(a)rise (from)	*develop*	*investigate*	*prove*	*require*
assume	*emerge*	*involve*	*provide*	*result (in)*
cause	*find*	*lack*	*reach*	*seem*
change	*follow*	*leave*	*reduce*	*tend*

(Adapted from Biber et al., 1999; Leech et al., 2001; Nation 1990, 2001)

Learning many of the essential verbs may take little effort because they can be encountered in all kinds of settings that are not necessarily academic (e.g., *change, find, follow,* or *leave*). These can be practiced in conversational activities, reading, or listening exercises. On the other hand, others have been traditionally difficult for students to learn and use appropriately (e.g., *affect, cause, form, lack,* or *matter*). In part, the reason for learners' difficulties with these verbs stems from the fact that they have identical noun–verb forms. The similarity in the spelling of these dual noun–verb forms can make identifying their syntactic functions particularly confusing.

Identical spelling and divergent syntactic functions of nouns, verbs, and adjectives have to be explicitly addressed in teaching. To determine whether a particular word is a noun or a verb, one needs to look around the sentence when an ambiguous word is encountered in reading and exercises. For instance, if an article or a possessive pronoun can be found in front of the word, it is probably a noun. On the other hand, if the word follows something that looks like a noun, it is likely to be a verb. Contrasting nouns and verbs that have identical spelling (e.g., *change, form, lack,* and *matter*) can clarify their uses as nouns or verbs:

1. *A lack of rain in the past few days has caused an increase in water consumption.*
2. *The companies lack funding for a new venture.*
3. *A change in the weather pattern may bring us a welcome precipitation.*
4. *The weather patterns will change in the next few days.*

For instance, in (1), *a lack* is preceded by the article *a*, and therefore, it is probably a noun. However, in (2), *the companies* is probably a noun phrase—the article again followed by *lack* and *funding*. In this case, *lack* is

[1]Some of the verbs on this list are discussed and exemplified later in this chapter.

likely to be a verb, and *funding* a gerund because *-ing* verbs require an auxiliary *be* to be present (*are funding*). Similarly, in (3), *a change* is a noun, and *will change* is a verb phrase with the future auxiliary *will*.

Because verbs such as *change, form, lack,* and *matter* are very common, they are easy to find in newspaper text or Internet news or business reports. To highlight the high frequencies of words with identical noun–verb(-adjective) forms, students can be assigned to find and bring to class news and magazine articles or printouts of Internet text with, for example, three uses of these words as nouns and three as verbs. Although locating the words in the media is not difficult, students need to learn to differentiate between noun or verb word forms of these words in contexts or sentences. To accomplish this learning goal, students need to become careful analysts of the basic English sentence structure.

THE FOUNDATIONAL ACADEMIC VERBS

As discussed in chapter 5 on nouns, the restricted vocabulary and syntactic range accessible to NNS students can effectively reduce their ability to write academic text. Thus, the crucial learning of the foundational nouns needs to extend to a similar learning of verbs (i.e., it may simply not be possible to construct academic text if one's vocabulary range is fewer than 1,000 words; Nation, 1990, 2001). The list of approximately 350 foundational verbs is presented next, and the words in the bold font are found most frequently and in highly varied texts across all academic disciplines.

Common Verbs in Introductory Course Texts at the University Level
(Extracted from the University Word List [Nation, 1990][2])

abandon	**affiliate**	**approach**	attain	coincide	compute
accelerate	**agitate**	arouse	avail	collide	conceive
access	**aid**	ascribe	benefit	commit	concentrate
accompany	**align**	assemble	bore	communicate	**conclude**
accomplish	**allege**	assert	breed	compel	condense
accumulate	**allude**	**assess**	cancel	compensate	conduct
achieve	**alter**	assign	capture	complement	confer
acquire	**analyze**	assimilate	cater	complicate	confine
adhere	appeal	assist	cease	**comply**	conflict
adjust	append	**assume**	challenge	compound	conform
administer	appraise	assure	circulate	comprehend	confront
advocate	appreciate	attach	clarify	comprise	conserve

[2]In many cases, noun and verb forms can be identical (e.g., *access, aid, influence, advocate*). These are included on both the list of common nouns and the parallel list of common verbs.

consist
console
constitute
construct
construe
consult
consume
contact
contaminate
contemplate
contend
contract
contradict
contrast
contribute
convene
converge
converse
convert
cooperate
coordinate
correlate
correspond
create
debate
decline
dedicate
defect
defer
define
deflect
degenerate
degrade
deliberate
demonstrate
denote
deny
depress
deprive
derive
design
detect
deviate
devise
devote
dictate
diffuse
digest
discern
dispense
disperse
displace
dispose
dispute
dissipate
dissolve
distinct
distort
distribute
diverge
dominate
edit
elaborate
elevate
elicit
eliminate
emancipate
embody
embrace
emerge
emphasize
enable
enhance
enlighten
enrich
ensure
enumerate
equate
err
establish
estimate
evaluate
evaporate
evoke
evolve
exclude
execute
exert
exhaust
expand
expel
exploit
export
expose
extract
facilitate
factor
fare
feature
fluctuate
focus
forgo
formulate
found
frustrate
fuel
fulfill
function
fund
fuse
generate
grant
guarantee
harbor
identify
ignore
illuminate
illustrate
impact
implement
imply
import
impose
impress
incline
incorporate
indicate
induce
infer
inhibit
injure
insist
inspect
institute
instruct
integrate
interact
interlock
interpret
interrelate
intersect
interview
intervene
invade
invest
investigate
invoke
involve
irrigate
isolate
issue
justify
label
launch
lecture
legislate
liberate
locate
maintain
manifest
manipulate
migrate
modify
notate
oblige
obtain
occupy
occur
orientate
oscillate
overlap
participate
perpetrate
persist
pervade
plead
plot
postulate
precede
precipitate
predict
presume
prevail
proceed
process
proclaim
procure
prohibit
project
propagate
prosper
protest
provoke
publish
purport
pursue
quote
react
rebel
recur
reform
refute
reign
reinforce
reject
release
rely
remove
render
repress
reproduce
repudiate
require
research
respond
restore
restrict
retain
retard
reveal
reverberate
reverse
revise
revive
revolt
revolve
rotate
route
saturate
schedule
scheme
score
seek
select
shift
shrink
signify
sketch
specify
speculate
starve
stimulate
stipulate
stress
structure
subdivide

subside	supplement	**sum**	transact	underlie	violate
subsidize	suppress	tape	transfer	undertake	withdraw
subtle	survey	team	transform	utilize	x-ray
suffice	suspend	tire	transmit	utter	
sum	sustain	tolerate	transport	**vary**	
superimpose	switch	trace	undergo	verify	

As with nouns, expanding the lexical range of verbs can take place by means of building semantic domains of verbs with similar meanings to increase writers' options in constructing text. For this purpose, two- and three-word verbs and formal idiomatic expressions (Moon, 1998) can also be practiced in context, together with other verbs with similar meanings. For example:

abandon—give up—leave

accelerate—speed up—quicken

access—enter—go in(to)

accompany—go hand in hand (with)

accomplish—achieve—fulfill—attain—realize

appear—emerge—show up

choose—select—elect—opt—pick (out)

continue—go on—keep on

discover—find out—learn—determine

discuss—take up—raise—talk over

finish—complete—get through

investigate—look into—research—examine

leave—go away—depart

maintain—keep up—continue

reject—turn down

remove—take off—take away

review—look over

search (for)—look for

The verbs in semantic domains can be practiced in editing or contextualized substitutions. The following example of a student text can benefit from an expanded range of verbs and a bit of editing:

> *As a development of science and technology, the research fields of human beings are changing into more variety. Medical technology is also changing, and computers are changing everything. Most of the projects cannot be completed by the person who just knows the one field. These projects require the researcher who knows many disciplines. This produces a contemporary scientific research approach that is also changing. With the development of microelectronics, much progress has been achieved in electrical engineering. The research area of electrical engineering has increased much more. On the other hand, people change to care about themselves more and more. There is much development in medical fields in recent years. Research has given us a lot of information that is always changing.* (An introduction from a junior-level term paper on the technological advancement in the 1990s.)

Although the basic ideas in this excerpt may not be difficult to understand, the student's repertoire appears to be severely limited. In a 122-word extract, the word *change* is repeated six times, *development* three times, and *know* twice. In this case, as in numerous other cases of L2 academic text, rudimentary vocabulary work can lead to a direct, even if superficial, improvement. For instance, both nouns and verbs can be somewhat more diverse (see chaps. 5, 7, and 12 on nouns, verb tenses, and hedges for additional information):

- *change (verb)—evolve—expand—develop—transform—modify—alter—advance*
- *produce (verb)—create—bring about*
- *know—be informed/trained/educated—be familiar with—be an expert in—have experience in—work in*
- *increase (verb)—advance—gain (momentum)—grow—broaden—spread—enhance—expand—rise—strengthen—boom* (if rapid)

Although few of these substitute expressions are lexically and syntactically sophisticated, their uses in L2 academic prose can make a noticeable difference in the linguistic variety of textual features.

ACTIVITY ("DOING") VERBS

Activity verbs comprise the largest class of verbs, and some of the following verb classes actually refer to actions that are a subclass of activity verbs (e.g., see Reporting Verbs and Relationship Verbs herein). Activity verbs refer to voluntary (e.g., *eat, give, take*) and nonvoluntary (e.g., *precipitation falls, the river overflows*) physical actions (Quirk et al., 1985). Two- and three-word verbs also belong in this class (e.g., *give up, look into, bring about*). Because activity verbs are numerous in English, practically every ESL vocabulary and reading skills textbook incorporates at least some practice with these items.

Activity verbs can be transitive and intransitive (i.e., used with or without direct objects), and they can be used with animate subjects (e.g., *the sociologist adheres to ..., the writer labors*) or inanimate subjects (*the valve turns, the conclusion sums up ...*). Nation's (1990) analysis showed that among vocabulary lists based on introductory university-level texts, activity verbs were not particularly frequent (see the complete list of verbs earlier in this chapter). Similarly, Biber's, et al. (1999) examinations of various English-language corpora found that in academic prose, activity verbs were far less common than existence verbs, although activity verbs predominate in conversations, fiction, and news reports.

For example, in Nation's (1990) list, activity verbs largely refer to physical actions, but not necessarily in their literal meanings:

abandon [a direction/venture]
accelerate [growth/development]
access [information/facilities]
accompany [innovation/change]
accumulate [resources/ capital]
acquire [meaning/business]
adhere [to rules/guidance /direction]
adjust [figures/course of action]

According to Biber's, et al. (1999) findings, in academic text the most common activity verbs include in declining order (including various forms and combinations with other words):

make	*use*	*show*	*provide*	*obtain*
give	*deal*	*move*	*apply*	*reduce*
take	*with*	*produce*	*form*	

These verbs also provide an effective venue for two- and three-word verb or idiom practice, e.g.

- *make up—consist (of)—form*; also idiomatic expressions: *make a difference, make do, make time, make way, make something up*
- *take up—start; take out—remove—omit*; *take on—undertake*; also idiomatic expressions: *take place, take part, take time (money/space), take something well/badly*
- *give off—emit—produce; give up—stop—leave—abandon; give in—agree (unwillingly*); also *give a thought, give time, give impression, give credit, give authority*

Practice materials for these common verbs can be found in various types of print media and used for group or individual work in context (see also Teaching Strategies later in this chapter). For example, newspapers (and news article titles) and other authentic materials provide a wealth of opportunities for exposure to activity verbs:

- *Heinz will <u>catch up</u> in California* (*Seattle Times*, January 31, 2001)
- *<u>Making way</u> for the New Student Center* (*The Spectator*, February 8, 2001)
- *New clam <u>showing up</u> in Oregon* (*Seattle Times*, March 23, 2001)
- *More college students <u>drop out</u> than graduate* (*Yahoo Daily News*, August 15, 2001)

On the other hand, such basic activity verbs such as *buy, put, pay, bring, meet, play, run,* or *wait* are hardly ever encountered in academic prose, even though they are prevalent in conversation and fiction (Biber et al., 1999). Relatively few activity verbs play a key role in academic discourse, and those that are actually needed can be learned incidentally when students are engaged in other types of L2 study (Jordan, 1997; Sinclair & Renouf, 1988).

REPORTING ("SPEAKING") VERBS

Lists of reporting verbs can be found in most ESL grammar books, beginning with those for intermediate-level students. Reporting verbs can denote such simple acts as *ask, say, speak,* or *tell.* Indeed these reporting verbs predominate in informal spoken discourse. On the other hand, in academic prose, the most frequent reporting verbs are more lexically and semantically complex:

acknowledge
address
admit
advise
announce
appeal
argue
call (for)
carry out
challenge
deny
describe
determine
discuss
emphasize
encourage
explain
express
indicate
inform
mention
note
offer
point out
propose
publish
question
quote
recommend
remark
report
respond
specify
state
suggest
teach
urge
warn
write

Reporting verbs are particularly important in paraphrasing, writing reviews of readings, and citing information from sources in rhetorical support of a writer's position and/or opinion. Reporting verbs are used to introduce indirect (and reported) statements in the form of noun phrases or noun clauses (see also chaps. 5 and 10). For example,

> *"... Sandra Scarr, Ph.D., has shown that fraternal twins who resemble one another enough to be mistaken for identical twins have more similar personalities than other such twins."*

> *"The researchers reported finding a gene nearly identical to the mouse obesity gene in humans."*

> *"This research indicates that people really are born with a tendency to have a certain weight...."*

> *"Earlier Simon LeVay, M.D., ... noted that an area of a brain's hypothalamus was smaller among gay than heterosexual men."* (All citations from Peele and DeGrandpre, 1999, pp. 73–75)

In academic discourse, citations of data, research findings, and scholarly studies citations are a ubiquitous means of demonstrating one's familiarity with readings and sources. In fact references to external sources of knowledge represent a requisite means of supporting one's position in rhetorical argumentation (Swales, 1990a). Thus, it is highly profitable for NNS writers to develop a stock of expressions to cite information from readings. In written assignments and papers, a varied stock of citation formats can help make the writers' text appear somewhat diverse.

The following examples of stock phrases and sentences with reporting verbs are organized by subject animacy, new/repeated reference mentions, and other linguistic and discourse features. In addition, however, it is important for students to know that in English the subject animacy makes no difference in the functions of reporting verbs used as predicates. That is, *Smith (2001) shows* or *the study/research shows* are equally grammatical and can be used in similar contexts (Hinkel, 2002d).

However, for many students the use of inanimate subjects with active verbs can seem ungrammatical, and the combinations of animate subjects with active verbs may be a better place to start (e.g., *Jones [2002] states that ...* or *According to Jones [2002], ...*). For further discussion of subject animacy, verb transitivity, and their importance in passive constructions, see chapter 7 on the functions and uses of the passive voice.

Stock Phrases and Sentences for Reporting Information From Published Sources

1. Reporting verbs in sentences with animate subjects
   (a) The first mention of the author's name/source

Smith (2002)	*states*	*that*
	notes	
	mentions	
	comments	
	remarks	
	indicates	
	explains	

Syntactically advanced construction with dual reporting verbs and infinitives

Smith/The author(s)	*describe xxx to show*	*that*
	explain xxx to demonstrate	
	present xxx to emphasize	

xxx can include such nouns as: data, information, examples, illustrations, facts, statistics, study results, observations

Adverbial constructions and hedges (see also chap. 12 on hedges)

According to Smith (2002), ...

(b) The second or subsequent mention of the author's name/source

The author(s)	*propose*	*that*
	report	
	comment	
	point out	
	remark	
	suggest	

(c) The second or subsequent mention in a paraphrase from the same source

The researcher(s)/this scholar	*goes on to*	*say*	*that*
	further	*writes*	
	additionally	*states*	

2. Reporting information in sentences with inanimate subjects
   (a) First or second/subsequent mentions of study results

Smith's (2002) study	*shows*	*that*
	proposes	
	emphasizes	
	maintains	
Smith's (2002) findings	*point out*	
The analysis of xxx	*suggests*	
The investigation of xxx	*argues*	
	denies	

(b) Advanced structures with object complements

Smith (2002)	*presents*	*the opinion*	*that*
	holds	*the position*	
	advocates	*the view*	

(c) Advanced constructions with various types of noun clauses and object complements

Their results	*help explain*		*that/how/why*
The study results	*explain*	*the reasons*	*that*
		the view	
		the position	
	challenge	*the argument*	*that*
		the claim	
The new findings	*offer*	*(the) explanations*	*that*

> When teaching the uses of reporting verbs in references to sources and literature citations, it may be helpful to present these constructions in columns for students to see clearly how the syntactic regularities in these constructions can work to the learners' advantage. That is, by simply replacing the subject noun or the verb with various proximate alternatives, L2 writers can actually come up with a great number of diverse and contextually appropriate expressions.

In real terms, however, few students may need a supply larger than five or six citational expressions, and practicing reporting verbs in the context of references to sources may help L2 writers become comfortable with their uses.

MENTAL/EMOTIVE (THINKING/FEELING) VERBS

On the whole, mental verbs are not popular in academic prose, and their rate of use in academic prose stands at approximately 0.42% in a large English-language corpus (Biber et al., 1999). In general, mental verbs refer to intellectual states (e.g., *know, learn, think*) and nonobservable intellectual acts (e.g., *notice, suspect, trust*). Other verbs in this class refer to mental and cognitive processes (*compare, calculate, recognize*).

The teaching of mental/emotive verbs needs to proceed judiciously. Although some of the verbs in this class are relatively common in academic writing, others are hardly ever encountered because they often impart personal and subjective tone to formal discourse. In classroom teaching, the former can be combined with reporting verbs, and the latter should be discouraged in L2 academic writing. Both of these types of mental/emotive are highlighted in this chapter.

The most common mental verbs found in academic text are actually fewer than 10 (listed here in declining order of frequency; Biber et al., 1999):

see	*consider*	*think*	*determine*	*read*
find	*know*	*assume*	*mean*	

A majority of mental verbs found in published academic text largely denote cognition, although this class also includes highly emotive verbs such as *bear, enjoy, face, hate,* and *want*. These verbs do not refer to physical actions of any kind and involve "thinking" or, in rare cases, receiving information (e.g., *observe, read, recognize*).

In addition to the most frequent verbs noted earlier, other mental verbs found substantially **less often** in large English-language corpora include other verbs that refer to mental/cognitive processes (Leech et al., 2001).

accept	*confirm*	*estimate*	*note*	*solve*
appreciate	*decide*	*examine*	*notice*	*study*
assess	*determine*	*identify*	*observe*	*suspect*
calculate	*discover*	*intend*	*prefer*	
choose	*distinguish*	*interpret*	*prove*	
compare	*doubt*	*judge*	*realize*	
conclude	*establish*	*learn*	*recognize*	

Mental verbs refer to "private" intellectual states and acts; for this reason, their uses in academic prose mark the text as somewhat subjective (Quirk et al., 1985). Indeed mental verbs are far more prevalent in conversational and informal discourse and fiction than academic text. Such verbs as *attempt, plan, try,* and *want* refer to the future time and are often employed in tentative or personal constructions with an element of uncertainty (Huddleston & Pullum, 2002; Quirk et al., 1985).

In formal papers, NNS students employ substantially more emotive and tentative verbs than do NSs because L2 writers rely on hesitation to avoid projecting an overly confident stance in propositions and claims (Johnson, 1989b), as is considered to be desirable and appropriate in many non-Anglo-American discourse traditions. For example, *I will try to graduate in spring* sounds more tenuous than *I will graduate in spring*. Another reason that NNS writers employ mental and tentative verbs significantly more frequently is that many learners are exposed to a great deal more informal conversational discourse than formal written prose (Hinkel, 2002a).

In addition to working with common academic verbs, it is also important to alert NNS writers to the fact that the mental/emotive verbs are hardly ever encountered in formal academic text and that their uses may make the text appear conversational and informal.

Conversational and Emotive Verbs Not Found in Academic Prose

attempt	*expect*	*like*	*plan*	*try*
believe	*feel*	*listen*	*remember*	*want*
desire	*hear*	*love*	*suppose*	*wonder*

The uses of these verbs may seem somewhat subjective in formal academic writing when discourse is expected to project objectivity, distance, and detachment (Swales, 1990a). For example,

> *Many American scholars have studied the history of American education. They have tried to find out what made education change. I feel that there are different causes for that.* (From a student text on early American history and education.)

Nonetheless, despite their apparent subjectivity and personal tone, certain mental verbs can be used effectively in the references to sources similar to reporting verbs:

assess	*calculate*	*conclude*	*confirm*	*observe*	*note*

However, it is advisable that L2 writers employ these verbs with caution. In the following example, the author's description appears to be somewhat personalized and even slightly obsequious (mental/emotive verbs are underlined):

> *Biologists like to work with each other because they feel that they need knowledge from other fields, such as chemistry and physics. They think that one person cannot work alone. We can notice the same in other fields, such as geology, when they share information, and everyone likes to take part that is related to his major. When biological research starts a new project, we want to listen to one another and plan what we will do because we expect to get results together. Knowledge grows rapidly in this world, and biologists try to keep up with the current knowledge by working together to design research. After research design is evaluated, we can recognize what went well and what didn't.* (Extracted from a students' paper about research design in biology.)

Due to the preponderance of mental verbs in this text, it may need to be thoroughly and laboriously edited to make the text appear more detached and objective. (Also repeated uses of first-person pronouns, characteristic of formal written discourse in various non-Anglo-American rhetorical traditions, seem to be distracting. See chap. 6 on pronoun functions and uses.)

LINKING (BEING/BECOMING) VERBS

Linking verbs refer to a syntactic "link" that exists between the subject on the left-hand side of the verb phrase and the subject complement on the right-hand side of the verb (see also chap. 3):

> *Deviance is universal; however, each society has a different view of what is deviant, and it changes from generation to generation. Even when it might appear that almost all societies agree on some general category of action as deviant ..., careful examination will show that they differ in their definitions of what specific acts are to be included in the category.* (Charon, 1999, p. 145)

> *Symbols are the basics for human thinking, and thinking in turn is basic to what we do in situations* (Charon, 1999, p. 173)

In these texts, the subject *deviance* is linked to the adjectives *universal* and *deviant* or the subject *it* is connected to the complement clause *that all societies agree on some general category of action as deviant*. Similarly, the noun *symbols* is linked to the complement phrase *the basics for human thinking*, and *thinking* is linked to *basic to what we do in situations*. In many cases, the function of the verb *be* can be taught as subject approximately equal to (≈) or directly referring to the complement. For example:

Jane is tall (i.e., *tall* refers directly to *Jane*). One of Jane's characteristics (≈) *tall*.

John is a student (i.e., *a student* directly refers to *John*). One of John's characteristics (≈) *student*.

Symbols are basics for human thinking (i.e., *symbols* [≈] *basics for human thinking*, and vice versa).

Although the fact that linking verbs are not very numerous in English, they are by far more predominant in academic text than in any other genre (Biber et al., 1999).

Highly Common Academic Linking Verbs

appear	*become*	*keep*	*remain*	*stay*
be	*grow*	*prove*	*seem*	*turn out*

The most common copula/linking verbs are *be* and *become*, and *be* is employed over 20 times more frequently than any other linking verb. *Be* often marks stative constructions (Huddleston & Pullum, 2002; Quirk et al., 1985)—that is, states and/or existence, but not actions, activities, or mental/emotive processes.

Other linking verbs prevalent in academic prose include *seem* and *appear*, which refer to likelihood or strong possibility (e.g., *the economy seems stable*). In addition, *seem* and *appear* refer to the process of reasoning or conclusions from reasoning that may not be completely certain (Chafe, 1985, 1986). In academic texts, these verbs are usually employed as hedges (Huebler, 1983; Hyland, 1998; see chap. 12 on hedges). Various linking verbs that refer to continuation, such as *remain, keep*, and *stay*, are far less common than *be, become, seem*, and *appear* (e.g., *This definition might seem simple enough;* Mankiw, 2001, p. 208).

The verbs *be* and *become* are followed by adjective complements in a vast majority of their uses (e.g., *be important, become necessary*). According to the Biber et al. (1999) corpus analysis, the most common adjectives that accompany linking verbs in academic text are:

true	*important*	*possible*	*necessary*	*present*
different	*difficult*	*likely*	*available*	*useful*

On the other hand, adjectives of subjective evaluation such as *nice, good, wonderful, terrible, good, pleasant, terrific,* or *terrible* are **not** employed in academic writing.

In academic prose, the verb *be* is very frequently followed by a noun phrase. Additionally, linking verbs can be followed by complement noun clauses and, rarely, prepositional phrases (Leech & Svartvik, 1994).

> *The reason that an economy's income is the same as its expenditure is that every transaction has two parties.... (Mankiw, 2001, p. 206)*

> *Gross domestic product (GDP) is the market value of all final goods and services produced within a country in a given period of time. ... Usually, the interval is a year.* (Mankiw, 2001, p. 208)

> *Although domestic quantity supplied and domestic quantity demanded differ, the steel market is still in equilibrium....* (Mankiw, 2001, p. 182)

Impersonal *it*-cleft constructions prevalent in academic writing are almost always followed by a linking verb (Quirk et al., 1985; see chap. 6 on pronouns):

> *It is the existence of values that underlies facts.*
> *... and it is reasonable to conclude that there is some "higher" being that is the ra-*

tionale behind such inconsistency.
It is at this point that the concept of moral worth plays a role in his [Sorley's] theory. It is through physical and mental adversity that happiness or pleasure are not properly to be construed at the end of our conduct. (All citations from Schoedinger, 2000, pp. 280–283)

In teaching, a small chart may be helpful to explain the syntactic regularities of the structure and uses of linking verbs.

Common Structures with Linking Verbs

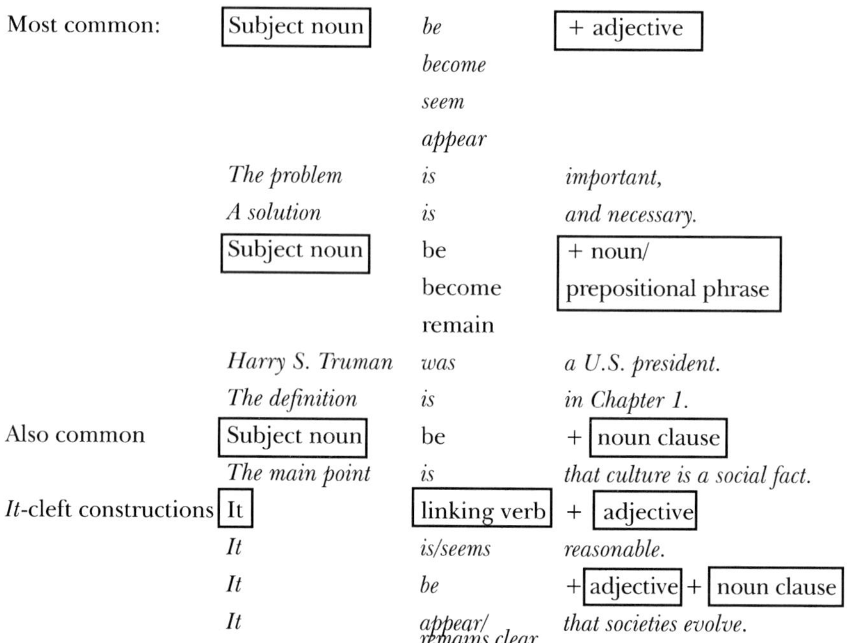

Most common:	Subject noun	*be*	+ adjective
		become	
		seem	
		appear	
	The problem	*is*	*important,*
	A solution	*is*	*and necessary.*
	Subject noun	be	+ noun/ prepositional phrase
		become	
		remain	
	Harry S. Truman	*was*	*a U.S. president.*
	The definition	*is*	*in Chapter 1.*
Also common	Subject noun	be	+ noun clause
	The main point	*is*	*that culture is a social fact.*
It-cleft constructions	It	linking verb	+ adjective
	It	*is/seems*	*reasonable.*
	It	*be*	+ adjective + noun clause
	It	*appear/ remains clear*	*that societies evolve.*

It is important to note, however, that the structures with linking verb + adjective are often overused in L2 academic discourse. As a result, a text that relies too much on linking verb + adjective constructions may appear simplistic and overly descriptive.

The use of predicative adjectives with linking verbs (*be wealthy, be important*) limits the amount and type of information that a sentence can convey (i.e., predicative adjectives can only refer to states or particular properties of the subject; Chafe, 1994). For example,

In history, science grows more complex, and it grows from general to specific. When science is still new, scientists do not have to have a special kind of knowledge. They work

in general knowledge. But when knowledge is more complex, scientists begin to choose special part from knowledge as a whole. Their jobs become more specialized. This special approach in science is important because scientists can accurately make conclusions.... The new approach in research is important because by this approach scientists can explain a phenomenon or solve a complicated problem. When science is mature, then research needs more special knowledge, and technical knowledge becomes essential. (From a student paper on the history of science.)

To deal with a high number of simplistic linking verb + adjective structures, the issue of sentence compactness needs to be explicitly addressed. For example, if the predicative adjective is moved and placed in front of the subject noun, the second half (the predicate) of the sentence can be "freed up" to include more information (see chap. 9 on adjectives).

science is complex → complex science (requires specialized knowledge)

science is mature → mature science

technical knowledge becomes essential → essential technical knowledge (can lead to more accurate conclusions)

jobs become specialized → specialized jobs

In classroom instruction, the teaching of copula and linking verbs often takes place at the beginning levels of proficiency because the uses and functions of these verbs are relatively uncomplicated. However, as the students' proficiency continues to increase in the course of language study, more diverse constructions and text functions of other lexical verbs should be brought to the forefront.

LOGICAL-SEMANTIC RELATIONSHIP VERBS[3]

In formal academic texts, certain verb classes refer to concepts, causes, proofs, embodiments of knowledge, and other complex relationships between actions and events (Halliday, 1994). The function of logical-semantic relationship verbs is to refer to the construction of knowledge by establishing cause and/or providing proof for events or denoting a change in the state of affairs. Although the lexical content of some of these verbs is advanced, their contextual uses do not need to be.

accompany	*allow (for)*	*approximate*	*belong to*	*change*
account (for)	*alternate (with)*	*arise (from)*	*cause*	*combine (with)*

[3]Some of these verbs are mentioned earlier in this chapter among the essential academic verbs.

complement	*contrast (with)*	*follow*	*involve*	*represent*
conflict	*contribute (to)*	*imply*	*involve*	*resemble*
consist of	*decrease*	*include*	*occur*	*result (in)*
constitute	*depend on*	*illustrate*	*precede*	*result (in)*
contain	*develop*	*increase*	*reflect*	
contradict	*differ from*	*indicate*	*replace*	

As with other types of lexical verbs, a productive approach to teaching relationship verbs can take place in the form of collocational expressions that can be learned in chunks. Collocations are combinations of two or more words that tend to be found together in text and discourse (Schmitt, 2000). These can include relationship verbs in combinations with nouns, prepositions and prepositional phrases, or other verbs. A few examples are presented next (for Teaching Techniques, see the next section of this chapter).

Identical Verb and Noun Forms

cause	*(verb)*	*cause concern*
		cause problems, cause inconvenience
	(noun)	*a root cause, an underlying cause*
		with good cause, without cause
		a cause for concern
		a common cause; a lost cause
		a cause of death
change	*(verb)*	*(leaves) change color*
		change (from xxx) to yyy (change from stocks to bonds)
		change jobs
		change direction, change course, change gears (conversational)
		change the subject (conversational)
		change sides
		change one's mind
		change hands (one million shares changed hands)
		change places with
	(noun)	*to be/represent a change (the new policy represents a dramatic change)*
		a change for the better
		a change of heart (= to change one's mind)
		in change, loose change, small change

For many learners, it is easier to work with relationship verbs and collocational expressions as lexical entities in contexts rather than trying to assemble phrases from their component parts (Nation, 2001; Wray, 2002). For example, collocational practice can take the form of news reportage and restatement of information from the Business section of a newspaper (e.g., "And now we bring you the latest from the stock market"). Other alternative formats for verb practice can take formal business plans or presentations to "the board of directors" or a company president, or poster sessions with formal explanations to report information to fellow-professionals, "stock holders," or potential "investors."

The key consideration in learning practice is to give learners an opportunity to use the lexical and syntactic structures that they would not otherwise have in their casual and informal interactions. For example, many relationship verbs can be employed in somewhat formal academic writing and presentations.

Verbs and Attendant Forms and Expressions

combine		*combine to do xxx*
		combine business with pleasure
		combined with xxx (acid combined with alkali)
		combined effort/action, combined income
	combination	*in combination with*
		a winning/perfect combination
		a combination of factors, combinations of (numbers/variables)
develop		*develop an idea, a plan (of action),*
		develop a relationship (with customers)
		develop into (a long-lasting peace, a full-scale war)
		(designed/created/positioned) to develop (markets/products)
		develop land
		develop film
		develop an illness
		developed country—developing country
	development	*child development*
		a new development, a significant development

Another popular venue for exposure to and usage of academic and advanced verbs is the traditional work with prefixes and suffixes. However, the teaching of prefixes and some types of suffixes may need to account for a few caveats.

- First, it is important to keep in mind that for many NNSs, who are not speakers of Romance, Germanic, or other Indo-European languages, learning the meanings of prefixes, roots, and suffixes, most of which have Latin or Greek origin, creates an additional learning burden (Nation, 2001). This is particularly true about the many words whose meaning does not represent the sum of its meaning parts (Schmitt, 2000). For example, does the *de-* in *demonstrate* have the same meaning as it does in *denounce* or *deliberate*? Also is the prefix in *antipollution* related to the one in *antiquity*?
- To further complicate matters, an ability to identify meanings of prefixes, word roots, and suffixes requires L2 learners to parse words correctly. As many teachers know from experience, this is certainly not an easy task even for NSs of English. Thus, having students work on prefixes, roots, and meaningful suffixes (e.g., *-less*, *-en*) may be of somewhat limited value when it comes to learners' actual ability to apply their skills to understanding and producing academic text. For this reason, learning new vocabulary by means of learning word parts may not always be the most efficient way to expand a student's lexical range.
- In spite of all the complexities associated with teaching prefixes and suffixes, a number of prefixes, suffixes, and word roots are so common in academic discourse that it may be difficult to do without them (e.g., *non-*, *il-*, *intro-*, *post-*). In teaching, productive and transparent word parts should be selected carefully because devoting effort to learning many others may bring benefits reduced relative to the invested labor and time.

An additional argument for teaching prefixes and suffixes is that some amount of incidental vocabulary learning can result because, first of all, learners are exposed to and work with advanced academic lexis. For example, relationship verbs include several with widely used prefixes *con-*, *de-*, and *in-*, and helping learners notice them and apparent similarities in verb meanings can create an additional opportunity for learning. Nation (2001) commented that "it takes time to learn the important prefixes and suffixes," and that for thorough vocabulary learning the needed time "is planned and provided" (p. 280). According to Nation, learning word parts "can help the learning of thousands of English words," with both high and low frequencies of use in academic vocabulary.

Verb Prefixes and Academic Verbs

con- (also: *col-, cor-, co-)*	*with, together, inside*	*conflict, constitute, contain, contradict, contrast*
de-	*not, away from, down from*	*decrease* (vs. *increase)* *decline* (vs. *incline, recline)*
in- (also: *im-, il-, ir-)*	*into or not*	*illustrate ([shine] light in)* *imply* (vs. *comply)* *include* (vs. *exclude)* *indicate* (i.e., *into point)* *involve* (i.e., *into volition/action)*
re- (also: *retro-)*	*back, again, backwards*	*reflect* (vs. *deflect, inflect)* *replace* (i.e., *place again/back)* *represent* (i.e., *before others again)* *resemble* (vs. *semblance; similar)* *result* (i.e., *as a consequence—back)*

To circumvent the tedium often associated with learning a high number of English affixes, students can learn whole words without parsing them into constituent parts in those cases when affixes appear to be particularly opaque (Adams, 2001; Schmitt, 2000). Numerous teaching materials are available for prefixes and suffixes practice, and lists, exercises, classroom activities, and homework assignments can be found in practically all reading and vocabulary textbooks for NNSs, as well as NS basic college-preparation textbooks.

Because in English derivational suffixes are less numerous than lexically abstract Greco-Latinate prefixes, teaching derived deverbal forms (e.g., *compete–completion*) is comparatively easier (Sinclair & Renouf, 1988). Most dictionary entries for verbs (and other words) provide all possible derivational suffixes, derived word forms, and essential syntactic information, as well as collocational expressions and sentence examples (see the dictionary exercise in the Teaching Section of this chapter).

Morphologically complex relationship verbs are a good place to start work on derivational forms and suffixes while providing learners an opportunity to learn words in other ways. In general terms, deverbal nouns (gerunds and nominalization) play a prominent role in academic discourse, and learning noun-forming derivational suffixes is essential for L2 academic writers (see also chap. 5 on nouns).

The following examples of such verbs as *alternate* and *approximate* and their attendant forms and other words with similar meanings illustrate only a few of the numerous possibilities.

> *alternate* (verb)— *alter—alternate* (adj.)—*alternative* (adj./noun)—*alternatively—alternating (current)*
>
> Noun relatives: *alternative* (see adjective form above); *alteration—alternation—alternator* (an engine part)
>
> Similar meanings: *modify—change—vary; alternation—modification—change—variation*
>
> *approximate* (verb)—*approximate* (adj.)—*approx.* (written abbreviation)—*approximately*
>
> Noun relatives: *approximation (*expressions*: close/rough approximation)*
> Similar meanings: *about, nearly, roughly, close to*

Studies of effective techniques for learning L2 vocabulary have demonstrated that words closely related in meaning and/or form are easier to learn and recall than unrelated words or antonyms (Nation, 1990, 2001). Although NNS associative word chains or networks do not necessarily approximate those of NSs, the learning of L2 words can be made more efficient if words are grouped by meaning similarities or synonymy because such groupings encourage a development of new word associations. Most important, however, for the purposes of learning new academic verbs (and other words) to be employed in text production, according to Nation (1990), learners do not need to remember every item in a synonym cluster (e.g., if the word *approximately* does not immediately come to mind, then easier words such as *about* or *nearly* may also work well in a context).

CHAPTER SUMMARY

Constructing university-level L2 academic prose places great demands on students' lexical and syntactic skills. One of the key domains in L2 vocabulary instruction must specifically address learners' range of and fluency with lexical classes of verbs, which are essential in all academic discourse and text. In addition to approximately 40 essential verbs that recur in formal academic prose across various genres and disciplines, 350 foundational verbs need to become a focus of L2 vocabulary teaching.

Overall, most verbs employed in academic texts can be roughly divided into five lexical classes: activity verbs, reporting verbs, mental/emotive verbs, linking verbs, and logical-semantic relationship verbs. In L2 text production, lexical verb classes do not have an equal importance (e.g., activity verbs and mental/emotive verbs play a less central role than reporting, linking, and logical-semantic relationship verbs). Therefore, the bulk of instruction in academic vocabulary dealing with verb functions and uses in formal prose needs to concentrate on the latter lexical classes.

In particular, reporting verbs play an instrumental role in demonstrating familiarity with readings, referring to sources, and citations of published works. These academic discourse tasks, as well as paraphrasing material from reading and literature, constitute a requisite component of formal academic discourse. Because academic text largely deals with descriptions of states and reports of abstract relationships among entities and events, linking verbs and logical-semantic relationship verbs are far more common in formal written prose than in any other genre. Hence, the teaching of appropriate contextual uses of relatively lexically simple linking verbs and, on the other hand, complex relationship verbs is crucial in L2 vocabulary and grammar instruction.

A variety of effective pedagogical approaches to vocabulary teaching have been developed during the decades of vocabulary research:

- The most valuable techniques entail helping learners build semantic domains (or associative networks) of verbs that are synonyms or near synonyms and that can provide readily accessible contextual substitutions in discourse.
- Teaching verb collocations with nouns, particles, and other words represents another important discourse-oriented technique in vocabulary instruction when learners can learn phrases or groups of words as lexical chunks, instead of incremental constituent parts.
- To expand the range of verbal semantic networks, the traditional foci of vocabulary teaching, such as formal two- or three-word verbs and idioms, as well as derivational prefixes and suffixes can also prove to be highly profitable because they provide additional venues for learning and expanding vocabulary.

STRATEGIES AND TACTICS FOR TEACHING AND TEACHING ACTIVITIES

The following six exercises are designed to increase students' mastery of English verbs.

(1) Dictionary Exercise

To show learners how to use an English–English dictionary to their best advantage, a copy of a dictionary entry can be blown up to make it easier to notice details. An example of the entry for the verb *occur* can be reasonably interesting to present and explain in class (adapted from *Webster's Dictionary,* 1996). Discussion points have been added to the definition inside square brackets.

---

occur /pronunciation symbols/ *v.i.* [verb intransitive, i.e. not taking a direct object], -**curred**, -**curring** [the spelling of the past and *-ing* forms requires two *-rr-*'s.

1. [the first and common meaning] to happen; take place; come to pass [these can be used as replacements/synonyms]: *When did the accident occur?* [the teacher can provide additional examples of phrases and sentences for this meaning, e.g. *The event occurs/takes place annually/frequently/in the summer.*]

2. [the second most common meaning] to be met with or found; present itself; appear [possible replacements for the second meaning].

3. to suggest itself in thought; come to mind (usually fol. by *to*); *An idea occurred to me.*

L [from Latin] *occurrere* to run, to meet, arrive, meet, equiv to *oc-* + *currere* to run.

—**Syn**. 1. befall [somewhat dated]. See **happen** [this is an important synonym] 2. arise, offer.

occurrence /pronunciation symbols/ *n.* [this is a derived noun] 1. the action, fact, or instance of occurring.

2. something that happens; event; incident [these can be possible noun synonyms]; *We were delayed by several unexpected occurrences.*

—**Syn**. 1. circumstance. See **event**.

In learners' dictionaries, additional information can be found, such as attendant prepositions (**occur** *in/among*, as in *Viral infections occur mainly among school children*) or collocations (*it occurs to somebody that*, as in *It occurred to him that new sports drinks may be popular among baseball fans*), or distinctions between formal and informal registers (**occur** *is formal and not common in spoken English*).

In general, dictionary exercises can provide learners with the necessary skills to navigate English–English dictionaries, which are daunting for many academically bound students even when they have outgrown their bilingual dictionaries. Such teacher-guided dictionary practice can also help learners notice occurrences of important words in reading.

(2) Building Semantic Clusters and Sets of Lexical Substitutions

(a) A list of verbs with various clusters of similar meanings can be provided in random order. Working in pairs or small groups of three or four, learners need to sort out verbs into the clusters according to the similarities of their meanings (e.g., Change-verbs or Organize-verbs). Then students need to supply additional verbs from their knowledge to bring the number of verbs in each cluster to 10 (or some other number). It is necessary to inform students at the outset that the pairs should be prepared to defend their choices and attributions during the extension portion of this verb practice.

The starting set can include:

analyze	elaborate	distinguish	propose	arrange	precede
investigate	operate	structure	fulfill	enlarge	remove
perform	schedule	state	coordinate	organize	follow
decline	balance	identify	debate	broaden	mention
decide	conclude	note	observe	work	move
research	run	view	expand	complete	
distribute	serve	reduce	notice	decrease	

The semantic clusters for categorizing the verbs can include several options, such as those next or some other broader or narrower combinations of these:

Change size/amount	Organize	Differentiate
Restate ideas	Function	Study in depth

It is important to keep in mind that more than one reasonable clustering of verbs is possible when the clusters are based on abstract semantic and lexical constructs such as *organize*, *function*, and *differentiate*. For example, the verb *observe* can fit well into the clusters Study in Depth and Restate Ideas or *precede* and *follow* into Organize and Differentiate. However, the teacher can take advantage of this conceptual fluidity and move to the next step of this exercise.

Here is one version of the verbs grouped by meaning (various possible options are listed in parentheses):

Change size/amount	**Organize**	**Differentiate**
decline	distribute	(distinguish)
(balance)	schedule	(structure)
reduce	(balance)	(identify)
expand	(structure)	(note)
(arrange)	(identify)	
enlarge	(coordinate)	
broaden	(arrange)	

(complete)	organize
decrease	precede
remove	follow
(move)	(move)

Restate ideas	**Function**	**Study in depth**
(elaborate)	perform	analyze
conclude	operate	investigate
(distinguish)	(schedule)	(elaborate)
conclude	run	(observe)
(identify)	serve	(expand)
(note)	fulfill	
view	(coordinate)	
propose	work	
(observe)	(complete)	
notice		
(expand)		
mention		

Unless the teacher is working with beginners, including simple action verbs (e.g., *giggle, laugh, cackle, chuckle*) in the starting set is less advantageous for learners because such verbs are rarely employed in academic prose and because they are concrete.

(b) When students have completed their clusters, they need to be given five minutes to review and assess their verb lists for each semantic group (*time to huddle*). Then two pairs (or groups) compare their verb lists in each cluster and defend their choices, which invariably differ from those made by another pair of students. Much productive direct and incidental learning takes place when students need to explain meanings of verbs to other students and the reasons for their choices. In fact the greatest benefit of the exercise lies in the follow-up discussion of verb meanings and the students' reasons for placing them in a particular cluster. Furthermore, students who are familiar with secondary and nonliteral meanings of abstract verbs have an opportunity to teach other students and verbalize their knowledge explicitly.

Usually the preparation for this exercise in terms of homework, classwork, and the final discussion of the verb meanings combined lead to almost immediate and noticeable productive uses of these verbs in students' academic text.

---

[4]I am grateful to Bruce Rogers, Ohio State University, for this exercise.

(3) Editing Practice and Word Replacements[4]

Students receive lists of sentences and/or text excerpts in which conversational or colloquial words are used (nouns or verbs). The students have to replace conversational vocabulary with academic equivalents or contextually appropriate items whenever possible (some possible replacements are noted in square brackets):

1. *These days, education is the most important thing* [objective, achievement, opportunity for advancement] *in people's lives since without education we cannot do* [accomplish, attain, carry out] *anything* [our objectives, goals, advancement] *in our lives.*
2. *People* [individuals, students, youth] *who get* [acquire, obtain, receive,] *better education will* [may, can] *get* [find, secure, compete for] *a better job, and people who get* [have] *less education will get* [have] *a hard time* [trouble, difficulty] *getting a job* [position, employment, job opportunities].
3. *Students use telecommunication and try* [attempt, undertake] *to search for* [find, learn, locate, obtain] *something* [information, fact, data] *that they want* [aspire, seek] *to gain through* [benefit from, increase their knowledge].
4. *When we discuss* [describe, examine, undertake to study, take a look at] *the history of western music, we discuss* [analyze, classify, categorize] *the music history by dividing it into several parts* [types, groups, categories, classes].
5. *Many scholars think* [believe, have the opinion, hold the view] *that since ancient times, music has not had a direct relation* [connection] *to painting.*

(4) Describing Graphs/Charts and Writing Data Analysis

Various graphs, charts, or data can be given to students with instructions to write a report based on the data. Individual students or pairs of students can each receive different graphs and data (e.g., Country A, Country B, Country C [The World Almanac, The World Book, and numerous encyclopedias contain a wealth of all sorts of information]), and company business graphs, stock prices, the stock market overview articles, and other sources can be used. In addition, students receive a similar or different list of verbs for each graph or set of data. The students' task is to write a report that presents the data and includes the verbs from the list. As an extension activity, students can also produce speculative explanations for the distribution of data in their graphs and set.

<u>Common Verbs for Various Graphs/Data</u>

combine	drop (off)	lead	reduce	slip
decline	fall	level	reflect	speculate

decrease	grow	notice	resemble
deduce	hold (up)	observe	result
determine	increase	precede	rise
deviate	judge	raise	sink

College Enrollments and the Cost of Tuition in State and Private Universities

Topic Specific Verbs

apply (for)	charge	enroll	pay
admit	drop out	fail	retain
afford	employ	graduate	teach

Normal High and Low Temperatures and Precipitation in Two to Four States

Topic Specific Verbs

coincide	cool off	fall	heat up	warm (up)
compound	deviate	flood	rain	
cool down	dry out	form	snow	

50 (or 5) Top Grossing Movies/Video Games in 2002

Topic Specific Verbs

award	generate	market (verb)	sell
come out	gross (verb)	reign	top
earn	import	release	win

Large U.S. Centers of Population 1900–2000

Topic Specific Verbs

arrive	locate	populate	revive	stimulate
gain	lose	relocate	seek	supplement
inhabit	maintain	reside	shift	sustain
leave	move (in/out)	reverse	stabilize	

(5) Word, Verb, or Prefix Competitions

Individual or pairs of students receive a list of verbs where each represents a lexical synonym starting point.

Report	*Research*	*Develop*

Each student or a pair needs to come up with as many lexical synonyms, associations, collocational phrases, or sentences for each verb in a limited amount of time. Then students can count and compare their lists to see which students won the competition.

With prefixes, students receive a list of similar starting points:

Re-	*Con-*	*De-*	*In-*	*Pro-*

Similarly, students need to come up with as many verbs, phrases with verbs, or sentences with these prefixes to see who can top the class counts.

It is important that at the completion of each competition, the winning student or team read out their list to the rest of the class. In addition, if the winners missed some verbs or phrases, the rest of the class can supplement it; as a result of the cooperative effort, the entire class arrives at the complete accessible list. Later the list can be photocopied and distributed to the entire class for all students to have and review. To maximize the learning benefits, students should be told a few days in advance of the competition when it is scheduled to take place so that they have the opportunity to study their words, verbs, and affixes for an extended period of time.

(6) Omitted Verbs

(see chap. 5 on nouns for a similar exercise)

In an excerpt from an academic text or textbook, all verbs should be deleted (whiteout would work well), and the list of the omitted verbs should be given to students on a separate sheet of paper. Individually or in pairs, students can replace all the omitted verbs. To add a level of complexity, students may be required to confirm that verb tenses are used correctly in the replaced structures. As in (1), when the task is completed, students can compare their replaced verbs with those of other students and see who has correctly replaced the most verbs. It is important that when comparing the replaced verbs, students or pairs of students discuss their reasons for making particular (correct) choices.

QUESTIONS FOR DISCUSSION

1. What would be an effective lesson plan for teaching verbs to beginning level students? To advanced students?

2. How would you make the best use of students' time teaching verbs for academic writing? With limited class time, what would you **not** devote much attention to?

3. Some classes of verbs are used less in academic writing than are other classes. Why do you think this is so? How can you help students differentiate between them?

4. How can the learning of new verbs (or nouns) be made more efficient? How can you as a teacher promote long-term retention of vocabulary items?

5. What may be the differences between idioms and collocations? Which type of expressions is more common in written academic prose? What are the possible reasons?

FURTHER READINGS ABOUT LEXICAL CLASSES OF VERBS AND TEACHING

Verbs in Academic Prose

Berkenkotter, C., & Huckin, T. (1995). *Genre knowledge in disciplinary communities*. Hillsdale, NJ: Lawrence Erlbaum Associates.

Chafe, W. (1985). Linguistic differences produced by differences between speaking and writing. In D. R. Olson, N. Torrance, & A. Hildyard (Eds.), *Literature, language, and learning: The nature and consequences of reading and writing* (pp. 105–123). Cambridge: Cambridge University Press.

Chafe, W. (1986). Evidentiality in English conversation and academic writing. In W. Chafe & J. Nichols, (Eds.), *Evidentiality: The linguistic coding of epistemology* (pp. 261–272). Norwood, NJ: Ablex.

Leech, G., & Svartvik, J. (1994). *A communicative grammar of English* (2nd ed.). London: Longman.

Leech, G., Rayson, P., & Wilson, A. (2001). *Word frequencies in written and spoken English*. London: Longman

Logical-Semantic Relationship and Other Types of Verbs

Halliday, M. A. K. (1994). The construction of knowledge and value in the grammar of scientific discourse, with reference to Charles Darwin's *The Origin of Species*. In M. Coulthard (Ed.), *Advances in written text analysis* (pp. 136–156). New York: Routledge.

Hunston, S., & Francis, G. (2000). *Pattern grammar.* Amsterdam: John Benjanims.

Palmer, F. R. (1994). *Grammatical roles and relations*. Cambridge: Cambridge University Press.

Partington, A. (1998). *Patterns and meanings*. Amsterdam: John Benjamins.

Scollon, R. (1993a). Maxims of stance. *Research Report No. 26*. Hong Kong: City Polytechnic of Hong Kong.

Verbs and Collocations

Moon, R. (1994). The analysis of fixed expressions in text. In M. Coulthard (Ed.), *Advances in written text analysis* (pp. 117–135). New York: Routledge.

Moon, R. (1998). *Fixed expressions and idioms in English*. Oxford: Oxford University Press.

Renouf, A., & Sinclair, J. (1991). Collocational frameworks in English. In K. Aijmer & B. Altenberg (Eds.), *English corpus linguistics* (pp. 128–143). New York: Longman.

Tadros, A. (1994). Predictive categories in expository text. In M. Coulthard (Ed.), *Advances in written text analysis* (pp. 69–82). New York: Routledge.

9

Adjectives and Adverbs in Academic Discourse

OVERVIEW

- Essential academic adjectives (and derived adverbs)
- Expanding the lexical range of adverbs and adjectives
- How to distinguish adjectives and adverbs
- Comparative and superlative adjectives and adverbs in academic text
- Prepositional phrases with adjectival and adverbial functions
- Participles and infinitives as modifiers
- Adjectives in thesis statements

Textual and discourse functions of adjectives and adverbs represents one of the key areas in L2 instruction on grammar and lexis. In written academic discourse, adjectives and adverbs can perform a variety of rhetorical functions, many of which are discussed in some detail in this chapter. Although adjectives and adverbs are not as numerous as nouns and verbs, adjectives, for instance, are extraordinarily frequent in academic writing—much more so than in conversational discourse or other types of writing (Biber et al., 1999). According to Huddleston and Pullum (2002), practically every sentence includes adjectives and/or adverbs.

For L2 learners, adjectives and adverbs often present a number of problems. To begin, various studies of NNS academic writing and text have shown that L2 writers often do not employ adjectives and adverbs in ways congruent with the norms of formal academic and professional writing (Hinkel, 1995b, 1997b, 1999a, 2003a; Hyland, 1998, 1999, 2002b; Hyland & Milton, 1997; Johnson, 1989b). For instance, advanced NNS writers use significantly fewer attributive adjectives and significantly more predicative adjectives than NS students with less training in writing and composition (Hinkel, 2002a). In addition, L2 academic texts often contain particularly high rates of intensifying adverbs (e.g., *really, very, totally*) and low frequencies of hedging devices to limit the breadth of generalizations and claims (e.g., *many/most, possible/possibly*) that are often expected in academic prose (Swales, 1990a; Swales & Feak, 1994; see also chap. 12 on hedges).

To compound some of these discourse-based complexities, syntactic and morphological irregularities among various classes of adjectives and adverbs can make L2 academic writing appear particularly error-prone. For instance, a vast majority of ESL teachers are familiar with **I work hardly and walk fastly* and **Students are confusing about the assignment* types of structures encountered all too often in L2 production. Although errors and misuses of adjectives and adverbs in student texts can appear to be a curse that cannot be broken, many of these problems can be addressed in instruction.

For instance, *hard* and *fast* are adverbs, and they do not take the *-ly* suffix. To find out whether a word is an adjective or adverb, one needs to ask questions *how?, when?, where?,* or *why?* All words that answer these questions are adverbs. Nongradable adjectives, such as those that refer to colors or shapes (e.g., *blue, long, tall*) cannot be turned into adverbs. To see whether an adjective can or cannot become an adverb, a command can be used: **Be blue/long/tall!* If the command does not work, an adverb cannot be derived. Similarly, answers to such ubiquitous student questions are actually not complicated: *Why can't I say in this month or in last year? Why is I am boring incorrect, if the movie is boring is perfectly fine? What's wrong with it is a good the time for going shopping? I can say it is a good day for going shopping, can't I?*

The truth of the matter is that many of the constructions that lead students to these types of errors and questions that teachers deal with daily are actually not difficult to address. These and other adjectival and adverbial mysteries are clarified in this chapter.

THE IMPORTANCE OF ADJECTIVES (AND ADVERBS) IN ACADEMIC PROSE

The syntactic function of adjectives is to modify nouns and noun phrases, and adverbs similarly modify verbs. Thus, it stands to reason that if nouns predominate in academic prose, so would adjectives to describe them. The following example, a short paragraph from an introductory textbook on business and economics, consists of 83 words and contains four definitions, all of which pivot on at least nine attributive and predicative adjectives.

> (1) ***Management*** *is the effective and efficient integration and coordination of resources to achieve desired objectives.* ***Efficiency*** *refers to the ratio of benefits to costs as resources are used and depleted to produce goods and services.* ***Effectiveness*** *refers to the degree to which the company's goals are being attained. Managers are those people who are responsible for ensuring that this happens. A* ***manager*** *integrates and combines human, capital, and technological resources in the best way possible to ensure that the*

organization's objectives are achieved.[1] (Zikmund, Middlemist, & Middlemist, 1995, p. 140; italics in original).

From this short excerpt, it may be easy to see that neither the definition of management or a manager can be constructed without the crucial role of adjectives.

On the other hand, adverbs are far less frequent. The next example is similarly extracted from an introductory textbook on macroeconomics to outline competitive markets:

> (2) ***Markets*** *take many forms. Sometimes markets are highly organized, such as the markets for many agricultural commodities. In these markets, buyers and sellers meet at a specific time and place, where an auctioneer helps set prices and arrange sales. More often, markets are less organized. For example, consider the market for ice cream in a particular town. Buyers of ice cream do not meet together at any one time. The sellers of ice cream are in different locations and offer somewhat different products.* (Mankiw, 2001, p. 66)

The text in (2), like that in (1), also contains 83 words, one definition, and seven adverbs, including one adverbial phrase (*in these markets*). However, the most important difference between the uses of adjectives in (1) and adverbs in (2) is that it may not be possible to define *management* and *a manager* in (1) without adjectives, whereas the brief description of *markets* in (2) is likely to remain clear even if most adverbs are dropped (see also chap. 3).

In academic discourse, adjectives play important cohesive, classificatory, and evaluative roles (Francis, 1994; Halliday & Hasan, 1976). For example, numerous nouns with broad meanings highly frequent in academic prose can be narrowed down by means of adjectives (Bhatia, 1992, 1993); as in *concept, decision, recommendation*, or *development* can be made more specific to fit in particular contexts:

> *new-innovative / difficult-complex / clear-transparent concept*
> *positive/negative/radical/creative/fantastic decision/ recommendation/development*

(See the sections on thesis statements and evaluative adjectives later in this chapter.)

Adverbs can play a similar focusing role for the meanings of semantically broad verbs or entire sentences. For example, the meanings of the verbs from the University Word List *dissipate*, *establish*, or *rely* can be delimited to such an extent as to make them different in their textual implications:

[1]Highlighting of keyterms is retained from the original texts in both Examples (1) and (2). Adjectives and adverbs are underlined.

dissipate	*quickly/immediately*	*vs.*	*slowly/eventually*
establish	*firmly/solidly*	*vs.*	*weakly/temporarily*
rely	*completely/greatly*	*vs.*	*sporadically/occasionally*

Adjectives have two main syntactic functions: attributive and predicative (see also chap. 4). Attributive (descriptive) adjectives precede nouns and noun phrases and modify them (e.g., *human and financial capital*). On the other hand, predicative adjectives mostly occur as subject complements following linking verbs (e.g. *Computer chip markets are new/competitive/profitable*). Thus, predicative adjectives actually belong to a different type of syntactic structures than attributive adjectives. The teaching of predicative adjective uses is discussed in some detail in chapter 4 on sentence and predicate constructions.

SYNTACTIC AND TEXTUAL FUNCTIONS OF ADJECTIVES AND ADVERBS

In most cases, adverbs, like attributive adjectives, represent optional phrase or sentence elements (the only exceptions are those that function as subject or object complements). The primary function of adverbs is to modify adjectives (e.g., *highly/ somewhat desirable*), other adverbs (e.g., *very/particularly quickly*), or entire sentences (e.g., *Occasionally/Usually, economists disagree about their conclusions*).

In general terms, adverbs can be classified by their meanings, such as time, place, reason, manner,[2] and duration. Adverbs, as modifiers of all types, supply information that deals with *How? When? Where? Why? How long? How often? To what extent?* Regardless of their meanings, however, among the main parts of speech (i.e., nouns, verbs, adjectives, and adverbs), adverbs are the least frequent in academic writing (Biber et al., 1999).

Adjectives, as modifiers of nouns, and adverbs, as modifiers of adjectives, adverbs, verbs, and entire sentences, can take a variety of forms: simple, usually one-word adjectives and adverbs (e.g., *tall/short* or *quickly/slowly*), as well as more complex, such as prepositional and other types of phrases (e.g., *the partridge in the pear tree* and *In the pear tree, we have a partridge*). Complex modifiers of nouns are usually referred to as **adjectivals**, whereas **adverbials** modify everything that adverbs do. Both terms—the adjectival and the adverbial—refer to functions rather than parts of speech.

Analyses of large written and spoken corpora have demonstrated that adjectivals of all types as well as nouns are particularly common in academic writing, whereas adverbials and verbs in conversation and fiction (Biber et al., 1999) are less so. In addition, other studies of academic L2 learners have also shown that many L2 writers rely on limited vocabulary and restricted

---

[2]For the textual and discourse function of the subclass of certainty and intensity adverbs, see chapter 12.

grammatical repertoire when constructing academic text and may simply lack syntactic and lexical repertoire to express their intended meanings (Jordan, 1997; Read, 2000). To put it simply, focused instruction is essential to help L2 academic writers expand their ranges of simple and complex adjectivals and adverbials they can use in their writing.

THE ESSENTIAL ADJECTIVES (AND ADVERBS)

Similar to the lists of nouns and verbs (see chaps. 5 and 8), a number of adjectives and adverbs have been identified as foundational and recurrent in introductory textbooks across various disciplines (Coxhead, 1998, 2000; Nation, 1990, 2001). In fact most of these lexical items are so common that it may be difficult to imagine doing without them in practically any context including academic (e.g., *annual, appropriate, classic, constant, identical,* or *incessant*).

In English it may be a little tricky to tell an adjective from an adverb or an adjective from a noun or a verb without context (e.g., *an abstract painting—the article abstract, a novel idea—a great novel*). This is one of the disadvantages of word lists. However, if L2 learners are aware that a particular word can have different syntactic functions and notice how these words are used in contexts, learning new and recurrent vocabulary and grammar structures can be made productive and contextually relevant (R. Ellis, 1990, 2002; Schmidt, 1990, 1994, 1995; see also chap. 8).

Most English adverbs are derived from corresponding adjectives and are marked by the suffix *-ly*, with the exception of those that have identical adjective/adverb forms and masquerade as either adjectives (e.g., *fast, hard, high*) or adverbs (e.g., *costly, early, friendly*). Because adverbs require an addition of the suffix *-ly*, adjectives are considered to be lexically and morphologically simpler than adverbs because they are the base forms from which adverbs are derived (e.g., *accurate—accurately, annual—annually, approximate—approximately*; Adams, 2001; Leech, Rayson, & Wilson, 2001).

For this reason, the University Word List developed by Nation (1990) includes just the adjective form for both adjectives and corresponding adverbs. In many analyses of large text corpora, word frequency counts rarely distinguish between adjective and adverb forms of the same lexical base (sometimes also called *word root*).

> Thus, it is possible to think of learning the 160 adjectives of the list as expanding one's vocabulary by approximately 250 to 260 words (not every adjective has a corresponding adverb—see stative and dynamic adjectives later). As discussed in chapter 3, research has established that, for a majority of L2 learners, learning 10 to 15 new words per day represents a reasonable and attainable learning goal (Nation, 2001). Thus, the entire list of essential academic adjectives can actually be learned in slightly under 2 weeks.

The 160 Most Essential Academic Adjectives (Nation [1990] Extracted[3])

abnormal	crucial	finite	liable	precise	supreme
abstract	crystal	fluent	linguistic	premininary	synthetic
academic	cumbersome	fundamental	magnetic	previous	tangible
accurate	deficient	genuine	major	radical	temporary
adequate	definite	homogeneous	meterial	random	tense
adjacent	dense	hostile	maternal	rational	tentative
amorphous	distinct	huge	mature	reluctant	thermal
angular	diverse	identical	mental	respective	tiny
annual	divine	imperial	miliarty	rigid	transparent
anonyous	domestic	implicit	minor	rudimenarty	trivial
appropriate	drastic	incessant	mobile	rural	tropical
approximate	dynamic	incompatible	moist	scalar	ultimate
automatic	dfficient	inconsistent	negative	secure	unduly
averse	elaborate	indigenous	neutral	similar	urban
aware	elicit	ingenious	novel	simulatneous	utter
capable	eloquent	inherent	nuclear	solar	vague
civic	empirical	initial	obvious	sophisticated	valid
classic	equidistant	innate	odd	spatial	vast
cogent	equivalent	intelligent	partisan	spontaneous	verbal
colloquial	eventual	intense	passive	stable	vertical
concentric	evident	intermediate	perpendicular	stationary	virtual
consequent	explicit	internal	perpetual	subjective	visual
constant	external	inverse	pertinent	subordinate	vital
contingent	feasible	judicial	physical	subsequent	
contrary	federal	kindred	positive	subtle	
corporate	fertile	legal	potential	superficial	
credible	final	legitimate	pragmatic	superior	

As with the teaching of nouns and verbs in academic writing, contextualized substitutions of adjectives represent one of the easiest techniques to produce lexically diverse constructions and text. In the case of some of the University List adjectives, lexical replacements may not be possible in some contexts. For example, it would be difficult to

[3]When adjective and noun forms or adjective and verb forms are identical, they are included on both lists.

come up with flexible and relatively context-independent substitutions for *abstract, angular, civic, concentric, divine, synthetic,* or *vertical*. On the other hand, numerous other highly common adjectives can have a variety of approximate and contextually appropriate descriptors, including words on the list (e.g., *amorphous—vague, definite—positive,* or *radical—drastic*).

For most instructors, compiling sets of lexical substitution for frequently used adjectives would not require much special preparation. It is easy to derive adverbs from most adjectives on the list as well as their substitutions:

accurate *exact, meticulous, precise, thorough*
accurately *exactly, meticulously, precisely, thoroughly*
adequate *satisfactory, sufficient, fair, acceptable, passable*
adequately *satisfactorily, sufficiently, fairly, acceptably, passably*
adjacent *next, nearby, adjoining, immediate*
adjacently *next, nearby, immediately*
amorphous *vague, unclear, undefined, unspecified*
amorphously *vaguely, unclearly*
annualyearly, per year, per annum
annually *yearly, per year, per annum*
appropriate *applicable, suitable, fitting, relevant*
appropriately *applicably, suitably, fittingly, relevantly*

According to Biber et al. (1999), the most common adjectives used in academic corpora of English number fewer than 25. These can be used both in attributive and predicative functions:

able	*clear*	*difficult*	*important*	*likely*	*necessary*	*small*
available	*common*	*great*	*impossible*	*long*	*new*	*sure*
better	*different*	*high*	*large*	*low*	*possible*	*true*

As mentioned, in academic prose adverbs are not nearly as common as adjectives, and even the most common are encountered at a rate of less than 1% (Biber et al., 1999). In academic writing, a handful make up the vast majority of adverbs and have the function of intensifiers, hedges, restrictives, or additives (Hoye, 1997; see also chap. 12):

Intensifiers: *even, very, quite, more, well*
Hedges: *sometimes, often, usually, relatively, probably, perhaps, generally*
Restrictives: *only, especially, particularly*
Additive: *also*

Most single-word adverbs or adverbial phrases in academic text occur in the medial position in the sentence, rather than at the beginning or end (e.g., *Measuring the temperature by hand and at uneven intervals proved to be …; It is often noted that air-born particles do not usually move in predictable patterns.*).

TELLING ADJECTIVES AND ADVERBS APART

Although most adverbs are marked by the suffix *-ly*, many are not. For example, adverbs without markers include:

almost	*now*	*seldom*	*today*
already	*often*	*sometimes*	*tomorrow*
here	*quite*	*then*	*yesterday*
next	*rather*	*there*	*yet*

On the other hand, some adjectives have the *-ly* suffix:

costly	*likely/unlikely*	*sickly*	*ugly*
early	*lively*	*silly*	*yearly*
elderly	*manly*	*shapely*	
friendly	*lovely*	*womanly*	

Some words can have the **functions of both adjectives and adverb** without changes in their form:

deep, early, fast, hard, hardly, high, late, long, low, near

To determine whether a particular word is an adjective or an adverb, a simple technique can be used: If a particular word or phrase answers the questions *where when, why, how, how often/long,* this word/phrase is an adverb.

For example,

Every business must operate (how?) *profitably to stay around* (when/how long) *for a while.*

With the exception of their occurrences as part of predicate following *be-* and linking verbs, all adverbs and adjectives represent optional sentence elements (see also chap. 3).

NONADVERBABLES AND NONCOMPARABLES

Adjectives can be divided into various semantic classes such as stative and dynamic, and gradable and nongradable. These classifications are important only inasmuch as their syntactic irregularities are concerned.

> The first two semantic classes of adjectives, **stative** and **dynamic**, are important and common in academic text because they usually denote shapes, measurements, colors, or nationalities. Stative adjectives refer to those qualities that cannot be changed by the noun they describe (the possessor; Quirk et al., 1985).

For example,

tall, short, old, young, fat, large, flat, round, square, long, hard, red, yellow, German, Korean

Because academic writing in general employs a high number of descriptors of size that are, in effect, stative adjectives, it is important that L2 writers be mindful of their syntactic idiosyncrasies (Biber et al., 1999; Channell, 1994). From this perspective, an important syntactic characteristic of these items is that they do not derive corresponding manner adverbs. Adverb forms of these adjectives that do exist have completely different meanings (e.g., *shortly* [soon], *hardly* [almost not], *broadly/largely* [generally], *widely* [in many places/among many people]). The most common academic stative adjectives are *long, small, high, low,* and *large*.

To test whether an adverb form of an adjective exists, it can be used in an imperative sentence (e.g., **Be tall/short/old/young/round/long*).

On the other hand, dynamic adjectives can be converted to adverbs by adding the suffix *-ly* (e.g., *anonymous—anonymously, arbitrary—arbitrarily, fair—fairly, feasible—feasibly, legal—legally, neutral—neutrally, objective—objectively, rational—rationally*).

Two additional classes of quirky adjectives include gradable and nongradable. Gradable adjectives can be used for comparisons, and nongradable adjectives cannot:

Gradable *more/most complex/drastic/fluent/flexible/intense*, vs.

Nongradable **more/*most potential/total/uncountable/countless/main/wrong*

Nongradable adjectives refer to everything-or-nothing qualities of nouns (either you are total or you are not). For the same reason, nongradable adjectives cannot be used with the intensifying adverb *very* or have sentence predicate functions (and occur after linking verbs). For example,

**The new project is more potential/main and very right/principal.*

COMPARATIVE AND SUPERLATIVE DEGREE OF ADJECTIVES AND ADVERBS IN ACADEMIC WRITING

Comparative and superlative degree adjectives have the function of comparing nouns (e.g., *big difference—bigger difference*). Comparative/superlative degree constructions can have a small number of syntactic constructions, of which three are prevalent in academic writing:

1. Comparative/superlative degree forms with the markers *-er/est*
2. Phrasal comparatives with more/most (e.g., more/most complex)
3. Structures with comparative clauses *than* and *as ... as:*
   The report is longer than I expected [it to be].
   The prices for commodities are (not) as high as analysts predicted [them to be].

For monosyllabic adjectives, as well as two-syllable adjectives with *-y*, *-ly*, or *-le* endings, comparative and superlative degrees are marked by *-er* and *-est* and discussed in practically every grammar textbook (e.g., *hot—hotter—hottest, pretty—prettier—prettiest*). In academic writing, comparative degree adjectives with *-er* are far more prevalent than other comparative constructions. In addition, academic writing in general employs more comparatives than other types of writing, such as fiction or news (Biber et al., 1999).

Other comparative degree adjectives adhere to a phrasal pattern with *more/most* + adjective (e.g., *more accurate, most prominent*). Like *-er* comparative forms, *more* and *most* phrases are also found more frequently in academic text than any other.

In addition to the *more/most* comparative and superlative degree adjectives, all adverbs with the *-ly* suffix also take *more/most* forms of comparative and superlative degrees. Such adverbs are far more numerous than those that take *-er/-est* comparative forms simply because more adverbs end in *-ly* than those that do not. Those adverbs that have forms identical to adjectives (e.g., *early—earlier—earliest, friendly—friendlier—friendliest, fast—faster—fastest, late—later—latest, low—lower—lowest*) follow the adjective comparative degree pattern for words with similar syllable structure.

What Not to Teach. Constructions with **comparative clauses** such as *-er than* and *as ... as* are actually relatively rare despite the fact that they are addressed in most ESL textbooks. Specifically, in corpus research, both these types of clauses are identified at the rate of approximately 0.03% per 1 million words of academic text (Biber et al., 1999). Thus, if ESL writing instructors have a limited amount of time and need to make choices, it does not seem that these constructions should have a high priority.

Similarly, superlative degree adjectives and adverbs are particularly rare in formal prose (e.g., *most impressive[-ly], most clean[-ly], most clear[-ly]*). Occasionally and in specific collocational contexts, simple adverbs without *-ly* can be used in superlative degree, but largely not in academic essays (e.g., *at your earliest convenience, at the earliest/soonest, most nicely,* or *most pleasantly*).

On the whole in their corpus of academic text, Biber et al. (1999) found only 800 superlative degree adjectives and adverbs per one million words (0.08%). These researchers pointed out that the markedly low frequency of superlatives "in academic writing probably reflects a general reluctance to make extreme claims" (p. 524). This finding can be contrasted with a much greater frequency of superlatives in news reportage or conversation.

What to Teach. The comparative and superlative degree adjectives and adverbs that do occur in academic writing are actually limited to only a few common items. These are presented next in two groups and organized by the frequencies of occurrence: first those with particularly high rates and then the second tier (Biber et al., 1999).

The Most Frequent Comparative/Superlative Degree Adjectives and Adverbs in Academic Writing (in declining order)

Pairs of One-Word Comparatives/Superlatives	One-Word Comparatives Only	Phrasal Comparatives/ Superlatives With More and Most
better—best	earlier	most important
greater—greatest	easier	more difficult
higher—highest	lower	more important
larger—largest	older	more likely
	smaller	most likely
	wider	

The second tier of common *more/most* combinations with adjectives in academic writing includes:

most common	*most effective*	*most significant*
more complex	*more frequent*	*more sophisticated*
more complicated	*more general*	*most suitable*

more convenient	*more powerful*	*more useful*
more detailed	*more recent*	*most useful*

Overall only a handful of attributive adjectives persistently recur in academic writing. Therefore, it seems reasonable that L2 students need to learn and use them interchangeably in their own writing.

ADJECTIVAL AND ADVERBIAL PREPOSITIONAL PHRASES

In academic writing, prepositional phrases are highly frequent—more so than in any other type of writing. Their functions can be either adjectival and adverbial depending on the word or phrase they modify. For example, a prepositional phrase can have the function of an adjective when it modifies a noun (e.g., *a dinner at a restaurant*) or an adverb when it describes a verb or an entire sentence (e.g., *Important clients eat at a restaurant* or *At a restaurant, we can observe an important separation of goods and services*).

> Because the contextual uses of prepositional phrases (and prepositions) are often lexicalized, it would be unreasonable to expect that L2 writers learn to use them correctly every time or even in most cases. At the very least, academically bound L2 students need to recognize prepositional phrases when they occur in the texts they read and their own writing.

Academic writing is particularly packed with prepositional phrases because they allow a writer to structure a great deal of information compactly. In fact several adverbial phrases can occur in one sentence, and often they do. It is this particularly high density of prepositional phrases in academic writing that makes them essential for students to know. As mentioned, prepositional phrases are flexible in their syntactic roles, modifying functions, and sentence positions. The extraordinarily high frequency of prepositional phrases, combined with their flexibility, is the reason that students have to learn to recognize prepositional phrases and use them appropriately in their own writing.

1. Many uses of prepositional phrases in academic writing are idiomatic and, thus, are difficult to use correctly without learning the specific idiomatic use (Channell, 1994; Huddleston & Pullum, 2002; Nattinger & DeCarrico, 1992). In fact several studies of L2 academic text have demonstrated that NNS writers employ adjectival and adverbial prepositional phrases significantly differently than NS students do (Hinkel, 1996a, 1997b, 2001a, 2002a, 2003a; Hyland, 1998, 1999). In light of these con-

siderations, it seems important that these prevalent features of academic writing need to be taught.

2. Like adjectives and adverbs, prepositional phrases serve key modifying functions of nouns and verbs and play a crucial role in constructing specific and clear sentences expected in academic writing in English (Johns, 1997; Jordan, 1997; Swales, 1990a).
3. Because of the flexibility in their sentence positions and functions, prepositional phrases located in various sentence slots can change the meaning of the sentence or a phrase (Hoye, 1997; Kay, 1997). For this reason, they need to be used with care. For instance, in many sentences, prepositional phrases occupy the obtrusive position between the subject and verb and make it difficult to identify the main subject noun and construct grammatical sentences (see chap. 4).

On the whole, there are only a few prepositions that are frequently encountered in academic writing. The six most common prepositional phrases with any type of function account for 90% of all uses, and they are limited to:

of *in* *for* *on* *to* *with*

The second frequent set of prepositions consists of only two: *at* and *by* (see also appendix to chap. 4). Among all these, however, the phrases with *of* and *at* are encountered far more frequently than others and usually in texts about nonhuman entities (inanimate objects—things; Biber et al., 1999).

Prepositional phrases with adjectival functions predominate in lexical chunks with *of* and can play various textual roles such as those of quantifiers (*one/two/of the ...; a set/number of*), possessives (*the door of the house*), classes of nouns (*type/kind/class of books*) containers (*a box of chocolates*), measures (*a gallon of gasoline*), direction or position, (*the back of the foundation of the building*), and time (*the beginning of the experiment*). Like adjectives, prepositional phrases with *of* have an important function—delimiting broad meanings of nouns (e.g., *the style of communication, the mode of rhetoric, the function of nouns, the role of verbs, the psychology of dreams*).

Additionally, lexical chunks with *in* also proliferate, but to a smaller extent than those with *of*. The phrases with *in* often follow a large number of nouns that deal with physical location and logical relations between two nouns/noun phrases. These are extremely common in academic text, and their examples abound:

increase/decrease/gain/growth/advance	in profit/sales/crime/the number of incidents
involvement/participation/part/role/lead	in politics/markets/research/the study of ...
factor/issue/component/element/ingredient	in this decision/development/plan/choice
difference/similarity/variation/contrast	in meaning/their performance/the level of ...
difficulty/success/progress/delay	in the analysis/determining ... /identifying ...
	(mostly followed by gerunds, see chap. 5)

In addition to their adjectival functions, prepositional phrases also play the role of adverbials in practically all academic texts. In fact they represent the most frequent form of adverbial modification, followed by single-word adverbs (Kucera & Francis, 1967; comparatively speaking, adverb clauses are much rarer; see chap. 10). Adverbials of manner predominate and describe **how** an action occurred or something was done (e.g., *with care, by air/water, piece-by-piece;* Quirk et al., 1985). The second most common type consists of agentive/instrumental adverbials (e.g., *by users/software developers, with/for this purpose;* Biber et al., 1999).

It is important to note that adverbial phrases of time, place, and condition are not particularly common in formal academic writing (e.g., *in January, at the lab/in this city,* and *if the company sells)*.... On the other hand, research has demonstrated that L2 academic writers overuse adverbials in these three semantic classes, and their prose often appears repetitive (Hinkel, 2002a). For example,

> *Nowadays, knowledge explosion is a term we often hear of. Knowledge explosion in technology today means massive accumulation of data. Sixty years ago, there is even no computer, but these days there is computer science. Computers are now used everywhere, in laboratories, on assembly lines, and in offices. Computers are used to control production on assembly lines and at the factory. If we need computers, we need to know how they work. Nowadays in offices, most paperwork can be done on computers. If computers do not function well, our society cannot work well either.* (Extracted from a student assignment on knowledge explosion and technology.)

This short excerpt from a student's text contains seven adverbials of place, six adverbials of time, and two conditional clauses (see chap. 10), not even to mention two manner adverbs, an intensifier, and a frequency adverb. Clearly the redundant adverbials of time and place need to be omitted and, possibly, replaced with other information.

Another large and important class of adverbials consists of various hedging devices that express hesitation (*possibly, perhaps*), an element of doubt and uncertainty (*probably, quite likely*), attribution of knowledge and information (*according to the article*), and limitation (*in this case, in my view*). These are discussed in chapter 12.

NOUN PHRASES OF TIME, MANNER, AND FREQUENCY

A subset of time adverbs can be particularly difficult for L2 writers to use correctly: those with demonstrative pronouns *this, that, these,* and *those*, as well as time phrases with *every, last, next, all*, as in **in this/that/last week/month/year.* This type of error occurs when these time phrases are formed similar to other time adverbials such as *in March/2001*. The main point to make to students about these constructions is that *this, that, these, those, every, last, next,* and *all* + time phrase do not take the prepositions *in* or *on* (as in **on this Monday*), although it is possible to say *on this day or during this/that/the last month/year.* As a general rule, nouns function as adverbials in contexts when they can answer the questions *When? How often? How long?* (see also chap. 4).

With all prepositional phrases, regardless of their functions, students must learn to recognize and use them appropriately in varied constructions. To construct coherent and grammatical sentences, students also have to separate prepositional phrases from the required key sentence elements such as subjects, verbs, and objects/complements. When working on academic text, L2 writers need to be aware of how the placement of the prepositional phrase in a particular sentence slot can change the meaning of the sentence.

PARTICIPLES AND INFINITIVES WITH MODIFYING FUNCTIONS

Present and past participles and infinitives represent other frequent types of adjectival and adverbial modifiers. For example, in the phrase *developing countries,* the present participle modifies the noun *countries* and therefore has an adjectival function, as does the past participle in *developed nations* or the infinitive in *a method to check the water level*. However, such constructions as *a solution emerged to simplify ..., to calculate the temperature, we ..., compared to the average increase,* or *by drawing a straight line,* all have adverbial functions because they modify verbs or entire sentences.

Participial Adjectives and Adverbs

Only a few things need to be mentioned about these modifiers because, on the whole, participials are relatively simple. However, participial adjective phrases (e.g., *the thermostat controlling the temperature ...* or *the temperature held constant at 50‡F*) are very common in academic writing, far more so than the adjective clauses from which they are derived (see the following discussion; Biber et al., 1999; Swales & Feak, 1994).

(1) The labels *present and past participle* actually have little to do with the present or past. Present participles that end in *-ing* (e.g., *amazing, boring, leading*) actually mark active adjectives (i.e., the noun that they describe performs the action expressed by the participle). In fact, it is possible to think of

these constructions as shortened (reduced) adjective clauses (see chap. 10). For example,

nations [that are] developing → developing nations

the research [that is] amazing → the amazing research

(2) Past participles that end in *-ed* or take the *-en* form (e.g., *reported, lost, hidden*) mark passive adjectives (i.e., the noun that they modify does not perform the action but some other entity does). For example,

the data [that are] reported → the reported data

the continent [that is] lost → the lost continent

The distinction between *-ing* and *-ed* forms of participial adjectives is often difficult for students, and such errors as *I am boring with this book* or *I am confusing about the homework* are common. Emphasizing active or passive (doing and receptive) functions of these adjectives is particularly helpful and can clarify a great deal of misunderstanding about the usage of these adjectivals. For example, in the sentence *I am boring* or *I am confusing*, *are you performing/doing the action? are you boring/confusing (to) someone? or is something else performing the action? in this case, are you boring or bored? confusing or confused?* Looking at the pairs *boring teacher—bored students* and *boring students—bored teacher*, can you tell me how this *boring/bored* structure works?

It is important to note, however, that most active or passive participial adjectives in English are lexicalized (i.e., they do not follow particular syntactic rules and can be impossible to derive; Hinkel, 2002d; Owen, 1993; Palmer, 1990, 1994). Thus, those constructions that students need to use frequently in their writing simply have to be learned as set (or fixed) expressions (e.g., *a winding road, a long-winded speaker*).

(3) One-word adjectives of any type precede the noun they describe as in *reported data* or *forgotten legends*. On the other hand, adjectival phrases are placed after the noun and do not move from their original position:

the objects [that are] moving slowly approach one another →
the objects moving slowly approach one another

the couples [that are] described in the journal article →
the couples described in the journal article

Like all other nouns, nouns with participial adjectives can occupy the subject or object sentence slot.

(4) Present or past participles can also perform the function of **active or passive adverbials** (aka reduced adverb clauses) in such constructions as:

Revolving around the earth, the moon is revered in many religions or
Revered in many religions, the moon revolves around the earth.

However, participial adverbial phrases are singularly rare in student academic writing (Hinkel, 2002a) and are not worth the time and effort expended on teaching them.

The Most Common Active and Passive Participles in Academic Writing (in any function)

Active Participles		Passive Participles		
being	concerning	based	caused	obtained
containing	involving	given	concerned	produced
using	having	used	made	taken

A side note. There are three types of *-ing* constructions in English: the progressive verb aspect (e.g., *I/he am/is singing*) (see chap. 6); the gerund that is, in fact, a noun derived from a verb (e.g., *Singing is enjoyable/Peter enjoys singing*) (see chap. 5); and the present participle that can perform the function of an adjective (e.g., *a singing bird*) or an adverb (*While singing, the bird ...*).

To tell the difference among the progressive verb aspect, the gerund, and the present participle, the sentence function of an *-ing* word needs to be determined. For instance, an *-ing* word that is part of the verb phrase is likely to be a progressive verb (e.g., *The cake is baking*). An *-ing* word in a subject or object sentence position is a gerund (e.g., *The key to learning is reading and writing*), and an *-ing* word that describes a noun or is a subject/object complement is likely to be an adjective (e.g., *an amazing story* or *the story is amazing [to me]*).

In many cases, however, it is impossible to tell the difference between the functions of various *-ing* words (e.g., *I am confusing* vs. *I am confusing you right now*). Also, for example, in the phrase *reading books*, the function of the word *reading* can be identified only when it is placed into a sentence (e.g., *Reading books are expensive* [adjective] vs. *Reading books is important* [gerund]).

Students need to be made aware of the various sentence roles of *-ing* words to be able to identify at least their important functions in sentences and contexts, such as gerunds or active/passive adjectives.

Infinitives as Adjectives and Adverbs

Infinitives have a large number of functions; for example, for postverb (predictative) positions of infinitives, some researchers identify as many as 10 (Biber et al., 1999) and others up to 20 functions (Huddleston & Pullum, 2002). The most common function of infinitives, noted in practically every ESL grammar book, is that of a nominal in the subject and/or object position (e.g., *To see is to believe* or *To know her is to love her*). Another ubiquitous type of infinitive is that with lexical verbs + noun/gerund/infinitive constructions as in *Young consumers prefer denims/wearing stiletto heels/to wear stiletto heels* (see also chap. 5 on nouns and (3)). In this section, only the adjectival and adverbial functions of infinitives are discussed.

In academic writing, only two types of infinitives occur in adjectival functions (Biber et al., 1999):

a/the way to + verb　　　　*a/the time to + verb*

Other modifications by means of infinitive phrases have adverbial functions. Infinitives as adverbials adhere to several lexicalized patterns that simply need to be learned.

1. Infinitives of purpose with omitted *[in order] to* constructions:
   The experiment was conducted [in order] to ...
   This type of constructions can be relatively easy to teach: If the phrase *[in order to]* can be inserted after the verb, an infinitive can be used; if not, a gerund may be an alternative. For example, which structure is correct: *Students went to the library for studying* or *to study*? In this sentence, the insertion seems to work: *Students went to the library [in order] to study*. Therefore, the infinitive is correct.
2. Infinitives after linking verbs such as *be, seem, appear, tend* (e.g., *The water level seems to increase/be constant/be held at ...).* This is the most frequent type of construction in academic writing.
3. Infinitives in academic texts following particular types of lexical verbs, the most common of which are *try, attempt, fail, allow, continue, enable, require*[4] *(e.g., The market continues to drop/rise ...).*

---

[4]Some of these frequent verbs can be used with infinitives that function as nominals (e.g., *fail to pass/the test, continues to fall/its decline*) or without modification/complementation (e.g., *The experiment failed, The downturn continues*).

4. Infinitives after specific adjectives that predominate in academic writing. The most frequent among these are: *possible/impossible, easy, difficult*, and *hard*, as well as a few others that can be grouped by their meanings (Hunston & Francis, 2000; Quirk et al., 1985; Swales & Feak, 1994).

Necessity adjectives: *important, essential, necessary, vital* (e.g., *Heat is essential boil the water* or *It is necessary to calculate ...*).

Evaluation adjectives: *better/best, appropriate/inappropriate, desirable, interesting, logical, reasonable/unreasonable, surprising, useful/useless, wise, wrong* (e.g., *The power of nonverbal communication can be useful to notice in routine interactions* or *By the age of twelve, most children know when it is appropriate or inappropriate to establish eye contact with another person*").

On the whole infinitives with adverbial functions are much more common in written than in conversational discourse, and they are so prevalent in practically any type of writing that it may not be possible to produce a written assignment without them.

THE-RICH-AND-THE-POOR CONSTRUCTIONS

The conversion of adjectives to noun phrases is actually quite rare and occurs only in limited contexts, such as highly general texts in humanities. In fact some analyses call these constructions *generic* (Huddleston & Pullum, 2002): *the young, the elderly, the impossible*. Because these constructions are rare in academic texts, only a couple of their characteristics need to be mentioned:

1. The-rich-and-the-poor phrases that refer to **groups of people never take singular verbs** (e.g., **the rich gets richer*). In fact these structures refer to concrete nouns (i.e., *those people who are rich* or *those people who are poor*).
2. *The-impossible* phrases, such as *the unlikely* or *the ridiculous*, can take singular verbs because they have abstract meanings (i.e., *what is impossible* or *that which is ridiculous*). However, **these structures are exceptionally rare in academic writing** (e.g., *the impossible*/the unthinkable has happened). These structures may not be worth the time and effort expended on teaching them.
3. Adjective-to-noun phrases are very inflexible and can only add the intensifier *very* (e.g., *the very old* and *the very young*). In fact, they cannot even take demonstratives or possessives (e.g., **these rich, *those very poor, *our old*).

KEY ADJECTIVES IN THESIS STATEMENTS

As noted at the beginning of the chapter, adjectives play a defining role in academic prose. Although common descriptive adjectives are found practically anywhere in academic text, noun modifiers play a key role in thesis statements and statements of purpose.

> Adjectives (and adjective phrases) can be used specifically for marking/signaling thesis statements considered to be obligatory in academic papers and essays (Swales, 1990a; Swales & Feak, 1994). Thesis statements are crucially important to provide coherence in academic prose, and their function is to highlight and summarize the central idea of the paper—usually in a single and clear sentence.

In many cases thesis statements in L2 academic papers appear to be broad and general, and one of the persistent problems that teachers need to work with students on is how to narrow the thesis down and make sure it has a clear focus.

> Relying on adjectives to delimit the power of nouns can be a practical and useful technique to accomplish this goal.

Research into academic text has shown that thesis statements can be narrowed down in two ways:

1. by marking the relational qualities of the essay (i.e., the strategic plan for its development—e.g., *two main arguments/different theories*), and
2. by restricting the breadth of abstract nouns widely prevalent in academic writing (e.g., *the main character's story of natural and personal disaster*).

Corpus analyses of academic prose have shown that the most common adjectives used to refer to the relational qualities of thesis statements include slightly over a dozen:

The top two:	*same, different*
The second five:	*whole, general, major, main, single*
Other possibilities:	*basic, common, following, individual, particular, similar, specific, various*
	(Adapted from Biber et al., 1999)

Relative qualities of the topic delimiters can be used in the following contexts:

1. *The main point of this paper is to discuss two/three major/different influences on/factors in ...*

2. *This paper evaluates the general/basic principles of Keynesian economics/economic injustice …*
3. *In this essay, I will argue that the single most important factor in the success of recycling/the increase of sports gambling is …*

Additional adjectives employed to delimit broad noun meanings in academic prose consist of the seven most frequent (Biber et al., 1999).

> Topic delimiters are usually derived from nouns (e.g., *finance-financial* or *politics-political*), and these are ubiquitously used in thesis statements, as well as introductory and opening paragraphs, when writers need to orient the reader to the main points made in the essay (Swales, 1990a).

The Most Common Adjectives Used as Topic Classifiers

economic	international	national	public
human	local	political	social

These adjectives have the function of narrowing down the scope of the main topic noun:

1. *My essay discusses and outlines the* ***political*** *beliefs held by Americans prior to/ before the beginning of the cold war.*
2. *This essay describes and explores* ***social*** *impact of television viewing on public attitudes and behaviors.*
3. *This paper explains the* ***human*** *and* ***economic*** *outcomes of/factors in/considerations of teen marriage.*

WRITING FROM SOURCES AND EVALUATIVE ADJECTIVES/ADVERBS

Most academic papers and assignments of any length are expected to be based on information obtained from published sources such as books, articles, reports, or print news. Thus, following the thesis statement, the discourse frame moves to supporting information that takes the form of summaries, paraphrasing, or citations from sources (Swales, 1990a; Swales & Feak, 1994). Usually in academic papers or assignments, in addition to simply making summaries and paraphrasing information, writers are expected to evaluate their sources and the opinions expressed in them critically. According to Swales and Feak (1994), for instance, in literature overviews and summaries, evaluative adjectives represent an integral part of the writer's description of a work or source.

> To this end, particularly in papers written for social sciences and humanities courses, after summarizing the information, writers are expected to signal their own views on the topic, issue, or author's tone.

Evaluations of the material obtained from sources necessitate uses of evaluative adjectives and adverbs. Familiarity with these modifiers can allow L2 writers to recognize them in text when they are reading and, additionally, employ them in their own writing. Analyses of written academic corpora in English have shown that evaluative adjectives belong to the largest class of adjectives followed by descriptors of size.

In academic prose, evaluations of information and the author's tone can be positive or negative depending on whether the main thrust of the **paper supports or rejects the ideas expressed in a particular source**. For this reason, **evaluative adjectives/ adverbs can also be positive or negative**. For example,

1. *In the history of the United States, the struggle for women's rights plays a very important/special role.* [positive]
2. *The author accurately presents a clear picture of today's life in Japan.* [positive]
3. *The currently popular account of causes of youth violence appears to be based on incomplete facts.* [negative]
4. *The articles blame the threat of overpopulation on controversial/misguided/questionable data.* [negative]

A number of both positive and negative evaluative adjectives and adverbs have been identified as more common in academic prose than in any other type of genre (Biber et al., 1999; Swales & Feak, 1994).

Positive Evaluative Adjectives and Adverbs

accurate(-ly)	competent(-ly)	impressive(-ly)	thorough(-ly)	
careful (-ly)	good/well	innovative(-ly)	significant(-ly)	useful(-ly)
clear(-ly)	important(-ly)	interesting(-ly)	special(-ly)	

Negative Evaluative Adjectives

controversial(-ly)	inconclusive(-ly)	misguided(-ly)	unconvincing(-ly)
inaccurate(-ly)	limited(-ly)	questionable(-ly)	unsatisfactory(-ly)
incomplete(-ly)	minor	restricted	

CHAPTER SUMMARY

The syntactic function of adjectives is to modify nouns and noun phrases, and adverbs similarly modify verbs, adjectives, or entire sentences. However, those descriptions do not convey the complexities L2 writers encounter with actual uses of adjectives and adverbs in contexts. Research has shown that L2 writers often employ adjectives and adverbs in ways that are not congruent with the norms of formal academic and professional writing.

- Students need to learn the most common adjectives and adverbs and understand how and where to use them.
- Students can tell adverbs from adjectives by asking whether a particular word or phrase answers the questions *where, when, why, how,* and *how often/long*, and, if so, then this word/phrase is an adverb.
- The comparative and superlative degree adjectives and adverbs that occur in academic writing are actually limited to only a few common items and should be taught to students.
- Prepositional phrases with adjectival or adverbial functions are particularly prevalent in academic text, and instruction and practice should explicitly address placement and use of prepositional phrases.
- Active and passive adjectivals (e.g., *bored/boring*) are confusing for NNS students and often misused, but grammatically correct usage can be explained by examining whether the noun modified by the adjectival is the doer of the action or whether something else is the source of the action leading to the condition indicated by the adjective (e.g., *The boring/bored teacher*—who is boring and who is bored?).
- Positive and negative evaluative adjectives are useful for narrowing the focus of thesis statements and extracting information from sources.

STRATEGIES AND TACTICS FOR TEACHING AND TEACHING ACTIVITIES

The following three exercises can help students increase their competence in adjective and adverb use.

(1) Expanding the Vocabulary Range for Adjectives and Adverbs

Students read a set of sentences with a variety of adjectives and adverbs used in contexts. The sentences should be extracted from academic textbooks, materials, or NS academic writing and can be made graded if desired, beginning with easier ones and progressing to the more complex. The number of sentences in each set should range between 5 and 10.

The fist step is to find new adjectives and adverbs in the sentences and remember their meanings in the sentences/contexts (this task can be assigned as homework). The second step involves the same sentences with lexical items omitted, when learners need to recall the meanings of the new words and complete the sentences. For additional flexibility or challenge, learners may be able to complete the sentence with lexical substitutes or list the new lexical item and additional substitute items. When the work is completed, students can discuss new words and substitutes in small groups or as a whole class.

This exercise can be used for learning any type of vocabulary items, not just adjectives and adverbs.

Step 1. Read the sentences/texts, identify the new words, and do your best to remember them. Some vocabulary items are repeated in different sentences.

1. *When faced with the need to identify an odor (smell), people are surprisingly imprecise and inconsistent.*
2. *The experiment that resulted in a rather low identification of 20 recognizable smells required participants to note as many unfamiliar odors as they could.*
3. *Even with corrections from the experimenters, the probability that the same vaguely familiar smell would be recognized remained low.* [Psychology]
4. *Perhaps the most dramatic change in the U.S. economy over the past six decades has been the increasing importance of international trade and finance.*
5. *Technological progress has also led to growth in trade in raw materials (such as steel) and perishable goods (such as food) by making transporting goods less costly.*
6. *Goods produced by modern technology are often light and easy to transport because they have low weight and relatively compact size.*
7. *Clearly, international trade policies of a particular country also affect financial and political decisions made by its government and often lead to important changes in the market place.* [Macroeconomics] (Adapted from Mankiw, 2001)

Step 2. Students receive sheets of paper with approximately half of the original sentences. However, the sentences on the sheets can include various combinations (e.g., Sentences 1, 3, 5, and 7, or 2, 4, and 6). Some of the lexical items in each sentence are omitted, and students have to complete the sentences with the original lexical items or their substitutes. When students complete the work on their first sheet with, for example, Sentences 1, 3, 5, and 7, they receive the second sheet with the other set of sentences (e.g., 2, 4, and 6).

Occasionally these can be collected and graded to evaluate students' progress. For pair or group work, when all sheets are completed, both sheets can be handed back to their authors, and students can discuss their results. Pairs or groups of students can also be asked to come up with as many substitutes as they can for each filled-in word.

Version 1.

(1) When faced with the need to identify an odor (smell), people are ____________ imprecise and ____________.
(3) Even with corrections from the experimenters, the probability that the same _________ familiar smell would be recognized remained low.
(5) ___________ progress has also led to growth in trade in ________ materials (such as steel) and ___________ goods (such as food) by making transporting goods less costly.
(7) Clearly, international trade policies of a _________ country also affect _________ and _________ decisions made by its government and often lead to important changes in the market place.

Version 2.

(2) The experiment that resulted in a ______ low identification of 20 recognizable smells required participants to note as many __________ odors as they could.
(4) ________ the most _________ change in the U.S. economy over the past six decades has been the increasing importance of international trade and finance.
(6) Goods produced by modern technology are often ________ and easy to transport because they have low weight and _________ compact size.

An important note: If this practice is repeated two or three times per week during the term, the number of new vocabulary items from the sentences will continue to grow. To provide students an opportunity to review vocabulary learned earlier, sentences can include a growing number of combinations: those with new items, as well as the vocabulary studied earlier in the week or during the previous week or two.

(2) What Is Your Function?

Modifiers are slippery characters because they occupy various slots in the sentence structure (see chap. 4) and, depending on their position, have the functions of modifying nouns, verbs, entire sentences, or other constructions. The practice with identifying the functions of modifiers can be particularly suitable for pair or group work. When the exercise is completed, pairs or groups can compare their results and discuss them.

Step 1

In the following sentences, please identify the function of the underlined modifying phrase(s) and indicate what word(s) or phrase(s) it modifies. Also please explain whether it is possible for this modifying phrase to be moved to a different position in the sentence. If so, how would the meaning of the sentence change? Please be ready to discuss and explain your choices.

1. *In the old days, mothers used to purchase clothes for their daughters. However, that approach didn't work anymore, because in the 1990s girls started to want independence at a younger age.*
2. *Good health care and maintenance, balanced diet, regular exercise, and sufficient amounts of sleep can lead to tangible benefits in the long term.*
3. *Long-term success of sales often depends on the ability of advertising and the sales personnel to build a good relationship with the buyer.*
4. *Advertising consists of any type of communication carried by a mass medium for a company selling the product. When consumers think of advertising, they normally think of television, radio, and magazines, but any mass medium may be used for advertising over the long term.*
5. *The ability to convey messages to a large number of people at once is the major benefit of advertising.*
6. *In the mass media, such as television and particularly radio, advertising companies have to follow strict guidelines and a number of federal regulations designed to control the types of messages intended for the public.*
7. *Publicity can also appear to be similar to advertising in the mass media. However, publicity is free, while advertising is not. Advertisers have a great deal of control over the content of promotional messages, and mass-media advertising has its disadvantages.*

(Adapted from Campbell et al., 2001)

Step 2.

In the following sentences, please identify possible positions/places where a prepositional phrase or a couple of prepositional phrases can be placed to make the sentence meaning as precise and clear as possible. Please be ready to explain your choices.

1. *Two psychologists interviewed 50 newlywed couples.*

   in several states *in an experiment*

2. *Happily married couples sat close, looked at each other, and talked to their spouses.*

   together *during the interview* *frequently*

3. *It turned out that the style of being together seems to continue.*

over time *in a follow-up stud* *ynine months later*

4. *The concept of self plays an important role, and we will explore two questions: "Who am I?" and "Why I am here?"*

   today *basic* *in interpersonal communication* *for this reason*

5. *We will move to the third question, "Who are these others?"*

   to complete the discussion *then* *necessary* *all*

6. *Charles H. Cooley proposed a novel idea about the formation of self-concepts beginning with first interactions.*

   at a young age *in 1902* *with others* *first*

7. *Our self-concepts are affected.*

   during childhood *by others* *deeply* *in addition*

(Adapted from Beebe, Beebe, & Redmond, 2001)

(3) Restatement and Paraphrase

(This exercise can be combined with work on nouns and/or verbs—see Strategies for Teaching in chaps. 5 and 8.)

In Part 1, the adjectives need to be replaced to restate the authors' text. In Part 2, please paraphrase the sentences whenever possible. (Optional definitions: Restatement uses different words to say the same thing in a short phrase or sentence. Paraphrasing means taking one or two sentences from the text and expressing their meaning in your own words. Good paraphrasing contains all the necessary information from the original text, but uses a different sentence structure and vocabulary.)

Please restate the adjectives in the following phrases:

1. a precise measure ______________
2. a negative impression ___________
3. an explicit statement ____________
4. believable evidence _____________
5. huge profits ________________
6. a contrary view ______________
7. an elaborate design ___________
8. pertinent information ___________
9. a potential improvement _________
10. indigenous people ______________

Please do your best to paraphrase the following sentences (Adapted from Campbell et al., 2001).

1. *In modern America, the reporter's job is to provide accurate information to enable citizens to make intelligent decisions.*

Paraphrase____

____

____

2. *A number of tough issues face the newspaper industry as it adapts to changes in the economy and technology.*
   Paraphrase____

   ____

   ____

3. *Modern technology began radically revolutionizing newspapers in the 1970s.*
   Paraphrase____

   ____

   ____

4. *Although newspapers remain a strong medium for communication, a number of significant concerns have been raised about their future.*
   Paraphrase____

   ____

   ____

5. *In the 1990s, the development of faster means of communication created intense demand for more efficient ways of transmitting data and the human voice.*
   Paraphrase____

   ____

   ____

QUESTIONS FOR DISCUSSION

1. In much of the traditional teaching of L2 writing, the meanings and discourse functions of adjectives and adverbs have not received a great deal of attention. In fact instruction is usually limited to the syntactic forms of these lexical items. Why do you think this development has occurred?

2. Please take a look at the following sentences. Can you explain the reasons for the meaning differences between Sentences (1) and (2) and between Sentences (3) and (4)?

   1. *With the professor, students discussed their problems.*
   2. *Students discussed their problems with the professor.*
   3. **With the book, students discussed their problems.*
   4. *Students discussed their problems with the book.*

Why do you think Sentence (3) does not make much sense even when Sentence (1) seems to be perfectly acceptable? Can you quickly formulate an explanation that students can use when working with sentence or word modifiers to reduced the number of similar ungrammatical constructions?

3. Can you explain why and how the placement of adverbials makes a great deal of difference in the following sentences?

The experiment was conducted, and the book was published later in 2003.
In 2003, the experiment was conducted and the book was published later.
In 2003, the experiment was conducted and later the book was published.
The experiment was conducted in 2003, and the book was published later.

4. As noted, adjectivals and adverbials play different modifying roles and can describe different sentence elements such as nouns, verbs, adjectives, or entire sentences. Do you think it is always possible to identify the modifying functions of adjectivals and adverbials unambiguously? Can you come up with a few examples/ sentences in which it is hard to tell what particular word or phrase is being modified? Can you also explain the reasons that make it difficult to clearly identify the function of these modifiers?

5. There is a certain intuitive order in which native speakers of English organize sequences of modifiers. For example, the sentence, *The scientists conducted the experiment* can be modified by means of the following adverbials:

at The Big University *in 2002* *with great fanfare*

(a) What is the order in which these modifiers can be arranged? In the sentence-initial position? In the sentence-final position? What would happen if you add the adverb of frequency *twice* to the mix? If you add another adverb of manner *brilliantly*? If you add another place adverbial *in Beautiful State*?

(b) Can you formulate a rule that students can use when constructing sentences with multiple adverbials?

FURTHER READINGS ABOUT ADJECTIVES, ADVERBS, AND TEACHING

Duffley, P. J. (1992). *The English infinitive.* London: Longman.
Halliday, M. A. K., & Hasan, R. (1976). *Cohesion in English.* London: Longman.
Hinkel, E. (1997). Indirectness in L1 and L2 academic writing. *Journal of Pragmatics, 27*(3), 360–386.
Hoye, L. (1997). *Adverbs and modality in English.* London: Longman.
Maynard, S. (1993). *Discourse modality: Subjectivity, emotion and voice in the Japanese language.* Amsterdam: John Benjamins.
McGloin, N. (1996). Subjectivization and adverbs in Japanese. In N. Akatsuka, S. Iwasaki, & S. Strauss (Eds.), *Japanese and Korean linguistics* (pp. 187–199). Palo Alto, CA: Center for Study of Language and Information.

Myers, G. (1996). Strategic vagueness in academic writing. In E. Ventola & A. Mauranen (Eds.), *Academic writing* (pp. 1–18). Amsterdam: John Benjamins.

Myers, G. (1999). Interaction in writing: Principles and problems. In C. Candlin & K. Hyland (Eds.), *Writing texts, processes and practices* (pp. 40–61). London: Longman.

Renouf, A., & Sinclair, J. (1991). Collocational frameworks in English. In K. Aijmer & B. Altenberg (Eds.), *English corpus linguistics* (pp. 128–143). New York: Longman.

Scott, M. (2000). Focusing on the text and its keywords. In L. Burnard & T. McEnery (Eds.), *Rethinking language pedagogy from a corpus perspective* (pp. 103–121). Frankfurt: Peter Lang.

Stevens, V. (1991). Concordance-based vocabulary exercises: A viable alternative to gap fillers. In T. Johns & P. King (Eds.), *Classroom concordancing* (pp. 47–61). Birmingham: University of Birmingham Press.

Tribble, C. (2000). Genres, keywords, teaching: Towards a pedagogic account of the language of project proposals. In L. Burnard & T. McEnery (Eds.), *Rethinking language pedagogy from a corpus perspective* (pp. 75–90). Frankfurt am Main: Peter Lang..

Tribble, C. (2002). Corpora and corpus analysis: new windows on academic writing. In J. Flowerdew (Ed.), *Academic discourse* (pp. 131–149). Harlow, UK: Longman.

Appendix to Chapter 9

Evaluative Adjectives and Noun Chunks Frequent in Academic Writing

Evaluative Adjective	Main (Head) Noun
good	judges, readers, separation, communication, relations, fortune, yields, indication (e.g., good judges, good fortune)
important	changes, advances, step, part, consequences, respect, role, point, factor (e.g., important changes, important step[s])
special	cases, process, regulations, class, types, method (e.g., special cases, special process[es])
right	principles, level, relation, direction, answer, criteria (e.g., right principles, right level[s])

Contrasting Pairs of Adjectives for Paraphrasing

large—small	long—short	young—old
low—high	final—initial	previous—following
general—particular	same—different	simple—complex
primary—secondary	necessary—possible	positive—negative

(Adapted from Biber et al., 1999; Swales & Feak, 1994)

III

TEXT AND DISCOURSE FLOW: THE SENTENCE AND BEYOND

The chapters in Part III move from the major sentence elements to clauses and rhetorical features of text. Chapter 10 covers the construction and discourse functions of adverbial, adjective, and noun clauses, and how these subordinate clauses can be taught.

Chapter 11 focuses on rhetorical features of text that can improve the cohesion and coherence of NNS text, including cohesive ties and lexical substitution, lexical and semantic cohesion, phrase-level conjunctions, parallel structure, and sentence transitions. Other rhetorical features that are discussed deal with rhetorical questions and exemplification.

Chapter 12 covers how to explain and teach academic hedging to NNS writers. The need for hedging statements, generalizations, and claims in academic prose is not an obvious consideration for many NNS writers and has to be explicitly addressed.

10

Backgrounding Discourse and Information: Subordinate Clauses

OVERVIEW

- Adverbial clauses of:
  - Time
  - Condition
  - Contrast/concession
  - Cause
- Adjective clauses and adjective participle phrases
- Noun clauses and reporting verbs

Similar to coordinating conjunctions (such as *and*, *but*, and *or*) that conjoin two or more simple sentences into more complex compound constructions, subordinate clauses can conjoin two or more simple sentences into much more complex sentence units. For example, two simple sentences can be conjoined by various means and turned into a number of compound (see chap. 3) or complex sentences:

Facial expressions are the most obvious emotional indicators.
Some emotions are easier to express facially than others.

These two sentences can be conjoined by various means:

1. *(a) Facial expressions are the most obvious emotional indicators, and/but some emotions are easier to express facially than others.*
   (b) Some emotions are easier to express facially than others, and facial expressions are the most obvious emotional indicators.

2. *(a) Facial expressions are the most obvious emotional indicators; however, some emotions easier to express facially than others.*
   (b) Some emotions easier to express facially than others; however, facial expressions are the most obvious emotional indicators.
3. *(a) Because facial expressions are the most obvious emotional indicators, some emotions are easier to express facially than others.*
   (b) Because some emotions are easier to express facially than others, facial expressions are the most obvious emotional indicators.
   (c) Facial expressions are the most obvious emotional indicators because some emotions are easier to express facially than others.
4. *(a) When facial expressions are the most obvious emotional indicators, some emotions are easier to express facially than others.*
   (b) Facial expressions are the most obvious emotional indicators, when some emotions are easier to express facially than others.
5. *(a) Although facial expressions are the most obvious emotional indicators, some emotions are easier to express facially than others.*
   (b) Facial expressions are the most obvious emotional indicators, although some emotions are easier to express facially than others.
6. *Facial expressions are the most obvious emotional indicators that some emotions are easier to express facially than others.*

Depending on how sentences are conjoined, the contextual meaning can change in dramatic ways even when all resulting sentences are perfectly grammatical. In seemingly simple variants of compound constructions in (1), the mere order of simple sentences in a compound sentences can result in two slightly different meanings. Also in the two compound sentences in (2), the order of simple sentences and placement of the conjunction *however* changes the meanings of the contrast. Important meaning differences can be noted among sentences (3a, 3b, and 3c) where the order of the simple sentences and placement of the causative conjunction *because* can completely alter the sequence of a cause and its result. Similarly, the placement of the concessive conjunction *although* in (5a and 5b) can differently mark two ideas for their importance in the context (and, possibly, contextual continuity). The most dramatic structural and meaning differences can be noticed in the complex sentence in (6) with a descriptive subordinate clause ... *that some emotions are easier to express facially than others*, whereas the clause actually explains what the *indicators* are.

Roughly speaking, most ESL grammar books identify three types of subordinate clauses: adverbial, adjective (also called *relative*), and noun (also called *nominal*) clauses. In complex sentences, adverbial clauses usually perform the function of simple adverbs or adverbial phrases (Chafe, 1986, 1994). For example, the function of the time adverbial can be performed by simple adverbs or complex adverbials alike:

Soon/Now/Today,	*most water is lost to plants*	*due to runoff.*
During spring/In the fall/After the rain,	*most water is lost to plants*	*due to runoff.*
When some of the vegetation on land is removed,	*most water is lost to plants*	*due to runoff.*

Similarly, adjective clauses perform the functions of simple adjectives or adjective phrases, all of which describe nouns or noun phrases:

Soil erosion and soil loss cause a change *in the ecology of the entire region.*

Soil erosion and soil loss cause a change *that affects the ecology of the entire region.*

Following the line of similarity, noun clauses perform the functions of nouns and noun phrases. Thus, noun clauses, like nouns, can be sentence subjects or objects (direct or indirect), as well as objects of prepositions. For example,

> *Experience tells us that males and females differ considerably* [noun clause—direct object] *in how they express emotion* [noun clause—object of the preposition *in*].

Subordinate clauses of all types represent advanced syntactic constructions. Thus, it is not particularly surprising that they are more common in academic writing than in speech or conversational register (Biber, 1988; Ford, 1993). On the other hand, analyses of L2 writing have shown that NNS texts include significantly fewer subordinate clauses of most types than those identified in the academic writing of NSs first-year students (Hinkel, 2002a).

For L2 writers, however, it is important to use complex sentences in academic text at the college or university level because a writer cannot credibly build an entire assignment or term paper using only simple or compound sentences (Davidson, 1991; Hamp-Lyons, 1991b; Vaughan, 1991), although some brave souls have been known to try. It is not just that L2 writers have to use complex sentences, but they have to use subordinate clauses correctly. Using complex constructions is not likely to win any accolades if the assignment contains numerous errors.

Practically all ESL grammar and writing textbooks provide explanations, recommendations, directions, and exercises for using subordinate clauses in academic writing to improve the organization of information and connections between ideas (Holten & Marasco, 1998; Leki, 1999; Smoke, 1999; Swales & Feak, 1994). However, as with the material discussed in earlier chapters, only a few varieties of subordinate clauses are usually employed in academic writing, and for L2 writers it may not be necessary to become excellent and proficient users of all the types of complex sentences found in ESL grammar books.

Among the three types of subordinate clauses, adverbial clauses are probably easier to teach and learn than adjective or noun clauses, and the material in this chapter is organized in the order of easier first.

ADVERBIAL CLAUSES

In general, adverbial clauses are more common in speech than in writing. However, in instruction in academic writing, and argumentative writing in particular, the uses of various types of adverb clauses such as causative, contrast/concessive, and conditional are often recommended in explication, reasoning, and analysis (Hacker, 2000; Raimes, 1992, 1999; Smoke, 1999; Swales & Feak, 1994).

> Earlier studies of L2 academic writing have demonstrated that NNS writers do not employ a great variety of clauses in their prose and largely use similar types of adverb clauses repeatedly. For this reason, the uses of complex sentences with subordinate clauses need to be encouraged in L2 writing, and students have to become familiar and comfortable with employing these constructions in their text.

What Adverbial Clauses Are For and What They Do

Adverbial clauses modify the entire sentences found in the main (independent) clauses. Adverbial clauses express a variety of contextual relationships, some of which refer to time, cause, contrast, and condition (Leech & Svartvik, 1994). Some adverb clause subordinators such as *while, since,* and *as* are ambiguous because they can be found in adverb clauses of cause, time, and contrast. However, for L2 writers, being able to name the types of particular clauses is not very important, and the fact that some of them are ambiguous does not matter a great deal.

ESL grammar books usually classify adverb clauses by the meanings of adverbial subordinators, and those found in most textbooks books include those with the following labels:

- Time clauses that are marked by such subordinating conjunctions as *after, as before, when, while, until* (e.g., *When water tables drop, water flow from springs and seeps diminishes,* or *As the air rises, it cools*).
- Cause clauses with the highly common subordinator *because* and an occasional *as* and *since* (e.g., *Because oceans cover about 70% of the*

earth's surface, the largest amount of water enters the atmosphere by evaporation from the ocean surfaces).

- Contrast clauses, also called concessive or concession clauses, identified by subordinating conjunctions such as *although, even though,* or *though* (e.g., *Although water evaporates from lakes and rivers, large amounts of water enter the atmosphere by transpiration from plants*).
- Condition clauses, in most cases marked by conjunctions *if,* sometimes *unless,* and rarely *even if* or *whether or not* (e.g., *If a river is diverted, ecological impacts may be difficult to predict*).

What is important for L2 writers to know is that structurally adverb clauses of all types are conjoined with (or attached to) the main clauses, and the meaning of the subordinate clause is always external to the meaning of the main. From this perspective, constructing adverb clauses is always optional because simple sentences can be conjoined in a variety of ways.

Syntactically, adverbial clauses are peripheral to the structure of the independent clause, but they play an important role in marking primary and secondary information in text (Quirk et al., 1985). In general terms, adverbial clauses are used to frame discourse for time and/or place, for example, and present background information relevant to that in the independent clause.

Because adverb clauses represent optional constructions (not integral to the syntactic structure of the main clause), combined with the fact that there can be numerous ways to conjoin simple sentences in the flow of text (see also chap. 4), various types of syntactic sentence errors with these constructions, such as fragments, can be encountered in L2 academic writing (see the following section on Common Errors in Adverbial Clauses).

> Essentially, when working with adverbial clauses, L2 writers need to decide what information is important in their sentences: The most important information goes into the main clause, and secondary/background information goes into the adverbial clause (Quirk et al., 1985).

In academic writing, the most common adverb clause varieties can have various meanings, but their prevalence differs a great deal. In teaching, particularly when time is a concern, the teacher needs to determine what structures are more useful for students to become familiar with and which are less fruitful. For example, adverb clauses of place or purpose are not very common even in the academic writing of native speakers, but clauses of time and condition are worthwhile to address in instruction (Hinkel, 2002a, 2003a).

Prevalent Clauses in Formal Academic Writing

- Condition clauses are common in contexts that introduce the writer's position or argumentation (Biber, 1988): *If a problem cannot be denied or repressed completely, some individuals distort its nature so that they can handle it more easily.* (Psychology)
- Time clauses are far less frequent than condition clauses: *When the Etruscans expanded their territory in Italy during the seventh and sixth centuries B.C., they controlled the monarchy in Rome.* (History)
- Concession (contrast) clauses are also prevalent in contexts where they play the role of hedges to limit the power of generalizations and claims, as well as account for opposing points of view: *Although irrigation can be costly, drip irrigation greatly reduces water use and waste.* (Environmental sciences) It is important to note, however, that concession clauses with *whereas* are hardly ever encountered in student academic texts.
- Cause clauses are not as prevalent in academic writing as clauses of condition, time, and concession, and they occur mainly in conversation (Leech et al., 2001): *Because marketing is primarily responsible for conception and development of products, marketing analysts also test and refine product ideas.* (Marketing) One of the reasons that cause clauses may not be very popular in academic writing is that in real academic analyses (as opposed to cause–effect compositions usually assigned in composition courses) direct and clear-cut causes of events and developments may be difficult to identify (Biber, 1988).

However, cause clauses are relatively frequent in student academic writing possibly because they are common in the conversational register. Other important adverb clauses, such as **concession** and **condition,** are rarely encountered in L2 student writing, and it may be that the importance of their contextual and academic uses needs to be emphasized in instruction (Hinkel, 2001a, 2002a).

Cautionary notes should be made in regard to the lists of adverbial subordinators ubiquitously found in composition textbooks and writing guides alike. Some of them are hardly ever found even in published academic prose (e.g., *as if, every time that, for* [purpose, e.g., *?for I need to study hard*], *in case, in the event that, in order that, now that, provided that, so that, whereas*). The long lists of seemingly redundant subordinators with similar meanings, as they are listed, can be confusing and discouraging for NNS learners. In teaching, the best approach may be to focus on a small number of practical subordinators (but not so small that writers have to use them repeatedly) that L2 writers can use in various contexts.

The Most Common Adverbial Clause Subordinators in Academic Writing

Condition	*if* (and rarely, *unless*)
Time	*when* (and occasionally, *as, after, before, until*)
Concession	*although, while, though* (in declining order)
Cause	*because*, (and occasionally, *since*)

In general terms, concessive clauses can be employed as sophisticated hedging devices that can also help writers have a balanced perspective on an issue/topic at hand.

> Prefabricated sentence chunks with concessive clauses can be highly useful and easy to employ in introductions, thesis statements, topic sentences, and generalizations:
> *Although/While xxx,* *yyy* (thesis/topic/generalization)

It is important for L2 writers to remember that their main point should be placed in the main clause (**the-main-for-main** types of constructions; Quirk et al., 1985):

Although many among minorities do not have money to go to school, they need to get education to win the struggle for power in society.
Need for achievement varies widely from person to person, although psychologists suggest a learned achievement motive.

On the other hand, cause clauses may need to be used sparingly and with caution.

Discourse Functions of Adverbial Clauses

The mobility of adverb clauses, just as that of adverbs and adverbial phrases (see chaps. 3 and 9), can be used to the writer's advantage. If the subordinate clause is placed at the beginning of the sentence, it can play an important role in establishing a cohesive and discourse-organizing link between the text and/or ideas that immediately precede the clause and the new information that follows (see also chap. 11 on text cohesion). On the other hand, adverbial clauses placed at the ends of sentences provide expansion of the information in the main clause (Celce-Murcia, 1998; DeCarrico, 2000). For example,

This ability to influence public opinion and mobilize the entire nation against a particular deviant activity ... illustrates the vast power of the mass media in defining devi-

ance and mobilizing support for strong social control. Because they need to capture the public interest, the mass media often sensationalize crime and deviance. (Thompson & Hickey, 2002, p. 183)

In this excerpt, the sentence-initial position of the because clause connects the information in the preceding sentence to that in the main clause (e.g., *public opinion—public interest, the mass media—they,* and *vast power—capture*). Specifically, adverbial clauses at the beginning of sentences play the role of connectives and transitions between ideas and information in keeping with the-old-information-first-and-the-new-information last pattern (see chap. 11). Some researchers have found that the majority of all initial clauses consist of *if*-conditionals that have the function of organizing discourse and establishing and maintaining topics (Ford & Thompson, 1986). On the other hand, corpus analyses of various genres have demonstrated that conditional clauses are less common in academic writing than in conversation or fiction (Biber et al., 1999; Leech et al., 2001).

The ability of the sentence-final adverb clause to expand the information in the main clause can be further noted in the following text, where the information in the clause provides an example for the point made in the main clause:

The annihilation of a minority may be unintentional, as when Puritans brought deadly diseases that Native Americans had no immunity to. (Thompson & Hickey, 2002, p. 237)

In addition to the sentence-initial and sentence-final positions, adverb clauses can also occur in the middles of sentences. However, these types of constructions require a break in the flow of information in a sentence, resulting in syntactically complex constructions that most (if not all) L2 writers probably would not miss a great deal.

Tenses in Adverb Clauses of Time and Condition

In adverb clauses of time and condition, only the present and past tense can be used:

When medical trials are completed, patients' records will be kept indefinitely.
If multinational companies increase their control of the global market, cross-cultural employment training will become an essential job requirement.

In complex sentences with clauses of time and condition, only the main clause can be marked for the future tense.

The future tense is never used in time and condition clauses marked by such subordinate conjunctions as *after, as (soon as), before, when, while, until,* and *if.* In time and condition clauses, perfect tenses are also singularly rare. As discussed in chapter 7, in general the uses of the future and perfect tenses are rare in academic writing.

Position and Punctuation of Adverbial Clauses

As mentioned earlier, complex sentences with adverbial clauses in effect represent two conjoined simple sentences, which can be moved around freely until they are conjoined:

1. *In the past, colleges and universities were primarily the domain of students in their late teens and early twenties.*
2. *Now increasing numbers of older students are returning to school.*

These two sentences can be combined in various ways depending on the writer's ideas and desired context: The main point of a sentence is placed in the main (independent clause) and secondary information in the adverb clause. The two sentences can be sequenced in a way that best fits the context as well:

3. *Although in the past, colleges and universities were primarily the domain of students in their late teens and early twenties, now increasing numbers of older students are returning to school.* [the adverb clause precedes the main clause]
4. *Now increasing numbers of older students are returning to school, although in the past, colleges and universities were primarily the domain of students in their late teens and early twenties.* [the same basic meaning can be conveyed when the adverb clause follows the main clause]
5. *Although now increasing numbers of older students are returning to school, in the past, colleges and universities were primarily the domain of students in their late teens and early twenties.* [the main and background information is switched, and the meaning of sentence (5) is different from that in either (3) or (4)]
6. *In the past, colleges and universities were primarily the domain of students in their late teens and early twenties, although now the increasing number of older students are returning to school, .* [the basic meaning of sentence (6) is the same as that in (5), and both (5) and (6) are different from (3) and (4)]

In L2 academic writing, there are only a couple of important things to remember about the placement and punctuation of adverb clauses:

> If adverb clauses are placed at the **beginning** of a complex sentence, a **comma** must be used to separate it from the main clause. **No comma** is necessary when the clause is at the **end** of the sentence.

COMMON ERRORS WITH ADVERBIAL CLAUSES

Three Steps Back: *Although ... but* Errors

The main discourse and contextual function of concessive clauses is to hedge the idea/generalization/statement in the main clause and present a balanced position by accounting for other perspectives:

> *Although not all communities and groups accept society's institutions, a majority of the citizens in any country do not challenge the social order and accepted social patterns.*
> *Economic descriptions of buying decision making assume buyers' purely rational purchase decisions, even though many buying decisions have emotional aspects.*

To put it simply, concessive clauses play a role analogous to "one step back" and the main clause "two steps forward." In this way, writers advance their ideas/positions gradually and diplomatically, as is usually expected in academic writing, rather than rushing forward (Swales, 1990a).

In L2 writing, however, when writers misunderstand the "one step back" function of concessives, they additionally employ the conjunction *but* with main clauses:

> **Although managers believe that a worker's salary is everything, but they forget to think about other benefits.*
> **Even though art was very important in the 18th century, but it is not so important now because technology is where the future is.*

In effect such structures result in one-step-back (*although*) + two-steps-back (*but* with the main clause) = three steps back, and the thrust of the writer's main point does not seem to advance.

> A common student error is using *although/even though* and *but* in one complex sentence. The teacher may have to persistently and emphatically warn against this use.

Sentence Fragments

The most common types of sentence fragments found in students' writing consist of separated adverb clauses or prepositional phrases. The first type of error is usually easy to notice and correct:

**Because engineering is a practical field of the application of science and math.*
**Although education and training are an investment.*
**When students earn more knowledge and hospital experience in nursing.*

To a large extent, such errors occur (in L1 and L2 writing alike) because separated adverb clauses are acceptable and highly common in conversations:

- *Why did you decide to study engineering?*
  —Because engineering is a practical field of application of science and math.
- *Education is expensive these days. Hmmm.*
  —Education and training are an investment though.
- *So, when do students get a chance to do clinical training?*
  —When students earn more knowledge and hospital experience in nursing.

The purpose of subordinate conjunctions such as *because*, *although*, *when*, and *if* is to conjoin the main and subordinate clauses. Thus, when conjunctions are used, they need to have two clauses to conjoin. In a sense conjunctions play the role of glue to glue two sentences together; if a sentence includes only one simple sentence and a bit of glue, there is nothing for the conjunction to conjoin.

> To correct separated adverb clauses, two options are possible: Either the glue must be removed (and the conjunction deleted), or another sentence needs to be added to make use of the gluing conjunction power.

Other types of sentence fragments such as separated prepositional phrases are also highly common in conversations:

- *Where did you read about xxx?*
  —In an article about the importance of visual art in advertising.
- *When did World War I begin?*
  —On the day when the Austrian crown prince was assassinated in Sarajevo.

In written text separated prepositional phrases are more difficult to notice and correct than abandoned adverb clauses. Fortunately, however, lonely prepositional phrases are less common.

As discussed in chapter 4, every English sentence must have at least a subject and a verb to be grammatical. Thus, to identify separated prepositional phrases, the **first** step is to ask the student to **find the sentence verb**. If there is **no verb**, it is a safe guess that there is probably **no sentence**. However, if one merely inserts a verb into a prepositional phrase to turn it into a sentence, the next step is to **find the subject**. As also discussed in chapters 4 and 9, **prepositional phrases cannot be sentence subjects**. For this reason the last step is to give the sentence **a subject, in addition to the verb**, and if the subject and verb "agree" in number (singular or plural), the sentence is finally complete.

ADJECTIVE (RELATIVE) CLAUSES

Adjective clauses have functions similar to those of simple adjectives or adjective phrases. An important difference among these adjectival constructions is that single-word adjectives (even a series of single-word adjectives) are placed in front of the noun they describe, whereas adjective phrases and clauses follow the noun they describe. For example,

- *Yellow ribbons play an important symbolic role in American culture.* [a single-word adjective]
- *Contemporary educational reform is an issue for the public debate.* [serial single-word adjectives]
- *A study carried out at the University of Kansas focuses on TV viewing among adolescents.* [an adjective phrase that describes the *study*]
- *Today, a typical American couple consists of a husband and wife, who both work outside the home.* [an adjective clause that describes *a husband and wife* noun phrase]
- *Many of the children who attend day care centers do not seem to pay much attention to their mothers' departure and return.* [an adjective clause that describes the noun phrase *the children*]

In academic writing, an advantage of using adjective clauses, as opposed to attributive (descriptive) adjectives, is that the amount of information included in a clause can be greater than that conveyed by single-word adjectives (Chafe, 1994). Adjective clauses can be used to modify practically any type of noun or noun phrase, and in these subordinate clause constructions the relative pronouns *that*, *who*, and *which* replace the noun that the adjective clause modifies:

1. *Livia (58 B.C.–A.D. 29), who* [~~Livia~~] *was Octavian's third wife, was admired for her wisdom and dignity.*
2. *In search of spices that* [~~spices~~] *were in extraordinarily high demand, the Portuguese went directly to the source, to India.*

In academic writing, among all types of relative pronouns, *who, that,* and *which* are used far more frequently than *whom,*[1] *whose, when,* or *why*. The fourth common relative pronoun is *where* to modify nouns that refer to places or nouns in prepositional phrases of place (e.g., *the regions where, in the city where,* or *at the site where*). Other types of relativizers occasionally found in academic writing include *in which* and *to which* (Biber et al., 1999). A list of chunks with nouns and relative pronouns that follow them in frequently encountered adjective clauses is included in the appendix to this chapter.

When working with adjective clauses, L2 writers must remember an important point:

> Relative pronouns (e.g., *that, who,* and *which*) "copy" the grammatical information from the noun phrase they replace (i.e., if the noun phrase is plural, then the relative pronoun remains plural and requires the plural form of the verb).

In Example (1), *Livia* is a singular noun, therefore the pronoun *who* is also singular, and therefore the verb *was* is also singular. On the other hand, in Example (2), the noun *spices* is plural, therefore the pronoun *that* is also plural, and therefore the verb *were* is plural.

In addition to these relatively simple adjective clauses, one more type of these constructions exists, and it is not so simple. In adjective clauses (1) and (2) with Livia and spices, the verb immediately follows the relative pronouns *who (was)* and *that (were)*. Thus, a conclusion can be made that *who* and *that* are subjects of the adjective clauses *who was Octavian's third wife* and *that were in extraordinarily high demand*.

However, adjective clauses can become far more complex (and far more error-prone) when the relative pronoun is the object of the adjective clause verb:

European expansion advanced outside the continent with the development of the sail and the gun. Western Europeans combined the sail and the gun in the form of the gunned ship.

European expansion advanced outside the continent with the development of the sail and the gun, which Western Europeans combined [~~the sail and the gun~~] *in the form of the gunned ship.*

In (3) and (4), the adjective clause modifies the noun phrase that actually has the function of the verb object. When the verb object in the adjective clause is turned into a relative pronoun (e.g., *who, that, which*), two things happen:

[1]The pronoun *whom* is required only when it follows a preposition (e.g., *to whom, for whom, about whom*). In all other cases, *who* would be appropriate (Leech & Svartvik, 1994; Quirk et al., 1985).

- The relative pronoun is moved to the first position in the clause to follow the noun it describes
- The object noun phrase (*the sail and the gun*) is omitted because it has taken the form of the relative pronoun[2]

The following points are important for L2 writers to know:

- The structure such as **European expansion advanced outside the continent with the development of the sail and the gun, which Western Europeans combined *them* in the form of the gunned ship* is incorrect because it includes two pronouns—*which* and *them*—to refer to the same noun phrase when only one is needed.
- Relative pronouns of any kind always follow the noun phrase they describe.
- In general, adjective clauses always immediately follow the noun phrase they describe.

Restrictive and Nonrestrictive Adjective Clauses

As mentioned, the purpose of adjective clauses is to modify (describe) the nouns that they follow. All grammar textbooks that deal with adjective clauses invariably mention restrictive and nonrestrictive adjective clauses. Restrictive clauses, by means of narrowly identifying a particular noun, restrict the range and type of nouns they modify only to one specific noun or type of nouns:

> A primary group consists of a small number of people who regularly interact on a face-to-face basis, have close personal ties, and are emotionally committed to the relationship. (Thompson & Hickey, 2002, p. 158)

In this example, the rather vague noun phrase *a small number of people* is "restricted" or limited by the specific definition in the adjective clause. Restrictive adjective clauses are never separated by commas because the information in the adjective clauses is necessary (and cannot be separated out) to define and identify the noun.

On the other hand, nonrestrictive clauses are those that supply additional information to describe nouns that are already known or well defined:

> *In preindustrial societies, most interactions occur in primary groups of friends, neighbors, and kin, who can consist of parents, siblings, aunts and uncles, cousins, and other relations.*

[2]In some languages such as Arabic, Hebrew, or Amharic, the repetition of the object noun or pronoun is required, and L2 writers who are speakers of these languages may make this type of error particularly frequently.

The adjective clause in this sentence largely defines the word *kin,* which actually may not need a specific definition and is likely to be known to most native speakers of English. Nonrestrictive clauses do not delimit the noun to one specific object or range of objects in the context because a narrow identification of this specific noun is not needed (e.g., *low rainfall regions, which …*) *the Romans, who …, feudal law, which …*). In this case, the adjective clause is separated by commas: It provides helpful but inessential information.

The greatest issues with the ever-popular discussions on restrictive and nonrestrictive adjective clauses, included in every grammar and composition book, is that they are extraordinarily difficult for L2 writers to identify. In an earlier example, for instance, the L2 writer would have to know the meaning of the word *kin* and then be able to figure out that this word already has a relatively limited meaning in English, and therefore be able to conclude that the adjective clause has to be separated out by commas. The teaching of restrictive and nonrestrictive adjective clauses and their punctuation may simply not be worth the time and work expended on their conceptual (and abstract) definitions and the ambiguous rules that govern their uses.

> In formal academic writing, only 15% of all adjective clauses are nonrestrictive, and the information included in them is usually tangential and somewhat unnecessary (Biber et al., 1999).

Undoubtedly, the quality and types of prose in the formal academic writing research in English language corpora are different from that in student writing.

> Nonetheless, in teaching ESL or academic L2 writing, the distinction between restrictive and nonrestrictive clauses, as well as this particular aspect of punctuation, may simply occupy very low priority.

In light of the lexical and conceptual complexities associated with the distinctions between restrictive and nonrestrictive clauses, a general rule of thumb may be useful for L2 writers:

> Adjective clauses with *that* relative pronouns are never separated by commas.

Adjective Participial Phrases

Adjective participial phrases are derived by reducing an adjective clause to an adjective phrase, and the functions of participial phrases are largely the same as those of single-word adjectives and adjective clauses (i.e., to modify nouns and noun phrases; Meyer, 1991). In formal academic writing, the main purpose of these advanced constructions is to package information as compactly as possible (Biber, 1988). In various studies of written discourse and the assessment of L2 writing, reduced clauses and participial phrases are often identified with formal written (rather than informal) discourse and advanced facility in writing and grammar (Davidson, 1991; Hamp-Lyons, 1991a, 1991b).

It is important to note that participial phrases of any type are hardly ever found in L2 academic writing, but using them occasionally (and correctly) in academic text may project a certain degree of linguistic sophistication.

Adjective participles can be active or passive (see also chap. 7):

Most water flowing in irrigation canals comes from nearby rivers [active participial phrase]

Water stored in artificial lakes evaporates during dry and hot summers [passive participial phrase]

When teaching advanced ESL/EAP writing classes, teachers need to be familiar with the mechanisms for adjective clause reductions even if they are not explicitly taught. For instructors, familiarity with the participial phrase derivation may come in handy when working with common student errors in the uses of active and passive adjectives (see chap. 7 for more information).

Adjective clauses are reduced by means of just a few steps:

1. The relative pronoun—the adjective clause subject (e.g., *who, that, which*)—is deleted
2. The adjective clause verb is converted to a **participle**.
   a. In the case of the **active** verb, *-ing* is added to the base form of the verb (e.g., *flow + ing, contain + ing, include + ing*)
   b. In the case of the **passive** verb, the auxiliary *-be* verb is deleted, and the past participle form of the verb is used (or simply retained without change as it is used in passive verb constructions; e.g., *[~~is/are~~] found, [~~was~~] reduced, [~~were~~] taught*)

Adjective Participial Phrase: Active

In regions ~~that~~ face the most serious water shortages, about 85% of the water is used in irrigation.

In regions face + ing the most serious water shortage, about 85% of the water is used in irrigation.

Adjective Participial Phrase: Passive

The volume of ground water ~~that is~~ found in underground reservoirs exceeds that of all surface water.

The volume of ground water found in underground reservoirs exceeds that of all surface water.

Adjective clause reduction in most contexts is considered optional (Chafe, 1970). According to a detailed study by Master (2002), the prevalence of adjective clause reduction depends on the discipline to some extent. For example, in biology, chemistry, psychology, computer science, geology, math, and physics, adjective clauses are reduced far more rarely than in humanities. On the whole, however, discipline-related distinctions are not very pronounced. Most important, however, Master (2002) found that **in a vast majority of cases, adjective clause reduction occurs when relative pronouns (e.g., *who, that, which*) occupy the clause subject position** (e.g., *the river flowing* ...). These types of participial phrases are far easier to teach (and for students to learn) than those where the relative clause pronoun occupies the clause object position (fortunately indeed).

A small number of active or passive adjective participles have been encountered repeatedly in formal academic writing, and these are derived from highly common academic verbs (see chap. 8). The frequent participles can be learned and used as needed in academic writing.

> With the exception of *using*, the *-ing* participles in the list hardly ever occur in the form of progressive verbs, and L2 writers do not need to be concerned about confusing them.

Common Academic Participles
Active (in declining order)

containing	*involving*	*relating*
using	*arising*	*requiring*
concerning	*consisting*	*resulting*
having	*corresponding*	

Passive (in declining order)

based	*caused*	*obtained*
given	*concerned*	*produced*
used	*made*	*taken*

(Adapted from Biber et al., 1999)

Some examples of the chunks with these participles can be taught in combinations with catch-all and other academic nouns found in chapter 4:

the issue concerning	*a solution requiring*
the experiment involving	*the result produced*
the problem relating to/resulting	*the information taken (together)*
the data containing/using	*given these facts*

As mentioned, however, the reduction of adjective clauses to adjective participial phrases is an optional and advanced syntactic operation. For this reason, it should only be taught in the case of highly proficient L2 writers or when a specific need arises in light of student errors with these constructions.

NOUN CLAUSES

Noun clauses are highly common in academic writing, and they are probably the most common type of subordinate construction. As the following information demonstrates, they are also by far the most structurally complex.

As mentioned earlier, the functions of nouns can be performed by single words, phrases, full clauses, and reduced clauses (such as infinitive or gerund phrases; see chap. 4). Noun clauses can fill the noun slot in a complex sentence (e.g., the subject, the object, the subject complement, or the adjective complement; see chap. 3). However, noun clauses that fill the object slot are by far the most frequent in academic writing (Biber et al., 1999). For example:

Psychologists know	*that information in short-term memory must be repeated.*
[Psychologists know	the fact/something/xxx—noun].

The sentence pattern with noun clauses in object slots, following the main verb phrase, is very common indeed:

> *Millions of students have learned that they need to repeat the multiplication table to remember it.*
> *Bartlett's research shows that material in long-term memory interacts in interesting ways.*

> The most important discourse function of noun clauses is to present and paraphrase information from sources. For this reason, noun clauses are particularly prevalent in academic writing when they follow **reporting** verbs in summaries, restatements, and citations (Leki, 1999; Swales, 1990a; Swales & Feak, 1994; see chap. 8 for information on reporting verbs).

Other types of constructions where noun clauses occur is following a specific and limited class of adjectives, such as:

> *It is apparent/clear/evident/well-known/true/vital that students learn vocabulary.*
> *The author is certain/clear/correct/right that students' writing needs improvement.*

Another function of noun clauses is to provide for extensive cohesive ties by means of recapitulation of the information stated earlier (e.g., *It was stated/mentioned previously/above that* ...) or predicting the development of discourse/argumentation moves, particularly in introductions (e.g., *This essay/I will show/argue/prove that* ...).

> As opposed to adverb clauses, in **noun clauses** the secondary information is presented in the main clause, **the most important information is presented in the subordinate clause**, which is almost always placed at the end of the sentence.

Noun clauses in the subject position (e.g., *That students study hard is a well-known fact*) are very rare in formal academic prose. Although most grammar books include them in their explanations of noun clauses, such structures practically never occur in student academic writing, native and non-native alike (Hinkel, 2002a).

Noun Clause Structure

Simple Sentences as Noun Clauses. Practically all simple sentences, as well as questions, can become noun clauses. Simple sentences that are sentences are embedded into complex sentences and marked by means of the subordinate (and occasionally optional) conjunction *that:*

Some psychologists believe	*(that)*	*changes occur in steps and stages.*
Others maintain	*(that)*	*changes take place in smooth, steady progression.*

> Although officially the clause marker *that* is optional, it serves an important function and marks the beginning of a noun clause. In formal writing, the omission of *that* can lead to confusing constructions that are somewhat informal. For this reason, L2 writers are best advised to keep their *that*s on.

By far the most common pattern of noun clauses entails reporting/belief verbs followed by *that* clauses (see also chap. 8). Additional lists of reporting and belief verbs are included in appendix to this chapter.

The Most Frequent Academic Reporting Verbs Followed by *That* Noun Clauses (in declining order)

say	*suggest*	*see*	*ensure*	*think*	*mean*
show	*know*	*find*	*indicate*	*believe*	*feel*

(Adapted from Leech et al., 2001)

As mentioned earlier, another type of construction with *that* noun clauses is the construction in which the clause follows an adjective. In these constructions, noun clauses have the function of adjective complement:

> *It is apparent that the current recycling policy is not working.*
> *The author is correct that the American pubic needs to be educated about waste.*

Such constructions are far more common in the conversational register than in any type of written prose, and they are relatively rare in formal academic writing. However, they occasionally appear in evaluative types of texts written by native and non-native students alike possibly because these structures occur in conversations (e.g., *I am angry/glad/happy/pleased/sorry/ sure you had problems* or *It is nice/great/incredible/ shocking/terrible that he was elected*).

The number of common adjectives followed by noun clauses is actually relatively small.

The Most Common Academic Adjectives Followed by *That* Clauses

General Purpose

accepted/acceptable	*doubtful*	*right*
apparent	*evident*	*true*
certain	*likely/unlikely*	*well known*
clear	*possible/impossible*	
correct	*probable*	

Evaluative Adjectives

critical	*vital*	*preferable*
crucial	*interesting*	*sufficient*
desirable	*disappointing*	*understandable*
essential	*notable*	*unusual*
important	*noteworthy*	
necessary	*noticeable*	

(Adapted from Leech et al., 2001; Swales & Feak, 1994)

Wh- Questions as Noun Clauses. *Wh-* noun clauses that represent embedded *wh*-questions also serve to delay the most important and new information to the secondary clause position and provide a lead to the topic the writer intends to introduce and address (Francis, 1994). This function of *wh*-clauses is particularly important in developing cohesive ties from the old-to-the-new information structure (see also chap. 11).

> In many cases with nouns clauses, it is the constructions with *wh*-questions, marked by *wh*-subordinators such as *what, where,* and *who,* that cause the greatest number of L2 errors.

In direct questions, subjects and verbs are inverted, and an auxiliary verb is added in almost all cases (with the exceptions of *who* and *what* questions to sentence subjects). For example:

What are some problems with Bentham's utilitarian theory?
How does the need for political theory arise?
What does Aquinas mean by "motion" and why cannot something be both "moved" and "mover"?

To convert direct **wh-questions to noun clauses** (and make them indirect questions), the questions need to be turned into statements—with **the subject (first)—verb (second)** word order as is required in all statements in English.

Also when *wh-* questions are converted to indirect questions in noun clauses, all wh- words must be retained. For example, when paraphrasing direct *wh-* questions, most of the work takes place inside the noun clause:

Main Clause	Noun Clause—Embedded Question
The author asks	*what [~~are~~] some problems are with Bentham's utilitarian theory.*
The article discusses	*how [~~doeS~~] the need for political theory ariseS.*
Philosophers continue to debate	*what [~~doeS~~] Aquinas meanS by "motion" and why [cannot] something cannot be both "moved" and "mover."*

It seems clear from the examples that *be-* and modal verbs (e.g., *can, may*) are moved to follow the subject slot. With other types of verbs, auxiliary verb information such as tense, person, and number (e.g., *does, do, did*) is merged with the main verb (e.g., *doeS ... mean → meanS, did ... mean → meanT, ariseS → arose*).

In teaching *wh*-questions to noun clause conversions, it is important to emphasize that students need to:

a) identify the **entire subject slot** to determine where to put *be*- and modal verbs
b) locate the **head noun** in the subject slot to figure out whether it is singular or plural to attend to subject–verb agreement

Embedding questions with subject wh- words immediately followed by main verbs does not require moving any elements of the noun clause:

	What determines status or class within society?
Hegel's theory explains	*what determines status or class within society.*
	What distinguishes philosophy from theology?
This essay presents Burke's views on	*what distinguishes philosophy from theology.*

Caveat: In examples such as *What are some problems with Bentham's utilitarian theory?*, the sentence subject is the noun phrase *some problems*, and not the relative pronoun *what*. As mentioned earlier, it is necessary to identify the entire subject noun phrase and head noun to convert *wh*-questions to noun clauses. To locate the subject and head noun, the litmus test is a full-sentence response to the question:

What are some problems with Bentham's utilitarian theory?
Some problems with Bentham's theory are xxx.
What distinguishes philosophy from theology?
YYY distinguishes philosophy from theology.

After direct questions are converted into statements, no question mark is needed: It is replaced by a period to mark the end of the sentence. This is an important point to make in teaching: The concept of a sentence and marked sentence boundaries is difficult even for NS students. To add to the mix, the **syntactic** distinctions between questions and sentences, marked by intonation alone in many languages,[3] may be particularly puzzling to speakers of many languages (e.g., the inverted subject–verb order, not to mention the separation of verbs into various parts, and questions marks).

Yes/No Questions as Noun Clauses. With **yes/no questions** that have no *wh*- words (e.g., *does utilitarian theory explain xxx?...*), a ***wh*- word must be added—*whether*.** For example,

[3]In many Indo-European and non-Indo-European languages, such as Russian, Ukrainian, and Arabic, questions are intonation marked.

	Is government in civil society a necessary evil [yes/no]
No one knows whether	*[~~Is~~] government in civil society is a necessary evil?*
	Does anarchy arise in the absence of government? [yes/no]
Taylor investigates whether	*[~~DoeS~~] anarchy ariseS in the absence of government.*

Contrary to explanations found in many ESL books that *whether* and *if* can be equally well employed in constructing noun clauses, in academic writing *if* occasionally occurs with only three verbs:

see (if) *determine (if)* *find out (if)*

As the examples demonstrate, to convert a question into a noun clause correctly, L2 writers need to be able to **identify the entire subject noun phrase** in the subject slot (in this case, *government in civil society*) because the verb follows the subject. Then it is necessary to identify the head noun with which the verb must agree in number. Clearly, noun clause construction is not a trivial task.

- To summarize, when L2 writers work with noun clauses, a number of syntactic operations need to be attended to:
  1. Embedding **statements** is the easiest task:
     - Build the main clause, add *that*, and then add the statement.
       *Biologists claim **that** cellular theories can explain aging.*
  2. With **wh- questions:**
     - Build the main clause, keep the *wh-* word, and identify the whole subject slot.
       *After years of research, it is still not known **what** the causes of depression are.*
     - Move *be-* or modal verbs to follow the entire subject slot. In the case of the auxiliary-and-main verb split, merge the verbs. **If the verb follows the *wh*-word, do not move anything.**
       *Entomologists continue to investigate **what eradicates** pests in food crops.*
     - Locate the head noun in the subject slot and make sure that the number of the head noun agrees with that of the verb phrase elements (including auxiliary verbs)
       What doeS carbon dating show researchers?
       The articles discusses what carbon dating showS researchers.
  3. With **yes/no** questions:
     - Build the main clause and add the conjunction *whether* after the main clause.
     - Identify the whole subject slot and move *be-* or modal verbs to follow the entire subject slot. In the case of the auxiliary-and-main verb split, **merge the verbs.**

Locate the head noun in the subject slot and make sure that the number of the head noun agrees with that of the verb phrase elements (including auxiliary verbs).

An important **rule of thumb** that applies to all noun clauses (and particularly embedded questions):

When questions become clauses, they are no longer questions—they are clauses, and clauses are actually sentences. For this reason, the question word order (the verb before the subject) and separated verbs (e.g., *what does it do? does it do …?*) cannot be used in statements even when a larger sentence includes a question in it.

A useful analogy can be a pencil box/pouch, a ring binder, a file folder, or any type of a container that includes smaller items in it: The main clause can include all sorts of items in it, such as noun (or adjective) clauses, but what is seen on the outside is the container and not its contents. So when the larger "container" is a sentence, the entire structure is a sentence. Helping L2 writers to **learn to notice** their own errors in the word order and the verbs in embedded noun clauses can take the form of simple prompting: Is this a question or a sentence? Is this a question? This is a sentence, right?

Tenses in Noun Clauses. As mentioned throughout this book, the distinctions between the conversational and formal written registers need to be explicitly addressed in teaching (Hinkel, 2001a, 2003a, 2003b). A majority of L2 learners in English-speaking environments have far greater exposure to and experience with conversational than written academic discourse, and many structures that may be common place in casual interaction find their way into formal writing:

?John said that he'll call me tomorrow; ?Mary told me that she'll be here at 8.

Although the uses of the past and future tenses in complex sentences with noun clauses is ubiquitous in conversational register, it is not acceptable in formal written English. As mentioned in chapter 7 on tenses, the usage of tenses in formal writing is highly conventionalized. A formal system of rules, also called the *sequence of tenses,* governs the uses of tenses in noun clauses:

- If the main verb takes the past tense, the subordinate clause can only take past or present tenses. Future markers and modal verbs undergo some of the following changes (these are only about half of all the rules):
  - Simple present turns into past (e.g., *He said that he studied every day*).
  - Simple past turns into past perfect (e.g., *She said she had studied*).

- The future marker *will* is turned into *would;* and *would have* in negative with the meaning of *did not* … (e.g., *He said that he would study for the test* [he did], and *He said he would have studied for the test* [he actually did not]).
- *Can* turns into *could* in positive constructions, and *could have* in negative also with the meaning of *did not* … (e.g., *She told me that she could help me*, and *She told me that she could have helped me*).
- *May* becomes *might* (e.g., *They mentioned that they might come*).
- *Should* and *might* do not change (e.g., *We said that we should/might go*).
- *Must* becomes *had to* (e.g., *They told us that we had to go*).

Given that these rules mention only some of the most important tense and verb changes in noun clauses, it is not difficult to see how implementing them may become hairy indeed. However, the conventionalized uses of tenses in academic writing can be used to L2 writers' advantage because the range of tenses and aspects in written prose is far more limited than that in conversational discourse (or most ESL grammar books).

In academic writing, the large number of rules and specific verb conversions in noun clauses can be simplified to a great extent:

> The verb tense in the main clause determines the tense in the noun clause. If the main clause is in the past, the noun clause verb can take the simple present or simple past tenses. The present tense is far easier to use in both main and noun clauses than to change verbs to past-tense forms (no positive/negative worries) or replace the verbs altogether.

In a sentence such as, *Researchers noted that it may/might be difficult to tell the difference between depression and learned helplessness*, the verb in the noun clause can be changed to the past tense or remain in the present tense, and both constructions can be perfectly usable, although their meanings differ slightly.

Another possibility for using tenses in noun clauses correctly is simpler still (see chap. 7):

> Whenever possible, the simple present tense should be used in the main and the noun clauses, with the exception of case studies and historical or biographical contexts, which are specifically flagged for the past tense by means of past time adverb phrases (or other markers).

In the following two examples, the present tense and past tense in the main and noun clauses work equally well:

Nancy Snidman showed that shyness represented a relative, culture-bound label. She found that no differences existed in the reactions of four-month-old babies.

Nancy Snidman shows that shyness represents a relative, culture-bound label. She finds that no differences exist in the reactions of four-month-old babies.

The flexibility of meanings and functions in the simple present tense makes it a highly versatile and practical construction. Simple is as simple does.

> In light of structural complexities in the uses of noun clause, it is hardly surprising that even advanced L2 writers continue to make syntactic errors in these structures. Most important, what is needed for these students is practice, practice, and practice.

A Side Note

In English, the pronoun *that* can serve many masters and do many things, and for this reason it is very confusing for L2 learners:

- The easiest form of *that* is **demonstrative**:
  That article was on achievement and learned motives, as in *this, that*, and *the other*

To identify the demonstrative *that*, it can be simply replaced by *this* or *the other*, and the sentence remains largely similar in meaning and structure: *this article was …, the other article was …* (see also chap. 6 on pronouns).

- The second form of *that* is the least useful because it introduces noun clauses but does not have a function in them:
  The author thinks that the earth is flat.

In this sentence, *that* can be simply omitted without any damage to or change in the sentence: *The author thinks the earth is flat.*

- In noun clauses that occupy the subject position of the entire complex sentence, the introductory *that* cannot be omitted:
  That students have trouble with noun clauses is understandable.

- The third form of *that* is probably the most complex: It replaces subject or object noun phrases in adjective clauses and, thus, takes over the functions and grammatical features of the noun phrases it replaces:

Social interaction that is found in many human activities plays an important role in socialization.

When the relative pronoun *that* is the subject of the adjective clause, it is easy to identify because it is immediately followed by the sentence predicate (verb). When *that* is not followed by the sentence predicate, it is the object of the adjective clause:

Emotions that people are not willing to discuss include aggression, envy, or disdain.

In this example, *that* is the verb object of the adjective clause: It is followed by the subject *people* and the verb *are*. In either case, when *that* is the subject or the object of the adjective clause, it cannot be merely dropped (as is the case with *that* in noun clauses) because without it the sentence would be ungrammatical.

CHAPTER SUMMARY

Subordinate clauses of all types represent advanced syntactic constructions. These clauses are necessary for L2 writers to use in academic writing to avoid having their writing appear too simple. However, to benefit from the sophistication subordinate clauses add to the students' writing, students must use these constructions correctly.

- Adverbial clauses are probably the easiest subordinate clauses for L2 writers to master, and they express a variety of contextual relationships, some of which refer to time, cause, contrast, and condition. Adverbial clauses are separate from the main clause of a sentence and contain supplemental information to the primary information in the main clause.
- Adjective clauses perform the same function that adjectives and adjective phrases perform, but where adjectives precede the nouns they describe, adjective clauses follow the nouns they describe. Adjective clauses can be used to modify practically any type of noun or noun phrase, and in these subordinate clause constructions the relative pronouns *that*, *who*, and *which* replace the noun that the adjective clause modifies. Adjective clauses are easier for students when the relative pronoun is the subject in the clause. When the relative pronoun is the object, students need to be taught to move the relative pronoun to the beginning of the clause and make sure that there is only one object to the verb.
- Noun clauses are probably the most common type of subordinate construction. Unfortunately, they are also the most structurally

complex. In addition to embedding simple noun clauses in the subject or object position of a sentence, students must be able to convert *wh*-question and yes/no question sentences into statement format when creating noun clauses from question sentences.

STRATEGIES AND TACTICS FOR TEACHING AND TEACHING ACTIVITIES

The following four exercises (some with extended activities) are designed to help students improve their use of subordinate clauses appropriate for academic writing.

(1) Reviewing the Reviewer

(a) Students are assigned to read an article, op-ed piece, or book/movie review. Their task is to assess the writer's position on the issue discussed in an article or evaluate the review. The first step is to identify the article writer's position conveyed in citations of the opinions and arguments of others, agreement/disagreement with these opinions/arguments, and points that the writer chooses to emphasize. In addition, students focus on reporting verbs and their contextual meanings by means of which the writer's position is established.

The reporting verbs and evaluative adjectives (see also Suggestions for Teaching in chaps. 8 and 9) can be organized into several groups such as positive–negative, supporting–rejecting, or neutral. As the next step, students can be asked to add their own items to supplement the lists (e.g., Positive Reporting Verbs, Positive Evaluative Adjectives, Negative Reporting Verbs, or Negative Evaluative Adjectives). Students can work in pairs to construct the lists.

Another option is to supply students with starter lists from which they can begin making their own:

Positive Reporting Verbs	Negative Reporting Verbs	Neutral Reporting Verbs
agree	deny	maintain
confirm	claim	demonstrate
assert	allege	note

When the lists are completed in pairs or individually, students write an evaluation of the article, op-ed piece, or review they read or another article/review. This tasks can be assigned several times throughout the term or a couple of times per week provided that students continue to build on the items already included in their lists.

(b) The same task can be carried out if students are asked to identify the writer's implications or possible outcomes of the argument/position expressed in the article/review. The reporting verbs in the starter list can include those in the belief verb list (see appendix to this chapter; e.g., *imply, forget, deduce, conclude*).

(2) Analyzing and Explaining Data

This activity can take 2 to 3 hours of class time and can be carried out in intermittent phrases with gaps of 1 to 3 days between phrases.

(a) Students can be presented with data in graph, charts, table, or text form. The data should deal with issues that most students find useful and interesting. For instance, the U.S. Census Web site (*www.census.gov*) contains a wealth of such information, including data on immigrants and immigration, education, men and women, college enrollments, cost of housing in a particular area of the country, or food. Sociological and demographic data can also be useful for students to practice their academic vocabulary in writing (see chaps. 4, 8, and 9).

Students can be asked to describe and explain the data. In some cases, it may be helpful for students if the data in the graphs or text are discussed without explanations before students begin writing. This exercise can be useful for students to work in pairs.

Sample 1. Figure 10.1 shows that the number of college students 25 years of age and older has grown dramatically over the past half century. The same can be said about traditional students who are younger than 25. What can explain these changes? In your opinion, why do older students in the United States attend colleges and universities?

Sample 2. According to the U.S. Census, in 1999, 54% of all college students were women. Among traditional students who are 25 years old or younger, 52% are women, and their proportion among older students overall constitutes 57%. In addition, in the age group of students older than 35 years, 62% are women. Approximately 3 million students attend graduate school, and graduate students consist of 1.8 million women and 1.4 million men.

(a) Please propose a tentative explanation (3–5 paragraphs) for these developments in U.S. education from a social and economic point of view. What do these figures demonstrate? What possible trends and changes in the social structure does the gender imbalance imply? What could demographers, sociologists, economists, and employers conclude from these census findings?

Please use some or all of the following verbs (or any other types of verbs) to help you construct your text:

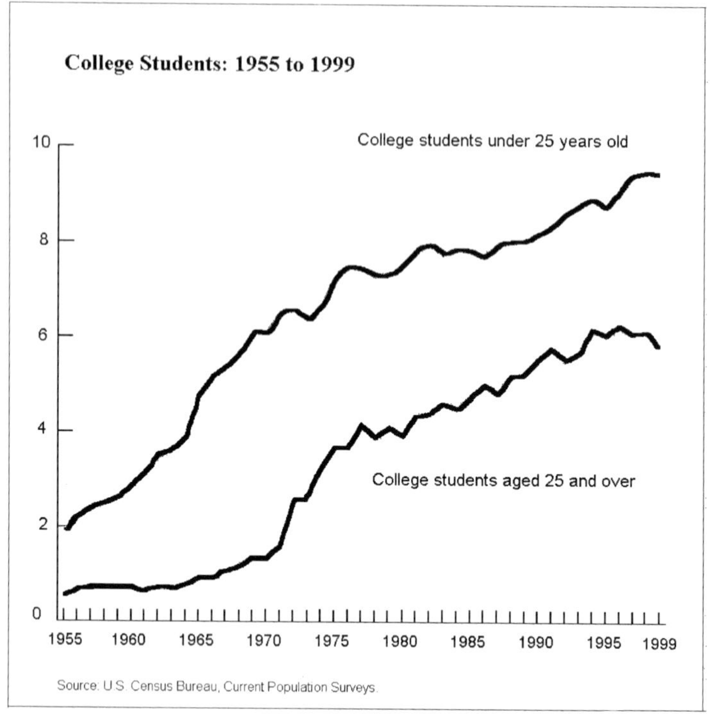

FIG. 10.1.

assume	conjecture	doubt	explain	infer	reason	suppose
believe	deduce	exemplify	illustrate	mean	reveal	
conclude	demonstrate	expect	imply	note	show	

Please do not forget such important modal verbs as can, may, *or* might *(see chap. 12).*

(b) When you are finished with your possible suggestions and discussion of the data trends, please exchange your proposed hypotheses to explain the data with another pair of students.

(c) Please read the alternative explanation of the data and suggested trends proposed by other students. Also please write a brief evaluation of the alternative explanation: Do you agree with other explanatory approaches suggested by another student/pair of students? What good points are observed and mentioned in the alternative discussion? What possible points or issues does an alternative explanation overlook? What broad conclusions can be made about the data if both your own and alternative explanations are combined to write a general comprehensive report?

Please do not forget some of the useful evaluative adjectives and adverbs such as (see chap. 9):]

Positive Evaluative Adjectives and Adverbs

accurate(-ly)	correct(-ly)	impressive(-ly)	significant(-ly)
careful(-ly)	good/well	interesting(-ly)	special(-ly)
clear(-ly)	important(-ly)	right(-ly)	thorough(-ly)

Negative Evaluative Adjectives

inaccurate(-ly)	limited(-ly)	misguided(-ly)	unconvincing(-ly)
inconclusive(-ly)	minor	questionable(-ly)	unsatisfactory(-ly)

Sample 3. In 2000, 84% of the U.S. population lived in the same place of residence they did 1 year earlier. Of the remainder, 10% moved to a different residence in the same area or city, 3% relocated from another area in the same state, 3% moved from another state, and 1% moved from abroad. In addition, 11% of the U.S. population are foreign-born, whereas 89% are native. Among the native population, 67% continue to live in the state of their birth.

Please propose a tentative explanation (3–5 paragraphs) for the reasons that a relatively large number of individuals move in the same area or city or from one state to another. What do these figures point to in the U.S. demographics and social and economic mobility? What do these census data imply about the number of immigrants in the United States? What could demographers, sociologists, and economists conclude from these census findings?

Teachers can also provide verb and adjective lists for Sample 3 as in Sample 2.

(3) Error Correction and Editing

The goal of this activity is to help students articulate and reason their editing of text.

Please correct the errors in the following texts and sentences and explain what you think needs to be corrected. Please keep in mind that some of the text needs to be completely rewritten.

1. The biologists and zoologists who study the environment where we live in they are called environmentalists. But in addition, social scientists who work in sociology, education, and public science, they also examine how do we talk about environment. Our thinking reveals more about what don't we understand about nature than about what

can we count on as we study. How to carry out the effective advocacy approach. I will take an environmental issue which is solid waste management to make an example to utter clearly how does the process of environmental education work on it.

Solid waste management defining as that an area of study associate with the control of generation, storage, collection, and disposal in a manner that are in accord with the principles of economics, public health, conservation, and other environmental consideration, and that are also responsibly to the public. Solid waste management includes administrative functions involving in the whole solution to the problems of solid waste thrust the community by its inhabitants. Because it is important for our future and for the life.

According to EPA Journal, 1989, it provided a general introduction to solid waste management and served as a way for understanding. To solve specific solid waste problems, the various elements that are combining in what is usually knows as a solid waste management system. In most cities, a solid waste management system that is existed for collection of solid waste. In below, these are relationships among four functional elements and solid waste concerns. (From a student paper on the importance of solid waste management for the environment).

2. The reason of I mention the culture of poverty can be relate with work incentive although different opinion for different people. In labor economics and with public assist that is providing in the field of social work, the author of the article states that as a dominating social perspective seen by higher social class on the poor people.

3. Because the brightest focus about this matter is that was put in our society in the dilemma that we should provide economic assist with the poor who are not working or not. Another matter that we should look for it further is if the culture of poverty is really existed in them and is maintaining generation by generation. (From a student assignment on the culture of poverty).

(4) What Is Your Point?

Students read an editorial, op-ed piece, or article from a newspaper or professional journal of their choice. The teacher can select articles for students or students choose their own. (Caveat: A common complaint, "But I couldn't find a suitable/interesting/good article," is easy to counter if the teacher has a small stock of articles—possibly saved back from earlier courses.) When students submit their work, they should be required to submit copies of their articles. If the work is done in class, they need to bring an additional copy to hand in with their writing.

Option: Students may be asked to read two articles on a similar topic, particularly when some "hot" issue is discussed in print media or on the Internet news sites, and articles are relatively easy to find.

Step 1. Please read the article, identify the author's thesis and main points/thesis supports [see appendix to chap. 11], *and underline them. Then build a paraphrase of the author's main points, point by point. Be sure not to copy the author's wording.*

For example, Skeleton Summary:

The author's main point is that ...

The article also states/notes/observes that ...

In addition, the author believes/thinks that ...

The conclusion of the article is that ...

A variety of sentence stems for summary making is presented in appendix to this chapter.

Step 2. *Please decide which of the author's points are valid and which are not. Then express your support or disagreement with each of the author's points. Please do not neglect to make your arguments balanced by acknowledging that even though you may disagree with a particular point. Expand on your Skeleton Summary and give it some argumentation muscle.*

For example, Muscular Summary and Solid Argumentation:

The author's main point is that.... Although I can see her point, xxx is not the only issue in yyy.

The article also states/notes/observes that.... I also think/believe that zzz.

In addition, the author believes/thinks that.... She supports her position based on xxx, but she may remember that zzz.

The conclusion of the article is that.... Other authors/reports/articles state that.... In my opinion, the author may need to consider that....

Step 3—Optional. Students can exchange articles and do it all again, Round 2, based on an article chosen by their classmate. Then when both Muscular Summaries and Argumentations are completed, students can compare (a) how they identified the article author's main point(s), and (b) what points in the article they chose to support or argue against.

QUESTIONS FOR DISCUSSION

1. In English, complex sentences with subordinate clauses represent highly advanced constructions that are difficult for L2 writers to use correctly. If you have a few students in your class who continue to

make errors in these constructions, will you consider these students to be ready for academic work in mainstream courses? Among the many types of errors that students are likely to make with these structures, which ones would you consider to be more severe or less severe? Why? Would you make such distinctions in the gravity of errors in subordinate clauses? Which ones and why?

2. As was discussed in chapter 4, it is important for L2 writers to learn to identify sentence elements such as subject phrases and head subject nouns, auxiliary verbs, main verbs, and objects. However, it is quite common that at the college level even native speakers of English are not always able to identify subject, verb, and object phrases correctly. In this case, how proficient should non-native speakers become in identifying sentence parts? Is it reasonable to expect non-native speakers to become better at identifying sentence elements than many native speakers are? Why or why not?
3. The following sentences include subordinate clauses. Can you identify their sentence functions and explain your decision? Are these sentence acceptable in formal academic written English?
   - *Many L2 writers dislike learning vocabulary—a common problem that can bother ESL teachers.*
   - *It goes without saying that learning to write academic essays in a second language takes a great deal of work.*
   - *Copernicus proposed that the Earth revolved around the Sun, which came as a complete surprise to his contemporaries.*
   - *In Wisconsin and other Great Lake states, snowstorms can produce large amounts of precipitation, which can impede transportation.*
   - *At a recent gathering of environmentalists, angry spats arose between the proponents and opponents of conservation, which were relished by the media.*
4. In your opinion, why do fewer sentence fragment errors occur with adjective and noun clauses than with adverb clauses?
5. In many constructions it is perfectly acceptable to mix the past and future tenses:
   - *This morning, psychologists announced to the media that they will finish the experiment next year.*
   - *John told Sue that he will buy a new computer when he is ready.*
   - *The spokeswoman for the president stated that no new taxes will be implemented in the forthcoming future.*

   In your opinion, in what contexts and under what circumstances is it acceptable to mix the past and future tenses? Can you come up with a quick rule to explain this distinction to students?
6. Would the semantic or structural regularities (and irregularities) of English be easier for L2 learners to deal with in their academic writing? Why? By the same token, would discourse organization or sen-

tence structure be easier for L2 writers to learn to use approp-riately? Why?

FURTHER READINGS ABOUT SENTENCE AND PHRASE STRUCTURE

Chafe, W. (1985). Linguistic differences produced by differences between speaking and writing. In D. R. Olson, N. Torrance, & A. Hildyard (Eds.), *Literature, language, and learning: The nature and consequences of reading and writing* (pp. 105–123). Cambridge: Cambridge University Press.

Croft, W. (1998). The structure of events and the structure of language. In M. Tomasello (Ed.), *The new psychology of language* (pp. 67–92). Mahwah, NJ: Lawrence Erlbaum Associates.

Davidson, F. (1991). Statistical support for training in ESL composition rating. In L. Hamp-Lyons (Ed.), *Assessing second language writing* (pp. 155–165). Norwood, NJ: Ablex.

Dixon, R. M. W. (1995). Complement clauses and complementation strategies. In F.R. Palmer (Ed.), *Grammar and meaning* (pp. 175–220). Cambridge: Cambridge University Press.

Ford, C. (1993). *Grammar in interaction.* Cambridge: Cambridge University Press.

Hamp-Lyons, L. (1991). Reconstructing academic writing proficiency. In L. Hamp-Lyons (Ed.), *Assessing second language writing* (pp. 127–153). Norwood, NJ: Ablex.

Hinkel, E. (2003). Adverbial markers and tone in L1 and L2 students' writing. *Journal of Pragmatics, 35*(7), 1049–1068.

Nash, W., & Stacey, D. (1997). *Creating texts.* London: Longman.

Ragan, P. (2001). Classroom use of a systemic functional small learner corpus. In M. Ghadessy, A. Henry, & R. Roseberry (Eds.), *Small corpus studies and ELT: Theory and practice* (pp. 207–236). Amsterdam: John Benjamins.

Vann, R., Lorenz, F., & Meyer, D. (1991). Error gravity: Response to errors in the written discourse of nonnative speakers of English. In L. Hamp-Lyons (Ed.), *Assessing second language writing* (pp. 181–196). Norwood, NJ: Ablex.

Appendix to Chapter 10

REPORTING AND BELIEF VERBS FOR ACADEMIC WRITING

Common Academic Reporting Verbs

affirm	assume	discuss	illustrate	presume
allege	claim	examine	imply	reveal
argue	contend	exemplify	maintain	state
assert	describe	explain	present	

Other Academic Reporting Verbs

add	comment	describe	object	report
agree	concede	discuss	present	reveal
allege	confirm	examine	presume	say
announce	convey	imply	promise	suggest
assume	deny	mention	remark	write

Belief Verbs Common in Academic Writing

accept	deduce	expect	mean	reason
assume	deem	forget	note	understand
believe	demonstrate	hold (the view	presume	
conclude	determine	that)	presuppose	
conjecture	doubt	imply	prove	
consider	establish	infer	realize	

(Adapted from Quirk et al., 1985)

REPORTING VERBS AND NOUN CLAUSE CHUNKS FOR SUMMARY MAKING

The author goes on to say/state/show that xxx
The author further argues/explains/shows that
The article further states that
(Smith) also states/maintains/argues/asserts that
(Smith) also believes/concludes/feels that
The article/report concludes that
In the second half of the article/report, (Johnson) presents xxx to show/explain that
(Adapted from Swales & Feak, 1994)

ADJECTIVE CLAUSE CHUNKS FOR ACADEMIC WRITING

Common Noun + Adjective Clause Chunks

Place

area(s) where	*case(s) where*
area(s) in/to which	*country where*

situation where	*conditions where*
situation in/to which	*examples where*
point where	

Time

time(s) when	*case(s) when*
time(s) in/at which	*period(s) when*

Other Frequent Noun + Adjective Clause Chunks

the way in which (the)	*extent to which the*
the ways in which	*the fact that the*
way in which the	*the fact that it*
such a way that	*the degree to which*
the extent to which (the)	*and the extent to which the*

(Adapted from Biber et al., 1999)

Academic Nouns Most Frequently Modified by That-Clauses
(in declining order, ***the fact that*** pattern)

fact	idea	view	report
possibility	suggestion	sense	sign
doubt	conclusion	notion	
belief	claim	hypothesis	
assumption	grounds	observation	

(Adapted from Nation, 2001; Biber et al., 1999)

11

Rhetorical Features of Text: Cohesion and Coherence

OVERVIEW

- Cohesive ties and lexical substitution
- Teaching lexical and semantic cohesion
- Expanding the range: lexical synonyms, near synonyms, and general words
- Phrase-level conjunctions
- Following the laws of parallel structure
- Sentence transitions and idea connectors
- Complex prepositions
- Clarifying and giving examples
- Structures not to use or to use sparingly
- Punctuation

This chapter addresses a number of rhetorical features of L2 academic writing, largely focusing on those that specifically require additional attention in L2 writing instruction. In particular various studies have noted that in academic writing cohesion represents an important characteristic of text and discourse flow and that for L2 learners constructing cohesive texts requires focused instruction and additional attention (Byrd & Reid, 1998; Carrell, 1982; Hinkel, 2001a, 2002a; Ostler, 1987; Reid, 1993).

In general terms, *cohesion* refers to the connectivity of ideas in discourse and sentences to one another in text, thus creating the flow of information in a unified way. In addition, in textbooks on writing and composition, cohesion can also refer to the ways of connecting sentences and paragraphs into a unified whole. Although the terms *cohesion* and *coherence* are often used together, they do not refer to the same properties of text and discourse. Cohesion usually refers to connections between sentences and paragraphs, and coherence can also refer to the organization of discourse with all elements present and fitting together logically. For example, the presence of an introduction, a thesis statement, rhetorical support, and a conclusion can create a coherent essay that is not necessarily cohesive (Carrell, 1982; Chafe, 1994; Scollon & Scollon, 2001).

Since the 1970s, a great deal of research has been carried out into the effects of features of text on discourse. Many studies have determined what syntactic and lexical constructions are used in writing, and how and when they are used alters the text's clarity, cohesion, contextual and social acceptability, and communicative effectiveness (Coulthard, 1985; de Beaugrande & Dressler, 1972; Halliday & Hasan, 1976; van Dijk, 1985, 1997).

The descriptions of a text's qualities, however, are constructed in abstract terms, and it is not always possible to define text clarity, cohesion, or effectiveness with any degree of precision. Any two well-educated native English speakers may disagree (and often do) about whether a particular text written in English is clear, cohesive, or developed. On the other hand, when it comes to L2 text written in English by non-native speakers, the imprecise terms in which the text's qualities are described acquire a whole new meaning.

As with other instructional fundamentals discussed at length in this book, the teacher's objective is not to try to develop learners' skills to write sharp journalistic prose or artful essays composed with grace, originality, and eloquence. Nevertheless, ESL teachers should not be satisfied with a quality of text that will doom the student to failure or barely passing grades in writing assignments in mainstream classes.

To this end, the approach to teaching cohesion, conjunctions, and the functions of prepositions and examples relies on concrete guidelines that are relatively easy for teachers to teach and writers to use in their written assignments, papers, essays, and reports, which are required in all academic disciplines and of all students.

The rhetorical features of academic text addressed in this chapter predominantly discuss matters of lexical and semantic cohesion, the syntactic and discourse functions of phrase coordinators, sentence transitions, as well as the appropriate types of examples in academic writing and areas where NNS writers typically encounter difficulties. Numerous studies of L2 written prose have pointed to the fact that these specific features of L2 text can benefit from specific and focused instruction.

COHESIVE TIES AND LEXICAL SUBSTITUTION

The terms *cohesive ties* (chains) and *lexical substitution* were originally developed by Halliday and Hasan (1976) to explain how cohesive elements act to conjoin text by direct reference to (or substitution for) another lexical item in the immediately preceding sentence. According to Halliday and Hasan, cohesive chains can refer back to not just the immediately preceding sentence but even three or four sentences in a sequence. In Example (1), the cohesive chain spans the entire text excerpt by means of a chain from *John de Witt* to *His, he*, and the final *He* while the reader does not lose track of the chain's starting point.

> (1) *John de Witt was one of the foremost European statesmen of the seventeenth century and grand pensionary (in effect, the first minister) of Holland. His international fame was all the more remarkable when we realize that he was one of the few representatives of a state who spoke on the behalf of the republic. He was an avid devote of reading and culture and belonged to a circle that discussed the latest ideas.* (Adapted from Perry et al., 2000).

In this excerpt, the pronouns *his* or *he* refer back to John de Witt, and the cohesive chain is established by means of personal pronouns across three relatively long sentences. However, such a clear-cut cohesive chain would require strict adherence to singular or plural noun–pronoun references.

Halliday's and Hasan's (1976, p. 279) lexical substitutions work in similar ways across several sentences in which a lexical item is not only repeated, but replaced by a related item, synonym, or near synonym of the original word—or a "general word" that can refer to an entire class of similar words. In the following example, the noun phrase *a baby boom* is substituted by the related phrase *this 75-million-person-bulge*, then a general word *people*, as in *middle-aged people*, followed by a pronoun *they*, and finally the repeated noun *bulge*.

> (2) *A baby boom took place in the United States between 1945 and 1965. This 75-million-person bulge will move upward through the country's age structure during the 80-year period between 1945 and 2025.... Today, these middle-aged people make up nearly half of all adult Americans. In sheer numbers they dominate the population's demand for goods and services. Companies not providing products and services for this bulge in the population can go bankrupt.* (Adapted from Miller, 2000)

This excerpt actually includes another lexical substitution chain that moves from *the United States*, to *the country*, then to *Americans, the population*, and again repeated *the population* (this lexical chain is underscored by a broken line). The second cohesive chain does not interfere with the first one originating from the phrase *A baby boom* at the beginning of the excerpt. The second chain of lexical substitutions largely follows the same pattern identified for the first: The original noun *the United States* is substituted by a related noun phrase *the country*, then by another related noun *Americans*, and finally by a near synonym repeated twice *the population*.

TEACHING LEXICAL AND SEMANTIC COHESION

The importance of lexical substitutions to expand the L2 writer's lexical range has been emphasized throughout this book. For this reason, when the teaching of lexical substitutes comes up again, this time in connection with helping learners develop cohesive and unified prose, it may seem a little tired. Without belaboring the topic, this section sets out to offer a few teaching techniques and tricks that have the goal of simplifying the matters of text cohesion as much as they can be simplified without a great deal of damage.

In 1981, Joseph M. Williams (Williams, 2002) created an intelligent and intelligible system for teaching text cohesion to anyone. His system was based on a few highly useful and accessible principles:

- It is more difficult to begin a sentence well than to end it well because the writer needs to decide which idea is the newest and most important.
- The newest and most important idea goes to the end of the sentence because it will be expanded on in the next sentence.
- However, the beginning of the sentence strongly sets up the reader's expectations about what follows, therefore the beginning of the sentence needs to be constructed carefully.

Figure 11.1 illustrates the organization of old–new information in a succession of several sentences. The first sentence starts with **known** information—for instance, a noun phrase that refers to the paragraph topic as it is stated in the title (or mentioned in the preceding paragraph).

The techniques to accomplish the goals of constructing cohesive text are practical and straightforward (Williams, 2002).

- Preliminary contexts and evaluative adverbs frame the sentence and are placed at the very beginnings of sentences (e.g., *in many ways, generally speaking, it is important to note that, perhaps*).
- The time and place of an action or event are also placed at the outset (e.g., *in the 20th century, during the experiment, at the time of the Reformation, in Rome, in American social structure*).
- After the preliminary elements, the sentence states what is already known and supplies the new information at the end.

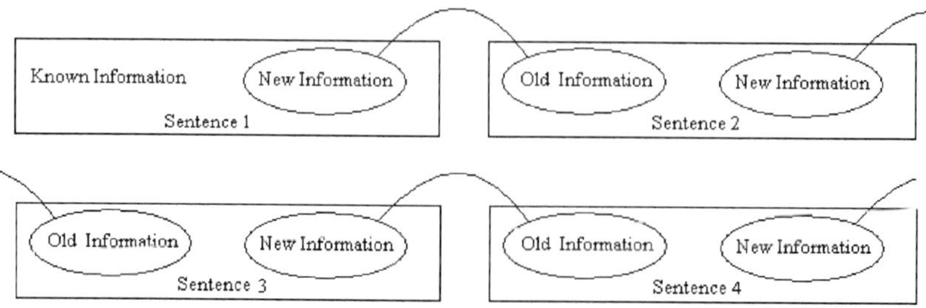

FIG. 11.1. Sentence cohesion: old–new information connectivity.

- In most cases, sentence topics are their grammatical subjects, and the rest of the sentence provides information about (comments on) the topic.

For example:

Unlike many lower animals that use their noses to detect mates, predators, and prey, humans [subject = topic] *do not depend on their sense of smell for survival* [information about the topic—new]. *Nevertheless, the sense of smell* [subject = topic—repeated/old information] *in humans is incredibly sensitive* [information about the topic—new]. (Adapted from Morris, 2002)

- Repeating short and specific sentence subjects/topics creates a cohesive text particularly in sentences with long predicate phrases (see examples in Strategies for Teaching at the end of the chapter).
- For L2 writers, to simplify the construction of a cohesive chain, the next sentence should repeat at least one word from the preceding sentence or provide its lexical/ semantic substitute (e.g., a near synonym or pronoun).
- The third sentence similarly repeats or substitutes one word from the second sentence to create an identifiable cohesive chain.

For example, in Excerpt (3), the cohesive chain is relatively easy to identify, and several cohesive chains are developed simultaneously without interfering with one another. Chain [1] moves from *coastal erosion* to *it* and then to *east coast and west coast, coastal erosion, coastal area,* and *coastal areas*, as well as related (and repeated) nouns *shoreline* and *shorelines*. *Environment and society* [2] is connected to *cities and villages* and then to *local people*. Cohesive line [3] begins with *changes* and moves to *changed, different*, and *adjust*, and line [4] connects *fishing* to *make their living, fishing*, and *their jobs* (also connected to *local people* by means of the pronoun *their* in *their living, their traditional ways,* and *their jobs*).

(3) *Coastal erosion* [1] *is a problem throughout the United States, and it* [1] *occurs on the east coast and the west coast* [1]. *The coastal erosion* [1] *will directly influence the environment and society* [2] *in the coastal area* [1]. *Cities and villages* [2] *that are located in coastal areas* [1] *will experience changes* [3] *in the shape of the shoreline* [1]. *When shorelines* [1] *have changed* [3] *shapes, fishing* [4] *in tide pools and from boats will also need to become different* [3]. *So, the local people* [2] *who make their living* [4] *by fishing* [4] *will also have to adjust* [3] *their traditional ways of doing their jobs* [4] *every day.* (Excerpted from a student paper on People and Environment: Coastal Erosion.)

Although the text in (3) is slightly repetitive, it is highly cohesive and unified. The technique of repeating a word from the immediately preceding sentence is easy to use for L2 writers at most levels of language proficiency.

ENUMERATIVE "CATCH-ALL" NOUNS

Halliday and Hasan's (1976) study of cohesion noted the importance of what they called *general words* with such broad and vague meanings that they can play the role of lexical substitutes for a variety of nouns. In various analyses of written academic corpora in English, these nouns are also called *enumerative* (Partington, 1996; Tadros, 1994; see chap. 6 for additional discussion and teaching suggestions). Enumerative nouns are far more common in academic than other types of writing. Highly prevalent items include the following.

approach	*event*	*manner*	*subject*
aspect	*experience*	*method*	*system*
category	*facet*	*phase*	*task*
challenge	*fact*	*problem*	*tendency*
change	*factor*	*process*	*topic*
characteristic	*feature*	*purpose*	*trend*
circumstance	*form*	*reason*	*type*
class	*issue*	*result*	
difficulty	*item*	*stage*	

These nouns can be very useful for establishing cohesive chains in academic text because, for instance, such nouns as *approach—method, subject—topic, problem—difficulty,* or *tendency—trend* can be employed interchangeably as lexical substitutes for other nouns with more specific meanings. A few examples from student papers illustrate the usefulness of enumerative catch-all nouns in text:

- *The author mentions pollution, water shortage, and loss of soil issues concerning the threat of overpopulation. In his article, he mostly talks about the environment but does not mention the health and nutrition problems. The health challenges are created when there are too many people in the world.*

  Lexical ties/substitutions: *issues—problems—challenges*

- *For a long time, philosophers have been discussing the factors that create a happy marriage. We find characteristics of happy marriages in the work of Aquinas, Singer, and sociologist Wallerstein, who argue about the aspects of marriage to show which ones are happy and which ones are not and why.*

  Lexical ties/substitutions: *factors—characteristics—aspects*

- *Americans are getting more and more uninterested in politics, and political scientists and educators have been trying to understand the trend that Amer-*

icans do not care about politics. In my country, people think that they are powerless to control the political system, and they don't care about politics either. So, American researchers have been studying the tendency that many people do not even go to vote.

Lexical ties: *trend—tendency*

On the whole, the number of enumerative nouns in English probably does not exceed a hundred, and learning them is well worth the time and effort because of the breadth of their meanings and their flexible contextual uses.

DEMONSTRATIVE PRONOUNS[1]

Demonstrative pronouns such as *this, that, these,* and *those* are also a prominent feature of cohesive discourse. For instance, Excerpt (2) showed how demonstratives can be used effectively to connect nouns and ideas across sentences.

Similar to articles or possessive pronouns, demonstrative pronouns belong in the class of determiners and play a prominent role in text cohesion. Demonstratives have referential functions in written English (Halliday & Hasan, 1976)—they point to particular objects or events discussed in earlier text. Quirk et al. (1985) identified several functions of demonstratives in discourse and pointed out that these pronouns are often ambiguous in their referential and determinative properties. Because demonstrative pronouns are relatively easy to use, L2 writers frequently employ too many of them in their writing (Hinkel, 2001a, 2002a).

In addition, in various languages such as Chinese, Japanese, or Vietnamese, the uses of demonstratives can be a great deal more elaborate than they are in English (Levinson, 1983; Palmer, 1994; Watanabe, 1993). Earlier studies have determined that L2 writers frequently transfer the meanings of demonstratives from their L1s and may attribute to these markers more referential implications than they actually have in English (McCarthy, 1991). For this reason, the limitations of demonstratives as a cohesive and "pointing" device need to be addressed in teaching (see chap. 6 for teaching suggestions).

PHRASE-LEVEL CONJUNCTIONS AND THE LAWS OF PARALLEL STRUCTURE

Officially, the function of conjunctions is to mark connections between ideas in discourse and text, and conjunctions are the most ubiquitous and proba-

[1]The uses of demonstratives and the pitfalls associated with their overuses in student text are discussed in detail in chapter 6. For this reason, the mention of demonstratives here serves merely as a reminder of their important cohesive function.

bly the most lexically simple means of developing text cohesion (Halliday & Hasan, 1976). Among the various types of conjunctions, coordinating conjunctions in particular determine a parallel relationship of ideas and syntactic units:

1. *Labor, management, owners,* ***and*** *buyers in a corporation are no longer confined to a single society. The laborers in Hong Kong, the owners in New York, the managers in both Hong Kong and New York,* ***and*** *the customers in Africa all make up the modern corporate world.* (Charon, 1999, p. 129)

Unofficially, however, coordinating conjunctions can be used to make sentences of practically any length one wishes:

2. *Some people seem to disagree with some of the aspects of advertising because they feel that some advertisements are too dangerous for their children,* ***and*** *one of the examples is alcohol advertisement,* ***but*** *according to the advertisers, the purpose of the advertisers is to attract more customers,* ***and*** *unique and attractive advertisements will lead people to buying more products, goods,* ***and*** *services,* ***and*** *companies attract their consumers by advertising in magazines* ***or*** *newspapers* ***or*** *TV,* ***and*** *most advertisements are shown on TV, especially during breaks of sports events* ***and*** *popular shows,* ***and*** *the customers can see these advertisements* ***and*** *find out about new products.* (Extracted from a paper written by an Arabic-speaking student on social impacts of advertising.)

Coordinating conjunctions such as *and, but, yet,* and *so* can establish parallel relationships between and among virtually any types of syntactic units: nouns, pronouns, verbs, adjectives, adverbs, phrases, and sentences. For example, the phrase *labor, management, owners,* ***and*** *buyers* consists of parallel nouns, all of which constitute the subject noun phrase of the sentence in (1). (Subject–verb agreement rules for parallel noun phrases in the subject position are discussed in chap. 4.)

However, the structure *the laborers in Hong Kong, the owners in New York,* and *the managers in both Hong Kong and New York,* in fact, represents two different parallel constructions: (1) the phrase *the laborers in Hong Kong* is parallel to *the owners in New York* and *the managers in* ... and (2) the next phrase *both Hong Kong and New York* contains yet another parallel construction—*Hong Kong and New York*—conjoined by the *both ... and ...* coordinator.

On the other hand, two simple parallel sentences or two subordinate clauses can also be conjoined into parallel constructions:

[Parallel simple sentences] *Marcus Tullius Cicero was a distinguished orator,* ***and*** *he was also a student of Greek philosophy.*

[Parallel subordinate clauses] *Cicero adopted the Stoic belief that natural law governs the universe* ***and*** *that all belong to common humanity.*

(Adapted from Perry, Peden, & Von Laue, 1999)

(For punctuation rules in parallel simple sentences, see chap. 4.)

The flexibility of the coordinating conjunctions that allows them to conjoin practically any types of parallel words, phrases, or sentences is unquestionably a wonderful characteristic. However, it is this very characteristic that can cause much turmoil among the parallel syntactic elements and lead some L2 writers into peril when sentences do not seem to end. Another problem with coordinators is that, as mentioned, they are by far the most common and simple of all cohesive devices in English, and no matter how long one's sentences are, they do not fool many people into thinking that their author is a sophisticated writer.

For instance, corpus analyses of spoken and written English have determined that *and* is one of the most frequent words and that it occurs at the rate of approximately 27,000 times per million words. *But* and *so* are also fairly prevalent, with rates of approximately 5,000 occurrences each (Leech, Rayson, & Wilson, 2001). Coordinating conjunctions are particularly common when they conjoin parallel phrases and simple sentences, whereas *but* is least frequent in academic text. It is interesting to note that in academic writing slightly over 30% of all occurrences of *and* conjoin simple sentences, with the large majority of these features found in parallel phrase constructions (Biber et al., 1999). Thus, when it comes to developing cohesion between sentences in formal academic text, employing coordinating conjunctions may not be the most impressive way to proceed. In fact, as mentioned, L2 writers greatly overuse *and, but,* and *so* to not-so-good effect (Hinkel, 2001a, 2002a). Simply including coordinating conjunctions in the text without connecting meanings of sentences and phrases results in a simple chaining of ideas and a fragmented writing style (Chafe, 1985).

However, the conjunction *or* finds many more uses in academic writing than in other types of text mostly due to the fact that academic definitions, explanations, and discussions often have the goal of providing descriptions of alternatives and options.

It is necessary to note that correlative conjunctions such as *both ... and, either ... or,* and *neither ... nor,* widely popular in the teaching of ESL grammar, are actually rare in any types of discourse, including spoken and/or written (Leech, Rayson, & Wilson, 2001). For instance, Biber et al. (1999) found *nor* to be far less common than all other coordinators in academic prose. In addition, according to their analysis, *both ... and* occur with frequency rates of 0.1%, *either ... or* with the rates of 0.05%, and *neither ... nor* hardly at all.

The Rigidity of the Parallel Structure

Using coordinating conjunctions that develop cohesion between sentences and sentence elements is not without pitfalls. L2 written text often contains various parallel structure errors that are actually relatively easy to teach because parallel sentence elements are highly regular and predictable in their rigidity.

To begin, the uses of coordinating conjunctions with simple sentences require that identical or repeated sentence elements be omitted. For example,

(1) ?*We measured the thickness of the bar before applying the solvent, and we measured the thickness after applying the solvent.*

In this sentence, several elements are repeated in the second sentence: the subject, the verb, and the object, as well as the gerund applying the solvent following the preposition *after*. It is possible to think of these repeated elements as simplifying a basic algebraic expression $2a + 2b = 2(a + b)$—when the common elements between the two sentences are placed at the beginning of the sentence and apply equally to all subsequent elements.

In this case, the **second** occurrences of *we measured the thickness of the bar* and *applying the solvent* would be extracted:

(2) ??*We measured the thickness of the bar before applying the solvent, and ... after ...*

Then the *and ... after* elements that are now left behind with nothing to conjoin should be moved forward to join the lonely *before* with *and ... after ...*:

(3) *We measured the thickness of the bar before and after applying the solvent.*

The same approach can also be used to eliminate repeated elements of phrases as in the following examples:

**can be measured and can be increased* →	*can be measured and ... increased*
**the metal spoon and the metal bowl* →	*the metal spoon and ... bowl*
**large factories, wholesalers, and big retailers* →	*large factories, wholesalers, and retailers*

Another important point to make about using coordinate conjunctions is that they conjoin **series** of elements that have to be of the same type (e.g., nouns, noun phrases, or gerunds [see chap. 5], verbs or verb phrases of the same tense and number, adjective or adjective phrases, or prepositional phrases). In effect, the term *parallel structure* refers to "a string" of elements that are similar to beads in a necklace: They can be a little bit different, but not dramatically so. Several examples from an authentic text on sources of the Western tradition are presented next.

Stoicism and its followers taught the universal principles or the natural law. [Parallel noun phrases in the subject position: The first element of the subject contains a simple noun and the second a noun phrase. Also identical parallel noun phrases in the object position: Both consist of an article, an adjective, and a head noun.]

Natural laws applied to all people and were grasped through reason.
[Parallel verb phrases in the predicate position: Both consist of a past tense verb + a prepositional phrase; however, the first verb is in the active voice and the second in the passive voice.]

In the tradition of Socrates, the Stoics believed people to be morally self-sufficient and capable of regulating their own lives.
[Parallel adjective phrases in the predicate infinitive phrase (see chap. 4): The first adjective phrase has no prepositional phrase and the second one does—*of regulating* ...]

The Romans valued the Stoic emphasis on self-discipline and the molding of character according to worthy standards.
[Parallel noun phrases inside two parallel prepositional phrases *on self-discipline* and *[on] the molding of character*, the second of which is omitted. Also, the second prepositional phrase includes two additional prepositional phrases at lower levels of importance *of character* and *according to....*]
(Adapted from Perry et al., 1999, p. 141)

If the string of parallel elements consists of more than two phrases, commas are used to separate them, and **the conjunction comes before the last item** (this is how readers know that they have arrived at the last item in the string):
Stoicism gave expression to the universalism of the Hellenistic Age, and it held that Greeks, barbarians, senators, patricians, gladiators, ***or*** *slaves were essentially equal because they all had capacity to reason.*

In constructions with parallel noun (or more rarely) adjective clauses, clause markers must be retained (even when they are identical in form and function) because dependent clauses are marked as clauses by means of these subordinators. For example:

[Augustine] ***cautions*** *the optimist that progress is not certain, that people, weak and ever prone to wickedness, are their own worst enemies, that success is illusory, and that misery is the essential human reality.* (Perry et al., 2000, p. 192)

Duns Scotus (1265–1308), a Scottish Franciscan, ***held*** *that human reason cannot prove that God is omnipotent, that he forgives sins, that he rewards the righteous and punishes the wicked, or that the soul is immortal.* (Perry et al, 2000, p. 289)

Such structures usually occur following reporting verbs (e.g., *cautions, holds, mentions, notes, states* [see chap. 8]), and, in general, in these and other contexts parallel clauses are not very common. In L2 prose, they may be particularly rare (Hinkel, 2002a).

Common Types of Errors in Parallel Structures

Common student errors found with the parallel structure largely involve similar problems when their parallel elements (head words or phrases) belong to different types and/or parts of speech. In most cases, they can be easy to correct and explain.

(1) Faulty Parallelisms: Infinitive—Gerund and Other Verb Phrase Elements

**The article describes how today young people do not like reading but to play computer games and other visual media.*

This sentence actually contains two errors in two different parallel structures. The first structure *do not like reading but *[to play]* hinges on the fact that gerunds mostly have the function of abstract nouns (see chap. 5), whereas infinitives have many adverbial characteristics (see chap. 9). To correct this error, the infinitive *to play* needs to be turned into a gerund (playing) or the gerund *reading* into an infinitive *to read* to make it parallel to *to play*.

The second error is somewhat more complex because it builds parallel construction between the two noun phrases *play games and [...] other visual media*. In this case, the structure would mean that young people *play ... other visual media*. However, visual media such as TV or the Internet cannot be *played*, but rather they are *used*. To correct this construction, the parallelism needs to be build on two verbs—*play* and *use* (or *enjoy, rely on, depend on*) instead of the noun phrases *games* and *visual media*.

(2) Un-Parallel Nouns/Noun Phrases

**Pascal was a philosopher, law scholar, educator, scientist, and he studied mathematics.*

In this sentence, the series of nouns is not parallel to the sentence *he studied mathematics*, which can simply be turned into another noun to match other elements: *mathematician*.

(3) Unparallel Simple Sentences in a Compound Sentence

Other common types of errors entail partial parallelisms of two simple sentences. In the following example, the second construction *exists the belief* is a sentence without the subject that attempts to be parallel to the complete simple sentence *this definition is obscure*.

**For the public, this definition is obscure, and exists the belief that engineers are technical people who don't have much knowledge in anything.*

Although the two simple sentences *this definition is obscure* and *exists the belief ...* are intended to be parallel, they are not because the second sentence does not have a subject. Two corrections are possible: *there exists [a] belief that* or *many believe that ....*

(4) Un-Parallel Adjectives—Noun Noun Modifiers and Linking/be-verbs—Activity Verbs

Sentence (4) contains two different parallelism errors: Adjective noun modifiers do not form very good parallels to noun modifiers that are nouns. In addition, linking and *be*-verbs, which often involve predicative adjectives (see chap. 4), do not get along with activity verbs (e.g., *read, write, measure*):

> **In urban and high-expense settings, a proper treatment of wastewater is necessary and preserve a healthy environment.*

The adjective *urban* is not parallel to the noun phrase *high-expense*, which can become *highly expensive* (or simply *expensive*). Similarly, the predicative adjective *necessary* does not match the verb *preserve*, nor does the first linking verb *is (necessary)* form a good parallel to the second activity verb *preserve (a healthy environment)*. In this case, the second predicate phrase may need to be rewritten as in *for the preservation of a healthy environment* or *to preserve a healthy environment* without the conjunction *and*. In either variant, the meaning may be slightly different from that originally intended by the writer.

(5) Un-Parallel Comparisons

One of the most confusing and difficult types of errors with the parallel structure entails faulty parallelism in complex comparisons in two conjoined sentences with omitted elements (see also chap. 4). The choice of which elements to omit, which to retain, and which to replace can cause a variety of problems:

a) **The precipitation rates in Portland are lower than Seattle.*

b) **The conventional treatment of wastewater is more expensive than mechanical equipment.*

c) **Math teaching in Japan is more than the U.S.*

In all these constructions, the necessary parallel (or replacement) elements have been omitted (i.e., the subject noun *those/that* + the preposition *in* or *by means of*; see the following complex prepositions):

a) *The precipitation rates in Portland are lower than [those] [in] Seattle.*

b) *The conventional treatment of wastewater is more expensive than [that] [by means of] mechanical equipment.*

c) *Math teaching in Japan is more [intensive/thorough] / [better] than [that] [in] the U.S.*

Replacing the omitted elements can usually correct the errors. However, it is important to make students aware of the complex comparative parallel structures with *than*.

SENTENCE TRANSITIONS AND IDEA CONNECTORS

Sentence transitions (also called sentences connectors or linking adverbials) have the primary function of connecting ideas between sentences and identifying the relationship between ideas (Swales & Feak, 1994). Practically every textbook on teaching college-level and academic writing to NS or NNS students presents detailed lists of sentence transitions, in which they are classified by their meanings (Bates, 1998; Hacker, 2000; Leki, 1999; Lunsford & Ruszkiewicz, 2001; Raimes, 1992, 1999; Smoke, 1999). In fact most textbooks for ESL learners encourage the use of sentence transitions because, as most textbook authors believe, they help novice writers establish clear cohesion between the ideas expressed in adjoining sentences and overtly mark the flow of information in discourse. Teachers also emphasize these sentence linkers because they are relatively easy to explain and also because the ideas in L2 writing may occasionally seem so disjointed that every little bit can help.

The major problem with sentence connectors in L2 academic writing is that, because these linkers are easy to understand and use, NNS writers employ far too many of them in their text. The second issue with these features of academic prose is that the use of sentence transitions does not necessarily make the L2 academic writing cohesive or the information flow easy to follow (Hinkel, 2001a, 2002a). The following example from a student's text illustrates this point:

> *First, the teenage crime rate is increasing very fast. Besides, the age of criminals is going down. Therefore, this is a serious problem. The society structure is toward the money principle, and moreover, everybody thinks that money is the most important thing. But, it is about the source of crime. In addition, the common crime for teenagers is stealing because they lack money. Nevertheless, sociologists have debated how to prevent teenage crime. Conclusively, family is the basic component of society, and family problems can cause teenagers to do maleficent things because their family cannot let them feel warm. Thus, they lack parents' love and care.* (Excerpted from a paper on the causes of youth crime, written by a Korean student.)

> In light of the emphasis on sentence transitions in writing instruction for university-level students, the misuse and overuse of these cohesive devices is not particularly surprising. In fact in teaching L2 writing, an important point to stress is that the uses of sentence transitions cannot make the text unified when the ideas in discourse flow are disjointed no matter how many transitions are employed.

In formal academic prose, the rate of sentence transitions is the highest among other types of written or spoken genre. However, sentence connectors account for less than 10% of all adverbials in the academic register. In addition to these facts, an interesting finding made by Biber et al. (1999) is that conversational discourse employs far more sentence transitions than academic writing does.

In academic writing, the most frequently encountered sentence transitions are actually not *first(-ly), second(-ly), third(-ly),* or *moreover* as undoubtedly many teachers have noticed in their students' writing. In fact by far the most common sentence transitions deal with contrast and concession (e.g., *however, on the other hand, instead, nevertheless*), as well as enumerative, additive, and summative meanings (Tadros, 1994) such as *to begin with, for one thing, in addition, further, also, similarly, in sum, to summarize, all in all,* and *overall*. The most common transitions number fewer than half a dozen.

The Most Common Sentence Transitions in Formal Academic Writing
(in declining order)

however thus therefore then so

According to corpus analyses by Biber et al. (1999), the most frequent sentence transition *however* occurs at the rate of 0.10%, followed by *thus* and *therefore* at the rates of 0.07% and 0.06% per million words, respectively. Other sentence connectors found in academic texts include *first, finally, furthermore, hence, nevertheless, rather, yet, in addition, on the other hand,* and *that is,* all of which are encountered at frequency rates of 0.01% each. To put it simply, in formal academic writing, sentence transitions are actually not common at all.[2]

COMPLEX PREPOSITIONS AND OTHER ALTERNATIVES

In general, the syntactic function of prepositions is to express a relationship between two entities; in this way they are similar to coordinating conjunctions and sentence transitions, which mark a relationship between ideas in two sentences. Complex prepositions are those that consist of more than word—usually of two or three words (e.g., *as for, except for, in line with*).

[2]In their research-based textbook for advanced academic writers at the graduate levels, Swales and Feak (1994) similarly reported that the uses of the following sentence transitions may be useful: *however, thus, also, in addition, finally, therefore, on the other hand, then,* and *nevertheless*. Based on these findings, these authors further pointed out, for example, that "conclusive" sentence transitions such as *in conclusion* are rare indeed.

Prepositions Versus Conjunctions

According to Quirk et al. (1985), sentence and discourse functions of prepositions (and complex prepositions as a subclass) have much in common with those of conjunctions and adverbs. Both prepositions and conjunctions have connecting functions:

the time when Ireland experienced a population crash in 1845
the time of a population crash in Ireland in 1845
the time of the 1845 population crash in Ireland
the time of the 1845 Irish population crash

In fact many prepositions and conjunctions have identical forms and, for this reason, can be confusing for learners (e.g., *after, as, before, since, until*).[3]

The key difference between conjunctions and prepositions is that prepositions are always followed by a noun, noun phrase, or nominalizations, including gerunds, but conjunctions conjoin the main and subordinate clauses, which necessarily have the predicate verb or verb phrase (see chap. 5 for nominalizations and gerunds). Thus, if the constructions following such words as *after* or *before* contain a verb, this sentence unit is a subordinate clause. If no verb can be identified, the word is the preposition in a prepositional phrase.

Distinguishing Prepositions and Conjunctions with Identical Forms

after	Preposition	*After a large-scale disaster, life begins to recolonize the site.* [no verb]
	Conjunction	*After a large-scale disaster occurs, life begins to recolonize the site.* [verb—occurs]
as	Preposition	*A few hardy pioneer species invade the environment as a start.* [no verb]
	Conjunction	*As the environment begins to renew itself, a few hardy pioneer species invade the site.* [verb—begins]
before	Preposition	*Before the restoration of the ecosystems, the pioneer species change the soil.* [no verb]
	Conjunction	*Before the ecosystems can be restored, the pioneer species change the soil.* [verb phrase—can be restored]

[3]Other identical forms of prepositions and conjunctions include *but* and *but* (except *all but one*) and *for* and *for* (because *for he loved his country*), but the latter of the two in these pairs is rare.

since	Preposition	*Since the 1960s, the urban growth has declined.* [no verb]
	Conjunction	*Since suburbs began to attract urban residents, a large number of jobs also shifted to smaller cities.* [verb phrase—began to attract]
till/until	Preposition	*Until the expansion of suburban job markets, most urban dwellers lived in central cities.* [no verb]
	Conjunction	*Until manufacturing job markets emerged in the early 1800s, only 5% of Americans lived in cities.* [verb—emerged]

(Adapted from Miller, 2000)

In addition to simple (one-word) prepositions and conjunctions with identical forms, many complex prepositions and subordinating conjunctions also have similar meanings and text functions. In academic writing, some can be used interchangeably provided that verbs are *not* included in constructions following complex prepositions.

Complex Prepositions

Complex prepositions can be divided into two groups: two-word and three-word units. They are relatively easy to identify.

> Two-word prepositions consist of a word + a simple preposition.
>
> Three-word sequences include a simple preposition + a Noun + a simple preposition.

The uses of complex prepositions, in addition to sentence transitions and subordinate conjunctions in complex sentences, can provide writers with a large number of options among lexical connectors. However, as with sentence transitions, the mere usage of connectives of any type does not serve to make disjointed text cohesive (see Suggestions for Teaching).

Many two- and three-word prepositions have similar connective functions and can be used in proximate syntactic constructions. In addition, the meanings of complex prepositions are also similar to those of sentence connectives such as transitions and subordinators (see chap. 10). Various constructions with the connective functions can be used interchangeably provided that the syntactic constructions they conjoin are modified accordingly (e.g., only nouns and noun phrases can be used following prepositions, and whole clauses after sentence transitions and subordinators in complex sentences). For example:

- *In spite of* [preposition] *such local and regional disasters* [noun phrase], *the overall human population on earth has continued to grow.*
- *Despite* [preposition] *joblessness and overcrowding* [noun phrase], *shantytown residents cling to life with resourcefulness, tenacity, and hope.*
- *Nevertheless/However* [transition], *municipal governments do not strive to improve the quality of life for new urban arrivals. Not only lacking the money, officials also fear that improving services will attract even more of the rural poor.*
- *Although/Even though* [subordinator] *disease is rampant in the squalor* [adverb clause], *most urban migrants do have more opportunities and are better off than the rural poor they left behind.*

Most Common Two- and Three-Word Prepositions and Their Substitutions

Two-Word Prepositions	Three-Word Prepositions and Substitutions
according to	Prepositions, etc.: *in accordance with, in line with, based on*
ahead of	Prepositions: *in front of (place), prior to (time)* Preposition/Transition: *before (place/time)*
along with, aside from, together with	Prepositions: *in addition to* Transitions: *also, further*
because of, due to	Subordinators: *because, since* Transitions: *therefore, as a result, so*
contrary to	Transitions: *however, on the other hand, on the contrary, in contrast to/with*
except for	Prepositions: *apart from, aside from, with the exception of*
instead of	Prepositions: *in lieu of, in place of*
prior to	Prepositions and Subordinators: *before (time), until*
subsequent to	Prepositions: *after, following*
Most Common Three-Word Prepositions and Their Substitutions	
by means of	Preposition: *with* (instruments/tools only)
in (the) case of	Subordinators: *if, as long as, unless, provided that*
in (the) process of	Preposition: *during* Subordinators: *while, when* Transitions: *meanwhile,in the meantime*
in spite of	Preposition: *despite* Subordinators: *though, although, even though* Transition: *nevertheless*
in view of, in light of	Preposition: *due to*

As many teachers know from experience, a common tendency among L2 writers is to employ a particular set of connectives repeatedly in their text (e.g., *according to, moreover, therefore*). However, the quality of academic writing is often evaluated based on lexical and syntactic variety, and providing writers with options for essential academic expressions may help create less stilted prose (Davidson, 1991; Hale et al., 1996; Read, 2000). To this end the usage of complex prepositions in addition to sentence transitions and subordinate clauses (see also chap. 10) can provide at least some degree of variation among lexical connectives and syntactic structures.

CLARIFYING AND GIVING EXAMPLES

In academic writing instruction, giving examples is often strongly encouraged. In most textbooks on academic writing, among other types of supporting evidence, examples are presented as a common means of rhetorical support for the writer's position in academic writing (Raimes, 1999; Reid, 2000a; Smoke, 1999). Many teachers emphasize that providing contextually relevant examples and illustrations represents a reasonable and valid means of thesis support in explaining one's position on an issue.

Instructional materials in L2 academic writing consistently point out that the examples employed in written academic discourse need to be representative of general points and ideas discussed in support of the writer's thesis. The types of examples included as supporting illustrations also need to be varied and rely on materials such as pertinent facts, statistics, descriptive details, and elaborate explanations (Raimes, 1999; Smalley et al., 2000).

However, what actually represents pertinent facts, descriptive details, and elaborate explanations is not clear cut. Although giving examples represents a prevalent explanatory and thesis support strategy in constructing persuasive text in English, teachers and researchers have found that college-level L2 writers rarely employ this strategy successfully and in accordance with the guidelines identified in L2 composition instruction (Dong, 1998; Hvitfeld, 1992). In fact in many cases, the strategy is counterproductive and leads to L2 writers' academic prose that seem to be particularly un-academic, when it includes high frequencies of discourse and text features incongruous with common characteristics of written academic discourse in English (Johns, 1991, 1997; Jordan, 1997). Some examples of incorrect and/inappropriate examples found in student writing can include: **For example, my brother/my country/my case; *For example, I do too; *For example, I agree/I hate it.* Other studies have noted that L2 writers frequently misunderstand how to provide appropriate exemplification and use brief mentions of situations or events rather than elaborated examples expected in formal college-level compositions (Hinkel, 1994). In many cases, students recount lengthy, highly personal narratives in lieu of representative examples (Hinkel, 2001c).

Examples provided in support of the writer's thesis or specific points made in the text can be used in the following contexts:

- To support a generalization
  - by means of information obtained from **published and citable sources** (such as statistical data, research findings, or opinions of experts; e.g., *For example, Peters (2004) has a different view and states that ...*)
  - by explicitly stating that generalizations indeed apply to **most (or many) cases/people/situations/events** (e.g., *For example, 42% of all high school students have part-time jobs* or *in U.S. universities today, only a minority of students are male, 49%*)
- To clarify and explain unfamiliar terms and abstract concepts
  - by means of specific cases that **demonstrably** apply to **most (or many) cases/people/situations** (e.g., *For example, when coastline changes its shape, the tide pools where people fish will also become different. In this case, the local people cannot go to fish where they used to before*)
  - by means of expanded/detailed descriptions that deal with the publicly known and verifiable events (such as political, financial, social, demographic, medical, natural, or historical developments), lives of public figures, communities, groups of people, or sets of circumstances, or explanations examined from several perspectives. For instance, an example of how the teaching of math in Japan is better than that in the United States has to include points about elementary and secondary schools, boys and girls, and/or teacher training and expectations of students.

In academic writing, examples and extended examples present factual information that is clear and well organized. Examples that are used to support the writer's thesis can provide the highlights or an outline of the rest of the information that follows. All extended examples usually begin with a statement of fact. For example:

Education is important for the economic survival of the poor. For example, in the course of his or her working life, an average high school graduate can earn 1.2 million dollars. College graduates can earn 2.1 million dollars, and people with master's degrees, on average, can make 2.5 million. It seems clear that the more education workers have, the more money they can make. Educated adults have greater earning power and can have a higher standard of living.

Students need to be warned that examples should NOT include:

- narrations of personal experiences, as well as those of one's family members, classmates, roommates, or neighbors

- explanations of personal opinions, which are not based on demonstrable and verifiable facts
- stories or rumors that one has heard from other people

In all cases, examples included in academic writing need to be selected carefully to include verifiably representative and accurate information. Occasionally (and only occasionally), an example of a dramatic situation or event can be used to illustrate how it relates to an extreme and untypical development.

STRUCTURES NOT TO USE OR TO USE SPARINGLY

Students need to be warned about using rhetorical questions and some presupposition words and phrases.

Rhetorical and Tag Questions

Many textbooks for writing usually recommend that writers ask provocative or disturbing questions in introductions or use questions as an attention-getting device, similar to their uses in journalistic prose (Axelrod & Cooper, 2001; Connelly, 2000; Hacker, 1994, 2000; Kennedy et al., 2002; McWhorter, 2000). However, in general, rhetorical questions are not considered to be appropriate in written academic texts in English because they can be excessively personal and subjective (Swales & Feak, 1994; e.g., *Why do these young people get married?*, *Who knows the truth?*, *Why does the U.S. government refuse to pay its U.N. debt?*, or *The anti-terrorist bodies of government should know what they are doing, shouldn't they?*).

Other studies indicates that direct questions in writing are often viewed as personal and artificial, and analyses of published English language corpora indicate that they are exceedingly rare in formal academic writing (Myers, 1989). Biber's, et al. (1999) study found that questions are used at the rate of 0.05% of all words in formal written text. Chang and Swales (1999) found that direct questions are actively discouraged in academic prose in many disciplines.

In various rhetorical traditions other than Anglo-American, rhetorical questions are often seen as an appropriate device to convey hesitation and/or uncertainty of facts, and their discourse function can be compared to that of hedging devices in English (Biq, 1990; Hwang, 1987; Maynard, 1993; Ohta, 1991; Sa'adeddin, 1989; Taylor, 1995). Studies of formal L2 academic writing have demonstrated that NNSs writers employ rhetorical questions significantly more frequently than NS students with less training in academic writing and composition (Hinkel, 2002a). Other studies have also established that L2 writers often transfer rhetorical uses of questions in formal writing from their L1s and employ them to excess (G. Taylor & Chen, 1991; Wong, 1990).

> On the whole, L2 writers should be strongly discouraged from using rhetorical questions in formal academic writing.

As Williams (2002) astutely commented, asking questions may be a bit dangerous because they can invite a wrong answer.

Presupposition Words and Phrases

Presupposition markers such as *obvious*, *obviously*, and *of course* are used to refer to assumptions that the writer believes to be common knowledge, widely known facts, and universal truths (and, in this sense, they are presuppositional; e.g., *Of course, if children watch violent TV shows, they become violent* or *Obviously, Exxon should pay for the cleanup because they were the ones who spilled the oil*). Halliday and Hasan (1976) noted that in formal writing these markers imply a slightly adversative force because they suggest that something is or should have been obvious, but may have been overlooked. Sinclair (1991) explained that the uses of *of course* have become largely idiomatic in spoken English because it functions as a one-word marker similar to other vague clichés that refer to assumed presuppositions.

Presupposition markers and similar references to universal truths make written texts particularly prone to misunderstandings and negative evaluations (Chafe, 1994; Moon, 1998). In academic and composition writing in English, *of course* and *obviously* often indicate flawed organization of information into given and new because in the Anglo-American rhetorical tradition the writer's responsibility for text clarity and minimal shared knowledge is customarily assumed (Tickoo, 1992).

> Presupposition words and phrases such as *obvious*, *obviously*, and *of course* should be avoided in formal academic writing.

PUNCTUATION OF COHESIVE ELEMENTS

In English academic writing, about a dozen punctuation rules make up the relatively rigid basics. An academic text written without using them can appear ungrammatical no matter how well it adheres to the rules of the English sentence structure. In all languages, punctuation rules are largely based on convention; for this reason, they may seem somewhat random and haphazard to L2 writers who were not exposed to them from the time they began reading. One of the outcomes of this view can be L2 writers' tendency to ignore punctuation rules altogether, with the exception of capitalization and periods, on which most writing teachers insist.

In English, the fundamental purpose of punctuation marks is to divide sentences into their component parts (see chap. 4). Therefore, to a great extent, the rules of punctuation follow those developed for sentence and phrase structures. It is possible to think of punctuation marks as sentence and phrase dividers or partitions that most often adhere to boundaries of sentence and phrase slots. A small number of punctuation rules depend on the meaning of sentences elements (e.g., restrictive and nonrestrictive clauses), and the semantic purposes of punctuation are usually the hardest for L2 writers to use correctly.

> In teaching it is important to emphasize that the purpose of punctuation (and the punctuation rules) is to make the sentence easy to read by visually dividing it into component parts.

The basic punctuation rules outlined next represent the bare bones of the punctuation system in English. These rules must be learned and used in the production of academic writing.

The Basic and Most Important Punctuation Rules

Sentence Transitions and Prepositional Phrases

- All sentence transitions at the beginnings of sentences have to be separated by a comma (e.g., *However, ... For this reason, ... In light of this information, ...*

Transition	,	the rest of the sentence	.

- Sentence transitions in the middle of a sentence are separated by commas on both sides (e.g., *Hill's research, however, emphasizes the importance of ...; The American democracy, on the other hand, ...*).

The beginning of the sentence	,	transition	,	the rest of the sentence	.

- In compound sentences, two short simple sentences can be separated by a semicolon (see chap. 4 for a detailed discussion).

Sentence #1	;	sentence #2	.

- If the short sentences in a compound construction are also conjoined by a transition, the transition has to be separated by a comma in all cases (e.g., *Soil depletion is very costly; however, it can be prevented; Factories concentrate in cities; additionally, distribution networks center around major water ways*).

Sentence #1 ; transition, sentence #2.

Example and Other Markers

- Example markers (e.g., *for example, for instance, namely*), information sequencers/discourse organizers (e.g., *in the first place, second, finally, also, then*), as well as adverbial emphasizers (e.g., *indeed, above all, most important*), play the role of connectives/transitions and follow the same punctuation rules.

Prepositional Phrases and Other Preliminary Information

- Prepositional phrases [preposition + phrase], adverbials of all types (time, place, and evaluation), and infinitives at the beginnings of sentences often play the role of sentence connectives and transitions (e.g., *In 2002, ... In the state capital, ... At the start of the 20th century, ... In the view of the author, ... In light of the study findings, ... In spite of the rain, ... Usually, ... Perhaps, ... Fortunately, ... To begin/conclude/summarize*).
- When they are placed at the beginnings of sentence, all elements that supply preliminary information and/or that have connective functions have to be separated by commas.[4]

Prepositional phrase/connective/adverbial , the rest of the sentence.

- Prepositional phrases in the middle or at the end of sentences are not separated out, and commas are not used (e.g., *The industrial revolution began in England in the mid-1700s. Mass production techniques emerged after World War I and formed the basis of advanced industrial societies*).

Parallel Structure

- In parallel structures, punctuation depends on the number of elements in the string.
- **Two** elements take **no commas** (e.g., *rain or snow; advertising and marketing staff; bought and sold*).

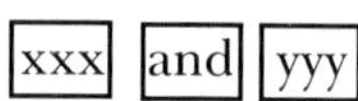

[4]Some grammar reference books suggest that the comma after a short introductory expression is optional. However, other reference books indicate the comma is required, and it is easier to explain to ESL writers that the comma is required so that they do not need to deliberate at what length of the introductory phrase the comma does become necessary.

- Three or more elements: **comma after each element**; a phrase conjunction (e.g., ***and/but/or***) is required **before the last element**. In fact the conjunction ***and*** marks the last element in the parallel structure (e.g., *soil, minerals, and water*; *production, trade, and distribution of goods; buy, sell, or trade commodities*).

[xxx] , [yyy] , [***and*** zzz] OR [aaa] , [bbb] , [ccc] , [***or*** ddd]

As mentioned in chapter 4, various punctuation marks have different "power," with the period being the most powerful sentence divider, followed by the semicolon and comma. In some contexts the semicolon and a conjunction + a comma can have the same power:

The United States is inhabited by 5% of the world population , but / ; it uses roughly 25% of the world's commercial energy.

The comma, possibly because of its relatively small dividing power, has a large number of uses. It can set off prepositional phrases, sentence transitions, elements of parallel structures (words or phrases alike), subordinate clauses, or short simple sentences when boosted by a conjunction. It is in part due to the comma's flexibility that L2 writers find the punctuation rules dealing with commas confusing (and who can blame them!).

CHAPTER SUMMARY

Cohesion refers to connections between sentences and paragraphs, and *coherence* can also refer to the organization of discourse with all elements present and fitting together logically. The following are techniques students can use to increase the cohesion and coherence of their writing:

- One effective way to teach cohesion is show students how to provide known information, usually with repeated lexical items or substituted lexical items in the first part or a sentence with new information presented at the end of the sentence. The new information from one sentence is presented as old or known information in the subsequent sentence. There can be multiple cohesive chains of old and new information in paragraphs.
- Enumerative nouns (e.g., *aspect, characteristic, issue*) are common in academic writing. Students can learn them and use them for lexical substitution to provide cohesion without undue redundancy.
- In coherent papers, examples are commonly used in support of points, but students need to focus on using academic types of examples in academic writing.

- For the most part students should avoid rhetorical questions and presupposition markers such as *obvious*, *obviously*, and *of course* in their academic writing.
- There are a few basic punctuation rules that are fairly straightforward. Students should be instructed on the application of these rules and held accountable for following them.

STRATEGIES AND TACTICS FOR TEACHING AND TEACHING ACTIVITIES

(See also Teaching Strategies and Tactics in chaps. 5 and 6, Nouns and Noun Phrases, and Pronouns for additional exercises with various types of nouns and personal and demonstrative pronouns.)

A number of effective teaching techniques may be useful in instruction dealing specifically with text cohesion in academic writing. These can focus on the judicious usage of sentence transitions, lexical and semantic cohesive ties, lexical substitutions, parallel structure, and punctuation.

(1) Identifying Cohesive Ties: Recognition Practice I

Students read excerpts of varied lengths from published sources, beginning with those that are one or two paragraphs long and ranging to those that consist of several pages (the lengthy reading/cohesive ties excerpts can be assigned as homework). The texts can be selected from newspapers for intermediate-level students, Internet news reports or society/human interest stories, or introductory university-level textbooks. The students' task is to identify and mark as many cohesive ties and lexical substitutions as possible. [To add a level of complexity, students can also be asked to identify known/old and new information in each sentence.] Then in pairs or small groups, students can compare their findings. In short text excerpts at the beginning of the practice, the teacher should spot check or guide the activity. Students can use numbers to mark cohesive ties, as is shown in Example (3) earlier in this chapter. A illustration is provided next.

The paragraph in (a) can be used as a stand-alone excerpt or used together with the paragraph in (b). Both tasks (a) and (b) have been completed as an example.

(a) Cooperation [1] is a pattern of interaction [2] in which individuals, groups, and societies [2] work together [1] to **achieve** [7] shared [1] goals [3]. Cooperation [1] is fundamental [4] to human survival [3], and without it social life [2] would be impossible [4]. Cooperation [1] sustains routine, face-to-face encounters [2]. It [1] is also necessary [4] for people [2] to raise children, protect themselves 2, and make a living. Some societies [2] place greater emphasis on cooperation [1] than others [2].

(b) Competition [5] is much like cooperation [1] because both individuals and groups [2] strive to **achieve** [7] a shared [1] goal [3]. However, competition [5] is different [6] in that instead [6] of joining [1] with others to **achieve** [7] valued goals [3], competitors [5] contest [5] for them [3] : society's prizes are in limited [6] supply, and only one [6] person or group [2] can **attain** 7 them. (Adapted from Thompson and Hickey, 2002).

Note: The cohesive chain of verbs 7 across the two paragraphs can be expected of advanced students: **achieve—achieve—achieve—attain.**

(2) Identifying Missing Cohesive Ties: Recognition Practice II

In addition to identifying cohesive ties and lexical substations that are established by the author of the text, it is also helpful for students to work with text lacking in cohesion. For this practice, the teacher may choose a student text without sufficiently developed cohesion. [The texts should be written by students who are not in the class, and the author's permission must be secured to use the text for teaching purposes.] To add a level of complexity, students can also be asked to add cohesive elements to the text. It is important that texts selected for correcting contain a variety of cohesion problems/errors, including repetitive transitions, faulty parallel structures, and redundant lexis.

In pairs or small groups, students can compare their additions and repairs, and results can be spot checked. Students can be asked to write in or rewrite phrases and sentences in need of correction. An example of text with insufficiently developed cohesion is presented next. Some corrections are suggested in [square brackets].

Assignment topic: Please choose one (or more) historical event, individual, or a group of individuals in American history that had an important influence on American education. Your paper needs to explain how this event or individual influenced or changed the currents in the norms of schooling widely accepted in their time.

Since puritans arrived in America, politics, economical [economy], *and other parts* [aspects of the United States] *have changed* [Sentence 1 is not related to the rest of the text and should be deleted]. *In the field of education, many things have occurred.* [Possible introductory sentence: it requires a specific mention of what has occurred to lead to changes in education throughout American history] *Many American scholars have studied American history. They have tried to find out what made education change. They state different causes about it* [non-referential pronoun]. *They* [the third use of the pronoun they—too far away from the original noun] *view history from different sights* [perspectives/positions]. [The last four sentences are redundant, vague, and very broad—probably should be deleted]

Some scholars argue that the political and economy situations and religion [politics, economy, and religion] *affect education. The content and method of political and education* [political and educational] *change* [no main verb] *not due to the problems* [the first mention of the problems—to what noun phrase(s)/text do the problems tie?] *in education itself, but due to the political and economy situations and religion* [politics, economy, and religion] *at that time* [the first mention of that time—to what noun/noun phrase does the pronoun that point?]. *They* [non-referential pronoun: it is too far from some scholars in the first line] *stated that the reason for the change* [no specific change has been mentioned, but only change in general—to what noun or noun phrase does the change tie?] *are outside of* [delete of] *education.*

The texts and the essays of [on/for?] *education, which were written at that time* [to what specific time does the pronoun that point?], *supported this interpretation* [to what interpretation does the phrase this interpretation point?]. *Noah Webster was a writer of texts, for example, Webster's spelling book* [Noah Webster is mentioned for the first time—who was he, when, what was his profession? Noah Webster may be a good topic for the paper, but his historical role needs to be the focus]. *Webster's Federal Catechism* [Webster's work is mentioned for the first time—what was it? what was it about? what was it for?], *which were* [how many Catechisms?] *the most popular textbooks* [how many textbooks? why were they popular?] *at that time* [at what time?] *in the late 18th and early 19th centuries. Webster believed that his texts would make good and patriotic Americans, develop American language, and unified nation spirit* [and build/create a unified national spirit; faulty parallelism: the third verb is missing in make—develop—??] [Why did Webster believe so strongly in his textbook? What did the textbook do, what did it include, and what was it for?].

(3) Lexical Substitutions: Odd Man Out

Students are provided sentences with words and a number of their near synonyms. Each set of near synonyms includes one word that has a different meaning and does not belong in the set. The task is to write another sentence or two to follow the first and make it cohesive with the first sentence. Possible idea continuations are provided in [square brackets].

(a) *The exact causes of various natural disasters, such as torrential rains and hurricanes, cannot always be* (established/determined/separated/identified) *because a number of natural phenomena can combine to bring about a particular weather event.* [A sentence or two about the work of scientists who work to predict/anticipate/foresee natural disasters or weather events.]

(b) *In the past several decades, it has become clear that individual physical* (features/characteristics/positions) *are hereditary and transferable from one generation to the another.* [A sentence about/a short discussion of the influence of heredity on physical appearance; e.g. height or the color of hair/eyes.]

(c) *Biologists and medical scientists* (collaborate/work together/correlate) *in their research devoted to the* (role/influence/method/influence) *of heredity on an individual's health, as well as psychological tendencies and habits.* [A sentence about/a short description of possible connections between heredity and psychology/habits.]

(d) *The paintings of the 17th and 18th centuries often* (focused/concentrated/ centered/leaned) *on a historical or religious scenes that* (depicted/portrayed/conveyed/ proclaimed) *a military victory or conquest.* [A sentence about other types of paintings, drawings, or a work of visual art.]

(e) *In many cultures, paintings and drawing usually include several* (main/prominent/crucial/essential) (elements/details/components/contributions) *that attract the attention of the viewer.* [A sentence about/a short description of a composition of a painting, a drawing, or a work of art.]

(f) *Cable TV broadcasts* (rely/depend/hinge) *on satellites to (transmit/relay/deliver/contain) the visual and audio signals to local stations that carry it further to their customers in the area.* [A sentence about/a short description of how other similar instruments work; e.g., cellular phones, radio, or computer networks.]

(4) Functions and Limitations of Sentence Transitions

The goal of this exercise is to demonstrate that sentence transitions alone cannot make the text cohesive, but can merely enhance textual cohesion that exists largely independently of transitional words and phrases.

Step 1. To highlight the function of sentence transitions as a relatively superficial cohesive device, students can be asked to produce text without using transitions at all.

Step 2. Then students can be requested to identify meaning-based relationships that exist between sentences or paragraphs in terms traditionally used in the semantic groupings of transitions found in many L2 writing texts—for example, additional information (*In addition, Additionally, Moreover*), result *(As a result, As a consequence)*, or concession *(although, even though)*. [This step can be combined with another for identifying a new idea in each sentence or a continuation of the same idea.]

Step 3. After students identify relationships between sentences (or portions of the text), they can be asked to decide which sentence or paragraph would be easier to understand with the addition of a sentence transition and which seems to be clear without one.

(5) Punctuation/Sentence Combining

(a) Any excerpt from student and/or authentic texts can be used for punctuation practice. All punctuation in the original should be eliminated before students are asked to insert punctuation marks (and/or combine simple sentences whenever possible).

(b) For students at the intermediate level of proficiency, the teacher may need to simplify authentic texts by replacing rare or advanced vocabulary items.

Retyped (but not copied) news media texts can also be useful for this type of practice.

QUESTIONS FOR DISCUSSION

1. In addition to cohesive ties and lexical substitutions, in what other ways can text cohesion be established? Please consider the following examples: Which ones are cohesive and which ones are not? Why is it that some of these short contexts seem to be more cohesive than others?
   (a) The end-of-the-year sales are a boon for merchants. The spring merchandise begins to ship in early February.
   (b) Florida's Apalachicola Bay is one example of pollution dangers. In economic terms, water contamination means that various sea products are threatened.
   (c) Only a few thousand people came to the opening night. The players were devastated.
   (d) This paper will discuss the decline in the importance of the Constitution and the standards of behavior expected of government officials.
   (e) Since the end of the WWII, European countries have not been the same. The changes in the mindsets of Europeans following the war have had a broad effect on their policies.
2. From the point of view of rhetorical features, it appears that L2 writing produced by NNSs almost always differs from that written by NSs in their L1, English. Multiple reasons can exist for these divergences between the rhetorical characteristics of L2 and L1 text. Can you identify the most important divergences and the reasons they exist?
3. In your opinion, what can be the reasons that textbooks for teaching writing to L1 and L2 writers alike emphasize particular features such as sentence transitions or examples, but not others (e.g., cohesive ties, lexical substitutions, or complex prepositions)?
4. In academic writing in English, it may be precarious to assume that the writer and reader share a good deal of common knowledge and are equally well familiar with certain universal truths. Yet to some degree such an assumption must be made for the writer to produce practically any piece of writing. How can new L2 writers strike a bal-

ance between explaining too much and not providing enough information for the reader to understand their text?

5. A number of structures and textual devices are discussed in this chapter. Please explain which of these would be the most difficult for teachers to teach or students to learn. Why? Are the difficult teaching structures the same as the complex learning structures?

FURTHER READINGS ABOUT RHETORICAL DEVICES AND COHESION

Biq, Y.-O. (1990). Question words as hedges in Chinese. In L. Bouton & Y. Kachru (Eds.), *Pragmatics and Language Learning* (Vol. 1, pp. 149–158). Urbana-Champaign: Intensive English Institute.

Carrell, P. (1982). Cohesion is not coherence. *TESOL Quarterly, 16*(4), 479–488.

Carrell, P. (1992). Awareness of text structure: Effects on recall. *Language Learning, 42*, 1–20.

Francis, G. (1994). Labelling discourse: An aspect of nominal-group cohesion. In M. Coulthard (Ed.), *Advances in written text analysis* (pp. 83–101). New York: Routledge.

Halliday, M. A. K., & Hasan, R. (1976). *Cohesion in English.* London: Longman.

Hinkel, E. (2001). Matters of cohesion in L1 and L2 academic texts. *Applied Language Learning, 12*(2), 111–132.

Kim, H. (1990). Continuity of action and topic in discourse. In H. Hoji (Ed.), *Japanese and Korean linguistics* (pp. 79–96). Palo Alto, CA: Center for Study of Language and Information.

Master, P. (2002). Relative clause reduction in technical research articles. In E. Hinkel & S. Fotos (Eds.), *New perspectives on grammar teaching second and foreign language classrooms* (pp. 201–231).Mahwah, NJ: Lawrence Erlbaum Associates.

McCarthy, M. (1994). It, this, and that. In M. Coulthard (Ed.), *Advances in written text analysis* (pp. 266–275). New York: Routledge.

Ostler, S. (1987). English in parallels: A comparison of English and Arabic prose. In U. Connor & R. Kaplan (Eds.), *Writing across languages: Analysis of L2 text* (pp. 169–185). Reading, MA: Addison-Wesley.

Scollon, R. (1991). Eight legs and one elbow: Stance and structure in Chinese English compositions. *Proceedings of the 2nd North American Conference on Adult and Adolescent Literacy* (pp. 26–41). Ottawa: International Reading Association.

Tickoo, A. (1992). Seeking a pedagogically useful understanding of given-new: An analysis of native speaker errors in written discourse. In L. Bouton and Y. Kachru (Eds.), *Pragmatics and language learning* (Vol. 3, pp. 130–143). Urbana-Champaign: Intensive English Institute.

Wong, H. (1990). The use of rhetorical questions in written argumentative discourse. In L. Bouton & Y. Kachru (Eds.), *Pragmatics and Language Learning* (Vol. 1, pp. 187–208). Urbana-Champaign: Intensive English Institute.

Appendix to Chapter 11

The diagram *The Structure of an Academic Essay* is intended to illustrate the fundamental structure of the classical, traditional, and sometimes deprecated academic essay. The structure of written academic discourse and text has not changed during the past two or three decades despite upheavals and revolutions in writing instruction (Johns, 1997).

The advantage of a clear and not-too-complex diagram is that it is easy to draw on a chalkboard, white board, or overhead transparency.

Academic essays usually include an Introduction, which names and briefly describes the topic. The essay must include a Thesis Statement, which specifies how the writer will approach the topic and what supporting points (1, 2, 3, or more) he or she will use to shore up the thesis. The thesis statement serves as an outline for the rest of the essay: The order of the Points made in the thesis statement always determines the order of Thesis Supports (1, 2, 3, or more). A useful analogy that can be made is that the Thesis Statement is the container that holds the entire essay together and in one place.

THESIS SUPPORT

Each Point made in the Thesis has to be supported. The information to support the Thesis should be divided into Paragraphs, one expanded and developed idea per paragraph (aka *one thought at a time*). Each paragraph should include a Topic Sentence that supports the Thesis Statement and is directly connected to a particular Point in the Thesis Statement, in the order of the Points.

The Structure of an Academic Essay

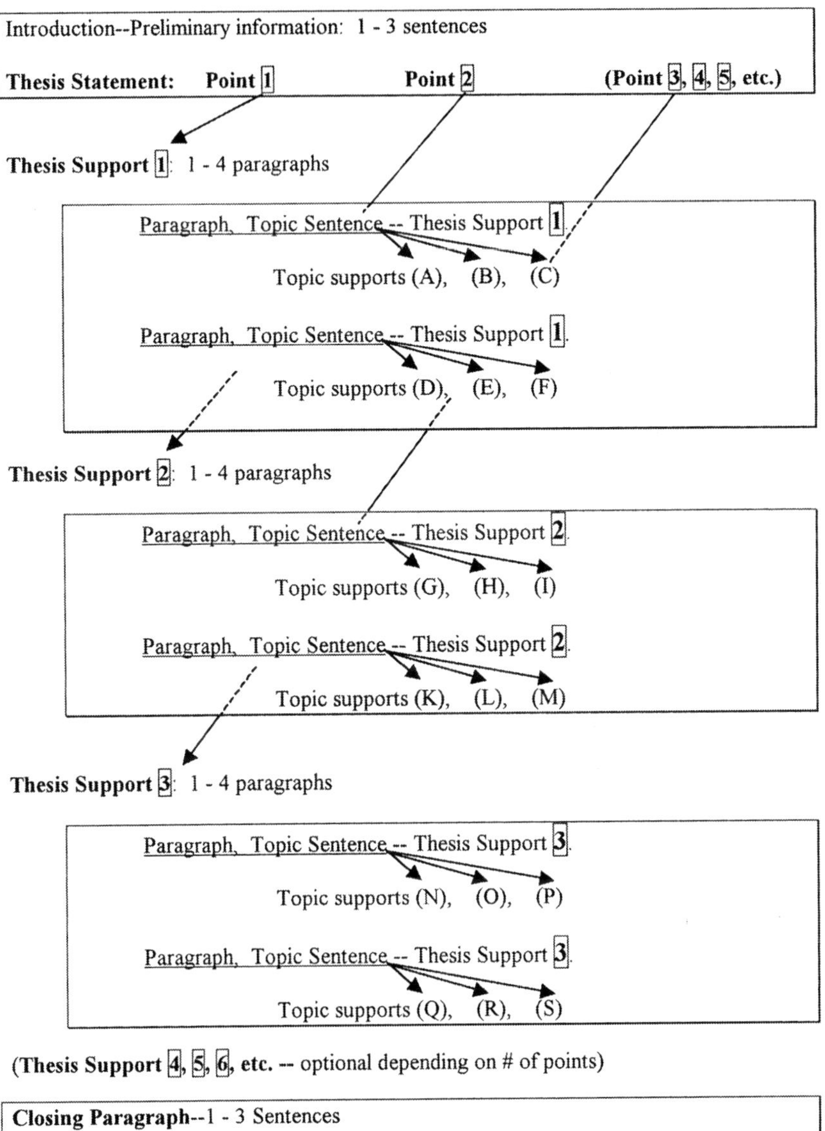
Introduction--Preliminary information: 1 - 3 sentences
Thesis Statement: Point 1 Point 2 (Point 3, 4, 5, etc.)
Thesis Support 1: 1 - 4 paragraphs
Paragraph, Topic Sentence -- Thesis Support 1.
Topic supports (A), (B), (C)
Paragraph, Topic Sentence -- Thesis Support 1.
Topic supports (D), (E), (F)
Thesis Support 2: 1 - 4 paragraphs
Paragraph, Topic Sentence -- Thesis Support 2.
Topic supports (G), (H), (I)
Paragraph, Topic Sentence -- Thesis Support 2.
Topic supports (K), (L), (M)
Thesis Support 3: 1 - 4 paragraphs
Paragraph, Topic Sentence -- Thesis Support 3.
Topic supports (N), (O), (P)
Paragraph, Topic Sentence -- Thesis Support 3.
Topic supports (Q), (R), (S)
(Thesis Support 4, 5, 6, etc. -- optional depending on # of points)
Closing Paragraph--1 - 3 Sentences

Similarly, each Topic Sentence also has to be supported by Topic Supports (A, B, C or D, E, F) directly connected to the topic sentence. If more than one paragraph is used to support a Thesis Point (1, 2, 3, +), other Topic Sentences in each paragraph also need to be directly relevant to the Thesis Point.

All Topic Supports (A, B, C and D, E, F) have to be related to their own Topic Sentence, and all Topic Sentences have to support the Thesis (every Topic Sentence wants to be the Big Kahuna—the Thesis).

When Thesis Point 1 is well supported, the essay moves on to Thesis Point 2.

THESIS SUPPORT 2

Thesis Support 2 consists of a number of paragraphs (1–4). Each paragraph includes a Topic Sentence that is directly connected to Point 2 in the Thesis. Topic Sentences are supported by Topic Supports (G, H, I and K, L, M). All Topic Supports are directly connected to their own Topic Sentences, which are directly connected to the Thesis Point 2.

A useful analogy: In an organization or business, employees in a department (or unit) have their direct boss, who is actually a small boss. The small boss, together with several other small bosses, has a medium-size boss. Several medium-size bosses report to an upper medium-size boss, and several upper medium bosses report to the Big Boss, the Kahuna (aka the Thesis Statement).

When Thesis Point 2 is well supported, the essay moves on to Thesis Point 3. When Thesis Point 3 is supported, on to Thesis Point 4, and so on.

In academic essays, a proper Conclusion is not always possible to make simply because many academic assignments and papers are written about issues that do not have conclusions. However, conclusion making is not required, but a Closing Paragraph is. To close an essay, it is also not necessary to repeat the Thesis Points (as students often do). A closing paragraph can look forward into the future and, for example, note possible developments, events, or steps than can be taken with regard to the essay topic or issue. Other types of Closing Paragraphs can include the writer's personal hopes/views/expectations that deal with the topic or simply a couple of summative sentences.

A practical exercise can be to ask students to underline the Thesis Statement in their assignment/essay and then underline the Topic Sentence in each paragraph and connect it to a specific Thesis Point, one at a time.

12

Hedging in Academic Text in English

OVERVIEW

- The role and importance of hedges in academic text
- Helping learners expand their hedging repertoire
- Various types of hedges such as frequency adverbs, possibility hedges, modal verbs, and adjective/adverb hedges
- Developing stock vocabulary and hedges
- Overstatements and learning to avoid them

In the past several decades, much research has been devoted to hedging in academic prose, among other types of discourse (e.g., Channell, 1994; Hinkel, 1997b; Holmes, 1984; Huebler, 1983; Hyland, 1998; Kay, 1997; Pagano, 1994). Analyses of large English-language corpora continue to underscore the importance and prevalence of various types of hedging devices in academic prose (Biber, 1988; Biber et al., 1999; Hoye, 1997).

According to Hyland (1998), the purpose of hedging is to reduce the writer's commitment to the truthfulness of a statement. In addition, hedging represents the use of linguistic devices to show hesitation or uncertainty, display politeness and indirectness, and defer to the reader's point of view (Hinkel, 1996a, 1997b). In academic prose, hedging has numerous social and rhetorical purposes, and it can take many linguistic forms, including adverbs, adjectives, modal and mental/emotive verbs, and conjunctions. In linguistic research, various definitions and classifications of hedging devices have been constructed to account for their complex and frequently culturally bound contextual uses.

In Anglo-American formal written text, hedges are used extensively with the general goal of projecting "honesty, modesty, proper caution," and diplomacy (Swales, 1990a, p. 174).

> The uses of hedges are highly conventionalized in academic writing and practically requisite in expressions of personal positions or points of view.

Based on his corpus analysis of published academic prose, Hyland (1998) confirmed that "hedges were by far the most frequent features of writer perspective" (p. 106) and stated that, in academic writing, this finding reflects the critical importance of distinguishing fact from opinion and rhetorical persuasion.

However, in composition textbooks and writing guides for basic writers, hedges, often called *limiting modifiers* (Hacker, 1994; Lunsford & Connors, 1997), are not discussed in detail. Despite the prevalence and importance of hedges in written academic prose, textbooks for teaching ESL and EAP writing rarely focus on hedges of any kind with the exception of modal verbs (Hyland, 1998). One notable exception is the work of Jordan (1997), who pointed out that hedging in academic writing in business, economics, medical sciences is not just desirable, but requisite. He emphasized that hedging is a "vitally important" (p. 241) skill in L2 academic writing and suggested various teaching techniques for giving students practice in the uses of hedges. Similarly, other researchers have noted that L2 learners need to gain an understanding of how hedging the extent of one's claims and certainty reflects the politeness of the academic genre because NNS writers need to correctly interpret the politeness strategies employed by other writers as well as produce appropriate text and language (Channell, 1994).

However, several studies have found that L2 academic text frequently contains overstatements, exaggerations, and forceful persuasion (Hinkel, 1997b, 2002a). In general terms, although there may be a variety of reasons for the impressions of overstatement and inflation projected in NNS texts, one important consideration may have to do with the fact that rhetorical uncertainty and the employment of hedges is valued greatly in the Anglo-American, but not necessarily in other, rhetorical traditions (Oliver, 1972; Sa'adeddin, 1989). Furthermore, research has shown that NNS writers have a restricted lexical repertoire that often leads to a shortage of hedging devices employed in L2 written text (Hinkel, 2003a; Hyland, 2002a). Therefore, focused instruction in appropriate uses of varied hedging is urgently needed.

The discussion of various types of hedging devices presented in this chapter is organized to begin with the lexically and syntactically simple devices and proceed to those of greater complexity. (For additional information about the hedging properties of conditional, concessive, and time [*when*] clauses, see chap. 10; the passive voice as hedging, see chap. 7; and indefinite pronouns as hedges, chap. 6.)

WHY HEDGING NEEDS TO BE TAUGHT

Because in various non-Anglo-American rhetorical traditions, rhetorical persuasion does not necessarily call for hedging, the desirability of hedging statements, generalizations, and claims is not an obvious consideration for many NNS writers. Therefore, the need for hedging in academic prose has to be explicitly addressed. Noting the distinctions in uses of hedges in informal conversational and formal written discourse is a good place to start.

For example, in casual conversations, English speakers often say, *I always forget to xxx!*, *You always do yyy!*, or *Everything is falling apart today*. Speakers of other languages say these things, too, in both English and their native languages. However, in all languages, informal conversations with friends require a different type of discourse and language features than, for instance, writing a petition to the dean. In fact, if someone talks to his or her friends and uses language features similar to those found in the petition, within a short time this individual would not have many friends left. So, the language features employed in formal academic writing are almost always substantially and markedly different from those used in conversations.

In many discourse traditions, overstatements and exaggerations can be so common that practically no one notices them. Also in English some conversational exaggerations are not likely to get much attention (e.g., *I have a thousand things to do today* or *Every time I get in the shower, the phone rings*). On the other hand, in formal writing, these sentences may become, *I am busy today* or *The phone often rings when I am in the shower.* Such exaggerations are usually assumed to be innocent hyperboles that are used to make a point, and both speakers and hearers are aware that the actual state of affairs is inflated. In contrast, the information in formal written discourse is expected to be far more precise and cautiously hedged, and in various types of formal prose, such as professional correspondence, memos, or reports, exaggerations and overstatements can be precarious and appear to be irresponsible and untruthful.

With conversational hyperboles, the speaker's and the hearer's shared and mutual assumptions apply to overstatements and exaggerations, allowing them to understand the intended meaning. Furthermore, apart from such shared and mutual assumptions that exist in the Anglo-American discourse tradition, there is little objective reason to believe that these assumptions should only apply to casual conversations, but not formal written prose. It may not be difficult to imagine that in non-Anglo-American rhetorical traditions, hyperboles can be a perfectly acceptable persuasion device when both the writer and the reader assume that the actual value of the information in a statement is smaller than the stated.

For example, in *Students always study hard*, the writer simply assumes that the reader knows that the intended meaning is *not* that *all (100%)*

students study hard at all times. The shared and mutual assumptions prevalent in various discourse traditions apply to allow the reader to understand that the writer knows that 100% of students do not work hard 100% of the time. In this case, the reader does not necessarily think that the writer's text is overstated, and reality hedging is assumed by both the writer and the reader.

THE SNOWBALL EFFECT TO EXPAND HEDGING REPERTOIRE

In L2 instruction, teaching NNS writers to hedge often requires persistence and effort because, in many discourse traditions other than Anglo-American, hedging is not considered to be an important feature of academic prose. In many cases, L2 writers have a restricted lexical range of accessible hedging devices. If a small number of hedges are used repeatedly, the L2 text may appear to be redundant and repetitious. Hence, teaching students to hedge their claims also has an attendant objective of helping them expand their lexical repertoire and advance their awareness of the important differences between academic writing and other written and conversational registers (Jordan, 1997).

The instruction on hedging may need to begin with lexically and syntactically accessible types of hedges, such as adverbs of frequency (*usually, often*) and quantifiers (*most, many, some*). These two types of hedges can be used by L2 learners even at the low to intermediate level of proficiency. Building on this base, teaching the meanings and hedging functions of modal verbs, such as *can* and *may*, can further help students increase their lexical range at a relatively low cost in terms of work and time.

Adjective and adverb hedges are by far the most numerous in English, and they include a wide variety of lexically simple items (e.g., *almost* and *only*) as well as semantically and syntactically complex items (e.g., *apparently* and *relative to*). However, even though adjectival and adverbial hedges are numerous, L2 writers certainly do not need to become fluent users of the entire group. In fact in combination with frequency adverbs, quantifiers, and modal verbs learned earlier, a relatively good range of hedges can become accessible for use in essays and assignments if only a portion of adjective and adverb hedges are addressed in instruction.

> An important ingredient in teaching NNS writers to construct academic text entails examining the features that should be avoided. These include hedging devices associated with informal and conversational register, which are rarely encountered in academic prose (e.g., *kind of, maybe*, and *to be supposed to*). A prevalence of such hedges can make a piece of writing appear conversational and inappropriate in tone.

In addition, overstatements and exaggerations are identified not only by absence of hedging, as noted earlier, but also explicit markers such as *completely, extremely, strongly,* and *totally*. Conversational hedges and exaggeratives are also dealt with in this chapter.

ADVERBS OF FREQUENCY AND POSSIBILITY HEDGES

With the exception of *always* and *never,* which mark the extremes of the frequency continuum, ***frequency adverbs*** such as *frequently, often, usually,* and *occasionally* represent one of the most common and simple hedging devices. In fact because these adverbs are lexically and syntactically simple, they can be accessible to most L2 learners, from those with intermediate to advanced L2 proficiency. In addition, due to their ubiquity, frequency adverbs can be employed to hedge the meanings of verbs or whole sentences and can be easier to use in editing than other more complex types of hedges. For instance, *sometimes, often, usually,* and *generally* are more common in academic prose than, for example, *ever* or *never,* which are particularly rare (Biber et al., 1999).

Although frequency adverbs can be definite (e.g., *hourly, daily, weekly, monthly*), the indefinite frequency adverbs have the function of hedges when used in appropriate contexts. These include (in the order of declining frequency rates in academic text):

- *frequently, often*
- *generally/in general, usually, ordinarily*
- *occasionally/on occasion, sometimes, at times, from time to time, every so often*
- *most of the time, on many/numerous occasions*
- *almost never, rarely, seldom, hardly ever* (negative meanings)
- *almost/nearly always, invariably*

Adverb phrases of frequency such as *on many occasions* or *at times* can be placed at the beginnings of sentences or at the ends of short sentences. For example, a student's sentence,

Cracks propagate when loads are applied to structural components,

can be relatively easy to hedge by means of adverbial phrases of frequency depending on the intended meaning:

> ***[In general/almost always/usually/on occasion/once in a while]****, cracks propagate when loads are applied to structural components.*

Single-word adverbs follow the general rules of adverb placement in a sentence:

- in front of the main verb, if the main sentence verb is not *be* (all examples are from student texts):
  Scientists ***[generally/usually/often]*** *think that by conducting research on human cloning, they will make a better quality human kind in the future.*
  The definition of workplace competence has ***[frequently/seldom/ occasionally]*** *included learning new knowledge and skills.*
- after *be*, if the main sentence verb is *be*
  This definition is ***[frequently/usually/sometimes]*** *too broad.*
  The reasons for the change are ***[generally/often]*** *not outside education, but they are connected to it.*

In many cases, uses of frequency adverbs are accompanied by the present simple tense.

Possibility hedges can be used as adjectives with nouns (*a probable/possible cause/reason*) and as adverbs in practically all other constructions (i.e., with verbs, adjectives, whole sentences, and other adverbs). Such adverbial hedges as *probably, perhaps, possibly,* and *in (this/that) case* are particularly common in formal academic writing (Hyland, 1998), and similar to frequency adverbs, they are lexically and syntactically easy to use. The placement rules of these adverbs follow those for frequency adverbs.

> Other types of possibility hedges are more characteristic of the **conversational** than the formal written register (e.g., *by [some/any] chance, hopefully,* and conditional clauses employed as clichés as in *if you know/understand what I mean [to say], if you catch/get my meaning/drift,* or *as everyone/the reader knows*).

As with adverbs of frequency, possibility hedges are not particularly complicated to teach. For instance, formal possibility hedges can be added to a student's sentences and conversational hedges and overstatements deleted as in (1) and (2):

(1) Statistics is ***[perhaps]*** *the newest science of mathematics. In our society, it is* ***[probably]*** *used [everywhere]* ***[in many places/for many purposes]****.*

(2) [As everyone knows,] ***[Good/careful]*** *judgment is* ***[possibly/probably]*** *the most important characteristic of a professional engineer.*

In these two excerpts, possibility hedges *possibly/perhaps/probably* can be employed to reduce the power of broad generalizations and claims made with regard to the universal usefulness of statistics in (1) and the single most important characteristic of an engineer in (2). In addition, the exaggerative adverb *everywhere* in (1) may not be particularly appropriate in an academic essay, and neither is the reference to common and assumed knowledge *as everyone knows* in (2). These two conversational overstatement markers can simply be deleted.

> In the context of academic prose, instruction should explicitly address the extent of the writer's full and unwavering commitment to the universal truthfulness, applicability, and knowledge expressed in statements such as (1) and (2). As the next step, the defensive stance and the power-reducing function of possibility hedges can be demonstrated and emphasized.

QUANTIFIERS AS HEDGES

Quantifiers refer to definite (*a half, a quarter*) and indefinite quantities and modify nouns. Indefinite quantifiers can function as hedges and include the following:

- *all, many/much*
- *some, a few/a little*
- *a number of* + noun/noun phrase
- *a good/great deal of* + noun/noun phrase
- *a bit (of)*

Clearly, the quantifier *all* would not make a very good hedging device, and its uses can make writers' claims appear somewhat overstated (e.g., *<u>All</u> teachers worry about how their pupils learn*). However, an addition of, for instance, *many/a few* and *much/a little* with countable and uncountable nouns, respectively, can help reduce the effect of broad generalizations in an essay about technological innovations:

> *[Many/Most] [P]eople have heard the concepts of facts, data, and knowledge. [Many/Some/A few] [S]cientists around the world seem to compete with each other for inventing new technology. [Many/Most/A number of] [People believe that technology cannot be limited, and it will keep going forever.*

Similarly, negative quantifiers such as *few/fewer* with countable nouns and *little/less* with uncountable nouns can hedge the somewhat extreme position implicit in the uses of indefinite pronouns *no one* and *nobody* in the following excerpt on fossil fuel consumption and passenger cars:

> ***[Few consumers/drivers/car owners]*** *[No one] want[s] to return to the energy crisis of the early 1970s. In those days, low fuel prices allowed consumers to focus on vehicle prices, performance, and comfort, and* ***[few individuals/drivers/engineers]*** *[nobody] cared about the fuel economy in passenger cars.... [Totally,] [t]his period can divided into three small periods for analysis.*

Investigations of student L1 and L2 essays have shown that NNS texts include significantly greater frequencies of *every-* and *no-* words (*everybody, everything, nothing, no one*) than the prose of NS writers (for additional discussion, see chap. 6 on pronouns; Hinkel, 2002a). However, research into formal academic prose shows that the quantifier *none* occurs at the rate of 0.01% and indefinite pronouns with *every-* 0.04%, as opposed to, for example, the quantifiers *many* and *some* with the rates of 0.1% and 0.28%, respectively. On the other hand, *no-* words and *none* are rarer still (Biber et al., 1999).

MODAL VERBS AS HEDGES

In general terms, in formal writing the meanings and functions of modal verbs can be divided into three classes (Hermeren, 1978; Quirk et al., 1985):

- Ability and possibility — *can, may, might, could, be able to*
- Obligation and necessity — *must, have to, should, ought, need to, to be to, to be supposed to* (highly informal)
- Prediction — *will, would*

Although most ESL grammar texts state that the primary purposes of modal verbs are to express meanings of ability (*can, could*), possibility (*may, might*), and obligation (*have to, must*), in academic texts the main function of modals is hedging. For example,

> *A life without mastery <u>may</u> produce vulnerability to depression.* (Seligman, 1999, p. 147)

> *Promotion provides information about the company and its products. It <u>may</u> convey a message that encourages consumers to respond.* (Zikmund et al., 1995, p. 293)

Will Versus *Can* and *May*

The meaning differences among modals largely deal with the degree of certainty, probability, and/or possibility. For instance, *will* refers to the future with a high degree of certainty, and *may* indicates a possibility. Therefore, because the function of *will* is to predict the future, unless the writer can assure the reader of the outcome certainty, the uses of the future tense in academic texts is considered to be somewhat inappropriate (see also chap. 7, the Future Tense).

Studies have shown that the future tense occurs significantly more frequently in L2 academic prose than in NS text. For example,

> *When parents take care of their children's social skills, their offspring <u>will</u> be far more successful than in families where children are ignored. Children from caring families*

> *will get along with their peer group and have a friendly environment.* (From a student essay on the parental role in child development.)

In this example, the uses of the future tense creates an impression of definiteness and a direct relationship between the parental care and children's success. In such cases, the discourse appears to contain exaggerated claims about definite outcomes. However, teaching appropriate structures in academic text in this case may be relatively simple (i.e., the future auxiliary *will* can simply be replaced with *may*).

In academic prose, modal verbs of possibility can have the function of hedges, and necessity modals can refer to reasoning and conclusion making (Chafe, 1994; Hinkel, 1995c, 1999a; Hoye, 1997). For example, the modal *may* expresses a possibility and *should* to a reasoned conclusion:

> *Ecological studies may give an answer to environmental problems in many countries. Our world should be healthier if pollution is controlled.* (From a student paper.)

> The meanings of *may* and *should* can be contrasted with those of *will*, which projects a great deal of certainty, and *must*, which conveys a high degree of obligation or probability.

An example of definitive predictions of future events demonstrates somewhat ambitious uses of will in a student paper:

> *For very sick patients with heart or lung diseases, doctors will use organs to help humans. The organs will be used as a "bridge" until doctors can find another human organ. However, animal rights activists will break into hospitals and laboratories where the operation takes place.... The doctors and the surgeons must practice their skills on animals before they do any surgery on humans.* (Excerpted from a student assignment about medical experiments on animals.)

In addition to the meanings of obligation, *must (not)* can also express prohibition, which is seldom employed in academic writing.

> The key distinction between the meanings of *may* and *can* lies in the fact that *may* refers to a possibility and *can* to an ability. Both *may* and *can* are rarely used in academic texts with the meaning of *permission* (Biber et al., 1999). Although *can* is common in the conversational register, in formal discourse *may* is more appropriate particularly in academic prose in humanities and social sciences (Hyland, 1998). In formal writing, *can* rarely refers to abilities, but rather possibilities and implications.

On the other hand, the negative modal *cannot* occurs in academic texts that have to do with denials, refutations, or counterexamples. The weak meanings of possibility in *could* and *might* do not project great confidence in an outcome, action, or event.

The predictive modal *would* in English may also have the function of a hedge in formal and informal academic writing, when it serves to reduce the writer's responsibility for the truth value and accuracy of evidence:

> *This would really help saving human lives, but there are also people who disagree with this*. (Excerpted from a student assignment about medical experiments on animals.)

However, because *would* conveys hypothetical and presuppositional meanings, it is often difficult for learners to use appropriately.[1]

In composition writing, the line between the meanings of modals of possibility, necessity, and prediction can be blurred (Raimes, 1992; Smoke, 1999). However, in general terms, in L2 academic writing modal verbs can be used effectively to moderate claims and avoid strong predictions and implications of certainty (Swales & Feak, 1994). Analyses of academic corpora have shown that *can* and *may* are by far the most common modals, whereas *must, should*, and *have to* are less frequent as are *will* and *would* (Biber et al., 1999; Hyland, 1998). For this reason, when teaching modal verbs as hedges, it is important to concentrate on the contextual meanings of only some, but not necessarily all, modal verbs.

> Teach the uses of *may, can*, and *could*. Do not spend time teaching the hedging uses of the other modal verbs.

ADJECTIVE AND ADVERB HEDGES

To put it simply, adjective and adverb hedges modify nouns and verbs, respectively. Adjectival hedges serve to reduce the force of noun meanings, and adverbial hedges have a similar effect on verb or sentence meanings (Quirk et al., 1985). In English the number of these hedges is large. In academic prose, many adverbial hedges function as markers of probability (e.g., *almost, nearly, practically*). Adjective and adverb hedges include advanced and diverse features that range from single-word adjectives such as *apparent, approximate*, and *essential* to more complex constructions such as *according to* + noun, *most* + adjective (e.g., *most advantageous*), and *relative to* + noun. Because complete lists of these devices differ among research findings, only the most common are presented next as identified in analyses of large corpora of written academic prose (Biber et al., 1999; Hoye, 1997; Hyland, 1998).

---

[1]Palmer (1990) specified that the predictive conditional *would* refers to future events that are contingent on a particular proposition that may be unreal or counterfactual. The predictive conditional with real or unreal meanings refers to the future in complex ways and depends on particular mixed time relations that preclude the use of the future tense maker *will*.

Adjective and adverb hedges differ in the degree of their formality, semantic complexity, and frequencies of occurrence. Formal hedges are predominant in academic written discourse. In teaching these can be contrasted with informal conversational hedges to bring learners' attention to distinctions between formal and academic writing and informal language uses.

> It is important for L2 academic writers to note the differences among various English-language registers, and focusing on hedges represents only one means of instructional practice.

Formal Hedges Employed in Academic Writing

about	*fairly*	*presumably*
according to (+ noun)	*likely*	*relative(-ly)*
actually	*merely*	*relative to*
apparent(-ly)	*most (+ adjective)*	*slightly*
approximate(-ly)	*nearly*	*somehow*
broad(-ly)	*normal(-ly)*	*somewhat*
clear(-ly)	*partially*	*sufficiently*
comparative(-ly)	*partly*	*theoretically*
essential(-ly)	*potential(-ly)*	*unlikely*

On the other hand, items such as those listed next are prevalent in conversational discourse. Therefore, their frequent use in academic writing can mark the text as excessively casual, informal, and somewhat inappropriate.

Common Informal and Conversational Hedges

almost	*enough*	*only*
at all	*(a) few*	*pretty*
at least	*hardly*	*quite*
basically	*just*	
dead (+ adjective)	*(a) little*	

In the teaching of L2 academic writing, however, it is not necessary that learners undertake to use many of these hedges. Students simply need to have ready access to a stock of these words and phrases that can be used interchangeably throughout their essays and assignments, in combination with other types of hedges discussed earlier. For instance, with practice *essentially*, *nearly*, and *slightly* can be accessible to learners who can use *basically*, *almost*, and *a little bit*.[2]

CONVERSATIONAL AND INFORMAL HEDGES

Lexical hedges represent a simpler variety prevalent in conversational and informal register that is often characterized by vagueness (Channell, 1994), and they have not been found in written academic corpora.

Informal Lexical Hedges Not Employed in Academic Prose

actually	*kind of*	*more or*	*pretty*	*sort of*
anyway	*maybe*	*less*	*something*	
in a way	*like*	*more*	*like*	

Informal lexical hedges are often considered inappropriate in formal academic writing, although individual instructors may be somewhat flexible with regard to their uses. According to Kay (1997), lexical hedges includes prepositional modifiers of nouns, verbs, and whole sentences that are particularly vague and mark a shortage of factual information or knowledge. For example,

> *Before this turning point [in the history of industrial production], everything was sort of undefined and sporadic. They just ran production using their own intuitions with a more or less successful manufacturing.... As a result, lots of creations could not be accomplished. This kind of working didn't hurt companies because there were not many competitors to share the market.* (From a student paper on the history of industrial production.)

The uses of such hedges as *sort of*, *kind of*, or *lots* in a formal academic assignment may actually create an impression that the writer is only vaguely familiar with the subject matter and is unable to cite specific information to make his or her text credible. The prior excerpt demonstrates that the student has a general idea of the history of industrial production, but did not make much effort or take the time for an in-depth study of the material. (See also Suggestions for Teaching at the end of the chapter.)

---

[2]Trying to teach semantic variance between such hedges as *essentially* and *basically* is not worth the time it takes for both the teacher and the student. In almost all cases, these and other hedging devices are interchangeable and should be used to avoid redundancy rather than express fine nuances of meaning.

References to Assumed Common Knowledge

Vague references to common and popular knowledge (e.g., *as we know, as people say*) function as hedges in conversational and informal registers, and in part for this reason they often find their way into L2 students' academic text (Hinkel, 2002a). This type of colloquial hedging has the goal of distancing the writer from the information by attributing it to an external source such as assumed common knowledge (Brown & Levinson, 1987). Their frequent uses in academic compositions, particularly when it comes to unsupported statements or claims, may create an impression of broad generalization making and a high degree of certainty without factual foundation.

Informal Common Knowledge Hedges

(as) we all know	*as the saying goes*
as far as we/I know	*(as) everyone/people/they say(s)*
as is (well) known	*from what I hear/know/see/understand*
as you/everyone/the reader know(s)	

For instance, references to assumed knowledge and sayings are not likely to warrant high praise in the context of academic papers and assignments. Earlier studies have shown, however, that these hedges are significantly more frequent in NNS academic essays than in those of NS students (Hinkel, 1996b, 2002a). All the following examples are from student texts:

Technology, as most people know, is a very important thing in this decade.

As readers know, studying history is necessary for us to understand our past.

People always seek happiness, money, and excitement, as of course everyone knows.

As they say, no pain, no gain. When deciding how to invest capital, investors have to be prepared to take risks.

Usually, referring to common knowledge and general truths that "everyone knows," is considered to be inappropriate in practically any type of student academic prose, with a possible exception of personal journal writing.

As the examples show, advanced students enrolled in degree programs may have the linguistic skills sufficient for producing grammatically accurate text. The issues of appropriateness, however, extend beyond grammaticality concerns and deal with what is and is not acceptable according to the norms of the academic discourse community (Swales, 1990a). In the case of references to common knowledge such as *as of course everyone knows*, informal and conversational hedges may simply not be acceptable in lieu of factual rhetorical support.

AVOIDING OVERSTATEMENTS, EXAGGERATIONS, AND EMPHATIC CLAIMS

A large class of adjectives and adverbs have the function of marking exaggerations and overstatements by inflating the value, truthfulness, or importance of information (Quirk et al., 1985; see also chap. 6 on indefinite pronouns). In this class, the adjectives usually modify nouns (*a significant work*), and adverbs increase the intensity of adjectives, other adverbs, and whole sentences (*I definitely/totally agree with this statement*). For instance, in academic writing in English, such extreme adverbs of frequency as *always* and *never* are often seen as inappropriate, and their inclusion in essays is not recommended (Smoke, 1999):

> *Managers always think that if employees are paid well, they will do their best on the job.* (From a student text.)

Exaggerative and emphatic adjectives and adverbs are prevalent in the conversational rather than formal written register and are often considered informal (Chafe, 1985). However, Hyland's (1998, 1999) corpus analyses of published academic articles show that the use of emphatics is comparatively more frequent in such diverse disciplines as philosophy, sociology, marketing, applied linguistics, physics, or mechanical engineering than biology and electrical engineering.

Exaggerations and overstatements often include numerous adjectives and adverbs commonly found in L2 writers' texts (Hinkel, 2002a).

Conversational Exaggeratives and Emphatics (Unfortunately) Frequent in L2 Academic Text

absolute(-ly)	*ever*	*perfect(-ly)*
a lot (+ noun/adjective)	*exact(-ly)*	*pure(-ly)*
always	*extreme(-ly)*	*severe (-ly)*
amazing(-ly)	*far* (+ comparative adjective)	*so* (+adjective/verb)
awful(-ly)	*forever*	*strong(-ly)*
bad (-ly)	*for sure*	*sure(-ly)*
by all means	*fully*	*terrible(-ly)*
certain(-ly)	*great(-ly)*	*too* (+ adjective)
clear(-ly)	*high(-ly)*	*total(-ly)*
complete(-ly)	*huge(-ly)*	*unbelievable (-ly)*

deep(-ly)	*in all/every way(s)*	*very*
definite(-ly)	*much* (+ adjective)	*very much*
enormous(-ly)	*never*	*well*
entirely	*no way*	
even (+ adjective/noun)	*positive(-ly)*	

In many rhetorical traditions other than Anglo-American, strong statements and claims are often intended to convey the writer's degree of conviction and/or rhetorical emphasis (Connor, 1996; Sa'adeddin, 1989; Zhu, 1996).

> Teachers need not only to direct students away from overuse of exaggerative, but also to help them develop alternatives.

Because many L2 writers lack a broad vocabulary base and their lexical means of expressing conviction and emphasis are limited, the number of exaggerated adjectives and adverbs in L2 text is significantly higher than in NS texts (Hinkel, 1997b; Hyland & Milton, 1997). In other words, when writers have to produce persuasive text within the confines of restricted language, they may have few accessible choices but the frequent use of emphatics and exaggeratives. The following example is extracted from a student essay on the necessary qualities of corporate managers:

> *Besides the skills leaders need to develop strongly, corporate culture nurturing leadership every day is extremely important. Cultivating a leadership-centered organization is definitely the most important goal of leadership. Today, some large companies have tens of thousands of employees, and they produce an enormous number of products and have scores of customers. These changes in the business environment create great pressure and high uncertainty. In business textbooks, leadership and management are very well defined and the definitions are well accepted by everyone.*

This example shows that a high degree of the writer's conviction can lead to increased frequencies of exaggeratives and emphatics in students' writing. The overstated tone of the text may not be difficult to correct by omitting or replacing several modifying adjectives and adverbs that combine to create rhetorically inflated prose.

CHAPTER SUMMARY

In general, the purpose of hedging in academic text is to project honesty, politeness, caution, and deference to the opinions of others. Many studies of large corpora of academic prose have demonstrated that hedging statements and claims are one of the essential characteristics of formal writing. In addition, investigations into academic writers' text have established that in many cases L2 writers do not employ hedging devices in accordance with the norms of the Anglo-American academic discourse community. However, in ESL and EAP writing instruction, the appropriate uses of hedging devices are often not addressed in sufficient detail.

In addition to the direct benefits of using hedging devices essential in academic text, focused instruction on hedges and their rhetorical functions can help learners identify distinctions between formal and informal and between spoken and written registers. Although overstatements and exaggerations are often considered acceptable in informal and conversational discourse in English, they need to be avoided in formal academic writing.

To provide L2 writers access to lexical and syntactic means of hedging, the instruction can begin with simple hedging devices and advance to those more linguistically complex. A cumulative effect of learning to use various types of hedges can lead to a noticeable reduction in frequencies of overstatements and exaggerations in L2 academic prose.

- Adverbs of frequency and possibility represent one of the simplest and most readily accessible hedges that can be effectively taught to L2 learners at the low to intermediate levels of proficiency.
- Instruction in the uses of quantifiers with countable and uncountable nouns, combined with uses of frequency adverbs, can also become an auxiliary goal in instruction in such fundamental L2 skills as reading, writing, and grammar.
- The teaching of modals verbs as hedges can also increase the students' repertoire of essential and relatively simple hedging devices to use in L2 writing.
- Although a large number of advanced adjective and adverb hedges in English has been identified in research, L2 writers should not be expected to employ all of them in their text with equal degrees of fluency. Adding just a few accessible complex hedges to an established base of simpler devices can provide learners a sufficient range of hedges appropriate in formal academic writing.
- Being familiar with and aware of conversational and informal hedges, as well as adjectives and adverbs associated with overstatements and exaggerations, allows L2 writers the option of avoiding them in formal written prose.

Hedging statements, generalizations, and claims are not universal characteristics of formal written discourse, and in rhetorical traditions other than Anglo-American hedging is not employed as it is in English. Furthermore, because a majority of L2 learners are exposed to conversational and informal discourse to a far greater extent than they are to formal writing, instruction on the functions and uses of hedging in English requires persistence and focused attention. On the whole, learning to hedge academic prose appropriately is unlikely to take place in informal conversations and/or by means of fluency activities.

STRATEGIES AND TACTICS FOR TEACHING AND TEACHING ACTIVITIES

As with other work on improving students' vocabulary as well as lexical and syntactic range, a practical approach can begin with helping students learn to notice that hedging devices are very common in written text in English, but not in conversations. Noticing the types of hedges in written prose can be followed by learning to distinguish between formal and informal registers as well as hedges. In addition to giving attention to the hedges frequent in formal written prose, it is also important to notice those that are not. The teaching suggestions and activities presented next are designed to enhance:

- Noticing the functions and uses of hedges in written text
- Distinguishing between the features of formal and informal registers
- Developing editing skills to hedge L2 students' writing and avoid overstatements

In teaching students how to use hedging devices appropriately, the snowball effect helps increase learners' range of hedges. "Growing" hedges represents one of the most effective and least work- and time-consuming strategies. To this end, the teacher needs to encourage students to employ diverse types of hedges in their writing because many hedges are not lexically or syntactically complex. Holding students accountable for the hedged quality of their written text may require both teachers' and students' attention to detail in working on the features of formal academic prose.

The teaching suggestions presented next rely on written texts easily obtainable from students' own writing, textbooks, and other print media sources, such as newspaper science, business, and society reports. For learning to notice the functions and uses of hedges, the teacher may also choose to begin with simplified juvenile formal prose usually found in books on environment, geography, wild life, plants, science, nutrition, sports, and other nonfiction literature.

(1) Noticing Hedges in Academic or News Media Texts

Students can be asked to bring samples of written materials from their disciplines or the teacher can supply a newspaper report on health issues, science, or the current news. Then a series of leading questions can focus on the analysis of the function and types of hedges in the text:

- What hedging (softening, politeness, power-limiting) devices can students identify?
- Why did the author use these hedging devices?
- In general, what is the author's responsibility for the truthfulness of his or her statements? In English? In students' L1s?
- Do writers in students' L1s also use various words and phrases to limit their responsibility for the truthfulness and/or inclusivity or breadth of their statements/generalizations (or to limit the power of their statements)? What are some of the examples of such softening/limiting words and phrases?
- In this particular text or sentence, what is the extent of the author's responsibility for the truthfulness of his or her text?
- Why did he or she use this particular type of hedge in this particular sentence?
- What is the difference in the "power" of the statement/sentence with the hedge or without the hedge? If the sentence is used without the hedge, can its meaning be seen as too strong or too inclusive? What can be possible meanings for various individual readers if the sentence is used without a hedge?
- Can students think of other ways to hedge this particular sentence or several sentences in a paragraph?

A few examples of sentences and text excerpts illustrate this activity.

(a) What are the differences in the "power" among the three sentences? Why are there differences in the meanings of these sentences? Can you identify the reasons for these differences?

People are totally against genetic engineering, but it provides benefits for humankind.

Some people are totally against genetic engineering, but it can provide benefits for humankind.

Some people are against genetic engineering, but it can provide many benefits for humankind.

(b) In your opinion, which sentence is more inclusive (and can be true in more cases)?

Genetic engineering improves the taste of food and the nutritional value of food products.

Genetic engineering can improve the taste of some types of food and the nutritional value of many food products.

(c) The following excerpt presents an author's opinion on a particular topic. Do you think the author accurately describes the situation? Why or why not? What particular words and phrases make the author's opinion appear very strong? Can this excerpt be made to describe the situation more accurately and the author's opinion less strong?

We really need the information on the Internet to be free. We must not pay money for all the advertising companies put on the Web. Information about smoking and alcohol leads to bad effects and will encourage people to become involved with them. It is also totally wrong to say that advertising is the main factor that causes these problems. People have to have all the information they need to make their decisions about their health. Therefore, advertisers have to reveal all the information about the products they sell.

(2) Hedges in Diverse Written Genre

Nonacademic, commercial prose such as tourism promotional fliers; company, product, and services advertisements; or beauty and fashion materials (i.e., texts intended to inflate rather than hedge the virtues of their products) can provide a useful venue for contrasting various types of written genres. These materials can also be analyzed, and the uses of exaggeratives and emphatics in promotional texts can be effectively compared with those in academic prose:

- What are the goals of the promotional materials?
- What is the purpose of academic texts?
- Why do the authors of promotional flyers employ inflated language features such as adjectives, adverbs, or nouns?
- Why are there fewer exaggeratives and overstatements in academic prose than in promotional materials?

In pairs or small groups, students can be assigned to write short texts (100–200 words) for a promotional flier to advertise travel to their home towns or their favorite travel destinations (e.g., cities, beaches, resorts, or hotels). Such fliers can promote shopping in students' favorite stores or food/service in favorite restaurants; other popular venues for writing can include beauty products, fashions and brand names (clothing, shoes, backpacks, handbags), athletic gear, as well as cars, computers, Web sites, computer games, music, TV shows, movies, magazines, or even celebrities (singers, movie stars, TV personalities, or sports figures). These promotional materials can be presented to other groups or the entire class in mock commercials or skits.

In a follow-up exercise, to contrast inflated and hedged prose, students can also write up academic descriptions of similar or different places, items, or people when writers need to scrupulously stay away from exaggerations and provide (real or imaginary) facts to support their claims.

(3) Distinctions Between Spoken and Written/Formal and Informal Registers

In addition to written promotional materials, audio- and videotaped commercials, infomercials, and/or casual conversation clips from movies, soap operas, talk shows, or situational comedies can be used to help learners identify important and numerous differences between formal and informal spoken registers. Distinguishing features of informal conversational and formal written texts can also be highlighted (i.e., academic essays cannot be written as if the writer were talking to his or her friends).

(4) Editing and Adding Appropriate Hedges and Weeding Out Exaggeratives

This is a very important exercise that can be used in stages throughout a course on learning to write academic prose. The learning goal of this practice is to focus students' attention on:

- Quantifiers: limiting the noun power
- Adverbs of frequency and modal verbs: limiting the verb power
- Predicting the future and modal verb hedges
- Identifying and replacing conversational hedges
- Avoiding exaggeratives and emphatics

Students can work in pairs, small groups, or individually to edit their own text or texts supplied by the teacher. The practice can be varied between work on "stripped-down" prose without any hedges or exaggeratives and text excerpts with added conversational hedges or exaggeratives that students need to find and correct.

(a) An example of a "stripped-down" text, in which students need to add hedges of various types (but not too many!):

These days, students plagiarize their papers by using the Internet. They do not write their own papers or do their own homework. Students easily access the companies that sell various course papers via the Internet. These students go to a website that sells papers and buy them. Plagiarized papers get excellent grades. In other cases, students get caught and expelled from the university. Educators feel that students need to fulfill their responsibilities in studying, and they say that students cheat by buying their papers. (Adapted from a student's essay.)

Another version of the same text with a few hedges added. Advanced-level hedges are underlined:

These days, [some/many] students plagiarize their papers by using the Internet. They do not write [some of] their own papers or do [much of] their own homework. Students [can] easily access the [many] companies that sell various course papers via the Internet. These students [can] [usually/<u>essentially</u>] go to a website that sells papers and buy them. [Sometimes/Occasionally] [Some/Many/Most] [<u>Perhaps</u>,] Plagiarized papers [can/may] get excellent grades. In other cases, students [may] get caught and [<u>possibly/potentially</u>] expelled from the university. [Some/Many/Most] Educators [usually/may] feel that students need to fulfill their responsibilities in studying, and they say that students [may/possibly] cheat by [<u>actually/apparently</u>] buying [some of/many of] their papers.

(b) Editing text with conversational hedges and exaggeratives (underlined):

There are <u>lots</u> of books written about the Four Great masters, and <u>everyone really</u> admires their paintings. The Four Great masters are well-known <u>all over</u> China; <u>all</u> of them played a very important role in the history of Ming painting. Wen Cheng-ming came from a <u>very</u> rich and educated family; therefore, he <u>never</u> had to worry about <u>any</u> financial problems and could <u>definitely</u> receive <u>great</u> education. He was one of Shen Choi's students; therefore, we can <u>clearly</u> recognize that his works were <u>totally</u> influenced by Shen Chou. But it as not Shen Chou but Wen Cheng-ming who was the most influential and the <u>most</u> widely copied among the local group of scholar-painters in the 16th century. In his early period, the structure of his painting is <u>sort of</u> similar to the style of Shen Chou, and both of them used the <u>world</u>-famous green-and-color style that presented <u>kind of</u> a tranquil feeling. (Excerpted from a student term paper in art history.)

Overstated examples such as this text can be easy to edit by correcting and replacing some of the inflated and colloquial features. Other editing practice can come from shorter excerpts or sentence-level contexts.

(c) Sentence-level editing practice (all examples are from student texts):

1. *Companies are really dealing with all kinds of businesses.*
2. *Computers are the most popular equipment because they absolutely make our work easier and faster.*
3. *A lot of students just go to the Internet instead of watching TV all day.*

4. *Nobody wants any trouble in their life, and risk management is the best course of action for all investors.*
5. *We have a lot of mass media to give us a lot of information about everything, so that we know what's going on in the world every day.*

QUESTIONS FOR DISCUSSION

1. In your opinion, why are overstatements and exaggerations believed to be an effective means of rhetorical persuasion in non-Anglo-American discourse traditions?
2. What can be the reasons that little attention is devoted to teaching the functions and uses of hedging devices in L2 composition instruction in some English-speaking countries?
3. How do culturally determined discourse conventions affect what is considered to be appropriate or inappropriate in various text genre (e.g., formal speaking or formal/informal)?
4. If one compares two or three different types of written prose (e.g., newspaper editorials/opinion pieces/letters to the editor vs. published academic articles), in addition to the employment of hedges, what other differences in the uses of linguistic and lexical features can be noted?

FURTHER READINGS ABOUT HEDGING

Hedges in Academic Prose

Channel, J. (1994). *Vague language*. Oxford: Oxford University Press.
Holmes, J. (1984). Hedging your bets and sitting on the fence: Some evidence for hedges as support structures. *Te Reo, 27*(1), 47–62.
Huebler, A. (1983). *Understatements and hedges in English*. Amsterdam: John Benjamins.
Hyland, K. (1998). *Hedging in scientific research articles*. Amsterdam: John Benjamins.
Myers, G. (1989). The pragmatics of politeness in scientific articles. *Applied Linguistics, 10*, 1–35.
Myers, G. (1996). Strategic vagueness in academic writing. In E. Ventola & A. Mauranen (Eds.), *Academic writing* (pp. 1–18). Amsterdam: John Benjamins.
Myers, G. (1999). Interaction in writing: Principles and problems. In C. Candlin & K. Hyland (Eds.), *Writing texts, processes and practices* (pp. 40–61). London: Longman.

Hedging in ESL/EAP Textbooks

Hyland, K. (1994). Hedging in academic writing and EAP textbooks. *English for Specific Purposes, 13*(3), 239–256.

Modal Verbs and Hedging

Coates, J. (1983). *The semantics of the modal auxiliaries*. Beckenham, Kent: Croom Helm.
Hoye, L. (1997). *Adverbs and modality in English*. London: Longman.
Hinkel, E. (1995). The use of modal verbs as a reflection of cultural values. *TESOL Quarterly, 29*, 325–343.
Hinkel, E. (1999). Objectivity and credibility in L1 and L2 academic writing. In E. Hinkel (Ed.), *Culture in second language teaching and learning* (pp. 90–108). Cambridge: Cambridge University Press.
Hoye, L. (1997). *Adverbs and modality in English*. London: Longman.

Hedging in L2 Academic Writing

Hyland, K., & Milton, J. (1997). Hedging in L1 and L2 student writing. *Journal of Second Language Writing, 6*(2), 183–206.
Hinkel, E. (1997b). Indirectness in L1 and L2 academic writing. *Journal of Pragmatics, 27*(3), 360–386.
Hinkel, E. (2002a). *Second language writers' text*. Mahwah, NJ: Lawrence Erlbaum Associates.

Conversational Hedges

Brazil, D. (1995). *A grammar of speech*. Oxford: Oxford University Press.
Chafe, W. (1985). Linguistic differences produced by differences between speaking and writing. In D. R. Olson, N. Torrance, & A. Hildyard (Eds.), *Literature, language, and learning: The nature and consequences of reading and writing* (pp. 105–123). Cambridge: Cambridge University Press.
Moxey, L., & Sanford, A. (1997). Choosing the right quantifier: Usage in context of communication. In T. Givon (Ed.), *Conversation: Cognitive, communicative, and social perspectives* (pp. 207–232). Amsterdam: John Benjamins.
Tsui, A. (1994). *English conversation*. Oxford: Oxford University Press.

References

Adams, V. (2001). *Complex words in English.* Harlow, Essex: Longman.

Allen, P., Swain, M., Harley, B., & Cummins, J. (1990). Aspects of classroom treatment: Towards a more comprehensive view of second language education. In B. Harley, P. Allen, J. Cummins, & M. Swain (Eds.), *The development of second language proficiency* (pp. 57–80). Cambridge: Cambridge University Press.

Arndt, V. (1993). Response to writing: Using feedback to inform the writing process. In M. Brock & L. Walters (Eds.), *Teaching composition around the Pacific Rim: Politics and Pedagogy* (pp. 90–116). Clevedon, UK: Multilingual Matters.

Ashwell, T. (2000). Patterns of teacher response to student writing in a multiple-draft composition classroom: Is content feedback followed by form feedback the best method? *Journal of Second Language Writing, 9*(3), 227–258.

Asian American Federation of New York. (2001). *New census estimates tell two stories about Asian and Pacific Islander students* [On-line]. Available http://www.aafny.org/proom/pr/pr_main.asp

Atkinson, D. (1991). Discourse analysis and written discourse conventions. *Annual Review of Applied Linguistics, 11*, 57–76.

Axelrod, R., & Cooper, C. (2001). *The St. Martin's guide to writing* (6th ed.). New York: St Martin's.

Bates, L. (1998). *Transitions* (2nd ed.). New York: Cambridge University Press.

Bean, J. (1996). *Engaging ideas.* San Francisco, CA: Jossey-Bass.

Beebe, S. A., Beebe, S. J., & Redmond, M. (2001). *Interpersonal communication* (3rd ed.) Boston: Allyn and Bacon.

Bereiter, C., & Scardamalia, M. (1985). Cognitive coping strategies and the problem of "inert knowledge." In S. Chipman, J. Segal, & R. Glaser (Eds.), *Thinking and learning skills: Research and open questions* (Vol. 2, pp. 65–80). Hillsdale, NJ: Lawrence Erlbaum Associates.

Bereiter, C., & Scardamalia, M. (1987). *The psychology of written composition.* Hillsdale, NJ: Lawrence Erlbaum Associates.

Bereiter, C., & Scardamalia, M. (1989). Intentional learning as a goal of instruction. In L. Resnick (Ed.), *Knowing, learning, and instruction* (pp. 361–391). Hillsdale, NJ: Lawrence Erlbaum Associates.

Berkenkotter, C., & Huckin, T. (1995). *Genre knowledge in disciplinary communities.* Hillsdale, NJ: Lawrence Erlbaum Associates.

Bhatia, V. (1992). Pragmatics of the use of nominals in academic and professional genres. In L. Bouton & Y. Kachru (Eds.), *Pragmatics and language learning* (Vol. 3, pp. 217–230). Urbana-Champaign: University of Illinois Press.

Bhatia, V. (1993). *Analysing genre: Language use in professional settings.* London: Longman.

Bialystok, E. (2001). *Bilingualism in development.* Cambridge: Cambridge University Press.

Biber, D. (1988). *Variation across speech and writing.* Cambridge: Cambridge University Press.

Biber, D. (1995). *Dimensions of register variation.* Cambridge: Cambridge University Press.

Biber, D., Johansson, S., Leech, G., Conrad, S., & Finegan, E. (1999). *Longman grammar of spoken and written English.* Harlow, Essex: Pearson.

Bickner, R., & Peyasantiwong, P. (1988). Cultural variation in reflective writing. In A. Purves (Ed.), *Writing across languages and cultures: Issues in contrastive rhetoric* (pp. 160–175). Newbury Park, CA: Sage.

Biq, Y.-O. (1990). Question words as hedges in Chinese. In L. Bouton & Y. Kachru (Eds.), *Pragmatics and language learning* (Vol. 1, pp. 149–158). Urbana-Champaign: University of Illinois Press.

Bizzell, P. (1982). Cognition, convention, and certainty: What we need to know about writing. *Pre/Text, 3*(3), 213–241.

Bratt Paulston, C. (1990). Educational language policies in Utopia. In B. Harley, P. Allen, J. Cummins, & M. Swain (Eds.), *The development of second language proficiency* (pp. 187–197). Cambridge: Cambridge University Press.

Bratt Paulston, C. (1992). *Linguistic and communicative competence.* Clevedon, UK: Multilingual Matters.

Brown, P., & Levinson, S. (1987). *Politeness.* Cambridge: Cambridge University Press.

Byrd, P., & Reid, J. (1998). *Grammar in the composition classroom.* Boston: Heinle & Heinle.

Byrd, P., & Nelson, G. (1995). NNS performance on writing proficiency exams: Focus on students who failed. *Journal of Second Language Writing, 4*, 273–285.

Campbell, R., Martin, C., & Bettina, F. (2001). *Media and culture: An introduction to mass communication* (3rd ed.). New York: St. Martin's Press.

Carlson, S. (1988). Cultural differences in writing and reasoning skills. In A. Purves (Ed.), *Writing across languages and cultures: Issues in contrastive rhetoric* (pp. 109–137). Newbury Park, CA: Sage.

Carrell, P. (1982). Cohesion is not coherence. *TESOL Quarterly, 16*(4), 479–488.

Carson, J., & Nelson, G. (1994). Writing groups: Cross-cultural issues. *Journal of Second Language Writing, 3*, 17–30.

Carson, J., & Nelson, G. (1996). Chinese students' perceptions of ESL peer response group interaction. *Journal of Second Language Writing, 5*, 1–19.

Carter, R., & McCarthy, M. (Eds.). (1988). *Vocabulary and language teaching.* Harlow: Longman.

Celce-Murcia, M. (1991). Grammar pedagogy in second and foreign language teaching. *TESOL Quarterly, 25*, 459–480.

Celce-Murcia, M. (1993). Grammar pedagogy in second and foreign language teaching. In S. Silberstein (Ed.), *State of the Art: TESOL essays* (pp. 288–309). Alexandria, VA: TESOL.

Celce-Murcia, M. (1998). Discourse analysis and grammar instruction. In D. Oaks (Ed.), *Linguistics at work: A reader in applications* (pp. 687–704). Fort Worth, TX: Hartcourt Brace College Publishers..

Celce-Murcia, M., & Hilles, S. (1988). *Techniques and resources in teaching grammar.* New York: Oxford University Press.

Chafe, W. (1970). *Meaning and the structure of language.* Chicago: University of Chicago.

Chafe, W. (1985). Linguistic differences produced by differences between speaking and writing. In D.R. Olson, N. Torrance, & A. Hildyard (Eds.), *Literature, language, and learning: The nature and consequences of reading and writing* (pp. 105–123). Cambridge: Cambridge University Press.

Chafe, W. (1986). Evidentiality in English conversation and academic writing. In W. Chafe & J. Nichols (Eds.), *Evidentiality: The linguistic coding of epistemology* (pp. 261–272). Norwood, NJ: Ablex.

Chafe, W. (1994). *Discourse, consciousness, and time.* Chicago: University of Chicago Press.

Chang, Y., & Swales, J. (1999). Informal elements in English academic writing: Threats or opportunities for advanced non-native speakers. In C. Candlin & K. Hyland (Eds.), *Writing texts, processes and practices* (pp. 145–167). London: Longman.

Channell, J. (1988). Psycholinguistic considerations in the study of L2 vocabulary acquisition. In R. Carter & M. McCarthy (Eds.), *Vocabulary and language teaching* (pp. 83–96). Harlow, Essex: Longman.

Channell, J. (1994). *Vague language.* Oxford: Oxford University Press.

Chapman, R. (1994). *Roget's thesaurus.* New York: HarperCollins.

Charon, J. (1999). *The meaning of sociology* (6th ed.). Upper Saddle River, NJ: Prentice-Hall.

Coady, J. (1997). L2 vocabulary acquisition through extensive reading. In J. Coady & T. Huckin (Eds.), *Second language vocabulary acquisition* (pp. 225–237). Cambridge: Cambridge University Press.

Coady, J., & Huckin, T. (1997). *Second language vocabulary acquisition: A rationale for pedagogy.* Cambridge: Cambridge University Press.

Collins, P. (1991). The modals of obligation and necessity in Australian English. In K. Aijmer & B. Altenberg (Eds.), *English corpus linguistics* (pp. 145–165). New York: Longman.

Connelly, M. (2000). *The Sundance writer.* New York: Harcourt.

Connor, U. (1996). *Contrastive rhetoric.* Cambridge: Cambridge University Press.

Connor, U., & Asenavage, K. (1994). Peer response groups in ESL writing classes: How much impact on revision? *Journal of Second Language Writing, 3*(2), 257–276.

Connor, U., & Carrell, P. (1993). The interpretation of tasks by writers and readers in holistically rated direct assessment of writing. In J. Carson & I. Leki (Eds.), *Reading in the composition classroom* (pp. 141–160). Boston: Heinle & Heinle.

Connor, U., & Kaplan, R. B. (Eds.). (1987). *Writing across languages: Analysis of L2 text.* Reading, MA: Addison-Wesley.

Coulthard, M. (1985). *An introduction to discourse analysis* (2nd ed.). London: Longman.

Cowie, A. P. (1988). Stable and creative aspects of vocabulary use. In R. Carter & M. McCarthy (Eds.), *Vocabulary and language teaching* (pp. 126–137). Harlow: Longman.

Coxhead, A. (1998). An academic word list. *Occasional Publications Number 18, LALS, Victoria University of Wellington, New Zealand.*

Coxhead, A. (2000). The new academic word list. *TESOL Quarterly, 34*(2), 213–238.

Cumming, A. (1994). Writing expertise and second language proficiency. In A. Cumming (Ed.), *Bilingual performance in reading and writing* (pp. 173–221). Ann Arbor, MI/Amsterdam: Language Learning/John Benjamins.

Cummins, J. (1979). Cognitive/academic language proficiency, linguistic interdependence, the optimal age question and some other matters. *Working Papers in Bilingualism, 19*, 197–205.

d'Anglejan, A. (1990). The role of context and age in the development of bilingual proficiency. In B. Harley, P. Allen, J. Cummins, & M. Swain (Eds.), *The development of second language proficiency* (pp. 146–157). Cambridge: Cambridge University Press.

Davidson, F. (1991). Statistical support for training in ESL composition rating. In L. Hamp-Lyons (Ed.), *Assessing second language writing* (pp. 155–165). Norwood, NJ: Ablex.

de Beaugrande, R. (1996). The "pragmatics" of doing language science: The "warrant" for large-corpus linguistics. *Journal of Pragmatics, 25*, 503–535.

de Beaugrande, R., & Dressler, W. (1972). *Introduction to text linguistics.* London: Longman.

DeCarrico, J. (2000). *The structure of English: Studies in form and function for language teaching.* Ann Arbor: The University of Michigan Press.

DeKeyser, R., & Juffs, A. (in press). Cognitive considerations in L2 learning. In E. Hinkel (Ed.), *Handbook of research in second language teaching and learning.* Mahwah, NJ: Lawrence Erlbaum Associates.

Dietrich, R., Klein, W., & Noyau, C. (1995). *The acquisition of temporality in a second language.* Amsterdam: John Benjamins.

Dong, Y. R. (1998). From writing in their native language to writing in English: What ESL students bring to our writing classroom. *College English, 8*(2), 87–105.

Dudley-Evans, T., & St. John, M. J. (1998). *Developments in English for specific purposes.* Cambridge: Cambridge University Press.

Ellis, N. (Ed.). (1994). *Implicit and explicit learning of languages.* San Diego: Academic Press.

Ellis, N. (1997). Vocabulary acquisition: Word structure, collocation, word-class, and meaning. In N. Schmitt & M. McCarthy (Eds.), *Vocabulary: Description, acquisition, and pedagogy* (pp. 122–139). Cambridge: Cambridge University Press.

Ellis, N., & Beaton, A. (1993). Factors affecting the learning of foreign language vocabulary: Imagery keyword mediators and phonological short-term memory. *Quarterly Journal of Experimental Psychology, 46A*, 533–558.

Ellis, R. (1984). *Classroom second language development.* Oxford: Pergamon.

Ellis, R. (1989). Are classroom and naturalistic acquisition the same. *Studies in Second Language Acquisition, 11*(2), 305–328.

Ellis, R. (1990). *Instructed second language acquisition.* Oxford: Blackwell.

Ellis, R. (1994). *The study of second language acquisition.* Oxford: Oxford University Press.

Ellis, R. (1997). *SLA research and language teaching.* Oxford: Oxford University Press.

Ellis, R. (2001). Investigating form-focused instruction. In R. Ellis (Ed.), *Form-focused instruction and second language learning (Language Learning 51: Supplement 1)* (pp. 1–46). Ann Arbor: University of Michigan/Blackwell.

Ellis, R. (2002). The place of grammar instruction in the second/foreign language curriculum. In E. Hinkel & S. Fotos (Eds.), *New perspectives on grammar teaching in second language classrooms* (pp. 17–35). Mahwah, NJ: Lawrence Erlbaum Associates.

Epstein, R. (1999). *The new Psychology Today reader.* Dubuque, IA: Kendall/Hunt.

ETS. (1996). *Test of Written English Instructional Guide.* Princeton, NJ: Author.

Fathman, A., & Whalley, E. (1990). Teacher response to student writing: Focus on form versus content. In B. Kroll (Ed.), *Second language writing* (pp. 178–190). Cambridge: Cambridge University Press.

Ferris, D. (1995). Teaching ESL composition students to become independent self-editors. *TESOL Journal, 4*, 18–22.

Ferris, D., & Hedgcock, J. (1998). *Teaching ESL composition*. Mahwah, NJ: Lawrence Erlbaum Associates.

Ford, C. (1993). *Grammar in interaction*. Cambridge: Cambridge University Press.

Ford, C., & Thompson, S. (1986). Conditionals in discourse: A text-based study from English. In E. Traugott (Ed.), *On conditionals* (pp. 353–372). Cambridge: Cambridge University Press..

Fotos, S. (1994). Integrating grammar instruction and communicative language use through grammar consciousness-raising tasks. *TESOL Quarterly, 28*(2), 323–351.

Fotos, S. (1998). Shifting the focus from forms to form in the EFL classroom. *ELT Journal, 52*(4), 301–307.

Fotos, S. (2002). Structure-based interactive tasks for the EFL grammar learner. In E. Hinkel & S. Fotos (Eds.), *New perspectives on grammar teaching in second language classrooms* (pp. 135–154). Mahwah, NJ: Lawrence Erlbaum Associates.

Fotos, S., & Ellis, R. (1991). Communicating about grammar: A task-based approach. *TESOL Quarterly, 25*(4), 605–628.

Francis, G. (1994). Labelling discourse: An aspect of nominal-group cohesion. In M. Coulthard (Ed.), *Advances in written text analysis* (pp. 83–101). New York: Routledge.

Friedlander, A. (1990). Composing in English: Effects of a first language on writing in English as a second language. In B. Kroll (Ed.), *Second language writing* (pp. 109–125). Cambridge: Cambridge University Press.

Fries, C. (1945). *Teaching and learning English as a foreign language*. Ann Arbor: University of Michigan Press.

Grabe, W., & Kaplan, R. B. (1989). Writing in a second language: Contrastive rhetoric. In D. Johnson & D. Roen (Eds.), *Richness in writing* (pp. 263–283). New York: Longman.

Grabe, W., & Kaplan, R. B. (1996). *Theory and practice of writing*. London: Longman.

Guiora, A. (1983). The dialectic of language acquisition. *Language Learning, 33*(1), 3–12.

Hacker, D. (1994). *The Bedford handbook for writers* (4th ed.). Boston: Bedford.

Hacker, D. (2000). *Rules for writers* (4th ed.). Boston: Bedford/St Martin's.

Hafiz, F., & Tudor, I. (1990). Graded readers as an input medium in L2 learning. *System, 18*(1), 31–42.

Hairston, M. (1982). The winds of change: Thomas Kuhn and the revolution in the teaching of writing. *College Composition and Communication, 33*(1), 76–88.

Hale, G., Taylor, C., Bridgeman, B., Carson, J., Kroll, B., & Kantor, R. (1996). *A study of writing tasks assigned in academic degree programs* (Research Report 54). Princeton, NJ: Educational Testing Service.

Halliday, M. A. K. (1994). The construction of knowledge and value in the grammar of scientific discourse, with reference to Charles Darwin's *The Origin of Species*. In M. Coulthard (Ed.), *Advances in written text analysis* (pp. 136–156). New York: Routledge.

Halliday, M. A. K., & Hasan, R. (1976). *Cohesion in English*. London: Longman.

Hammerly, H. (1991). *Fluency and accuracy*. Clevedon, UK: Multilingual Matters.

Hamp-Lyons, L. (1990). Second language writing: Assessment issues. In B. Kroll (Ed.), *Second language writing* (pp. 69–86). Cambridge: Cambridge University Press.

Hamp-Lyons, L. (1991a). Reconstructing academic writing proficiency. In L. Hamp-Lyons (Ed.), *Assessing second language writing* (pp. 127–153). Norwood, NJ: Ablex.

Hamp-Lyons, L. (1991b). Scoring procedures for ESL contexts. In L. Hamp-Lyons (Ed.), *Assessing second language writing* (pp. 241–277). Norwood, NJ: Ablex.

Hargreaves, L. (2001, May). Dropout rate among Chinese physics PhD students seems high; community considers why. *Physics Today,* p. 42.

Harley, B. (1989). Transfer in the written composition of French immersion students. In H. Dechert & M. Raupach (Eds.), *Transfer in language production* (pp. 3–19). New York: Ablex.

Hermeren, L. (1978). *On modality in English: A study of the semantics of the modals.* Lund: CWK Gleerup.

Hinds, J. (1983). Contrastive rhetoric. *Text, 3*(2), 183–195.

Hinds, J. (1987). Reader versus writer responsibility: A new typology. In U. Connor & R. B. Kaplan (Eds.), *Writing across languages: Analysis of L2 text* (pp. 141–152). Reading, MA: Addison-Wesley.

Hinds, J. (1990). Inductive, deductive, quasi-inductive: Expository writing in Japanese, Korean, Chinese, and Thai. In U. Connor & A. Johns (Eds.), *Coherence in writing* (pp. 87–110). Alexandria, VA: TESOL.

Hinkel, E. (1992). L2 tense and time reference. *TESOL Quarterly, 26*(3), 556–572.

Hinkel, E. (1994). Native and nonnative speakers' pragmatic interpretation of English text. *TESOL Quarterly, 28*(2), 353–376.

Hinkel, E. (1995a, April). *Projecting credibility in academic writing: L1 and L2 discourse paradigms.* Paper presented at the Ninth International Conference on Pragmatics & Language Learning, University of Illinois, Urbana, Illinois.

Hinkel, E. (1995b, March). *What is your point? Indirectness in L2 writing.* Paper presented at TESOL, Long Beach, CA.

Hinkel, E. (1995c). The use of modal verbs as a reflection of cultural values. *TESOL Quarterly, 29,* 325–343.

Hinkel, E. (1996a, March). *Audience and the writer's stance in L2 writing.* Paper presented at TESOL, Chicago, Illinois.

Hinkel, E. (1996b). When in Rome: Evaluations of L2 pragmalinguistic behaviors. *Journal of Pragmatics, 26*(1), 51–70.

Hinkel, E. (1997a). The past tense and temporal verb meanings in a contextual frame. *TESOL Quarterly, 31*(2), 289–313.

Hinkel, E. (1997b). Indirectness in L1 and L2 academic writing. *Journal of Pragmatics, 27*(3), 360–386.

Hinkel, E. (1999a). Objectivity and credibility in L1 and L2 academic writing. In E. Hinkel (Ed.), *Culture in second language teaching and learning* (pp. 90–108). Cambridge: Cambridge University Press.

Hinkel, E. (1999b). Introduction: Culture in research and second language pedagogy. In E. Hinkel (Ed.), *Culture in second language teaching and learning* (pp. 1–7). Cambridge: Cambridge University Press.

Hinkel, E. (2001a). Matters of cohesion in L1 and L2 academic texts. *Applied Language Learning, 12*(2), 111–132.

Hinkel, E. (2001b). Building awareness and practical skills for cross-cultural communication in ESL/EFL. In M. Celce-Murcia (Ed.), *Teaching English as a second or foreign language* (3rd ed., pp. 443–458). Boston: Heinle & Heinle.

Hinkel, E. (2001c). Giving examples and telling stories in academic essays. *Issues in Applied Linguistics, 12*(2), 149–170.
Hinkel, E. (2002a). *Second language writers' text.* Mahwah, NJ: Lawrence Erlbaum Associates.
Hinkel, E. (2002b). Expressing L1 literacy in L2 writing. In D.S. Li (Ed.), *Discourses in search of members: Festschrift in honor of Ronald Scollon's 60th birthday* (pp. 465–482). Greenwood, CT: Ablex.
Hinkel, E. (2002c). Teaching grammar in writing classes: Tenses and cohesion. In E. Hinkel & S. Fotos (Eds.), *New perspectives on grammar teaching in second language classrooms* (pp. 181–198). Mahwah, NJ: Lawrence Erlbaum Associates.
Hinkel, E. (2002d). Why English passive is difficult to teach (and learn). In E. Hinkel & S. Fotos (Eds.), *New perspectives on grammar teaching* (pp. 233–260). Mahwah, NJ: Lawrence Erlbaum Associates.
Hinkel, E. (2003a). Adverbial markers and tone in L1 and L2 students' writing. *Journal of Pragmatics, 35*(7), 1049–1068.
Hinkel, E. (2003b). Simplicity without elegance: Features of sentences in L2 and L1 academic texts. *TESOL Quarterly, 37.*
Holmes, J. (1984). Hedging your bets and sitting on the fence: Some evidence for hedges as support structures. *Te Reo, 27*(1), 47–62.
Holten, C., & Marasco, J. (1998). *Looking ahead: Mastering academic writing.* Boston: Heinle & Heinle.
Horowitz, D. (1986a). What professors actually require: Academic tasks for the ESL classroom. *TESOL Quarterly, 20*(4), 445–462.
Horowitz, D. (1986b). Process, not product: Less than meets the eye. *TESOL Quarterly, 20*(1), 141–144.
Horowitz, D. (1991). ESL writing assessment: Contradictions and resolutions. In L. Hamp-Lyons (Ed.), *Assessing second language writing* (pp. 71–86). Norwood, NJ: Ablex.
Hoye, L. (1997). *Adverbs and modality in English.* London: Longman.
Huckin, T., Haynes, M., & Coady, J. (Eds). (1993). *Second language reading and vocabulary learning.* Norwood, NJ: Ablex.
Huddleston, R., & Pullum, K. (2002). *The Cambridge grammar of the English language.* Cambridge: Cambridge University Press.
Huebler, A. (1983). *Understatements and hedges in English.* Amsterdam: John Benjamins.
Hulstijn, J. (1990). A comparison between the information-processing and the analysis/control approaches to language learning. *Applied Linguistics, 11*(1), 30–45.
Hulstijn, J. (1992). Retention of inferred and given word meanings: Experiments in vocabulary learning. In P. Arnaud & H. Bejoint (Eds.), *Vocabulary and applied linguistics* (pp. 113–125). London: Macmillan.
Hulstijn, J. (1997). Mnemonic methods in foreign language vocabulary learning. In J. Coady & T. Huckin (Eds.), *Second language vocabulary acquisition* (pp. 203–224). Cambridge: Cambridge University Press.
Hulstijn, J., & Laufer, B. (2001). Some empirical evidence for the involvement load hypothesis in vocabulary acquisition. *Language Learning 51*(3), 539–558.
Hunston, S., & Francis, G. (2000). *Pattern grammar.* Amsterdam: John Benjamins.
Hvitfeld, C. (1992). Oral orientations in ESL academic writing. *College ESL, 2*(1), 29–39.
Hwang, S. J. (1987). *Discourse features of Korean narration.* Arlington, TX: The Summer Institute of Linguistics and The University of Texas.

Hyland, K. (1996). Talking to the academy: Forms of hedging in science research articles. *Written Communication, 13*, 251–281.
Hyland, K. (1998). *Hedging in scientific research articles.* Amsterdam/Philadelphia: John Benjamin Publishing Company.
Hyland, K. (1999). Disciplinary discourses: Writer stance in research articles. In C. Candlin & K. Hyland (Eds.), *Writing texts, processes and practices* (pp. 99–120). London: Longman.
Hyland, K. (2002a). *Teaching and researching writing.* Harlow, Essex: Longman.
Hyland, K. (2002b). Authority and invisibility in academic writing. *Journal of Pragmatics, 34*(8), 1091–1112.
Hyland, K., & Milton, J. (1997). Qualification and certainty in L1 and L2 students' writing. *Journal of Second Language Writing, 6*(2), 183–205.
Indrasuta, C. (1988). Narrative styles in the writing of Thai and American students. In A. Purves (Ed.), *Writing across languages and cultures: Issues in contrastive rhetoric* (pp. 206–227). Newbury Park, CA: Sage.
Institute of International Education. (2001). *Open doors* New York: Author.
James, C. (1998). *Errors in language learning and use.* London: Longman.
Johns, A. (1981). Necessary English: A faculty survey. *TESOL Quarterly, 15*(1), 51–57.
Johns, A. (1990a). L1 composition theories: Implications for developing theories for L2 composition. In B. Kroll (Ed.), *Second language writing* (pp. 24–36). Cambridge: Cambridge University Press.
Johns, A. (1990b). Coherence as a cultural phenomenon: Employing ethnographic principles in the academic milieu. In U. Connor & A. Johns (Eds.), *Coherence in writing* (pp. 211–225). Alexandria, VA: TESOL.
Johns, A. (1991). Faculty assessment of ESL student literacy skills: Implications for writing assessment. In L. Hamp-Lyons (Ed.), *Assessing second language writing* (pp. 167–180). Norwood, NJ: Ablex.
Johns, A. (1997). *Text, role, and context: Developing academic literacies.* Cambridge: Cambridge University Press.
Johns, A., & Dudley-Evans, T. (1991). English for specific purposes: International in scope, specific in purpose. *TESOL Quarterly, 25*, 297–314.
Johnson, D. (1989a). Enriching task contexts for second language writing: Power through interpersonal roles. In D. Johnson & D. Roen (Eds.), *Richness in writing* (pp. 39–54). New York: Longman.
Johnson, D. (1989b). Politeness strategies in L2 written discourse. *Journal of Intensive English Studies, 3*, 71–91.
Johnson, P. (1988). English language proficiency and academic performance of undergraduate international students. *TESOL Quarterly, 22*, 164–168.
Johnstone, B. (1989). Linguistic strategies and cultural styles for persuasive discourse. In S. Ting-Toomey & F. Korzenny (Eds.), *Language, communication, and culture* (pp. 139–157). Newbury Park, CA: Sage.
Jones, C. (1985). Problems with monitor use in second language composing. In M. Rose (Ed.), *When a writer can't write: Studies in writer's block and other composing-process problems* (pp. 96–118). New York: Guilford.
Jordan, R. (1997). *English for academic purposes.* Cambridge: Cambridge University Press.
Jourdenais, R. (2001). Cognition, instruction and protocol analysis. In P. Robinson (Ed.), *Cognition and second language instruction* (pp. 354–376). Cambridge: Cambridge University Press.
Kachru, Y. (1999). Culture, context, and writing. In E. Hinkel (Ed.), *Culture in second language teaching and learning* (pp. 75–89). Cambridge: Cambridge University Press.

Kaplan, R. B. (1983). Contrastive rhetorics: Some implications for the writing process. In A. Freedman, I. Pringle, & J. Yalden (Eds.), *Learning to write: First language/second language* (pp. 139–161). London: Longman.

Kaplan, R. B. (1987). Cultural thought patterns revisited. In U. Connor & R.B. Kaplan (Eds.), *Writing across languages: Analysis of L2 text* (pp. 9–22). Reading, MA: Addison-Wesley.

Kaplan, R. B. (1988). Contrastive rhetoric and second language learning: Notes toward a theory of contrastive rhetoric. In A. Purves (Ed.), *Writing across languages and cultures: Issues in contrastive rhetoric* (pp. 275–303). Newbury Park, CA: Sage.

Kaplan, R. B. (2000). Contrastive rhetoric and discourse analysis: Who write what to whom? When? In what circumstances? In S. Sarangi & M. Coulthard (Eds.), *Discourse and social life* (pp. 82–102). Harlow, UK: Longman.

Kay, P. (1997). *Words and the grammar of context.* Stanford, CA: CSLI.

Kelly, P. (1986). Solving the vocabulary retention problem. *ITL Review of Applied Linguistics, 74,* 1–16.

Kennedy, G. (1991). Between and through: The company they keep and the functions they serve. In K. Aijmer & B. Altenberg (Eds.), *English corpus linguistics* (pp. 95–110). New York: Longman.

Kennedy, X., Kennedy, D., & Holladay, S. (2002). *The Bedford guide for college writers* (6th ed.). Boston: Bedford/St Martin's.

Kjellmer, G. (1991). A mint of phrases. In K. Aijmer & B. Altenberg (Eds.), *English corpus linguistics* (pp. 111–127). New York: Longman.

Kroll, B. (1979). A survey of writing needs of foreign and American college freshmen. *ELTJ, 33*(2), 219–227.

Kroll, B. (1990). What does time buy? ESL student performance on home versus class compositions. In B. Kroll (Ed.), *Second language writing* (pp. 140–154). Cambridge: Cambridge University Press.

Kucera, H. and Francis, N. (1967). *Computational analysis of preesnt-day English.* Providence: Brown University Press.

Kumaravadivelu, B. (1993). Maximizing learning potential in the communicative classroom. *ELT Journal, 47*(1), 12–21.

Larsen-Freeman, D. (1991). Second language acquisition research: Staking out the territory. *TESOL Quarterly, 25,* 315–350.

Larsen-Freeman, D. (1993). Second language acquisition research: Staking out the territory. In S. Sliberstein (Ed.), *State of the Art TESOL Essays* (pp. 133–168). Alexandria, VA: TESOL.

Larsen-Freeman, D., & Long, M. (1991). *Introduction to second language acquisition research.* New York: Longman.

Laufer, B. (1994). The lexical profile of second language writing: Does it change over time? *RELC Journal, 25*(1), 21–33.

Laufer, B., & Nation, P. (1995). Vocabulary size and use: Lexical richness in L2 written production. *Applied Linguistics, 16,* 307–322.

Leech, G., Rayson, P., & Wilson, A. (2001). *Word frequencies in written and spoken English.* London: Longman.

Leech, G., & Svartvik, J. (1994). *A communicative grammar of English* (2nd ed.). London: Longman.

Leki, I. (1991). The preference of ESL students for error correction in college-level wring classes. *Foreign Language Annals, 24,* 203–228.

Leki, I. (1995). Coping strategies of ESL students. *TESOL Quarterly, 29*(2), 235–260.

Leki, I. (1999). *Academic writing: techniques and tasks* (3rd ed.). New York: Cambridge University Press.

Leki, I., & Carson, J. (1997). "Completely Different Worlds": EAP and the writing experiences of ESL students in university courses. *TESOL Quarterly, 31*(1), 39–70.
Leslie, L. (2000). *Mass communication ethics.* Boston: Houghton-Mifflin.
Levine, D., & Adelman, M. (1993). *Beyond language: Cross-cultural communication.* Englewood Cliffs, NJ: Prentice-Hall.
Levinson, S. (1983). *Pragmatics.* Cambridge: Cambridge University Press.
Lewis, M. (1993). *The lexical approach.* Hove, UK: LTP.
Lewis, M. (1997). Pedagogical implications of the lexical approach. In J. Coady & T. Huckin (Eds.), *Second language vocabulary acquisition: A rationale for pedagogy* (pp. 255–270). Cambridge: Cambridge University Press.
Lunsford, A., & Connors, R. (1997). *The every day writer.* New York: St Martin's Press.
Lunsford, A., & Ruszkiewicz, J. (2001). *Everything's an argument.* Boston: Bedford/St Martin's.
Mankiw, N. G. (2001). *Principles of macroeconomics* (2nd ed.). Fort Worth, TX: Harcourt.
Master, P. (1991). Active verbs with inanimate subjects in scientific prose. *English for Specific Purposes, 10*(1), 15–33.
Master, P. (2002). Relative clause reduction in technical research articles. In E. Hinkel & S. Fotos (Eds.), *New perspectives on grammar teaching second and foregin language classrooms* (pp. 201–231). Mahwah, NJ: Lawrence Erlbaum Associates.
Matalene, C. (1985). Contrastive rhetoric: An American writing teacher in China. *College English, 47*, 789–807.
Matthiessen, C. (1996). Tense in English seen through systemic-functional theory. In M. Berry, C. Butler, R. Fawcett, & G. Hwang (Eds.), *Meaning and form: Systemic functional interpretations* (pp. 431–498). Norwood, NJ: Ablex.
Maynard, S. (1993). *Discourse modality: Subjectivity, emotion and voice in the Japanese language.* Amsterdam: John Benjamins.
Maynard, S. (1997). *Japanese communication.* Honolulu: University of Hawaii Press.
McCarthy, M. (1991). *Discourse analysis for language teachers.* Cambridge: Cambridge University Press.
McCarthy, M., & Carter, R. (1994). *Language as discourse.* London: Longman.
McWhorter, K. (2000). *Successful college writing.* Boston: Bedford/St. Martin's.
MELAB. (1996). *Technical manual* Ann Arbor, MI: English Language Institute, The University of Michigan.
Meyer, C. (1991). A corpus-based study of apposition in English. In K. Aijmer & B. Altenberg (Eds.), *English corpus linguistics* (pp. 166–181). New York: Longman.
Miller, T. (2000). *Environmental science: Working with the Earth* (8th ed.). Belmont, CA: Brooks/Cole..
Mitchell, R., & Martin, C. (1997). Rote learning, creativity, and "understanding" in classroom foreign language teaching. *Language Teaching Research, 1*(1), 1–28.
Moon, R. (1997). Vocabulary connections: Multi-word items in English. In N. Schmitt & M. McCarthy (Eds.), *Vocabulary: Description, acquisition, and pedagogy* (pp. 40–63). Cambridge: Cambridge University Press.
Moon, R. (1998). *Fixed expressions and idioms in English.* Oxford: Oxford University Press.
Morris, C. (2002). *Understanding psychology* (6th ed.). Englwood Cliffs, NJ: Prentice-Hall.
Muranoi, H. (2000). Focus on form through interaction enhancement: Integrating formal instruction into a communicative task in EFL classroom. *Language Learning, 50*(4), 617–673.

Myers, G. (1989). The pragmatics of politeness in scientific articles. *Applied Linguistics, 10*, 1–35.

Myers, G. (1996). Strategic vagueness in academic writing. In E. Ventola & A. Mauranen (Eds.), *Academic writing* (pp. 1–18). Amsterdam: John Benjamins.

Myers, G. (1999). Interaction in writing: Principles and problems. In C. Candlin & K. Hyland (Eds.), *Writing texts, processes and practices* (pp. 40–61). London: Longman.

Nation, I. S. P. (1990). *Teaching and learning vocabulary*. New York: Newbury House.

Nation, I. S. P. (2001). *Learning vocabulary in another language*. Cambridge: Cambridge University Press.

Nation, P., & Waring, R. (1997). Vocabulary size, text coverage, and word lists. In N. Schmitt & M. McCarthy (Eds.), *Vocabulary: Description, acquisition, and pedagogy* (pp. 6–20). Cambridge: Cambridge University Press.

Nattinger, J., & DeCarrico, J. (1992). *Lexical phrases and language teaching*. Oxford: Oxford University Press.

Nelson, G., & Murphy, J. (1993). Peer response groups: Do L2 writers use peer comments in revising their drafts? *TESOL Quarterly, 27*(1), 135–142.

Norris, J., & Ortega, L. (2000). Effectiveness of L2 instruction: A research synthesis and quantitative meta-analysis. *Language Learning, 50*(3), 417–528.

Norris, J., & Ortega, L. (2001). Does type of instruction make a difference: Substantive findings from a meta-analytic review. In R. Ellis (Ed.), *Form-focused instruction and second language learning [Language Learning 51: Supplement 1]* (pp. 157–213). Ann Arbor: University of Michigan/Blackwell.

Ohta, A. S. (1991). Evidentiality and politeness in Japanese. *Issues in Applied Linguistics, 2*(2), 183–210.

Oliver, R. (1972). *Communication and culture in ancient India and China*. Syracuse, NY: Syracuse University Press.

Ostler, S. (1980). A survey of needs of advanced ESL. *TESOL Quarterly, 14*(4), 489–502.

Ostler, S. (1987). English in parallels: A comparison of English and Arabic prose. In U. Connor & R. Kaplan (Eds.), *Writing across languages: Analysis of L2 text* (pp. 169–185). Reading, MA: Addison-Wesley.

Owen, C. (1993). Corpus-based grammar and the Heineken effect: Lexico-grammatical description for language learners. *Applied Linguistics, 14*(2), 167–187.

Pagano, A. (1994). Negatives in written text. In M. Coulthard (Ed.), *Advances in written text analysis* (pp. 250–265). New York: Routledge.

Palmer, F. R. (1990). *Modality and the English modals* (2nd ed.). London: Longman.

Palmer, F. R. (1994). *Grammatical roles and relations*. Cambridge: Cambridge University Press.

Paltridge, B. (2001). *Genre and the language learning classroom*. Ann Arbor: The University of Michigan Press.

Paribakht, T., & Wesche, M. (1993). The relationship between reading comprehension and second language development in a comprehension-based ESL program. *TESL Canada Journal, 11*(1), 9–29.

Paribakht, T., & Wesche, M. (1997). Vocabulary enhancement activities and reading for meaning in second language vocabulary acquisition. In J. Coady & T. Huckin (Eds.), *Second language vocabulary acquisition* (pp. 174–200). Cambridge: Cambridge University Press.

Partington, A. (1996). *Patterns and meanings*. Amsterdam: John Benjamins.

Pawley, A., & Syder, F. (1983). Two puzzles for linguistic theory: Nativelike selection and nativelike fluency. In J. Richards & E. Schmidt (Eds.), *Language and communication* (pp. 191–227). New York: Longman.

Perry, M., Chase, M., Jacob, J., Jacob, M., & Von Laue, T. (2000). *Western civilization: Ideas, politics, and society.* Boston: Houghton-Mifflin.

Perry, M., Peden, J., & Von Laue, T. (1999). *Sources of the Western tradition* (4th ed.). Boston: Houghton-Mifflin.

Peters, A. (1983). *The units of language acquisition.* Cambridge: Cambridge University Press.

Pica, T. (1994). Questions from the language classroom: Research perspectives. *TESOL Quarterly, 28*(1), 49–79.

Pike, K. (1964). A linguistic contribution to composition: A hypothesis. *College Composition and Communication, 15*(1), 82–88.

Poole, D. (1991). Discourse analysis in enthnographic research. *Annual Review of Applied Linguistics, 11*, 42–56.

Prior, P. (1998). *Writing/disciplinarity: A sociohistoric account of literate activity in the academy.* Mahwah, NJ: Lawrence Erlbaum Associates.

Quirk, R., Greenbaum, S., Leech, G., & Svartvik, J. (1985). *A comprehensive grammar of the English language.* New York: Longman.

Raimes, A. (1983). *Techniques in teaching writing.* Oxford: Oxford University Press.

Raimes, A. (1992). *Exploring through writing* (2nd ed.). New York: St Martin's Press.

Raimes, A. (1993). Out of the woods: Emerging traditions in the teaching of writing. In S. Silberstein (Ed.), *State of the Art: TESOL essays* (pp. 237–260). Alexandria, VA: TESOL.

Raimes, A. (1994). Language proficiency, writing ability, and composition strategies: A study of ESL college student writers. In A. Cumming (Ed.), *Bilingual performance in reading and writing* (pp. 139–172). Ann Arbor, MI/Amsterdam: Language Learning/John Benjamins.

Raimes, A. (1999). *Keys for writers: A brief handbook.* Boston: Houghton-Mifflin.

Read, J. (2000). *Assessing vocabulary.* Cambridge: Cambridge University Press.

Reid, J. (1993). *Teaching ESL writing.* Englewood Cliffs, NJ: Prentice-Hall.

Reid, J. (2000a). *The process of composition* (3rd ed.). New York: Longman.

Reid, J. (2000b). *The process of paragraph writing* (3rd ed.). New York: Longman.

Renouf, A., & Sinclair, J. (1991). Collocational frameworks in English. In K. Aijmer & B. Altenberg (Eds.), *English corpus linguistics* (pp. 128–143). New York: Longman.

Richards, J. (2002). Accuracy and fluency revisited. In E. Hinkel & S. Fotos (Eds.), *New perspectives on grammar teaching in second language classrooms* (pp. 35–50). Mahwah, NJ: Lawrence Erlbaum Associates.

Riddle, E. (1986). Meaning and discourse function of the past tense in English. *TESOL Quarterly, 20*(2), 267–286.

Rosenfeld, M., Leung, S., & Oltman, P. (2001). *The reading, writing, speaking, and listening tasks important for academic success at undergraduate and graduate levels* (MS 21). Princeton, NJ: ETS.

Rutherford, W. (1984). *Second language grammar learning and teaching.* New York: Longman.

Rutherford, W., & Sharwood Smith, M. (1985). Consciousness-raising and universal grammar. In W. Rutherford & M. Sharwood Smith (Eds.), *Grammar and second language learning* (pp. 274–82). New York: Newbury House.

Sa'adeddin, M. A. (1989). Text development and Arabic-English negative interference. *Applied Linguistics, 10*(1), 36–51.

Santos, T. (1984). Error gravity: A study of faculty opinion of ESL errors. *TESOL Quarterly, 18*(1), 69–90.

Santos, T. (1988). Professors' reactions to the academic writing of nonnative-speaking students. *TESOL Quarterly, 22*, 69–90.

Schachter, J. (1990). Communicative competence revisited. In B. Harley, P. Allen, J. Cummins, & M. Swain (Eds.), *The development of second language proficiency* (pp. 39–54). Cambridge: Cambridge University Press.

Schmidt, R. (1983). Interaction, acculturation, and acquisition of communicative competence. In N. Wolfson & E. Judd (Eds.), *Sociolinguistics and second language acquisition* (pp. 137–174). Rowley, MA: Newbury House.

Schmidt, R. (1990). The role of consciousness in second language learning. *Applied Linguistics, 11*(1), 129–158.

Schmidt, R. (1993). Awareness and second language acquisition. *Annual Review of Applied Linguistics, 13*, 206–226.

Schmidt, R. (1994). Implicit learning and the cognitive unconscious: Of artificial grammars and SLA. In N. Ellis (Ed.), *Implicit and explicit learning of languages* (pp. 165–210). San Diego: Academic Press.

Schmidt, R. (1995). Can there be learning without attention? In R. Schmidt (Ed.), *Attention & awareness in foreign language learning* (pp. 9–64). Honolulu: University of Hawaii Press.

Schmitt, N. (2000). *Vocabulary in language teaching*. Cambridge: Cambridge University Press.

Schmitt, N., & McCarthy, M. (Eds.). (1997). *Vocabulary: Description, acquisition, and pedagogy*. Cambridge: Cambridge University Press.

Schoedinger, A. (2000). *Our philosophical heritage* (3rd ed.). Dubuque, IA: Kendall/Hunt.

Schumacher, E. (1999). *Small is beautiful: Economics as if people mattered*. Vancouver, BC: Hartley & Marks/Harper Collins.

Scollon, R. (1991). Eight legs and one elbow: Stance and structure in Chinese English compositions. *Proceedings of the 2nd North American Conference on Adult and Adolescent Literacy*, pp. 26–41. Ottawa: International Reading Association.

Scollon, R. (1993a). *Maxims of stance* (Research Report No. 26). Hong Kong: City Polytechnic of Hong Kong.

Scollon, R. (1993b). Cumulative ambiguity: Conjunctions in Chinese–English intercultural communication. *Working Papers of the Department of English, City Polytechnic of Hong Kong, 5*(1), 55–73.

Scollon, R., & Scollon, S. (2001). *Intercultural communication* (2nd ed.). Oxford: Blackwell.

Seligman, M. (1999). Fall into helplessness. In R. Epstein (Ed.), *The new psychology today reader* (pp. 142–147). Dubuque, IA: Kendall/Hunt.

Sharwood Smith, M. (1981). Consciousness raising and the second language learner. *Applied Linguistics, 2*(1), 159–168.

Sharwood Smith, M. (1991). Speaking to many minds: On the relevance of different types of language information for the L2 learner. *Second Language Research, 7*(2), 18–32.

Sharwood Smith, M. (1993). Input enhancement in instructed SLA: Theoretical bases. *Studies in Second Language Acquisition, 15*(2), 165–179.

Sharwood Smith, M., & Rutherford, W. (1988). *Grammar and second language teaching*. New York: Newbury House.

Shaw, P., & Liu, E. T. K. (1998). What develops in the development of second language writing? *Applied Linguistics, 19*(2), 225–254.

Silva, T. (1990). Second language composition instruction: Developments, issues, and directions in ESL. In B. Kroll (Ed.), *Second language writing: Research insights for the classroom* (pp. 11–23). New York: Cambridge University Press.

Silva, T. (1993). Toward an understanding of the distinct nature of L2 writing: The ESL research and its implications. *TESOL Quarterly, 27*(4), 657–676.

Silva, T. (1997). On the ethical treatment of ESL writers. *TESOL Quarterly, 31*(2), 359–363.

Sinclair, J. (1991). *Corpus, concordance, collocation*. Oxford: Oxford University Press.

Sinclair, J., & Renouf, A. (1988). A lexical syllabus for language learning. In R. Carter & M. McCarthy (Eds.), *Vocabulary and language teaching* (pp. 140–160). Harlow, Essex: Longman.

Smalley, R., Ruetten, M., & Kozyrev, J. (2000). *Refining composition skills* (5th ed.). Boston: Heinle & Heinle.

Smoke, T. (1999). *A writer's workbook* (3rd ed.). New York: Cambridge University Press.

Swain, M. (1985). Communicative competence: Some roles of comprehensible input and comprehensible output in its development. In S. Gass & C. Madden (Eds.), *Input in second language acquisition* (pp. 235–253). Rowley, MA: Newbury House.

Swales, J. (1971). *Writing scientific English*. Walton-on-Thames, UK: Thomas Nelson.

Swales, J. (1990a). *Genre analysis*. Cambridge: Cambridge University Press.

Swales, J. (1990b). Nonnative speaker graduate engineering students and their introductions: Global coherence and local management. In U. Connor & A. Johns (Eds.), *Coherence in writing* (pp. 189–207). Alexandria, VA: TESOL.

Swales, J., & Feak, C. (1994). *Academic writing for graduate students*. Ann Arbor, MI: University of Michigan Press.

Swan, M., & Smith, B. (2001). *Learner English: A teacher's guide to interference and other problems* (3rd ed.). Cambridge: Cambridge University Press.

Tadros, A. (1994). Predictive categories in expository text. In M. Coulthard (Ed.), *Advances in written text analysis* (pp. 69–82). New York: Routledge.

Taylor, G., & Chen, T. (1991). Linguistic, cultural, and subcultural issues in contrastive discourse analysis: Anglo-American and Chinese scientific texts. *Applied Linguistics, 12*, 319–336.

Taylor, I. (1995). *Writing and literacy in Chinese, Korean, and Japanese*. Amsterdam: John Benjamins.

Thompson, W., & Hickey, J. (2002). *Society in focus: An introduction to sociology* (4th ed.). New York: Allyn & Bacon..

Tickoo, A. (1992). Seeking a pedagogically useful understanding of given-new: An analysis of native speaker errors in written discourse. In L. Bouton and Y. Kachru (Eds.), *Pragmatics and Language Learning* (Vol. 3, pp. 130–143). Urbana-Champaign: Intensive English Institute.

Tsui, A., & Ng, M. (2000). Do secondary L2 writers benefit from peer comments? *Journal of Second Language Writing, 9*(2), 147–170.

U.S. Census. (2000). *Enrollment status of the population 3 years old and over, by age, sex, race, Hispanic origin, nativity, and selected educational characteristics: October* [On-line]. Available http://www.census.gov/population/socdemo/school/ppl-148/tab01.txt

U.S. Department of Commerce, Bureau of the Census. (1995). *Dropout rates in the United States.* Washington, DC: Author.

van Dijk, T. (Ed.). (1985). *Handbook of discourse analysis* (4 vols.). London: Academic Press.

van Dijk, T. (Ed.). (1997). *Discourse as structure and process* (2 vols.). London: SAGE.

Vann, R., Lorenz, F., & Meyer, D. (1991). Error gravity: Response to errors in the written discourse of nonnative speakers of English. In L. Hamp-Lyons (Ed.), *Assessing second language writing* (pp. 181–196). Norwood, NJ: Ablex.

Vann, R., Meyer, D., & Lorenz, F. (1984). Error gravity: A study of faculty opinion of ESL errors. *TESOL Quarterly, 18*(3), 427–440.

Vaughan, C. (1991). Holistic assessment: What goes on in the raters' minds? In L. Hamp-Lyons (Ed.), *Assessing second language writing* (pp. 111–126). Norwood, NJ: Ablex.

Warden, C. (2000). EFL business writing behaviors in differing feedback environments. *Language Learning, 50*(4), 573–616.

Watanabe, S. (1993). A note on so-called "donkey sentences" in Japanese: A preliminary study. In P. Clancy (Ed.), *Japanese and Korean linguistics* (pp. 299–315). Stanford, CA: CSLI/Standford University Press.

Widdowson, H. (1983). New starts and different kinds of failure. In A. Freedman, I. Pringle, & J. Yalden (Eds.), *Learning to write: First language/second language: Selected papers from the 1979 CCTE Conference, Ottawa, Canada* (pp. 31–47). London: Longman.

Wilkins, D. (1972). *Linguistics in language teaching.* London: Edward Arnold.

Williams, J. (1999). Learner-generated attention to form. *Language Learning, 49*(4), 583–625.

Williams, J. M. (2002). *Style: Ten lessons in clarity and grace* (6th ed.). New York: Addison-Wesley.

Wong, H. (1990). The use of rhetorical questions in written argumentative discourse. In L. Bouton & Y. Kachru (Eds.), *Pragmatics and Language Learning* (Vol. 1, pp. 187–208). Urbana-Champaign: Intensive English Institute.

Wood, D. (2001). In search of fluency: What is it and how can we teach it? *Canadian Modern Language Review, 57*, 573–589.

Wray, A. (2002). *Formulaic language and the lexicon.* Cambridge: Cambridge University Press.

Wray, A., & Perkins, M. R. (2000). The functions of formulaic language: An integrated model. *Language and Communication, 20*, 1–28.

Zamel, V. (1982). Writing: The process of discovering meaning. *TESOL Quarterly, 16*(1), 195–210.

Zamel, V. (1983). The composing processes of advanced ESL students: Six case studies. *TESOL Quarterly, 17*(1), 165–187.

Zhang, S. (1995). Reexamining the affective advantage of peer feedback in the ESL writing class. *Journal of Second Language Writing, 4*, 209–222.

Zhu, W. (2001). Interaction and feedback in mixed peer response groups. *Journal of Second Language Writing, 10*(4), 251–276.

Zhu, Y. (1996). Modality and modulation in Chinese. In M. Berry, C. Butler, R. Fawcett, & G. Hwang (Eds.), *Meaning and form: Systemic functional interpretations* (pp. 183–209). Norwood, NJ: Ablex.

Zikmund, W., Middlemist, R., & Middlemist, M. (1995). *Business: The American challenge for global competitiveness.* Burr Ridge, IL: Richard Irwin/Austen Press.

Author Index

T

V

W

Z

Subject Index